The Workwoman's Guide

Library of Congress Cataloging-in-Publication Data

Lady.
  The Workwoman's guide.

  "Containing instructions to the inexperienced in cutting out and completing those articles of wearing apparel, &c., which are usually made at home; also, explanations on upholstery, straw-platting, bonnet making, knitting, &c."
  Reprint. Originally published: London : Simpkin, Marshall, 1838.
  Includes index.
  1. Sewing. 2. Knitting. I. Title.
  TT705.L27 1986   646.2   86-28550

Printed in the U.S.A. on Acid-Free Paper by ACADEMY BOOKS, Rutland, VT

FOREWORD

With the production of this facsimile edition of *The Workwoman's Guide*, Old Sturbridge Village inaugurates a new collaboration with Opus Publications. Through it, scarce and out-of-print materials relating to the early 19th century will be made available from the collections of the Research Library which enrich the Village interpretation of New England rural life between 1790 and 1840.

The value of *The Workwoman's Guide* is that it provides in its text and illustrations the original 19th-century instructions for making and cleaning clothing and accessories. Described are hundreds of objects that were stitched from cloth, knitted from yarn, braided, dyed or otherwise converted into utilitarian and ornamental objects of clothing and household furnishing. As the Industrial Revolution transformed the marketplace with the addition of easily acquired textiles in great abundance, so *The Workwoman's Guide* chronicles the use of these new products in the domestic arts.

Since *The Workwoman's Guide* was added to the collections some years ago, the instructions in the book have been incorporated into our household demonstrations. Along with hearth cooking, which is not treated in this book, domestic crafts like sewing, knitting and bonnetmaking are central to the emerging definition of home life in New England in the first half of the 19th century.

Old Sturbridge Village is a non-profit educational institution visited by approximately half a million people yearly. About 100,000 of these visitors are school students, whose visits are part of their curriculum. Among the exhibits are a working farm, water-powered mills and demonstrations of such trades as printing, blacksmithing, shoemaking and tinwork. For more information about visiting the museum village, call or write for the seasonal calendar of events.

Old Sturbridge Village
1 Old Sturbridge Village Road
Sturbridge, MA 01566
(617) 347-3362

OPUS PUBLICATIONS, INC.
669 Boston Post Road, Guilford, Connecticut 06437

FRONTISPIECE.

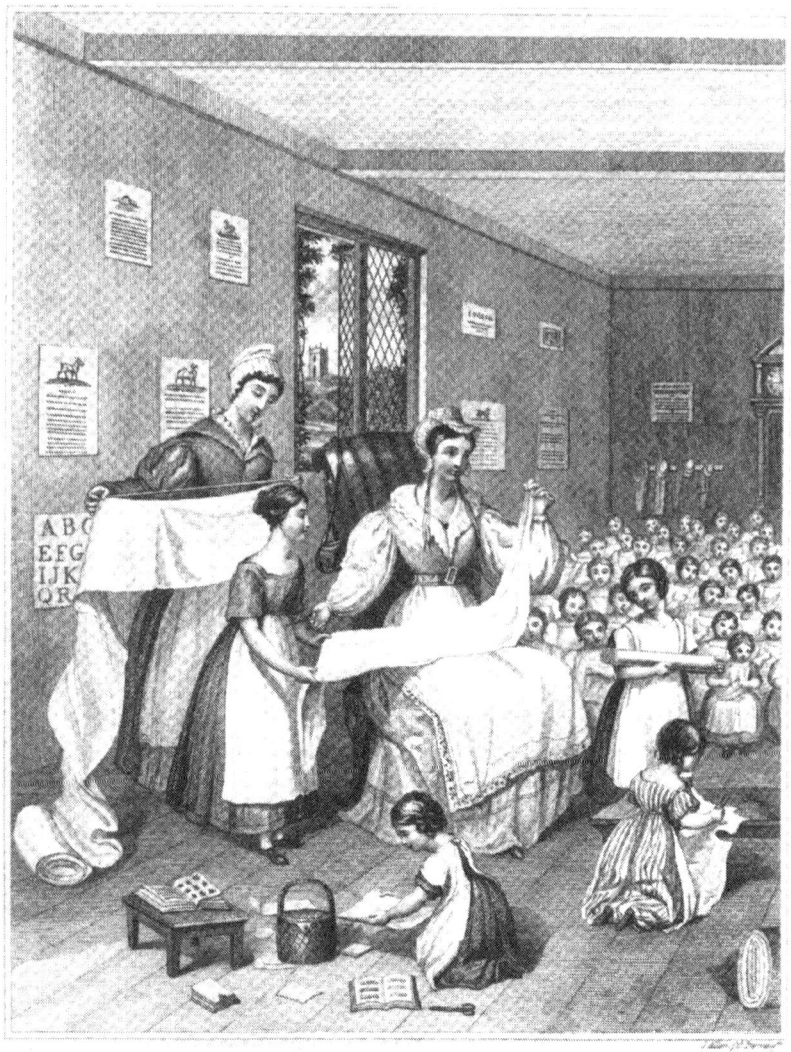

She stretcheth out her hand to the Poor —
She looketh well to the ways of her Household.   Prov. 31 Ch.

THE

WORKWOMAN'S GUIDE,

CONTAINING

INSTRUCTIONS TO THE INEXPERIENCED IN CUTTING OUT AND COMPLETING

THOSE ARTICLES OF WEARING APPAREL, &c., WHICH ARE USUALLY

MADE AT HOME; ALSO, EXPLANATIONS ON UPHOLSTERY,

STRAW-PLATTING, BONNET-MAKING, KNITTING, &c.

BY A LADY.

"*METHOD SHORTENS LABOUR.*"

LONDON:

SIMPKIN, MARSHALL, AND CO., STATIONERS' HALL COURT:

THOMAS EVANS, COLMORE ROW, BIRMINGHAM.

1838.

BIRMINGHAM:
PRINTED BY THOMAS EVANS, COLMORE ROW.

PREFACE.

"But to know
That which before us lies in daily life;
Is the prime wisdom."
MILTON.

The Author of the following pages has been encouraged to hope, that, in placing them, after much deliberation, in the hands of a printer, she is tendering an important and acceptable, however humble, service to persons of her own sex, who, in any condition of life, are engaged, by duty, or inclination, in cutting out wearing apparel in a family, or for their poorer neighbours. She trusts, in particular, that Clergymen's Wives, Young Married Women, School-mistresses, and Ladies' Maids may find, in the "Workwoman's Guide," a fast and serviceable friend.

The patterns, which comprise all the necessary parts of clothing in great variety, to suit both rich and poor, have been some years in collecting, and are given as the most generally approved shapes and sizes in present use. Economy and neatness of appearance have been equally consulted in choosing them, and all have been successfully tried. In selecting and arranging the Infant's wardrobe, the comfort of the little wearers and ease of dressing, have been accurately studied. Interested by the feelings of a Mother in this division of her book, the Author has worked at it with especial zeal and assiduity, and submits it with particular confidence.

To assist the unpractised in understanding the written descriptions, almost every pattern is likewise drawn twice (see Plates), so as not only to represent its appearance when cut out, but also when made up. The difficulty of describing irregular and complicated shapes has been obviated by enclosing each in a square, marked with a scale of nails; by which means, even sleeves, collars, capes, and bonnets can be cut out with unfailing precision. In a charity school, for which the Author was much interested, and for the use of which, both her collection of patterns was originally begun, and her drawings made, girls from ten to sixteen years of age were in the constant habit of cutting out correctly and easily, with no other guidance than the drawings. To sketch the pattern on a slate, and to cut it out first in paper, was all the facility afforded to, or needed by, beginners.

The Reader, as she advances, will see that this work is not confined to the simply cutting out and making up articles of dress, but likewise includes the important subjects of House Linen and Upholstery, and that the minor branches of knitting and straw-platting have their places. Directions which, it is trusted, will be found useful, respecting various other points of domestic industry, are not omitted.

On the general plan of the work, and the motives which have induced the writer to venture it before the Public, she need not, perhaps, say more. A few words are near her heart, which she does not resist the temptation of adding.

A woman, who in the upper classes of society, has taken her place at the head of a family, has undertaken a high and responsible situation; but one, in which, by daily attention to certain humble details, she can essentially serve the welfare of some who are dear to her, and of many who are dependent on her.

The Author, as an Englishwoman, reflects with pride upon the number of her country women, whom the gifts of nature, and a brilliant or careful education enables to grace their place in society. She believes that very many of them are further qualified, as far as good will and natural intelligence can go, to discharge those humbler, but not less honourable, parts of their calling, to which she has alluded, but are deterred from applying to them (or much embarrassed if they do), from finding that, whilst they are proficients in many beautiful accomplishments, and not without cultivation in the more solid parts of information, they are yet mere novices in other unostentatious attainments, that have become indispensable to their domestic efficiency. The complete remedy for this inconvenience can only be found in making some further knowledge of domestic arts and economy a prominent part of the education of our daughters; home and school must both be called upon to contribute. Amongst the arts in question, the homely one of cutting out is entitled to rank high, for subserviency to comfort and elegance, as well as to economy, whenever this is an object, and in what fortune can it wisely be neglected? It is one which may seem peculiarly fitted to be taught in schools, by the conveniency of the means for teaching, by its cleanliness, and, if the Author may be allowed to say so, by its intellectual character, since to cut out well, it is necessary to think, and indeed the art, continually depending upon exact measurements, proportions and even correct diagrams, or figures, must be considered as a sort of unassuming household mathematics. Dress, it seems, has of late been admitted by philosophical critics to the dignity of a fine art: it both requires and cultivates taste, and the consideration of a pleasing effect and air in dress is first applied in the cutting out.

No one who has not been a frequent visitor in the homes of the poor, is aware of the extravagance and waste usual among women of a humble class, arising from their total ignorance in matters of cutting out and needle-work, nor how much instruction they want on those points, even to the making of a petticoat and a pinafore. The same ignorance and unskilfulness, and the same consequent waste of laborious and scanty earnings is common among our female household servants; who, by putting out their clothes to dress-makers, pay nearly half as much for the making up as for the materials. The direct saving of expense upon articles of dress, were they qualified to work for themselves, would, with all persons in these conditions of life, be an important annual item. But the indirect and further benefit would be of infinitely more account. The thrifty disposition, the regularity and neatness, the ideas of order and management, inspired by the conscious ability and successful exertion, in one leading branch of good housewifery, cannot be too highly prized or diligently cultivated; for the result is *moral*. The orderly house but reflects the orderly mind; the humble wife and mother, whose active indefatigable hand, silently executing her careful ingenious thought, improves the comforts, the visible respectability, and real condition of her husband and children, is mistress of a secret for blending her best and tenderest affections with the employment of every day: she contrives judiciously what she constantly and earnestly meditates, and finds no weariness in the labour to which strength continually flows from a deep fountain in her heart.

Personal investigation alone can satisfy those ladies who interest themselves in the welfare of the poor, how useful a kindness they would exercise in making efficient systematic instruction, in these arts, an ordinary and important part of school business.

Could the Author hope that the little work, in which she has endeavoured to arrange the elements of cutting out progressively, would ever be admitted as a manual in the village school-room, a cherished wish of her heart would be gratified; in the mean time, she will be glad to think, that she may have saved some wives and mothers, entering upon their arduous vocations, a part of the inconveniences experienced by herself, although accounted a tolerable workwoman in the general acceptation of the term, when, on assuming the former of these characters, she was compelled to rely on her own resources.

The Author must here acknowledge her obligations to that valuable little work "Cottage Comforts;" also to the "Teacher's Assistant in Needlework" and "Knitting," and a few others, for some useful suggestions.

TABLE OF CONTENTS.

CHAPTER I.   GENERAL OBSERVATIONS ON NEEDLE-WORK. Comprising Plain Stitches, Fancy Stitches, Marking, Darning, Braiding, &c. General Rules for completing Work.

CHAPTER II.   A FEW OBSERVATIONS ON PURCHASING GOODS.

CHAPTER III.   GENERAL RULES FOR CUTTING OUT.

CHAPTER IV.   THE WORK-BOX.

CHAPTER V.   ON BABY LINEN, WITH SCALES FOR THE CLOTHES OF OLDER CHILDREN. Caps; Cockades; Rosettes; Infants' Open Shirts; first Flannel Gowns; Flannel Bands; Night-gowns; Pinafores; Petticoats; Robes; Receiver; Shawl; Flannel Cloak; Child's Bib; Infants' Pelisses and Cloaks; Infant's Hood; Cots; Cribs; Cradles; Basket; Pincushion.

CHAPTER VI.   LINEN FOR MEN, WOMEN, GIRLS, AND BOYS. Women's Shifts; Child's Shifts; Child's Trowsers; Girl's Trowsers; Trowsers for Girls or Boys; Leglets; Women's Drawers; Turkish Trowsers; Men's Drawers; Women's Night Jackets; Night-gowns; Flannel Waistcoat for a Lady; Boys' Waistcoats; Man's Under Waistcoat; Boy's Upper Waistcoat; Child's Night Vest; Child's Day Vest; Bathing Gown; Women's Night-caps; Caps for poor Women; Caps for Servants; Caps for School-girls; Bathing Cap; Dressing-gowns for Men; Dressing-gowns for Women; Cloak Dressing-gown; Dressing Jacket; Flannel Petticoats; Pockets; Frills; Cuffs; Tidy Cuffs; Mourning Cuffs; Aprons; Dress Aprons; Working Aprons; Apron Pockets; Grocers' Aprons; Cooking Apron; Pantry Apron; Gentleman's Working Apron; Neck-tie; Scarfs; Women's Stays; Nursing Stays; Men's Stays or Belts; Children's Stays; Bustles; Veils; Long and short Sleeves for Children; Long and short Sleeves for grown-up Persons; Old Woman's Sleeve; Boy's Sleeve; Shoulder-pieces; Capes; Collars; Riding Collar; Habit-shirt; Chemisette; School-girl's Tippet; Petticoats; Nursing Petticoat; Gowns; General observations on Colours; On the making up and choosing Dresses; General observations on cutting out Dresses; Bodies of Gowns—high, low, full, plain; On trimming Bodies of low Dresses; Nursing Gowns; Children's Frocks and Tunics; Boy's Surtout; Child's Pelisses; Day-caps; Morning Caps; Bonnet Caps; Cap for an Old Lady; Caps for the Society of Friends; Lappets; Widow's Cap; Velvet or Silk Cap; Care of the Lady's Wardrobe; To fold up Dresses and Frocks; General observations on Packing; Care of the Gentleman's Wardrobe; Mourning and Dress at Funerals; Pinafores and Saccarines for Children; House-maid's Pinafore; School-girl's Pinafore; Surgeon's Pinafore; Waggoner's Smock-frock; Shirts for the Labouring Classes; Gentlemen's Shirts; Gentlemen's Shirt Fronts; Boys' Shirt Fronts; Gentlemen's Stocks; Clergyman's Dress; The Cassock; The Gown; The Surplice; The Sash; Scarf; Bands; The Clerk's Gown; Children's Bonnets; Hats and Caps for Boys; Travelling Caps; Lady's Riding Cap; Working Man's Cap; Women's Bonnets; Old Women's Bonnets; Bonnet for a Member of the Society of Friends; School-girl's Bonnet; Oiled Silk Hood; Calèche; Women's Cloaks; Mantelet or short Cloak; Carriage Cloak; Old Woman's Cloak and Hood; School-girl's Cape or Cloak; Boy's Cloak; Shawls; Shawl for a Member of the Society of Friends; Quilted Shawl; Mourning Shawl; Spencers for Children; Tippet and Sleeves; Neck Handkerchiefs; Pocket Handkerchiefs; Bridal Favours; Men's Slippers; Ladies' Slippers; Travelling or Over-shoes; Half-slippers; Carriage Slippers; Babies' Shoes; On covering Shoes; Gloves; On Down and Fur; Muffs; Boas; Tippets; Operas or Ruffs; To clean Fur and Down; To preserve Fur.

CHAPTER VII.   HOUSE LINEN. Division into Bed-room, Table and Pantry, House-maid's, Kitchen, and Stable Linen; Number required, kinds to be chosen, size and price of each; Sheets; Pillow-slips; Towels; Toilette or Dressing Table Covers; Table Cloths; Dinner Napkins; Doyleys; Knife-box Cloths; Pantry Knife Cloths; Pantry Dresser Cloths; Plate-basket Cloth; Pantry China Cloths; Pantry Glass Cloths; Pantry Lamp Cloths; Waiting Gloves; House-maid's Dusters; Scouring Flannels; Paint Cloths; Chamber Bottle Cloths; Chamber Bucket Cloths; Clothes Bags; Kitchen Table Cloths; Dresser Cloths; Roller Cloths; Dusters; Tea Cloths; Jelly Bags; Ham Bags; Cheese Cloths; Stable Linen; General observations on Linen; On marking House Linen; Linen Press; Washing Books—Nursery Washing Book; Lady's Washing Book; Gentleman's Washing Book; House Linen Washing Book.

CONTENTS.

CHAPTER VIII. UPHOLSTERY. General observations; Bedsteads—all their parts and the different kinds; Hints on putting up Beds; On furnishing Beds; General observations on the choice and arrangement of Drapery for Beds; On the Heads and Tops of Beds; Foot-boards; The Half-tester; French Pole Bed; French Arrow Bed; French Bed; French Block Bed; French Canopy Bed; Turn-up Bed; Press Bed; Stump Bed; Trestle Bed; Hanging Bed or Cot; Mattresses; Beds; Bolsters and Pillows; Blankets; Counterpanes; Watch Pockets; Carpets; List of different kinds; General observations on making up Carpets; Window Curtains—Various kinds of Drapery for Windows; Curtains for a Passage or Church Window; Muslin Curtains; Half Curtains; Full Curtains; Rod Curtain; Window Blinds; Chair, Sofa, and other Covers; Divan; Footstools and Hassocks; Church Basses; Church Seats; Table Covers; Screens.

CHAPTER IX. COVERS, CASES, &c. Night-gown Bag; Travelling Dressing-case or Tidy; Glove Cases; Pocket Handkerchief Case; Shoe or Brush and Comb Bags; Shoe Bags; Mat; Boot Bags; Nursery Bag; Book Covers; Trunk Cover; Knife or Fork Case; Card Case; Candlestick Case; Nose-gay Case; Wool Case; Housewife; Yard Measure; Pincushions; Bags; Needle Case; Work Basket; Travelling Bag; School-girl's Badge; Carriage Case or Portfolio; Travelling Portfolio; Seaman's or Traveller's Case; Gentleman's Travelling Dressing Case; Watch Pocket; Invalid's Chair.

CHAPTER X. RECEIPTS. Marking Ink; Red Marking Ink; To remove Marking Ink; Salts of Lemon; To take out Ink without Salts of Lemon; Bleaching Liquid; To remove Stains; Scouring Drops; To remove Grease; To take out Mildew; To take out Iron-moulds; To remove Paint Spots; To clean Silks and Cottons; To restore scorched Linen; To clean Calico Furniture; To clean Chintz; To scour Carpets; To wash Silk Handkerchiefs; To wash coloured Muslins, &c.; To restore the colour of Linen; To wash China-crape Scarfs, &c.; To wash Blonde; To wash Lace; To wash Kid Gloves; To clean white Satin Shoes; To keep Blonde, &c.; To dye Gloves like York tan or Limerick; To dye white Gloves purple; Wash for Leather Gloves; To dye Cotton a Nankeen colour; To dye the Linings of Furniture buff or salmon colour; To clean Gold and Silver Lace; To preserve Linen from Moths; To preserve Woollens and Blankets; To preserve Furs and Woollens from Moths; To varnish old Straw or Chip Hats; To raise the surface of Velvet; To make Starch; To make Court Plaister; Lavender Water; Eau de Cologne; Powder for Infants' Dust Bags; Pot Pourri; Scent Bags; To make Shoes Water-proof; Remedy against Fleas; Remedy against Bugs; To destroy Bugs; To destroy Flies; General observations on Washing and Ironing; List of Articles required in a Laundry; Washing; Hanging to dry; Mangling and Ironing; Clear Starching; Gaufiering.

CHAPTER XI. KNITTING. Knitting Pins; Materials for Knitting; Knit Stitches; Casting on Stitches; Common Knitting Stitch; Dutch common Knitting; Turn or Seam Stitch; Widening; Narrowing; Slipping a Stitch; Finishing off; Welting; Binding; Fancy Stitches; Double Knitting; Open Hem Stitch; Honey-comb Stitch; French Stitch; Fantail Stitch; Network Stitch; Open Cross Stitch; Berlin Wire Stitch; Plain open Stitch; Crowsfoot Stitch; Chain Stitch; Embossed Hexagon Stitch; Common Plat; Elastic Rib; Rough-cast or Huckaback Stitch; Embossed Diamond Stitch; Ladder Stitch; Imitation Double Knitting; Herring-bone Stitch; Purse Stitch; Lace-wave Stitch; Herring-bone Bag Stitch; Improved Open Stitch; Shawl Pattern; Cross-stitch Pattern; Curb Stitch; Ribbed Stitch; Diamond Stitch; Raised French Stitch; Two-coloured Chain Stitch; Rug Stitch; The Nondescript; A New Stitch; Muffatee Stitch; Knit Fringes; Fringe and Border; Stockings—General proportions for Stockings; Scale for Stockings; Socks; Garters; Socks for Babies; Babies' Socks or Slippers; Child's long Sock; Child's first Stocking; The Ribbed Boot; The Over-shoe; The Snow-heel; Little Night Boots; Socks for Invalids; Knit Boots; Scale for Knit Boots; Night Socks; Knit Sole; Knee Cap; Knit Gloves; Driving Mits; Mittens for Babies; Mittens; Armlets; Muffatees; Frill or Ruff; Scarf; Comforter; Handkerchief; Knit Habit-shirt; Knit Half-handkerchief; Honey-comb Shawl; A Tippet; A Purse; A Baby's Knitted Cap; Baby's Hood; Gentleman's Night-cap; Knitted Bags; Kettle Holders; Knit Open Braid; Mats; Coverlet; Blankets; Knit Cotton Doyleys.

CHAPTER XII. GENERAL OBSERVATIONS ON STRAW PLATTING. Apparatus required; Bleaching Box; Mill for the Plat; Bonnet Stand; Box Iron; Dying Kettle; Straw Splitter; On preparing Straw; On Bleaching Straw; Dying Straw black; Directions for Platting; Plats; Plats of Three; Plat of Four; Angular Plat of Four; Plat of Five; Plats of Six; Plats of Seven; Plats of Eight; Plats of Nine; Plats of Ten; Plats of Eleven; Plat of Twelve; Plats of Thirteen; Plat of Fourteen; Plat of Fifteen; Plat of Sixteen; Hollow Spiral Straw-work; The Tuscan Hat; English Leghorn Plat; Bonnets; Receipts for Stiffening; On cleaning Bonnets; Turning Bonnets; Hats; Mats; To make Bobbin Tape.

PLATE. 1.

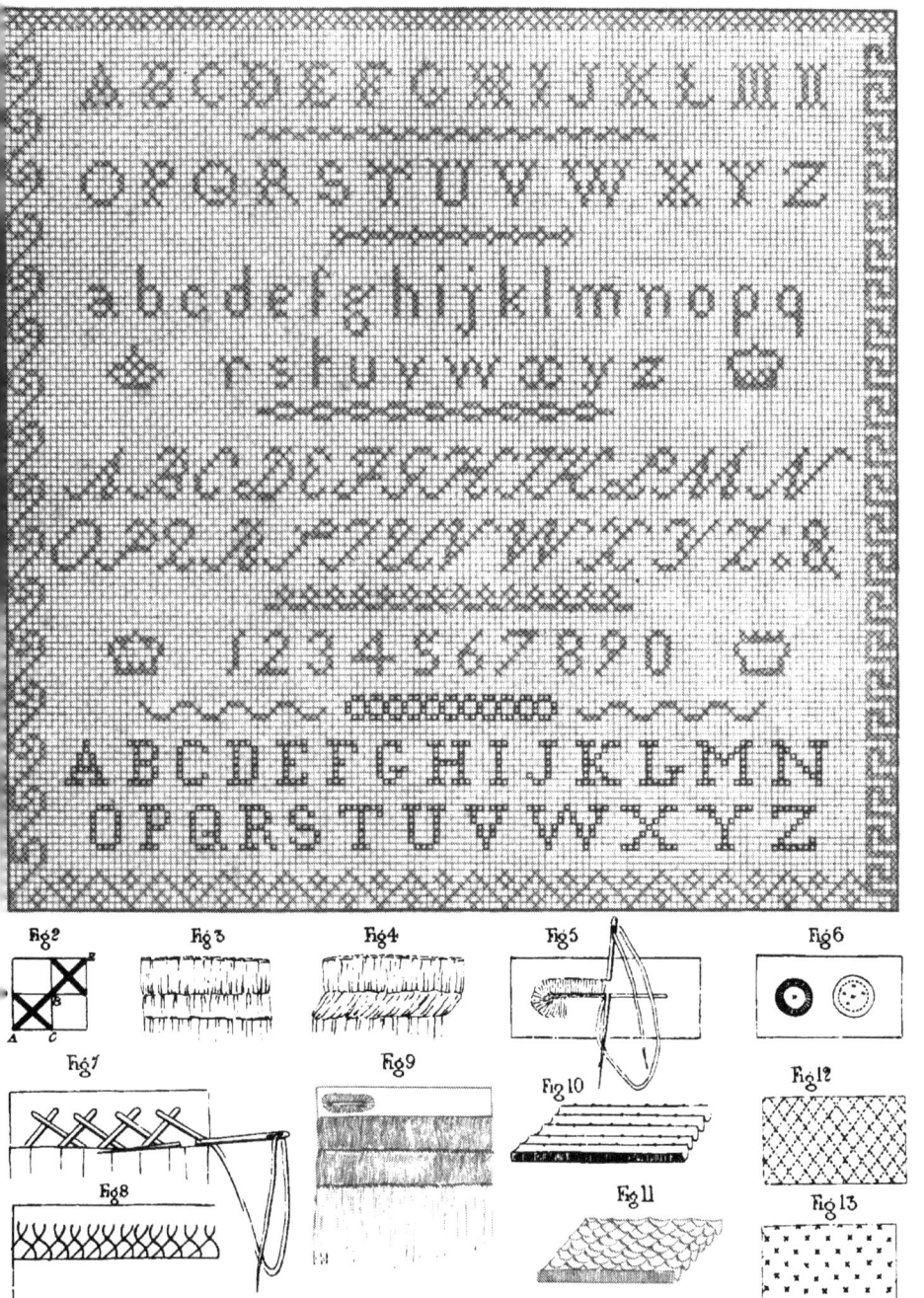

PART FIRST.

CHAPTER I.

A FEW GENERAL OBSERVATIONS ON NEEDLE-WORK.

"But here the needle plies its busy task."—COWPER.

SEE that the edges of the work are perfectly even before turning down, which should be done to a thread, unless the work is not cut straightwise.

The needle and cotton should be adapted to the quality of the work, and when the latter is very fine, rovings taken from it, and used as thread, are very good for the purpose.

The cotton should be always worked the way it unwinds from the reel, for this reason, the needle had better be threaded before cutting off the cotton.

The thimble should be worn on the second finger of the right hand. The needle, while being threaded, is held in the left hand, and the cotton in the right.

The scissors, when used, should have the thumb placed in the upper ring, and the third finger in the lower: they should also be held with the sharper point uppermost.

When work is very strong, the thread used in making it up should be strengthened by waxing.

Thread is much more durable than cotton, and it should therefore be used in working all kinds of linen. Cottons are better for calico, muslin, &c.

All kinds of threads and cottons, especially when coloured, should be kept (when not in use) wrapped up in brown paper, as the air is apt to decay them.

Sewing silks should be wrapped up in soft wash leather.

Buttons, hooks and eyes, tapes, &c. are all better kept folded up, as they are apt to tarnish and decay.

Needles, scissors, and all kinds of steel, injure materially when exposed much to the air, especially at the sea coast.

HEMMING.

Turn down the raw edge twice very evenly, and flatten it with the thumb and finger, taking care to arrange the corners nicely.

In *beginning* to hem, point your needle from your chest towards the right, and after drawing the thread nearly through, stroke the end under the hem, so as to keep it fast without the assistance of a knot, which is always untidy. When your needleful is used, cut off the end, leaving just sufficient to stroke under the hem. In fastening off effectually, sew several stitches close together, and cut off the thread closely. Hem from right to left.

B

SEWING AND FELLING.

The work for sewing is thus prepared: the two selvages are placed together, or if there are no selvages, the raw edge of one piece is turned down once, and the edge of the other piece is turned down double the width, and then half the width is turned back again for the fell. The two pieces are pinned or basted together, with the parts turned down face to face, and held firmly between the finger and thumb: the thread is fastened on by pressing the end carefully into the seam with the needle, and working over it. The stitches should be just deep enough to keep the parts strongly together; they should also lie in a slanting direction, at even distances from each other. When the seam is sewn, the finger should be placed under it, while the thumb nail flattens it down. Turn the work on the other side, and fell the seam just the same as in hemming.

MANTUA-MAKERS' HEMMING.

This is often used instead of sewing, for bags and sleeves that have no linings, or skirts of petticoats, &c., and the work is prepared as follows. Lay the raw edge of one piece a little below that of the other, then turn the upper edge over the lower, twice, as in hemming, and fell it securely down.

STITCHING.

Having observed that your work is quite even, turn down a piece to stitch to, count twelve or fourteen threads from the edge, and draw a thread to stitch upon. In stitching, take two threads back, and pass the needle so as to come out from under two before. Join on a fresh piece of thread by passing the needle between the edges, and bringing it out where the last stitch left off.

GATHERING.

Observe that the part going to be gathered is cut evenly and straight. Divide the piece into half, and then into quarters, putting pins at the divisions as marks; do the same with the piece to which it is to be gathered, by which means the fulness will be equal.

Begin about twelve or fourteen threads from the top, take up three threads on your needle and miss four, more or less according to the fulness required: when a quarter is done, draw the gatherings pretty closely, and secure the thread by twisting it round a pin; then stroke the gathers nicely down, one at a time, with a large needle, so as to make them lie closely and evenly together. Afterwards, untwist the thread from the pin, and loosen the gathers till you have made the quarter gathered, correspond with the quarter to which it is to be sewn. Fasten the thread again firmly to a pin, and sew the gathers strongly on, one at a time, letting the stitches take a slanting direction, so as to slip between the gathers.

RUNNING.

The work for running must be prepared by putting the two edges exactly together, if they are both selvages; but if they are raw edges and afterwards to be felled, one raw edge must be turned down once, and the other laid upon it a few threads from the top. It should be run about six threads below the turned down part. Take three threads and leave three, and back-stitch occasionally, to keep the work firm.

DOUBLE GATHERING OR PUFFING.
PLATE 1. FIG. 3, 4.

Double gathering or puffing is sometimes used in setting on frills, and gives a very neat finished appearance; it is done in the following manner. Gather your frill at the top, in the usual way, and stroke it strongly down; then gather it again below the first gathering, according to the depth of the puffing you wish to make, about half an inch, more or less according to fancy, and sew on the first gathering to the dressing-gown, frock, or whatever you wish to trim, at a distance that corresponds with the width of the puffing: the second gathering is to be sewn to the edge of the dress, so that the part between the two gatherings forms a full hem. Some people make three gatherings, and proceed in the same way, forming the two full hems or puffings. It is usually put on straight, but sometimes in sewing on, the hem is drawn obliquely, or to one side, which makes a little variety, and when there are three gatherings, one hem is drawn to one side, and the other to the opposite one, but this requires much exactness to do it equally.

GERMAN HEMMING.

German hemming or felling is a neat substitute for sewing, where it is desirable that the seam should lie very flat; it is sometimes employed with great advantage for sleeves, and even in the long seams of shifts. It is quite as strong as the old method of a seam and fell, and looks better, as it is all done on the wrong side.

Turn down the raw edges of both your pieces of cloth once, (having them both turned down next you,) and lay one below the other, so that the smooth top of the lower one does not touch the edge of the upper one, but is just below it, then hem or fell the lower one to the cloth against which it is laid, still holding it before you, as you had prepared it, which is exactly like hemming upside down. When you have got to the end of your seam, open your sleeve, or whatever you are doing, and lay the upper fold over the lower edge, which you must then fell neatly down, and it is completed.

WHIPPING.

The edge for whipping should be cut particularly smooth, and divided into halves and quarters; the muslin is then rolled very tightly with the left thumb upon the finger, about ten threads from the edge. The cotton with which you whip should be very strong and even, and the needle should be stuck in on the outside, and brought out on the inside, the needle pointing towards your chest. Take the stitches very evenly, and so as to draw easily. Draw the whipping up to the width of the piece to which it is going to be sewn; pin it down, and sew it firmly, holding the whipping towards you, and letting the stitches lie athwart, so as to be hidden between the whips. If you stroke whipping with a large pin or needle, in the same way as in gathering, it adds much to its neat appearance in setting on, and makes it more easy to do.

BUTTON-HOLES.
PLATE 1. FIG. 5.

Cut the button-hole with a chisel (or the proper scissors made for that purpose) by a thread, the same size as the width across the button. In holding the work, let the button-hole lie lengthwise along the fore-finger. Begin at the side opposite the thumb farthest from the point of the finger. Put the needle in through the wrong side of the hole, and bring it out five threads down on the right. The stitch is made by putting the needle through the loop of the thread before it is drawn close. Observe that you keep your work evenly by the thread, and do not turn the corners too soon; the needle should be put in between every two threads, else the work will not be thick enough. It has a neat effect to stitch all round the button-hole.

HERRING-BONING.

PLATE 1. FIG. 7, 8.

This is a stitch generally used for flannels and other woollens, also, for carpets, druggets, window-blinds, &c. when a hem would be thick and clumsy from being turned down twice; whereas in herring-boning the edge is turned down only once, and lies flat and more compact.

Turn the work down once evenly, first cutting off any woollen fuzz at the raw edge which looks untidy, and then beginning to work from the left of your piece of work towards the right, take a stitch of two or three threads close under the raw turned-down edge, then put in your needle half way up the turned-down part, and four or five threads towards the right hand, and make another stitch of three threads; bring down the needle, and make another stitch as before under the raw edge, still working a few threads each time farther to the right hand, and so on forming a stitch something like the backbone of a fish, and therefore termed herring-bone. This same stitch done on muslin with fine cord or braid is very ornamental, and is often used at the tops of hems or bodies of infants' robes.

DARNING.

"A stitch in time saves nine."—POOR RICHARD.

The stocking or work should be held across the first and second fingers of the left hand. In beginning to darn, the needle should be held pointed from the chest. The work should be begun a few threads before the hole, or even the thin place, to give a firmer hold to the cotton. Take one thread and leave one, alternately till the row is complete; afterwards, point the needle towards the chest, and take up the intermediate threads which were left before. The cotton must not be drawn tight, as it is apt to shrink in washing, therefore a loop should be left at each end. Continue darning backwards and forwards till the hole and thin parts are covered, afterwards begin to darn cross-wise, being particularly careful to avoid splitting the threads or pulling the loops tight.

Some people make a point of running the feet of new stockings all over, which is very advisable for men and boys who wear boots, as it preserves them much longer.

There are a variety of stitches in darning, some of which have a very neat appearance, among others the following:—

Take up 1 thread and leave 2
Take up 2 2
Take up 1 3
Take up 2 4
Take up 3 3

Table linen, when darned, looks neater if the work is done in some pattern; thus, a diamond or circle looks more tidy than an irregular patch of darning.

ON MENDING A CRACK.

In taking up a crack in a stocking, fasten the thread firmly on, and then take the two half loops which are next each other on one side of the crack, upon the needle, and having drawn the thread through them, do the same on the other side, making the half loop, which was last taken up on either side, the first of the next stitch.

ON TAKING UP A LADDER.

A ladder is caused by the fall or dropping of a stitch, which it is necessary to pick up as soon as possible, by putting the needle into the loop that has fallen, and drawing the bar immediately above through the loop, thus the bar becomes a loop in its turn, and the next bar above is in like manner drawn through it, till all are taken up, when the last loop is well secured and darned over.

ON MAKING BUTTONS.
PLATE 1. FIG. 6.

Cover your piece of wire with a square piece of calico, which you must double over the corners, and sew firmly in the middle; afterwards stitch the button round close to the wire, or else work over the wire the button-hole stitch, and in the centre, work a little regular star to set it off.

ON MAKING TUCKS.

Tucks should be very even; for this purpose, have a bit of card on which is notched the depth of each tuck, and also the space between them. Tucks should be run firmly in small regular stitches, constantly taking a back-stitch as you go on.

MARKING.

In marking, two threads are generally taken each way. There are three ways in which the needle is passed before the stitch is perfect. One is aslant from you towards the right hand; the second is straight downwards towards you; the third is across or aslant from you towards the left hand, taking care to bring out the needle at that corner of the stitch nearest the one you are going to make. The generality of markers make the first stitch aslant twice over, to make it clearer before proceeding onwards; thus, in Plate 1, Fig. 2, the thread, being brought out at A, passes across to B, and out again at A; again, across to B, and out at C; then, aslant to D, and out again at B, ready to proceed to the next stitch. Where there are two or three letters to be marked, the thread should be neatly fastened off at the end of each letter and not carried on from one to the other. Two or four threads are left between the letters, according to the quality of the article to be marked. In linen, eight threads are generally left. In gentlemen's families, house linen is either marked with the gentleman's initials, or else with those of the lady's christian name added to the gentleman's full initials, his christian name coming first: thus, supposing Edward Montagu's wife is named Louisa, the initials would be E. L. M., afterwards the name of the cloth and the number are marked thus:

E. L. M.
G. C.
8
. . 37.

signifying, Edward Louisa Montagu, Glass Cloth, Number 8, 1837. There are many pretty marking patterns for samplers, flat canvass pincushions, or needle-books. In noblemen's families, the marks are surmounted by coronets. There are also two other kinds of marking; the one is the same stitch as that above described, but differing in the form of the letters, which are in writing or Italian characters; this may best be done by copying written letters accurately: the other kind of marking is, by making the letters perfectly straight, as in printing, and instead of the marking stitch, working them in small oylet holes.

In Plate 1, Fig. 1, the sampler drawn gives an accurate idea of the canvass, and the shape of all the letters in the different alphabets. The first alphabet is that in most general use; the second contains the small letters; the third is a correct representation of the Italian characters, which are much used for marking pocket handkerchiefs and other fine articles of dress; the fourth and last is quite a fancy stitch, and rarely employed. The oylet holes are formed by working in small stitches round each square, about four stitches in the four corners, and four intermediate stitches between, are necessary to form each oylet hole.

PIPING

Is a neat mode of finishing capes, sleeves at the wrist, waistbands, tops of bodies, &c., and is sewn on in the following way.

Cut crosswise strips of silk, (or whatever other material you are piping with,) sufficiently wide to admit well the cord, run these strips neatly together, to make them of a proper length for the piping you want. Some people run the silk on the cord first, before sewing it to the piece of work; others, however, merely lay the cord neatly inside the silk, which is then placed on the edge of the work to which it is piped, so that the two raw edges of the strip of silk enclosing the cord should lie on the raw edge of the work; the three thicknesses are then all firmly run together, the stitches being made just below the cord. When it is sewn on, the raw edges are pressed inwards, so as to make the cord set at the edge. The lining is then neatly put in, which covers these edges and makes all look tidy.

PLAITING.

Care should be taken that the plaits lie evenly one against another, and that they are of the same size, especially in frills, sleeves, &c. In double plaiting, the plaits lie both ways, and look very handsome and full in frills: it requires great care to do them evenly, without which they will not look well.

ON LINING SLEEVES, BAGS, &c.

After cutting out the lining exactly the same size as the sleeve, fold it very carefully, so as to make the raw edges lie exactly one on the other; do the same with the sleeve, taking care to fold the wrong side outwards. Place the lining on the sleeve and pin them evenly together; after which, run all the four thicknesses strongly down the seam. Put your hand in the sleeve, and turn it inside out, drawing the lining inside; the seam is then quite neat, both inside and outside, as the stitches lie between the lining and the outer silk. The same should be done with bags, and any other thing that will admit of it.

ON BRAIDING.

This work can scarcely come under the head of plain work, still, as children's dresses are so much ornamented with it, a few observations may be useful. The very fine flat braid should be used, as it looks so much neater than that which is thick; it is sold in knots. Silk braids look well on silk, merino, or muslin; but cotton is the best for jean, prints, or stuffs. The pattern should be drawn on silver paper, which is tacked on the piece of work, and the braid worked on it with the same coloured sewing silk, as thread washes white. To sew on silk braid, you should use the silk drawn out of the braid, as it is finer and more even, and will match the colour better than any other you can procure: cut off, therefore, a bit the length of a needleful, to keep for the purpose of unroving. If you want to take the pattern of a piece of work upon paper, place some letter paper on the work, and while holding it firmly, rub the paper well with half a nutmeg, which will mark the pattern correctly, and sufficiently distinct on the paper to admit of its being inked afterwards. Two shades of braid sewn close together have a pretty effect.

BIASSING.
PLATE I. FIG. 9.

In biassing, the first part of the stitch resembles gathering, and after stroking in down with a large needle or pin, you lay, upon the right side of the gathers, a thread very much thicker than that you are using in your needle; you then sew over this thread, taking hold, at the same time, of the gathering thread, and pointing your needle to your chest; you must be very careful to put your needle between every gather: the thick thread, thus worked upon the gathering, has a very neat effect, and adds much to its strength; two or three rows of it, at short distances from each other, look very well: it is particularly suitable for the shoulders and sleeves of dresses, and for children's saccarines, pelisses, &c. It is a good plan to bias with sewing and netting silk, in preference to thread, as it is much stronger.

GAGING.

This is very suitable for the fronts of children's dresses, and the tops of the cuffs of sleeves; it is done as follows. Take up the stitches at regular intervals of half an inch, for the first row. For the second, continue doing the same; letting the needle, however, take up the intermediate parts. The third row resembles the first, and so on. For the purpose of securing the gathers firmly, work them as follows, with very strong netting silk. Take on your needle the two first gathers, and the thread on which they run, pulling your thread firmly through. For the next stitch, again take two gathers and the thread upon your needle, letting the first of them be the last gather that was taken up at the former stitch, so that the work proceeds but by one gather at a time. Observe to draw the netting silk as tightly as possible, so as to make the stitches lie very closely together, in a slanting position.

HONEY-COMBING.
PLATE 1. FIG. 10, 11.

This sort of work is much used for the inside of the tops of work-boxes, and sometimes for the tops and heads of beds; it is usually done with silk, satin, or velvet, for the former; and highly-glazed chintz or calico, for the latter. Crease your material in even folds, taking care to have them very regular, and of a proper depth to suit the purpose for which it is intended; with a strong thread, tack the folds together with long stitches, so as to make them lie compactly one against another; then, with sewing silk of the proper colour, stitch firmly together, at moderate equal distances, the first and second folds: afterwards, stitch the second and third folds, at equal distances, taking your stitches in the intermediate intervals (see Plate 1, Fig. 10 and 11). The third and fourth folds are only repetitions of the first and second, and by continuing your work in this way, the stitches of the alternate rows will accord with each other. When the piece is completed, and the tacking thread drawn out, pull your work open, and it will form puffings, in the shape of diamonds, on the right side.

BINDING.

Flannel is generally bound with sarsenet ribbon, or a kind of thin tape called flannel binding. This is generally put on so as merely to shew a little way over the edge on the right side, and should be neatly and firmly hemmed down. On the other side, run the binding down with small neat stitches, so as to look very tidy on the right side. Some people, in binding flannel, turn half on the other side of the edge, but this is not nearly so neat in appearance.

QUILTING.
PLATE 1. FIG. 12, 13.

Is generally employed for coverlets, silk shoes, cushions, linings of work-baskets and boxes; also, for babies' bonnets, hoods, &c. &c.; and is well adapted to those purposes for which warmth and softness are essential.

It is done in the following manner. Lay a piece of flannel, demet, or other soft substance, between the satin (or other material forming the outside) and the lining of whatever you are going to make.

Run it firmly together, taking care that the stitches go through, not only the satin, but the flannel and lining. The running is done in diamonds, squares, octagons, or any other pattern with very small stitches, in silk the same colour as the material. Coverlets are often quilted with patterns of birds, fishes, stars, &c. &c.

Another kind of quilting, which looks very neat, is done as follows. Baste the piece of work in diamonds, with very long stitches of thread, and then, with your needle, work a little star at each of the intersections or points of the diamonds, putting in your needle between the material and the lining, when the thread is ready to be carried from one star to another, to conceal the stitches.

MAKING ROULEAUS.

These are used for trimming dresses, capes, &c., and are made of satin, silk, or velvet, in the following manner. Cut pieces of the material crosswise, about one or more nails, and join a sufficient number of them to form the length required; after which double the strip in two, on the wrong side, and run along near the edge. When you have got to the end, see that your needle is fastened firmly, with strong thread to it, and turn your needle inside the roll, running it through as you would a bodkin, and, on pulling it gently out, it will pull the rouleau inside out, and make it look neat; after which, draw sufficient wool through the rouleau to fill it.

CORONATION BRAID.

This kind of braid is bought in knots, and resembles Fig. 10, Plate 1. In putting it on frocks, it may be sewn in various patterns of leaves, &c.: it looks pretty, and both wears and washes well. (See Plate 5, Fig. 28, 29.)

CORD SEWN ON.

This is often put on infants' frock bodies, it looks neat and washes remarkably well. It is sewn on in waves, diamonds, vandykes, or any other pattern. The thread for sewing it on should be fine, and the stitches very small.

CHAIN STITCH.
PLATE 5. FIG. 21.

It is a kind of ornamental work, which, as it is often used in frock bodies for children, will be here explained; together with some other fancy stitches, although they do not strictly come under the head of plain work.

Chain stitch is done as follows. Thread your needle with fine round union cord, braid, or bobbin; tie a knot at the end of it, and draw the cord through to the right side of your work. Let your cord hang loosely in front, while you stick in your needle, as in the Plate, and bring it out below, inclining it a little to the left, passing your needle over your thread as you draw it out, so as to form a loop. Draw out the needle, taking care not to pull the stitch tightly, and repeat the same, putting the needle in a little higher, and to the right hand of the place where it was last drawn out: thus each new loop begins within the lower part of the preceding one, and you produce the effect of a chain.

FANCY CHAIN STITCH.
PLATE 5. FIG. 22.

This is a very pretty stitch for ornamenting babies' dresses, and especially their hats, and should be worked in netting silk, silk cord, or braid. The stitch resembles that of the common chain stitch above mentioned, excepting that very little is taken up on the needle at a time, and the stitches made far apart. The stitch may be varied according to whether the needle slants little or much. If it is made to lie quite horizontally before the work, it becomes button-hole stitch at once.

CHAIN STITCH ON GATHERS.

This has a remarkably neat effect, and if done with coloured worsted upon Holland dresses, when biassed or gaged, it will wash and wear well. Take up two gathers at a time for each stitch, always taking one old, and one new gather on the needle at a time.

FANCY BOBBIN EDGING.
PLATE 5. FIG. 18.

This is pretty for the edges of frocks and robings, and is a very simple stitch, which wears well. After hemming the edge, tie a knot at the end of your bobbin, and draw it through to the right side of the work, just below the hem. Carry the bobbin over the hem, by sticking in your needle at the wrong side, bringing it through; after which, on drawing the loop to the proper size, pass your bobbin through it, and begin the next stitch, and so on, forming a succession of loops.

FANCY HERRING-BONING.
PLATE 5. FIG. 23.

This stitch resembles that of the common herring-bone, except that it is worked perpendicularly instead of from left to right, and the thread is brought round behind the needle, as represented in Plate 5, which gives a greater finish to the stitch.

DOUBLE HERRING-BONING.
PLATE 5. FIG. 27.

This pattern is too intricate to describe, farther than by saying it is a kind of double herring-bone on each side. The Plate gives a tolerably accurate idea of the stitch. As great care is requisite to keep the pattern even, it is better to run a tacking-thread, as a guide, down the middle of it.

THE ANGULAR STITCH.
PLATE 5. FIG. 24.

This is a neat ornament for capes, cuffs, and the skirts of children's pelisses, and resembles the button-hole stitch, but is carried angularly from right to left, to form the pattern. Care should be taken to make the pattern of equal width and very even and straight, as much of its merit depends upon its regularity.

THE SERPENTINE STITCH.
PLATE 5. FIG. 25.

This is a peculiarly pretty work, and much employed for children's dresses. It is worked with the hand, and sewn on to the material when made. Take the cord, knot it so as to form a loop at one end, and pass the other end through the loop towards the front, to form another loop to the right hand; continue passing the bobbin first through the loop on one side, and then through the loop on the other, directing the cord so as to pass from the outer side of the work invariably towards the inner, or that part next the work. The Plate will give a clearer representation of this than can be easily done by words.

THE HORSE-SHOE STITCH.
PLATE 5. FIG. 20.

This stitch is worked from left to right, as seen in the Plate, and is pretty when worked near to the edge of robings, hems, &c. The Plate gives so clear a representation of the way to hold the needle and thread, that no explanation is necessary. It is done with thick loosely twisted cotton or bobbin.

FANCY BUTTON-HOLE STITCH.
PLATE 5. FIG. 19.

This is very pretty for the fronts of bodies, also for the bands and shoulder-bits, and above the broad hems or tucks of frocks. It resembles a very wide button-hole stitch. It washes and wears well.

CORAL PATTERN.
PLATE 5. FIG. 26.

This pattern is particularly suitable for the tops of broad hems, or the waistbands of children's frocks. It requires great accuracy in the working; and if attempted by an inexperienced person, it would be desirable to run lines, in long stitches, to determine the middle and outer sides of the pattern. It can be best understood by reference to the Plate, merely remarking that the stitch is begun on the left hand, and continued alternately from left to right, always pointing the needle towards the centre.

GENERAL RULES FOR COMPLETING WORK.

" The threaded steel
Flies swiftly, and unfelt the task proceeds."—COWPER.

In making up dresses, all openings of pocket-holes, of sleeves near the wrist, &c. &c., should be very firmly fastened off, as they are apt to tear. There are two or three modes of making them strong: one is by working round the part in button-hole stitch, and also by making a bar from one side to the other, by passing the needle backwards and forwards several times, working the button-hole stitch upon the bar; a second is by sewing a piece of strong tape upon the hem, about an inch on each side from the bottom; and a third way, which can only be done when the pocket-hole is in a seam, is by making one side lap over the other considerably, by which means the slit is not only strengthened, but it does not gape open, which always has an untidy appearance. To prevent dresses from opening at the slit below the band, it is a good plan to extend the gathers, on one side, an inch beyond the band, by joining a piece of strong tape to the end of it, and sewing the gathers neatly upon it. This piece of tape must be contrived so as to hook or button on to the band on the other side, so as to lap over the slit, and thus prevent its opening.

In fastening on tapes, sew firmly in close small stitches round the three outer sides, and back-stitch across the fourth.

In sewing on buttons, it is best to put the needle in and out, so as to form a cross stitch in the centre over and over again, till firmly fastened.

In sewing on the long tapes to the bands of petticoats, gowns, &c., it is an excellect plan to make a large button-hole near one end, through which the tape of the other end is passed, before brought to tie in front.

The gussets of sleeves, &c., are put in as follows. Take the piece intended for the gusset and prove, by folding it crosswise, that it is a perfect square; after which, it is the best and most durable plan to hem it all round: next hem the two ends of the sleeve, and fix on the gusset by sewing one end of the sleeve firmly to one side of the gusset, and the other end of the sleeve to the next side of the gusset, immediately round the corner. The easiest mode of ascertaining which sides of the gusset are joined to the sleeve, is by folding the gusset corner-wise, and the two sides that lie one above the other are sewn to the two ends of the sleeve, and the other two sides, lying also one above the other, form that part of the sleeve fastened to the body of the dress. Sometimes the gusset is cut out much smaller than the ends of the sleeve, especially for baby clothes, in which case the sides of the gusset forming the part fastened to the skirt, ought to be still placed so as to continue in a line with those sides of the sleeve sewn on to the skirt. That part of the ends of the sleeve which is longer than the gusset should be sewn together.

Some sleeves are cut with the gussets in one length, so that it is only necessary to turn up the one corner of the piece, like a half handkerchief, so as to make it lie upon the side of the strip which is folded just in half, and when the second end is sewn to that part which meets it, the sleeve is formed, and only requires hemming at the bottom to complete it, before putting it in.

In setting a long sleeve, such as a shirt or night-gown sleeve, into a wristband, let the slit be sufficiently long to admit of the wristband being laid open and easily ironed. The gathers at the top of the sleeve should be set into a space exactly the same as the wristband, to make it lie flat also. These little attentions are a great assistance to the washer-woman.

CHAPTER II.

A FEW OBSERVATIONS ON PURCHASING GOODS.

"Many have been ruined by buying good pennyworths."—POOR RICHARD.

IT is very bad economy to purchase, for articles of clothing, cheap bargains. They generally consist of damaged goods, or are otherwise inferior in their quality, as it stands to reason that no mercer would feel inclined to sell his stock at a lower rate than its worth.

The only parts of dress which it may be sometimes advisable to purchase at a cheap rate, are gloves, ribbons, and such articles as are easily soiled long before being worn out, and cannot well be cleaned: in large towns and dirty neighbourhoods they are soon discoloured, and therefore their durability is of little consequence.

Linens, calicoes, woollens, prints, &c., should be carefully chosen from the best, as they are in constant wash and wear, and would soon become worn and threadbare if not good and strong. Two sets of good linen will wear out three or four sets of inferior, which, when the expense of making up is considered, becomes, in its turn, far more expensive, besides the extra trouble and time, both of which are well worth saving.

Observe that the cloth is the proper width for the articles wanted, so as to cut out to the best advantage. Much waste may arise from its being one nail too wide or too narrow. Take notice that the selvages, and also the threads, are even and good both ways.

CALICO.

Observe that it is free from dress, which is a preparation of lime employed by the manufacturers to make it of a better colour, as, if (as is often the case) the dressing is too high in proportion to the strength of the threads, it becomes rotten, tears, and wears badly, and after washing, is poor and thin, like canvass; choose your calico, therefore, undressed, for then you can more exactly judge of its quality and strength. It should be soft, without specks, and the threads and selvages even. It is often cheaper to buy the whole piece, if much is wanted, as a small allowance is made per yard. If a small quantity is wanted for a baby's caps, shirts, &c., it is often good economy to purchase remnants, fencings, or felts, by which means you sometimes get the best qualities for very low prices. Calico runs of various widths and qualities: the unbleached, or grey, is the best for shifts, boys' shirts, &c., for the lower orders, being warmer and stronger than the white.

The following are the useful widths, with the general prices at the present time, though, of course, they are constantly varying.

Unbleached calico, from 13 nails wide to 2 yards 4 nails, price from 4d. to 1s. 6d.

Fine white calico for caps, aprons, &c., from 12 nails upwards to 1$\frac{1}{2}$ yard, price from 4d. upwards.

Stout calico, from 14 nails upwards to 3 yards wide, price from 8d. to 3s.

LINEN.

The Suffolk hemp is considered the best. The threads should be particularly even. The useful widths are from 13$\frac{1}{4}$ nails to 16, for shirting. The common linen is sometimes as low as 8d. or 9$\frac{1}{2}d$. per yard, and the best at 2s. 9d. or 3s. Linen should be scalded before it is cut out and made up, as it is too stiff to allow of its being sewn with ease.

LAWN.

Lawn is merely a finer quality of linen, and is sometimes used for the fronts of gentlemen's shirts, also for babies' night-caps, shirts, frilling, &c. Its width varies from 13 nails upwards, and the price from about 4s. to 8s.

CAMBRIC.

Cambric is a finer sort of lawn. Its width is about three-quarters of a yard, and the price from 4s. to 12s.

MUSLIN CHECKS.

The small check which is used for caps generally wears the best. Observe that the thin places between the checks are good, and the threads even. They are generally 1$\frac{1}{4}$ yard wide, and from 9d. to 20d. or 2s. per yard.

BLUE CHECKS.

This is very serviceable for aprons, and should be entirely linen, if wanted to wear well. It runs from 1 yard wide to 1$\frac{1}{4}$ yard, and is from 3d. to 16d. per yard.

The cotton check answers very well for children's pinbefores, though not nearly so durable as the other. It is of various widths, and from 6d. to 1s. per yard.

PRINTS, CHINTZES, AND GINGHAMS.

These often wash very badly: if, therefore, you are buying a doubtful colour, it would be advisable to beg a piece as a pattern, and wash half of it, which, when compared with the other half, will shew at once whether the colours are fixed or not. They are better when the pattern is the same on both sides.

Dark and light blue, lilac, buff, bright brown, red, and pink are good wearing colours.

Green, chocolate, and violet are very fading colours. They vary in price from 3d. to 10d., or even 1s. The usual width for gowns is 11 nails. The width sold for aprons is 14 nails.

FLANNELS.

The Welsh is far superior to the Lancashire, and both washes and wears better; the latter is, however, cheaper. It is generally of a yellowish colour, while the Welsh is more of a blue grey.

Purchasing large quantities at the fairs at Welsh-Pool, Newtown, and other Welsh markets, is good economy, as several yards are often given in to the hundred. The common flannels for petticoats are 9d. to 14d. per yard, and the finer upwards, to 2s. or 3s. 8d.: they vary in width from 9 nails to 16. New flannel should be plunged in scalding water, and hung out to dry without wringing.

CLOTH.

Cloth should be smooth, with a good nap.

STUFFS.

Observe that they are evenly dyed, as they are often dashed. Hold them up to the light, that you may better judge of their quality. The black dye is apt to decay the stuff. Brown and dark green are particularly good wearing colours. Width from $\frac{1}{2}$ and $\frac{3}{4}$ yard, upwards. Price from 8d. to 2s.

CRAPE.

Crape is often dashed and spotted, as it is a difficult article to take dye evenly. Have it spread over white before buying it, when you can more easily detect blemishes. The width is 1 yard, and the price 2s. to 4s. 6d.

SATIN.

It should be soft and thick, unless for trimming caps, when a poorer kind may be used. When wanted for trimmings, satin should be cut crosswise.—(See the end of Chapter III.) It is from $\frac{1}{2}$ yard to 10 nails wide, and from 2s. 6d. to 7s. 6d.

SILKS

Should not be too stiff, thin, or papery, as they are apt to tear or slit in the plaits and folds. See that they are soft, without specks or stains; and, as silk dresses turn well, and even dye afterwards, it would be advisable to have no wrong side—that is, the pattern equally good on both sides. They are generally $\frac{1}{2}$ yard wide, though black silk of 1 yard in width can be bought for aprons.

In cheap silks, a kind of camel's hair is frequently woven to make them appear richer and thicker to the touch, but this is highly injurious to the silk, as it causes it to wear very ill, and cut in all the folds and creases. The way to detect the existence of camel hair in silks, is to take a little bit in the hand and pull it gently crossway, and if there be any camel hair interwoven with the silk it will spring back as if elastic, making a soft kind of whistling sound.

CHAPTER III.

GENERAL RULES FOR CUTTING OUT.

"Waste not, want not."
"Cut your coat according to your cloth."

ARTICLES of clothing are measured by cloth measure.

     2¼ inches make 1 nail.
     4 nails — 1 quarter.
     4 quarters — 1 yard.
     5 — — 1 English ell.
     6 — — 1 French ell.

All linens, calicoes, &c., to be washed before cut out.

All linens, including lawn, cambric, and Holland, should be cut by the thread.

All calicoes, muslins, and flannels will tear, though the former, unless very stout, pull a good deal awry.

All small articles, as gussets, should be cut, in preference to being torn.

Cutting out whole sets of things together often prevents much waste; hence it is better to cut out six or twelve shirts at once, than only one at a time.

Skirts, sleeves, wristbands, shoulder-straps, collars, waistbands, and every thing liable to be stretched in wearing, to be cut selvage-wise.

Frills, flounces, and pieces fulled between bands, are usually cut the width way.

Frills for caps are generally twice as long as the article they are to be frilled upon; three times is very full, and is sometimes used for neck frills.

Linings of hats, bonnets, fronts, and backs of gowns, tippets, most women's collars, and every thing intended to set well and closely, of an irregular shape or surface, to be cut crosswise.

Pipings and linings to broad hems always to be cut crosswise.

In cutting crosswise, first fold the end of the piece like a half-handkerchief, so as to lay the raw edge evenly against the selvage side, and cut off the half square, from which cut the strips for piping, &c.

To cut off a yard crosswise, measure a yard along each of the selvage sides, (after the half square has been cut off) crease it slantingly across, and cut it.

Satins, velvets, and some silks, may be purchased cut the cross way, as well as the straight.

CHAPTER IV.

THE WORK-BOX.

> " Your thimble gone ? Your scissors, where are they?
> Your needles, pins, your thread, and tapes all lost.
> Your house-wife here, and there your work-bag tost."—POEMS.

THE next thing which will come under our observation is the work-box, or basket, and of this it may be useful to say a few words, as much of the comfort of a good workwoman depends on the choice and arrangement of her tools (if they may be so termed) and materials.

A work-box, or basket, should be large enough to hold a moderate supply of work and all its requisites, without being of such a size as to be inconvenient to carry about, or lift with ease. There should be in it divisions or partitions, as they assist in keeping it in order; but some persons are apt to run into the extreme of over-partitioning their boxes, which defeats its own purpose and becomes troublesome: this should be carefully avoided.

A work-box should contain six or eight of the useful sized white reel sewing cottons, black cotton, and silks, white, black, and coloured, both round and for darning; a few useful tapes, bobbin, galloon, buttons of all kinds, including thread, pearl, metal, and black; also, hooks and eyes. An ample needle-book, containing a page of kerseymere for each sized needle, not omitting the darning, glove, stay, and worsted or carpet needles.

There are various kinds of scissors; the most useful are,

A large pair, for cutting out linen;
A medium size, for common use;
A small pair with rounded points;
A smaller pair with sharper points, for cutting out muslin work, &c.;
Lace scissors with a flat knob at one of the points;
Button-hole scissors.

A pincushion, an emery cushion, a waxen reel for strengthening thread, a stiletto, bodkins, a thimble, a small knife, and a yard measure, made like a carpenter's foot rule, only with nails instead of inches marked upon it: for a further description of it, see explanation to Plate 24.

These complete the list of things necessary for a good workwoman; other things, as shield, tweezers, which are often added, may be considered as superfluities.

It is a good plan to fit up a square basket for the use of each working servant in the house, as for instance, the lady's-maid, the nurse, the house-maid, the laundry-maid. These baskets should vary sufficiently in form and size to be easily distinguished one from the other; the kind usually sold for babies' baskets is the most convenient, being large enough to hold plenty of work, and yet shallow, so as easily to search for things at the bottom.

To these baskets should belong, a small tin box for buttons, hooks and eyes, bodkins, &c.; a large pair of scissors and sheath tied to each other, and fastened by a long string to the handle of the basket. A heavy pincushion, formed of a brick or piece of iron or lead, placed in a bag full of bran, padded with flannel, and covered over with print or calico. A large needle-book. A bag to contain tapes, silks, darning cottons, &c. It is advisable to mark the scissors-sheath, needle-book, pincushion, bag, and even basket, with the initial of the maid by whom it is used, as H. B. for house-maid's basket.

A rag bag is a desirable thing to have hung up in some conspicuous part of the house, into which all odd bits, and even shreds, of calico, print, linen, muslin, &c. should be put; as they are useful to come in when a gusset or chin stay, or other small article is wanting. Those bits too small for this purpose may still be used by school children, for practising stitches of needle-work upon; or, at all events, may be disposed of to the rag merchants, and thus prove of some value at last. Another family bag, for the purpose of containing stray tapes, or shoe strings, hooks, eyes, odd buttons, pieces of silk, or bits of ribbon, may be kept with advantage; especially where there is a large family of children, whose demands for these small articles are daily and constant.

CHAPTER V.

ON BABY-LINEN, WITH SCALES FOR CLOTHES OF OLDER CHILDREN.

*"The mother, wi' her needle and her shears,
Gars auld claes look amaist as weel 's the new."*—BURNS

THE following articles are necessary to be prepared for an infant's first dress, and are equally applicable (with some exceptions) to the poor as well as the rich, though the quality of the materials, of course, must differ. The average number of each article usually provided by ladies for an infant's wardrobe, may here be introduced with propriety, though they must vary according to circumstances. Persons to whom economy is a great object may find a much smaller stock answer as well, if they are able to send the linen often to the wash.

Shirts	12 to 18	Plate 2	Fig. 23
Flannel bands	2 — 4	— 3	— 12
Flannel caps	2 — 3	— 2	— 8
Night-caps	6 — 12	— 2	— 4
Day-caps	3 — 6	— 2	—
Napkins (dozens of)	4 — 6	— 3	— 11
Pilchers	4 — 6	— 3	— 10
Pinafores	6 — 12	— 3	— 18
Bedgowns	4 — 6	— 3	— 16
First day-gowns	3 — 4	— 3	— 14
Night-flannels	3 — 4	— 3	— 1, 2
Day-flannels	3 — 4	— 3	— 3
Flannel cloak	1 — 2	— 4	— 19, 24
Flannel shawl	2 — 3	—	
Robes	4 — 6	— 4	— 2 to 8
Petticoats	4 — 6	— 4	— 1
Socks	4 — 8	—	—
Hood	1	— 4	— 29
Cloak or pelisse	1	— 4	— 20, 21, 23

Also, the following et ceteras:—

One receiver; 1 basket-cover; 1 flannel, and 1 India-rubber apron; 6 nursery soft towels; 1 cradle, bassinette, or crib-cover, and bedding; 1 pincushion.

LENDING LINEN FOR THE POOR.

Linen is often lent by ladies to the poor, at their confinements, in bags, boxes, or baskets, containing the following articles:—

WOMAN.	Pl. Fig.	BABY.	Pl. Fig.
2 shifts	6..2	3 shirts	2.27
2 night jackets	8..2	3 caps	2..4
2 caps	9..2 or 20	1 flannel cap	2..8
1 flannel petticoat	8..9	1 flannel band	3.12
1 flannel gown (or shawl)	10..4	3 night-gowns	3.12
1 pair of sheets		2 flannel gowns	3..6
1 roll of flannel, 4 breadths long, and ¼ yard deep		12 napkins	3..4
		2 soft towels	3.11

Also, may be added, a baby's crockery bottle, bed-pan, dust-bag, pair of blankets, bottle of castor oil, sal volatile, with proper directions pasted on, some large pins, strong thread, and a few books.

The most convenient kind of basket for containing these articles of clothing, is a light wicker-work one, about 20 inches long, 12 inches wide, and 20 inches high. This size holds two folded sheets, side by side, at the bottom, and all the rest above. It should have two handles, sufficiently high to allow of the lid opening easily. (See Plate 5, Fig. 14.)

A FEW GENERAL OBSERVATIONS.

Baby-linen should be cut out with great exactness and precision, and made up with the most scrupulous neatness. In all the patterns, an eye should be had to their being contrived so as to put on with the greatest comfort and ease to the infant, and made to button or tie readily. No hard seams, buttons, or runners should come in contact with their tender skin, therefore all strings should be made to tie on the outside.

To each head a scale is affixed, by which the same patterns may be cut out of various sizes, in proper proportions, to suit children of different ages.

There are three lengths for the skirts of baby-linen; the first and longest, for the rich, is generally 18 nails, and for the poor, 16; the second size, commonly called three-quarters, is about 15 nails for the rich, and 13 for the poor; the third size, or short coats, is about half a yard.

To prevent mistakes, observe, that on all occasions, the number of nails marked on the Plate, refers to the size of the article when cut out, and not when made up.

CAPS

Are generally made of soft calico, or checked muslin, with muslin frills, for the poor, and of fine lawn or cambric, with cambric frills or lace borders for the higher classes. Babies' caps, of whatever size they may be, are generally cut so as to form a square when they are doubled, after allowing for runners, &c.

FOUNDLING CAP.

PLATE 2. FIG. 1, 2, 3, 4.

SCALE.

	Baby's 1st size.	Child of 2 years.	Child of 4 years.
	Yds. nls. in.		Yds. nls. in.
Width of calico, to cut to the best advantage ...	16..0	13¼ or 18 nls.	15..0
Quantity required for twelve caps	1 .. 2..0	or 1 yd. 12 nls. 1 yd. 5 nls.	2..0..0
Width of cap	4..0	4¼ nails	5..0
Length of cap down to the selvage	6..0	7 do.	8..0
Distance from the bottom to the slit behind......	1..0	1¼ do.	1¼.0
Depth of slit into the cap	1..0	1 do.	1..0
Depth in front to be turned back	1..0	1 do.	1..0
Depth of frill	1	¾ do.	¾.0
Length of frill	1..10..0	2 yards	2¼..0..0

BABY'S FIRST SIZE.

Choose your calico soft and fine, of 12 or 16 nails wide, so as to enable you to cut exactly three or four caps in the width, the depth of the cap, from front to back, being 4 nails; the whole length, from ear to ear, is 6 nails, which you must measure down the selvage way of the cloth (see Fig. 2). One yard and 2 nails will cut into twelve caps, if the calico is 16 nails wide.

When you have divided your calico into pieces for caps, cut them out as follows:—

Take one piece, and fold the edge backwards one nail down the long side, and then, by doubling the cap in half the other way, it should form a square (Fig. 1): the nail thus doubled back, (see Fig. 3, A upon B), is to be hemmed down neatly, and a runner formed for a bobbin (see Fig. 4, T). The corners, by the ears, are rounded off (see Fig. 4, S), and another runner formed all round the edge. (Observe, in all the Plates the letter D denotes the folded, or doubled part of the material.) The back is shaped by first measuring one nail from the bottom (see Fig. 3, DD), and cutting into the cap one nail (Fig. 3, D E), taking care to cut it very evenly by a thread: afterwards slope off the crown, above the slit, in a semi-circular form (Fig. 3, E F G).

The cap is made up by neatly felling and back-stitching the seam from D to D, Fig. 3, and gathering the semi-circular part into the straight piece, E D, and felling it over. A strip of calico is often neatly sewn on the inside, over the gathers, to make them set softer to the child's head, and is called a back-stay. These strips, together with the chin-stays, should be cut selvage-wise of the cloth.

A chin-stay is three nails long, and half a nail wide, therefore cut off three nails from down the selvage, and then divide from this piece as many chin-stays as are wanted; afterwards cut the back-stays, which are only two and a half nails long, and a quarter of a nail wide. The chin-stay should be neatly sewn up the whole length, with a small button-hole at one end; they are generally sewn on at the left corner of the cap, and the button on the right.

Some persons prefer having two buttons sewn on the cap, one at each ear, and the stay made with two button-holes, so as easily to be changed and washed, without changing the cap also, as babies are apt to wet them, which makes them hard and rough to the chin. The frills should be cut width-wise

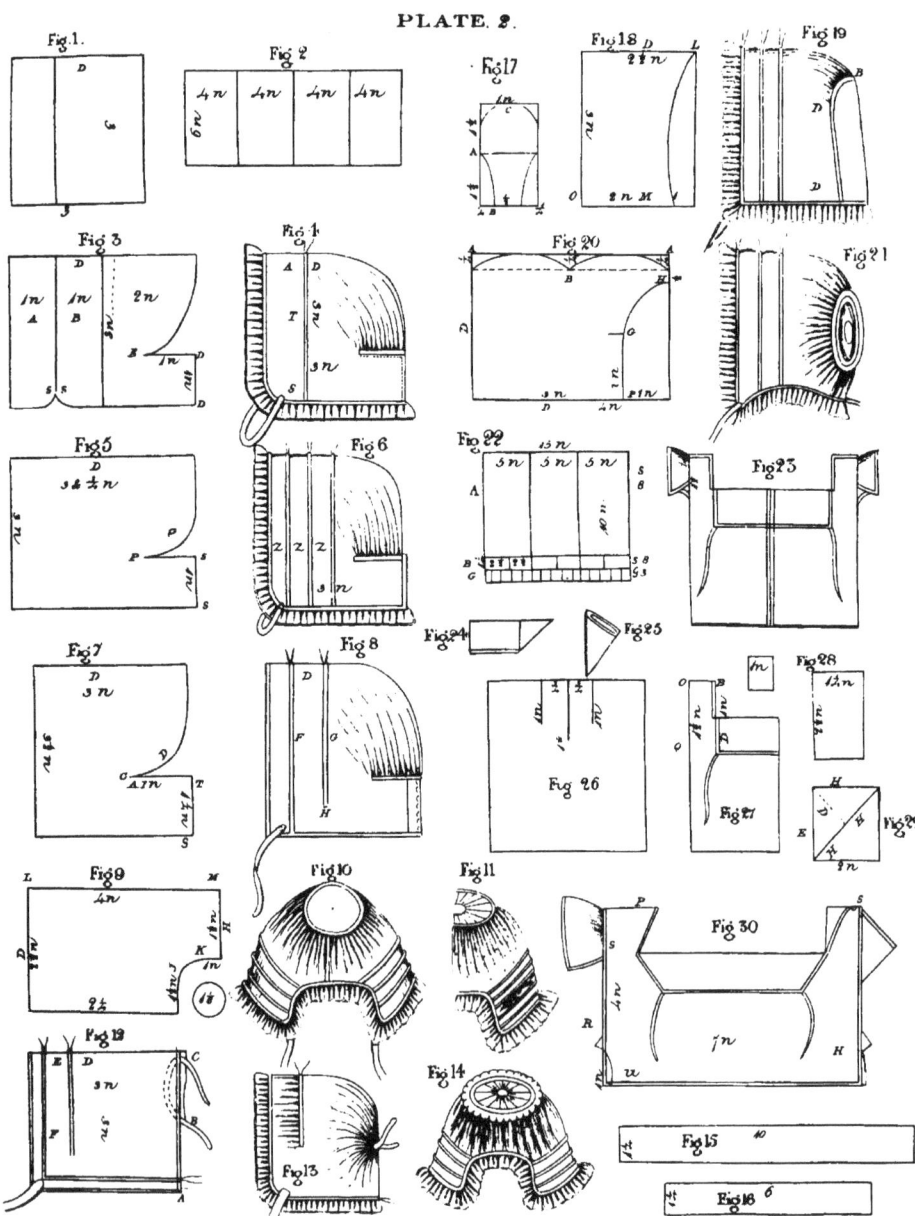

of the muslin; the strips should be one inch wide. The length is generally determined by the width of the muslin, and is from a breadth and a half to two breadths, so as to prevent waste as much as possible. For a cap this size, about a yard and ten nails length of frilling is sufficient.

ANOTHER CHILD'S CAP.

PLATE 2. FIG. 5, 6.

SCALE FOR DIFFERENT SIZES.

——	First size.	Child of 2 yrs.	Child of 7 yrs. and upwards.
	Yds. nls.	Yds. nls.	Yds. nls.
Width of calico, to cut to the best advantage ...	15	17	14¼
Quantity of calico required to cut twelve caps...	1 .. 2	1 .. 5	2 .. 0
Width of cap..	3¾	4¼	4¾
Length along the selvage	6	7	8
Distance from the bottom to the slit behind......	1	1¼	1½
Depth of the slit into the cap.......................	1	1	1
Depth of frill	1	½	¾

INFANT'S FIRST SIZE.

This sort will answer for either day or night-cap, and, when nicely made, looks neat and pretty. The calico should, if possible, be 15 nails wide, to allow of exactly four caps being cut in the width, to prevent waste, as these caps are to be 3¾ nails wide: should any waste arise, it will, however, come in for chin-stays, &c. The cap is 6 nails long. Double the piece in half, and it will form a square, by allowing the ¾ of a nail for the runners in front. Measure one nail behind from the bottom, S S, and slit into the cap one nail, S P. Slope off the crown in a semi-circular form, P Q.

In making up the cap, make three or four runners at regular intervals, Z Z, and a neat hem all round, to admit of bobbins. The semi-circular part, P Q, is gathered into the straight part, P S, and neatly felled over, the seam, S S, being previously sewn up. Hem the back-stay inside the gathers, and put on the chin-stay and frill.

CHILD'S FLANNEL CAP.

PLATE 2. FIG. 7, 8.

SCALE FOR DIFFERENT SIZES.

——	First size.	Child of 3 yrs.	Child of 6 yrs.
	Nails.	Nails.	Nails.
Width of cap, cut in width of cloth	3	3½	4
Length cut down the selvage	7	8	9
Distance at the bottom to the slit behind	1¼	1½	1¾
Length of slit	1	1¼	1½

INFANT'S FIRST SIZE.

These caps are of use after washing an infant's head, to prevent its taking cold, till its hair is sufficiently dry to put on its usual cap. Choose very soft fine Welsh flannel, of 15 nails wide, so as to cut five caps in the width, of 3 nails each. Let them be 7 nails long, so as to come well over the ears, and admit of shrinking in washing. Fold the pieces in half, measure at the back 1¼ nails from the bottom, S T, and slit into the cap, T A. Slope off the crown from C to D. In making them up, they should be neatly hemmed, and the hem run at the edge with very fine thread, to make it lie flat, or else herring-boned with very small stitches. Ladies generally have these caps bound with white sarsenet ribbon (see explanation of binding, page 7). The back ought to be herring-boned with very small regular stitches, and the circular part, C D, plaited and herring-boned into the straight part, A T, and a piece of fine calico or sarsenet ribbon hemmed inside, over the plaits. Two runners, or string cases (Fig. 8, F G), are then made by hemming neatly two bits of soft tape or sarsenet inside, at proper distances. The one marked G not to be carried lower down on each side than H, which is nearly opposite the slit at the back. All the tapes are tied outside, and the tape holes neatly worked round in button-hole stitch. Two tapes for strings.

INFANT'S DAY-CAP.
PLATE 2. FIG. 9, 10, 11.

No scale necessary, as this shape is generally worn only by infants.

INFANT'S FIRST SIZE.

This shape is the most suitable for a day-cap for the higher classes, and is generally made of worked cambric or spotted lace. The cap is 8 nails long, to be cut down the selvage, and 2½ nails wide; your material would, therefore, cut to the best advantage if 15 nails wide, to admit of six caps being cut in the width. The crown or circular piece is 1 nail across when hemmed, therefore, cut it as much larger as will allow for the turning down.

It is finished as follows: make the runners and hem in front very small and firm, either at regular distances from each other, or otherwise, according to fancy. Sew up the back, H, and make a small neat hem at the bottom, J K, to admit another bobbin; afterwards, whip the top, L M, having previously with pins divided it into quarters. Hem the circular piece and crease it into four also, and gather the cap into the crown, drawing the whipping evenly, and making each quarter correspond.

Fig. 11 is the same shape, but more ornamented, having a worked crown, and made of spotted cambric. These caps look very pretty with a white or delicate blue or pink satin or silk inner cap, to set off the work. A piece of insertion work is also put between the runners in front, which adds to the lightness of their appearance.

PLATE 2. FIG. 12, 13.

This is much used by the poor, and is easily made and as easily washed. Take of the material a piece 6 nails down the selvage, and 3½ nails wide. Double it, letting D be the doubled part. Sew up the back from A to C, leaving a small hole or button-hole at the top, C; make a runner all round the front and behind, at half a nail's distance from the edge, which is hemmed with a very narrow hem to form a frill: also, lay in a runner from E to F; next, sew a bobbin at B, letting one end of the string hang outside, and the other, being pulled through the seam, remains inside the cap. This end is carried up and brought out through the hole at C (see the dotted line in the Plate which represents the top inside); when worn, the tapes, on being tied together at B, draw up the cap into shape, and if neatly arranged and pulled out with the fingers, it looks very neat and pretty. (See Fig. 13.) Some put a loop of bobbin inside at B, which, on being brought out through C, fastens to a button at B, on the outside.

THE FULL FRENCH CAP.

PLATE 2. FIG. 14, 15, 16.

This is exceedingly pretty, but is rather troublesome to get up at the wash, and sometimes requires unpicking to be neatly done.

Take a piece of cambric 10 nails wide width-way, and 1¼ deep selvage-wise (see Fig. 15). Take another piece, 6 nails long selvage-wise and 1¼ wide (see Fig. 16). The latter piece is that part in which runners are made to admit of bobbins.

A crown of 1 nail across is then cut, to which the long strip (Fig. 15) is evenly fulled all round with a piece of lace or edging let in all round. The other side is fulled to the front of the cap, and the border being put on, the whole is completed.

CHILD'S HORSE-SHOE CAP.

PLATE 2. FIG. 17, 18, 19.

SCALE FOR DIFFERENT SIZES.

	First size.	Second size.
	Nails.	Yds. nls.
Proper width of material to cut to best advantage	15	12
How much wanted for twelve caps	14	1 .. 12½
Length of cap down the selvage	6	8
Depth of cap cut in the width of material	2½	3
Quantity sloped off at M	½	½
Length of horse-shoe crown	2	2¼
Width of ditto	1¼	1½
At what distance from the top begin to slope off	½	¾
To how much at the bottom, when doubled, it is to be sloped off	¼	½

EXPLANATION OF THE FIRST SIZE.

This is commonly called the horse-shoe cap, from the resemblance of the crown in shape to a horse-shoe. The length of the cap down the selvage is 6 nails, and the width 2½ nails. Double it, (see Fig. 18, D being the double part,) and slope at the top of the front, L, to the back, M. The distance from M to O is 2 nails, therefore, half a nail is thus sloped off. For the horse-shoe or crown (Fig. 17), cut a piece 2 nails long and 1¼ wide; fold it length-wise in half, and half a nail from the top, begin to round off the corner towards C, to form the horse-shoe; then measure off at the bottom of the piece, while still doubled, a quarter of a nail, which cut off from A to B, curving it a little to give it a prettier shape. The cap is made up with two or three runners in front: the head-piece is put into the crown, the gathers to be rather fulled at B (Fig. 19), and nearly, if not quite, plain from D to D. The frilling is one inch deep.

INFANT'S FRENCH CAP.

PLATE 2. FIG. 20, 21.

FIRST SIZE.

This shape is only used for infants, therefore, a scale is unnecessary. It is very pretty, though but little worn, and never used for the poor.

22   THE WORKWOMAN'S GUIDE.

The cap is 8 nails long down the selvage, and 2¾ wide. After doubling it in half, fold it again from A to A, and then from A to B; shape a quarter of a nail off the corners, in a semi-circular form. In the front, D, measure 3 nails, and cut off the 1 nail, taking care to cut by the thread, in an upright direction, for the distance of 1 nail, (P G,) and then slope it off in a corner, to half a nail below the top. In making it up, sew up the back neatly, and full the cap very equally into the crown, which must be one nail across, when hemmed. Three or more runners in front, and double frills, complete the cap.

Ribbon chin-strings to draw through loops on each side, on account of washing.

COCKADES, ROSETTES, &c.

A few words on the rosettes and bows usually put on children's caps, hats, and bonnets, may not be unacceptable.

There are several kinds of these bows, of which the following are the principal.

A cockade for an infant boy's cap or hat. This is made of narrow white satin ribbon, sewn on a small circle of buckram, which should be about the size of half-a-crown. Begin at the outer edge of the buckram, and sew the ribbon on in small loops or bows, round and round, until you fill it quite up to the centre.

Lace cockade for a boy. This is often made of some costly kind of lace, generally Valenciennes, and requires four yards. It should be whipped at the edge, and sewn on to a piece of buckram or stiff muslin, beginning at the outer edge of it.

When intended for a girl, it is called a rosette, and instead of being round, it is an oval or long shape, and looks like several frillings of lace sewn together, perhaps 1½ nail long. It is made in the same way as the cockade.

A pretty and less expensive lace cockade or rosette, may be made by sewing edging on each side of a broad piece of net, gathering the net in the middle and running it upon a buckram circle or oval beginning in the centre of it and working to the edge, making the lace stand as full and close as possible.

Infants' hats and bonnets have pretty trimmings of satin cut the cross way, and about 1½ or 2 nails broad, on a buckram foundation, either round for a cockade, or oval for a rosette; they are merely gathered at one edge, and sewn on the buckram, as described above, beginning in the centre. Being cut the cross way prevents the outer edge roving out easily.

A simple little bow for a bonnet, or to fasten the neck of a dress or pelisse, may be made as follows. Cut off a piece of ribbon 2¼ nails long, and plait or gather it up in the middle; this is for the ends: take another piece 3½ or nearly 4 nails long, gather it up in the centre, and turn the two ends of it underneath, to the middle, gathering them up also, thus forming two bows; lay these bows upon the first piece, and sew them together in the centre, with strong thread: to conceal the gathering, fold a small piece of the ribbon very narrow, and tie or sew it round the middle of the bow, as if to hold it together; this finishes it neatly.

INFANTS' OPEN SHIRTS.
PLATE 2. FIG. 22, 23, 24, 25, 26.

Infants' shirts are generally made of soft calico for the poor, and very fine lawn or cambric, for the higher classes.

SCALE.

———	Small size.	Large size.
	Yds. nls.	Yds. nls.
Width of material, to cut out to best advantage	15	16½
Quantity requisite for twenty-four shirts	5 .. 13	6 .. 10
Depth of shirt to be cut in the width	5	5½
Length of shirt to be cut down the selvage	10	11
Length of sleeve to be cut down the selvage......	1¼	1½
Width of sleeve	2½	3
Gusset	bare nail.	full nail.
Slit down for the arm-hole	1½	1¾
Space for shoulder	¾	¾
Slit for flaps...	full nail.	full nail.

Either of the above sizes is very good for babies' first shirts. The small size fits the best for the first five or six weeks after the infant's birth, but with a large baby would soon be too small; the second size, therefore, though rather too large to begin with, is eventually the most useful. As it is advisable to avoid waste as much as possible, the width of the material would best determine the size, taking care, however, that it does not exceed the one, or be smaller than the other of the above scales.

In cutting out 24 shirts (see Plate 2, Fig. 22), cut eight lengths of 10 nails for the skirts (see A), eight lengths of 1¼ nails for sleeves (see B), and three lengths of 1 nail (see C) for gussets.

In cutting out the first size, choose your calico of exactly 15 nails, to admit of three shirts being cut in the width, of 5 nails long each. The width of the shirt down the selvage is 10 nails. Fold the shirt in half, and then double it again, so as to fold it in quarters (Fig. 27), cut a slit down the two doubled parts in front for the arm-holes (see O Q); take care that you do not cut your arm-holes at the wrong end of the doubled part, they should be slit at the end where there are two folded parts to slit down: make them 1½ nails deep, then leave a full three quarters of a nail for the shoulder (Fig. O B), and slit down a full nail to form the bosom and back flaps (Fig. B D). The sleeves are 1¼ nails long, to be cut down the selvage, and 2½ nails wide, so that three pairs will cut exactly in the width of the calico, if 15 nails wide.

The gussets are a bare nail square; about eight pairs will cut in the width. Fig. 26 is the appearance of the skirt after being cut out, when half opened, so as to be doubled once. In making a shirt, hem it neatly with a very narrow hem, unless there is a selvage at the bottom: hem, also, the two sides and the flaps, taking care to do the last properly, so as when falling over, to lie the right side outwards. Two narrow tape strings are sewn to the corners of the middle flap, 7 nails long. The shoulders are sewn and felled with very narrow seams; the gussets are then sewn on the sleeves, which are very neatly hemmed. The sleeve is set into the shirt, and fulled at the top in neat and very small gathers. All the seams should lie particularly flat, and be as narrow as you can make them.

INFANT'S SECOND OR CLOSE SHIRT.

PLATE 2. FIG. 27, 28, 29, 30.

When infants are about nine months old, they generally leave off using the open or first shirt, and begin to wear the close shirt (Fig. 30) until they reach the age of seven or eight years, when the usual shaped shirt or shift is worn.

SCALE FOR DIFFERENT SIZES.

——	Child of 8 months.	Child of 2 yrs.	Child of 5 yrs.	Child of 7 or 9 yrs.
	Nails.	Nails.	Nails.	Nails.
Width of material	14	15	16	18
Full breadth of shirt to be cut in width	14	15	16	18
Length of shirt to be cut down the selvage	4	5¾	7	9 or 10
Length or depth of sleeve cut down the selvage	1	1	1½	2
Width of sleeve	3	3	3	3½
Gusset	1	1	1¼	2
Slit down the arm-hole	1¾	2	2¼	3
Space for shoulder	1½	1½	1¾	2
Slit for flaps	1½	1½	1½	2
Slit for tail	1	1¼	1½	2

EXPLANATION OF THE FIRST SIZE.

Choose your lawn or calico 14 nails wide, if possible, to admit exactly of one shirt in the width. Cut 4 nails down the selvage-way for the length of the shirt.

Fold the piece in half, which will make it 7 nails wide when thus doubled, make a slit down the doubled part of 1¾ nails deep for the arm-hole, and put a pin in the two selvages to mark the depth of the other arm-hole. Fold the shirt once more, so as to lay the two arm-holes one upon the other, (see Fig. 27), and, at the top, from O to Q, measure 1½ nails for the shoulder, and slit 1½ nails, making the slit B D slope outwards towards the sleeve, about half a nail out of the straight line, as bosom flaps shaped thus, set much better to the figure, and also that part of the shoulder (Fig. 30, P) can be turned over, and confines all straps, tapes, &c. neatly, so as to prevent their being seen from under the frock sleeve.

The sleeve usually put in is 1 nail deep, to be cut down the selvage, and 3 nails wide. The sleeve gusset a full nail square, and the skirt gusset half a nail square. (See Fig. 24.)

The shirt is made up as follows (see Fig. 30). Sew the two selvages together (see R) with fine strong thread, leaving 1¾ nails above for the arm-hole, S, and 1 nail below for the opening, or tail of the shirt, U. The corresponding side, H, is double, so that the slit for the arm-hole and for the tail have to be cut. Hem the bottom of the skirt and up the tails, after putting in the gussets (or tail bits as they are generally called). Some people think these tail gussets unnecessary for young children; but they add so much to the strength of the shirt, and give so little extra trouble, that they are well worth the pains. Sew and fell the shoulders with flat narrow seams, hem the bosom flaps, taking care to turn down your hems so as to be the right side outwards, where the flap falls over. Set in your sleeves quite plain, till nearly the top of the shoulder, and full in the remainder, in very small neat gathers. Two tape strings are sewn at the corners of the front bosom flaps

Fig. 25 is another pattern of a sleeve which is very neat when worn, as it is never seen below the frock sleeve; but it has a less finished appearance than the other. This last shape, however, is preferable for children from four to six years of age, from its strength and simplicity, and is made as follows:— Cut a piece of calico two nails square, which fold and cut in half, corner-wise (see Fig. 29); fold this half square again, and the double part, D, falls under the arm, E is set into the shirt, and H is hemmed neatly for the arm to go through. The great advantage of this shape is, that the shift sleeve is never seen from beneath the child's frock, and therefore always sets neatly (see Fig. 30, the sleeve to the right).

PLATE 3.

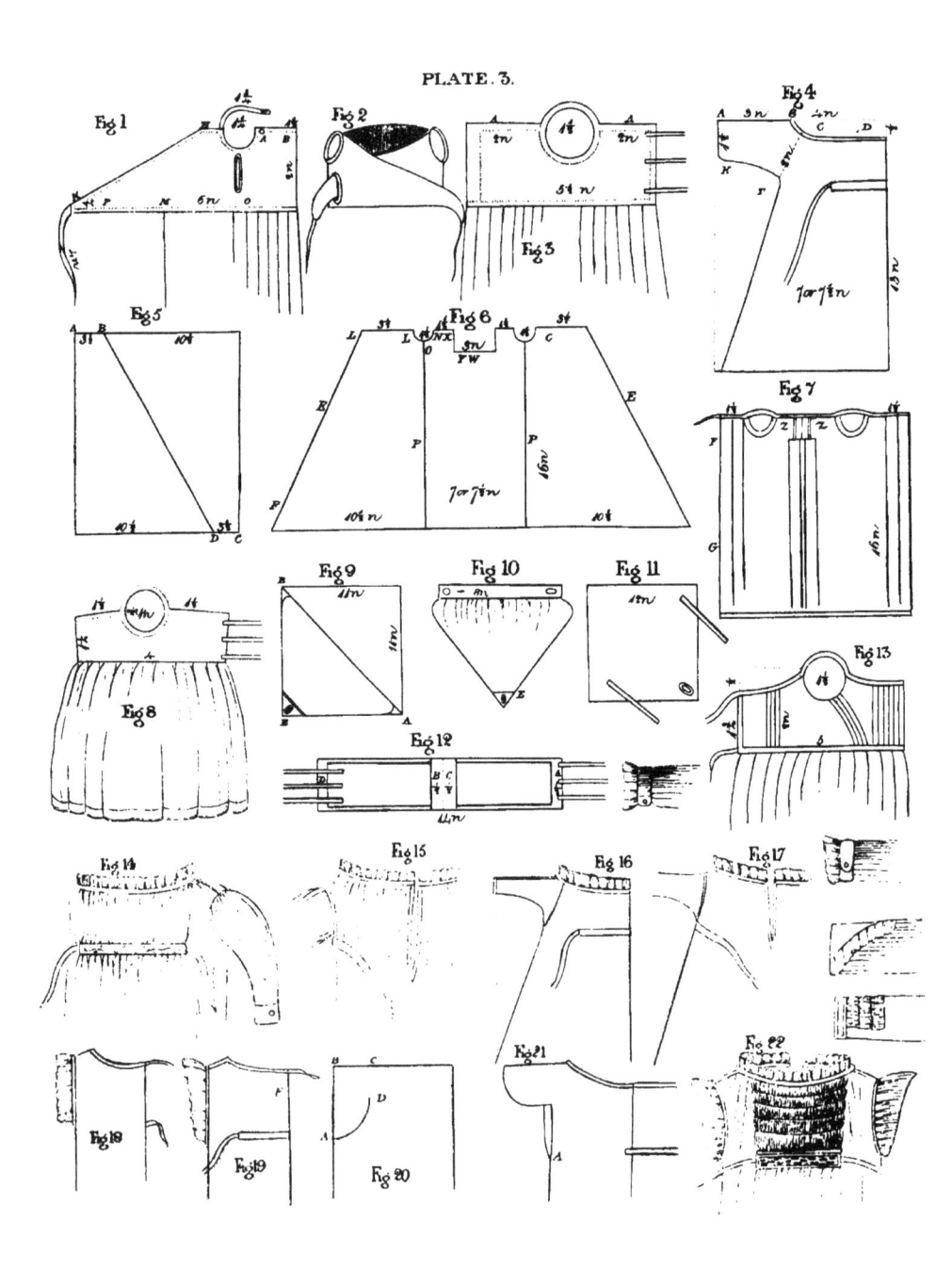

INFANTS' FIRST FLANNEL GOWNS.
PLATE 3. FIG. 1. 2.

This is an excellent pattern for an Infant's first gown, either day or night, from the ease with which it is put on, and also for the warmth and support it gives to the child. The body is made of flannel, lined with very fine soft calico or lawn.

In cutting out the skirt, tear off two breadths of the proper length. The long clothes of babies of the higher classes are longer than those of the poor, as the latter would soon be tumbled and dirty, they should be 13 or 14 nails, and for the former, about one yard is ample. Some ladies dress their children in very long flannels and robes, but this is as unnecessary as it is ill-judged; for the weight of the long petticoats must be painful, besides the perfect inability of the poor infant to stretch and kick about its little limbs, is obvious.

Divide one of these breadths in two, and pin a half breadth to each side of the whole breadth. Run firmly down the two seams, and herring-bone them back again, and then bind with the flannel binding neatly down the two sides of the front, and at the bottom of the skirt. The body is 12 nails long to be cut down the selvage, and 2 nails wide. About seven bodies can be cut in the width, flannel being generally 14 nails wide. Double the piece for the body length-wise, and stick in a pin $1\frac{1}{2}$ nail from the front or doubled part (see A B) to mark where the beginning of the arm-hole lies. The arm-hole is $1\frac{1}{4}$ nail across, and $\frac{3}{4}$ nail deep; after cutting it out, slope the remainder of the body from H to K in a straight line, to within a $\frac{1}{4}$ nail from the bottom at the end, so as not to finish off in a point. A large opening, or sort of button-hole is next made under the left arm-hole, to be $\frac{3}{4}$ nail long, leaving about $\frac{1}{4}$ nail above and below it. It is thus made up: place the soft lining upon the flannel, taking care that the wrong side is outwards, and run them firmly together, pretty near the edge, along the two sides, the top of the body, and round the arm-holes; after which, finish your thread firmly off, turn the body inside out, and stroke the lining and flannel smoothly together, by putting your hand inside and pressing it gently all round. Next put the skirt into the body; measure the middle of each and pin them together; afterwards, pin the front or opening of the skirt at M, exactly half way between the arm-hole and the end of the body (see O P). The skirt from M to O to be set in plain, and then the remainder plaited up in about twelve small equal plaits to the middle, taking care to turn the plaits so as to lie outwards from the centre towards the point; the other half is then to be fixed in, and with a strong thread, stitch the plaits to the flannel body, laying the two rough edges together. When done, smooth down the stitched part, and hem the calico lining to it.

The body should next be run neatly and firmly with very small stitches all round, about $\frac{1}{4}$ inch from the edge. In the part from P to M, the lining should be made so as to be a little seen on the outside, and be hemmed down to represent flannel binding. The lawn or calico shoulder-straps should be cut $1\frac{3}{4}$ nail long, and a button-hole worked at one end, while the other is sewn on that end of the arm-hole towards the middle. The slit or button-hole should be turned over neatly by the lining, to appear as if bound all round. Two narrow tapes of 4 nails long, sewn to the points, complete the whole. In dressing the infant, the one end is drawn round through the slit, which makes it fit closely and compactly to the figure, and yet be soft and elastic. Fig. 2 is the representation of one folded as if on.

ANOTHER SHAPE FOR AN INFANT'S FIRST FLANNEL NIGHT-GOWN.
PLATE 3. FIG. 5, 6, 7.

This is a very good kind also, and the one in most general use, though not equal to the one just described. It takes a breadth and a half to make this petticoat, therefore it prevents waste if you cut out two at once.

Cut your two breadths 14 nails long, or a yard, according to pleasure, and measure along the width of one breadth (Fig. 5) 3½ nails from the selvage (see A B), and put in a pin as a mark. Measure the same at the other end of the width of the flannel, making your measurement from the opposite selvage (see C D); then double your flannel smoothly across from B to D, and cut it evenly along the sloping line.

The other breadth of flannel is torn exactly down the middle. Take one of these halves, and let one of the above-mentioned sloped pieces be pinned on each side of it, taking care to place them with the sloped part outwards (see Fig. 6, E E), and the smaller part of each sloped piece be at the top. After running and herring-boning the two seams, P P, you must cut out the top part of the skirt to form the body. First, therefore, double the skirt very evenly in half, and beginning at the end which is open, leave 3½ nails for the back, L L, and place a pin as a mark; and also in order that the flannel, when once laid correctly, may not slip out of its place. Measure 1¼ nail for the arm-hole, which you must also pin; then cut it out to the depth of ½ nail, L O N, measure 1½ nail beyond for the bosom, N X, and then cut down 1 nail deep, in a straight line, X Y; after which, cut off the flannel in a straight line, Y W, to the end. The gown, when opened, has the appearance of Fig. 6, with a large piece cut out of the bosom in the middle. The two sides of this gap in the bosom should be very firmly run together about one inch from the edges; these edges then should be laid open, so as to turn back, one on the one side, and the other on the other, and very neatly herring-boned down; it will thus have the appearance of two hems (see Z Z, Fig. 7). The skirt, which of course is very full, must be set into two equal double plaits, and herring-boned upon the body in the inside. The skirt at the sides must next be set in two or three plaits (see F G, Fig. 7), so that, when plaited up, the space from the arm-hole to the back be but 1½ nail. Bind or herring-bone the top of the bosom, and make a string-case of soft tape at the top of the back. Put in the tapes, sew on shoulder straps of soft calico or tape, with button-holes, and put on the buttons at the end of the arm-hole, towards the back.

ANOTHER INFANT'S FLANNEL GOWN.
PLATE 3. FIG. 4.

This shape is the one generally used by the lower classes, not only for flannels, but for print gowns and petticoats; and is preferred to others on account of the ease with which it is cut out, and also because there is much less needle-work in the making up: there is, however, some waste, which is an objection. The gown is 13 nails long, but as there should be no seam on the shoulder, the two breadths must be cut in one length of 26 nails, which is 1 yard 10 nails. Double it in two, so as to be 13 nails long, and then fold it in half very evenly down the middle, so as to make the four selvages lie exactly one upon the other, and pin them firmly down to keep the folds in place; then, after measuring 3 nails from the selvages at the top (see A S), to determine the length of the sleeves, cut out the part S C D, to form the neck of the gown. Observe that the part from S to C is a nail deep, which should be nicely rounded off, and from C to D, the bosom is cut straight along.

The gown is next shaped at the side; and to do so properly, put in a pin at S, and fold it in a regular slope down to the bottom of the gown. Measure down the slope from the top, S, the distance of 2 nails, and put in a pin as a guide; cut off from the bottom upwards to T, and rounding it off at the corner, slope along T K for the sleeve, allowing 1¼ nail width for the wrist. In making it up, the seams should be joined with a mantua-maker's hem, and a band should be sewn on the inside of the front, to be 6 nails in length, and about 1½ nail below the neck. Cut a button-hole in the gown at each end of the band, draw with a bodkin a piece of tape through one hole, and fasten it down at the other extremity of the band; do the same with the other button-hole, so that on pulling the tapes, the gown will be drawn up, and neatly fulled in front.

INFANT'S SECOND SIZE NIGHT-FLANNEL.
PLATE 3. FIG. 3.

This shape is used when infants are six or eight months old, and is merely a double flannel body sewn upon the skirt, which is two breadths of 12 nails in length.

The body is 11 nails long, to be cut down the selvage, and 2½ nails deep when doubled; therefore cut it 5 nails wide, and double it down all the length very carefully. You must pin or tack it together evenly, to enable you to cut out the arm-holes correctly. Then fold the body in two, measure from the end two nails for the back, A, and cut out the arm-hole 1 nail deep, and 1½ nail across. Open the body again, unpick the tacking threads, and run round the arm-holes with small firm stitches on the wrong side of the flannel, also up the sides; after which, turn the body inside out, and then make a large plait in front as a support to the child; this plait ought to be so large, that when made, only 2¾ nails will remain between the arm-holes, instead of 4 nails. After herring-boning this plait neatly down, run in small stitches all round the body (see the dotted line) at about a ¼ of an inch from the edge, to make the flannel lie flat, and give it a finished appearance. Some people back-stitch it, and others prefer making a line of very small herring-bone, or else chain-stitch it all round. These last two modes are certainly more ornamental, but the simple running is quite as neat, and saves much time; three tapes must be sewn on one end of the body, at equal distances from each other, and at scarcely a nail from the edge; the three tapes at the other end to be sewn on close to the edge, and to correspond with the others, so as to tie neatly with each other, and to allow of the body lapping over nearly a nail. The shoulder straps of tape are sewn on, and are 2 nails long, after allowing an extra half nail for turning in.

The skirt is sewn up, and not open as the others; the bottom is neatly bound, the pocket-hole is torn down the middle of one of the breadths, and is two nails long; it must also be bound all round. The skirt is set into the body in small plaits.

INFANT'S FIRST SIZE DAY-FLANNEL.
PLATE 3. FIG. 8.

SCALE OF DIFFERENT SIZES.

	Infant.	Child of 6 months.	Child of 2 or 3 yrs.	Child of 4 or 6 yrs.
	Nails.	Nails.	Nails.	Nails.
Length of skirt	16	12	5	6
Length of body down the selvage	8	9	10	11
Depth of body	1¼	1½	2	3
Space across the arm-hole	1	1¼	1½	2
Depth of arm-hole	¾	1	1¼	1¼

*** The space for the bosom and back is ascertained by dividing the body in four, and cutting out the arm-holes according to the Scale.

The body is made of fine jean or twill, lined with lawn; or, if for the lower classes, of soft coarse calico, with plenty of nap upon it. The body is 8 nails long, to be cut down the selvage, and 1¼ deep, so that twelve bodies could be exactly cut in the width, if your stuff were 15 nails wide.

Fold the body in two, and, after measuring 1½ nail from the edge, cut out the arm-holes, which are 1 nail across, and ¾ nail deep. Slope off, both at the top of the back and at the bosom, about a ¼ of an inch, to make it set better. The lining is next cut out, and both are run neatly together, the wrong side outwards, near the edges, along the sides and top, and round the arm-holes: when done, turn the body inside outwards, and flatten it between your finger and thumb, so as to make it lie flat. Afterwards back-stitch it, in beautifully even stitches, all round the top and sides, at a little distance from the edge. Sew on the shoulder-straps and tapes, putting three on each side; those on one side to be set close to the edge, and the other three at about half a nail's distance from it. The skirt is about 14 nails or a yard long: the two breadths are sewn together, and the pocket-hole torn in the middle of the back breadth about 2 nails. The bottom is bound, as also the pocket-hole, and the skirt set in the body in regular small plaits at the sides, leaving it plain in the middle for about 2 nails.

ANOTHER CHILD'S DAY FLANNEL.
PLATE 3. FIG. 13.

This pattern is intended for children of six to ten years, previous to their wearing stays. The body is made of fine jean, and lined with calico; pieces of cord or bobbin are placed between the two in rows, and fastened in by the needle, running the body and lining together between each two rows. Rows of cord may be thus run in various patterns, and, if neatly done, look very pretty.

The Plate is a sufficient guide for cutting out the body, without further description. The skirt should be set in plaits in the middle, and towards the ends. The shoulder-straps should also be of jean.

INFANT'S FLANNEL BAND.
PLATE 3. FIG. 12.

Infants require great warmth and support round the stomach and hips, and for that purpose, wear flannel bands for the first ten or twelve months.

Cut the flannel down the selvage 14 nails long, and 2½ nails wide. It should be exactly 15 nails in width, to enable you to cut out six without waste.

Herring-bone very neatly the top and bottom, and herring-bone a deep hem of ½ a nail (see A) at one end, and a narrow one (see D) at the other; then make two large plaits in the middle, to reduce the length to 11 nails (see B C). These plaits will be about half a nail deep, and should fall one on each side of the middle, and be herring-boned down. The three strings on each side to be sewn as seen in the Plate; those of the one side to be put at 3 nails from the end.

INFANTS' FLANNEL PILCHERS OR SAVERS.
PLATE 3. FIG. 9, 10.

Infants often wear pilchers or savers, put over their napkins, to prevent their clothes from being wetted. They are made as follows:—

Cut a piece of flannel 11 nails square, fold it in half, and cut it crosswise, A B: it will make two pilchers. It must next be rounded off a little at the two corners, A B, and at the third corner, E, (which, observe, is opposite the cross-way of the flannel,) sew on a piece of calico, in which cut a button-hole. The crossed part, A B, is then neatly plaited into a calico band, 1 nail deep, when doubled, and 8 nails long, and a button and button-hole sewn on at the ends. In putting it on, first button the band round the waist in front, bring the corner between the legs, and button it to the same button.

ON BABY-LINEN.

INFANTS' NAPKINS.
PLATE 3. FIG. 11.

Babies napkins should be made of soft diaper, or, if for the poor, old sheeting, table-linen, or strong fine linen answers well. Choose your material exactly 10 or 20 nails wide. Napkins are generally made by cutting the diaper in lengths of 20 nails, and doubling each length in two. Sew nearly all round the doubled piece, taking care to turn the raw edges outwards instead of inwards, as usually done, because the napkin is turned inside out, when it is sewn all round, with the exception of a space large enough to admit the hand, to enable it to be turned. This opening is afterwards neatly sewn up with small stitches. It is essential that the seam or outer edge of napkins should be as smooth and soft as possible, on account of the tender skin of infants: it is very desirable to soak and scald the material often before it is used. Two strings and a tape loop may be added, to be used instead of a pin, to fasten it on.

ANOTHER MODE OF MAKING NAPKINS.

The pieces, when cut off, should be merely hemmed like towels, and, when used, are doubled and put on as the others. The grand advantage of this simple sort is, that when there is but one baby, they come in, after nursery use, for towels and other purposes, whereas the others are comparatively useless.

INFANT'S NIGHT-GOWN.
PLATE 3. FIG. 14, 15.

Night-gowns are generally made of calico or dimity, and sometimes of fine twilled muslin. The calico are most frequently used, but the dimity look the prettiest; they, however, often split, and are not so durable as the former.

This pattern is the one usually adopted by ladies for infants: it requires great neatness in the making up, to look well.

Let your material be about a yard wide, and cut two breadths of 18 nails long each. Fold each breadth very evenly down the middle, and at one end stick a pin, exactly 2 nails from the selvages. Crease the stuff from this point to about a nail from the bottom, and cut off the gore. These gores come in for the two bands and wristbands. The former are each 10 nails long, and 1 nail deep; the wristbands are $2\frac{1}{4}$ nails wide, and, when double, are $\frac{3}{4}$ nail deep: they should be nicely rounded at one end. The sleeves are cut in the shape and to the size of Plate 4, Fig. 15.

After sewing up the seams, the neck and arm-holes are formed The shoulder is a little sloped, and is $1\frac{1}{4}$ nail long. The arm-holes are a little curved, and $1\frac{3}{4}$ nail deep. The bosom and back are hollowed, and the slit behind is 3 nails deep.

Procure a piece of strong insertion-work, $2\frac{1}{2}$ nails long, and $\frac{2}{3}$ of a nail deep.

In making it up, first hem the neck of the gown, and, at $\frac{3}{4}$ of a nail below the bosom, run the finest gathers possible, leaving a space of $1\frac{1}{2}$ nail on each side, between the end of the gathers and the sleeve. The gown is again gathered across, about a nail below the first gathering, and then the insertion muslin is very neatly sewn on the gathers, with very small even stitches; the two bands are next stitched, one at each end of the insertion-work, and are rounded off at the ends. A narrow frill of lawn is put round the bosom. The sleeves are fulled at the top, and set in; they are either merely hemmed to admit a tape, and a lawn frill sewn on them, or are put into wristbands, which should button over. Instead of putting in insertion-work, some bias it at the waist, which is thought to make it wear better.

Fig. 14 represents the front, and Fig. 15 the back of the gown.

ANOTHER INFANT'S NIGHT-GOWN.
PLATE 3. FIG. 16, 17.

The skirt of this pattern is cut out exactly like the one before mentioned, but is made up in a more simple manner. The gown, instead of being gathered in front, is left loose, and a strip of calico, ⅓ a nail deep, is sewn on in the inside, about ¾ of a nail deep from the bosom, and of such a length as to leave, on each side, but two nails space between it and the arm-holes. This piece of calico is to be used as a string-case, and two small slits for tape-holes must be cut in the gown, at about a ¼ of a nail distance, within each end of the strip. The tapes should be rather broad, and each, on being drawn by a bodkin through its slit, should be carried along the string-case and firmly fastened down to the opposite end, so that, on pulling the two strings, the gown is drawn up in neat gathers, forming a body. The sleeves are cut down the selvage instead of crosswise, and are nearly straight, the top being 4 nails wide, and the bottom or wrist, 2½ nails. A small frill may be put on the bosom and wrists; or, if it is a coloured gown for a poor child, a small runner to admit a bobbin, at the distance of the width of a narrow frill from the edge, will, on being drawn up, form a very neat frill both for the bosom and sleeves.

ANOTHER INFANT'S NIGHT-GOWN.

This sort is only used by the poorer classes. It is made of coloured print or soft calico, and is cut out exactly after the pattern of the flannel bed-gown (see Plate 3, Fig. 4). The frills are formed by making runners near the edge of the neck and wrists.

INFANTS' PINAFORES.
PLATE 3. FIG. 18.

Pinafores are made of diaper, Holland, linen, or print. The former are for ladies' infants—the latter for the poor. The patterns vary according to sex and age. The one generally used at first is as follows:—

SCALE.

	First size.	Child of 2 yrs.	Child of 6 yrs.
	Nails.	Nails.	Nails.
Length down selvage	8	10	12
Width of material	11	14	15
Depth of arm-hole	2	2¼	2½
Piece left for shoulder	¾	1	1¼
Quantity hollowed out of neck	¼	½	½
Length of frill to each arm-hole	10 or 11	—	—
Depth of frill	⅜	½	¾
Distance from top for the second tape to be sewn on	2	2¼	2¾
Size of gussets	½	½	¾

Procure your material exactly the proper width for the pinafore, to prevent waste. After cutting off the pieces of the proper length and width for the pinafores, take one piece and fold it down the middle,

ON BABY-LINEN. 31

length-wise, in two; then again fold it, and cut the slits for the arm-holes by a thread. Pin it carefully together, still folded in four, whilst you hollow out the neck, leaving the proper space for the shoulders. Hem it at the top as you would a shift, by turning down the hem, and then turning it backwards, the more readily to hold it while you sew the hem firmly all round. The arm-holes should have narrow hems, and be very firmly sewed at the bottom, or they will tear. Whip and sew on the frills, hem the bottom, sew on the tapes, and the pinafore is completed. Some people put gussets in at the shoulder: and it is better to do so for elder children.

For further sizes, see School Girl's Pinafore.

PINAFORE WITH LAPPETS.
PLATE 3. FIG. 19.

This shape is very much used by the poor, as it protects the sleeves. The pinafore is cut out exactly as in Fig. 18; but instead of putting on frills, little capes or lappets are substituted. These capes are cut width-way of the size, according to the Scale.

SCALE OF LAPPETS.

	First size.	Second size.
Length down selvage	10 nails	1 yard
Depth	1 ditto	1¼ nail

The cape is rounded off towards the ends, and, after being neatly hemmed, is whipped and sewn all round the arm-hole, making the ends come under the arm. In front, the pinafore is confined with a band, which is stitched firmly on in two places before, and which, passing round the waist, buttons behind.

THE WASTE-NOT PINAFORE.
PLATE 3. FIG. 20, 21.

This is a particularly simple shape, being cut without any waste whatever.

Divide the pinafore in four, and cut it according to the Plate.

SCALE.

	Nails.
Width of material	12
Length of ditto	8
Space from A to B	1½
Space from B to C	¾
Space from C to D	¾

Cut from A to D, by which means a shoulder-flap is made, and, when on, the shoulder-piece is raised sufficiently to prevent the necessity of hollowing out the neck. A double plait should be sewn under the arm-hole (see Fig. 21, A). This cape, being plain, is improved by an edging of work, or a little braid, to add lightness to its appearance.

A BABY'S DRESS PINAFORE OR TIDY.
PLATE 3. FIG. 22.

Intended to be worn when the child's frock is tumbled or untidy. It is made of cambric or jaconet muslin. There are two breadths in it of 14 nails wide—one breadth in front, and the other cut in two, and sewn on each side. The arm-holes are made in the seams, and frilled round, or lappets sewn on. At the top in front, from shoulder to shoulder, the pinafore is drawn up by a tape in the hem, and secured to the proper size. The front is biassed into a band of insertion-work, to go partly round the waist. The back is drawn by a string at the top, and again below by a string-case. The front may be either simply biassed once into the band, or it may have three or four rows of biassing. Round the top is an edging of work, or a frill.

INFANTS' PETTICOATS.

PLATE 4. FIG. 1.

SCALE.

——	First size.	Child of 18 months.	Child of 2 yrs.	Child of 5 yrs.	Child of 8 yrs.
	Nails.	Nails.	Nails.	Nails.	Nails.
Width of material	14	14	16	16	18
Length of body down the selvage	9	10	11	12	13
Depth of body	1¾	2	2¼	2½	2¾
Depth of arm-holes	¾	1	1¼	1	2
Width of arm-holes	1½	1¾	2	2	2¼
Depth of slit behind............................	3	3	3	3	3
Length of shoulder-straps	1½	1¾	2	2	2¼
Length of short sleeve when opened out ...	4½	7	8	9	10
Greatest depth of ditto.........................	2¼	2½	3	3½	4
Least depth of ditto	¾	1	1¼	1½	2

Petticoats are generally made of jaconet muslin, twilled muslin, or fine calico, and should be about 14 nails wide. The skirt is 2 breadths in width, and cut to the length required, after allowing for the deep hem or tucks. They are usually cut the following sizes for the rich and poor.

	Nails.		Nails.
First size	17	....	15
Three-quarter size	13	....	12
Small size	8	....	7

In cutting out the body, double the strip in two, and again in half, so as to be folded exactly in four, and cut out the arm-holes according to the depth and width wanted, as seen by the Scale. The sleeves are cut out according to the pattern in Plate 4, Fig. 12 or 13; the shoulder-straps are cut out, and the body is ready for making up. Hem it along the top, sufficiently wide to admit a tape, stitch on the shoulder-straps, sew and hem the sleeves, and gather them into the shoulder-straps. The body should have rather wide hems at the two ends, and a sufficiently wide hem at the bottom to admit a narrow tape. Full the body in front, and sew it firmly to the skirt (which should be previously gathered), making it lie pretty evenly all round. The top strings should draw from the shoulder-straps only, and another string may be run in the front to draw it, and tie on one side.

INFANTS' FROCKS,

PLATE 4,

Are generally made of jaconet muslin, twilled muslin, and print, and, when the children are older, sometimes of nankeen, jean, Holland, merino, cloth, stuff, and silk. Those for the poor are usually of

PLATE 4.

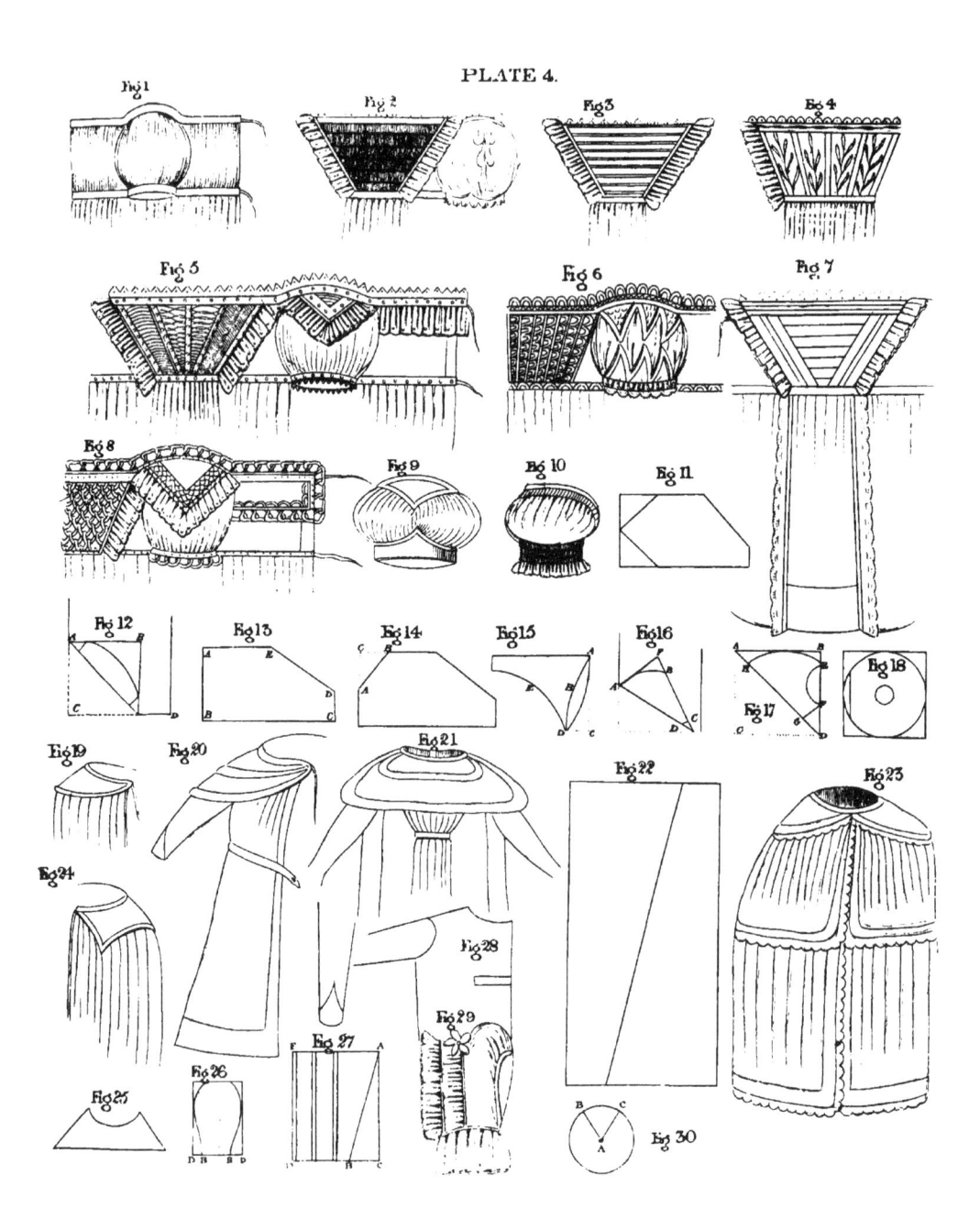

print, and are made according to the pattern for petticoats (see Plate 4, Fig. 1); those for the rich are made in various ways, among which are the following:—

The full body.
The plain body, cut in one piece.
The plain body, with backs and fronts cut crosswise.

SCALE FOR THE SKIRTS.

Width of skirt 2 or 3 breadths, so as to form from 14 to 16 nails wide, when the skirt is double, as if made up.

	Rich.	Poor.
	Nails.	Nails.
Length of skirt for first size	18	15
Ditto three-quarters size	12 or 14	10
Ditto short coats	8	8
Depth of hem at the bottom	4	1
Depth of slit to the skirt	2½	2½

There are so many ways of making up skirts, that only a few will be described.

Broad hems and tucks of various depths are the simplest and prettiest; others are more ornamented by letting in work at the top of the broad hem, or working with braid, bobbin, or cord. Robings are often brought down in front, in continuation of the little capes sewn on the bodies. These robings should be 1½ nail broad, sloped off to ½ nail, and carried down to the bottom of the skirt, or to the top of a deep hem. They should be sewn on so that the edge of the work is turned outwards.

The sleeves are made according to fancy, and are of the sizes marked in the Scale, pages 35, 36.—(See also, Plate 4.)

FULL BODIES.

PLATE 4. FIG. 1.

SCALE.

——	First size.	Child of 1 yr.	Child of 3 yrs.	Child of 5 yrs.	Child of 8 yrs.
	Nails.	Nails.	Nails.	Nails.	Nails.
Depth of body down the selvage	1½	2	2¼	2½	3
Length of body width-way of the cloth	14	16	20	20	20
Depth of arm-hole	1	1¼	1½	1¾	2
Width across arm-hole	1½	2	2¼	2½	3
Length of waistband	8	9	10	11	13
Length of band for the hem at top	8	9	11	12	13
Length of sleeve-bands	3	3½	4	4¼	4½
Length of shoulder-strap, if wanted	1¾	2¼	2½	2¾	3

In cutting it out, double the strip for the body once, and again in half, and then cut out the arm-holes the proper depth and width. The full body is made up in either of the following ways:—the first and most simple, is by merely hemming it at the top and bottom, putting wid ehems at the ends, and then setting it upon the skirt, making more fulness at the back and in front than at the sides. The sleeves are put into the body with shoulder-straps.

The tapes are put in to draw from the shoulder-straps behind, at the top, and another string to draw in front, also a tape all through the waist-hem.

These simply-made frocks are very useful for fast-growing children, as they will let out to the size wanted.

ANOTHER MODE OF MAKING UP.

PLATE 4. FIG. 2.

The other mode of making them up is the neatest in appearance. The body is gathered at the top and set into a long narrow band, which forms the hem and the shoulder-straps. The bottom of the body is also firmly gathered, aud sewn on with very strong thread to the skirt, which is also gathered so as to let the fulness lie principally in front. Sometimes the body is biassed in front in two or three rows, as in Fig. 2.

PLAIN STRAIGHT BODY.

SCALE.

——	First size.	Child of 1 yr.	Child of 2 yrs.	Child of 4 yrs.	Child of 8 yrs.	Child of 10 yrs.
	Nails.	Nails.	Nails.	Nails.	Nails.	Nails.
Length of body down selvage......	10	11	12	14	16	18
Depth of body	1½	1¾	2	2½	2¾	3
Depth of arm-hole	¾	1	1½	2	2½	3
Width across arm-hole	1½	1¾	2	2¼	2¾	3
Length of band, if wanted	8	9	9½	10	11	12
Length of shoulder-straps	1¾	2	2¼	2½	2¾	3¼
Length of sleeve-bands	3	3	3	3½	4	4
Length of band at top	9	10	10	10	11	12
Length of each cape..................	9	10	11	13	14	14
Depth down selvage..................	¾	¾	1	1¼	1¼	1¼

Straight bodies are generally used for ladies' children, and are ornamented in different ways. Some are worked in bobbin-work, coronation braid (see Fig. 4), common braid, or else work is let in; and others with satin-stitch worked on the muslin, or very fine small tucks, either horizontal or perpendicular (see Fig. 3). One or two bodies will be more minutely described here, as a guide by which to make others.

PLATE 4. FIG. 5.

Divide the body in half, so as to ascertain the middle, and run a tacking-thread down it; run two others, one on each side, at the distance of little more than ½ a nail from the middle, at the top, and slanting down to the middle point at the bottom of the body; run two others, at the distance of ⅔ of a nail on each side of the last, slanting them towards the centre, at the distance of ⅓ a nail on each side from the centre. These tacking-threads serve as a guide, by which means the pattern can be done more regularly. Sew two bobbin-lines, one on each side of each tacking-thread, leaving a small space between them sufficiently wide for little oylet holes, or some other ornamental pattern, to be worked. Afterwards, sew on the bobbin neatly in patterns, according to fancy. Put in the sleeves next, having worked the bands and the triangular shoulder-bits to correspond with the front. Next put on the capes. The whole should be trimmed with a little edging or narrow work.

ON BABY-LINEN.

PLATE 4. FIG. 8.

The front is worked in fancy button-hole stitch, as in Plate 5, Fig. 19. The bands round the sleeves and the triangular shoulder-bits are worked in rows of the same stitch. The capes are worked near the edge with the horse-shoe stitch, as also the ends of the body (Plate 5, Fig. 20), and the edging is entirely of fancy bobbin edging (Plate 5, Fig. 18).

PLATE 4. FIG. 6.

Procure some pretty open work, in the style of that in the Plate, and sew several strips together, always making the pieces narrower at the bottom than at the top, in order to make them point towards the centre, as in the Plate. A body made thus generally wears and washes very well. The capes should be of some pretty work, and the whole trimmed with edging to match the rest. The triangular shoulder-bits have a piece of insertion-work inlaid in them.

BODY WITH HONEY-COMB STITCH.

This body has the side-bits cut as above, and the front is a triangular piece of honey-comb stitch worked and let in. In making the triangular bit, lay the plaits very narrow and even, before working it in honey-comb. For a description of the stitch, see Plate 1, Fig. 15, 16.

SLEEVES.
PLATE 4.

There are various sorts of long and short sleeves, some of which it is impossible to describe clearly, and it will not, therefore, be attempted. The most simple are the following:—

THE ROUND SLEEVE.
FIG. 1, 18.

SCALE.

	First size.	Child of 1 yr.	Child of 3 yrs.	Child of 6 yrs.
	Nails.	Nails.	Nails.	Nails.
Size of square piece out of which the circle for the sleeve is cut...	7	8	9	10
Diameter of inner circle	1	1¼	1½	2
Length of shoulder-strap	1¼	1¼	1¾	2
Length of sleeve-band	3	3¼	3½	3¾
Depth of sleeve-band	½	¾	1	1¼

FIG. 18.

Cut your material into square pieces of the size wanted (in proportion to the Scale), and double the square in half, so as to make it triangular, or three-cornered in shape. Fold it in the same manner again and again, as often as it will admit of being done; one side is longer than the other, mark it with your scissors the same distance on the long side from the point, as it is on the short, and cut it directly across; by which means the square will become a circle, as will be seen when opened. This circle should be hollowed out at one side (Plate 4, Fig. 18), in order to make it set better under the arm. Before opening the circle, a small hole should be cut at the pointed end, to form the opening for the arm in proper proportion. The shoulder-strap and band are next cut. Set the inner circle very neatly into the band; after which, gather the outer circle and sew it to the shoulder-strap, ready to put into the body. This sleeve is sometimes confined by loops of ribbon, or little triangular pieces of work, as in Fig. 2 and 6.

ANOTHER SHAPE.

PLATE 4. FIG. 13.

PRINCIPALLY USED FOR PETTICOATS AND PLAIN FROCKS.

SCALE.

	Baby's first size.	Child of 2 yrs.	Child of 4 yrs.
	Nails.	Nails.	Nails.
Measure of the largest depth	2	2¼	3
Length of sleeve, when open, to cut crosswise of the material	7	9	11
Measure of the smallest depth	½	¾	1
Length of band	3	3¼	3¼
Length of shoulder-strap	1¼	1½	2

It is better to cut this pattern (and indeed all patterns of sleeves) in paper, before cutting your material, to prevent waste. The pattern, when folded in half, resembles Fig. 13, being for the first size, and is 2 nails deep from A to B, and 3½ nails long from B to C. The top, from A to D, is sloped down, beginning at E, which is about half the length, by which means the depth from D to C is only 1 nail. When opened, the sleeve resembles Fig. 12. In cutting it out, turn up a corner of your material (Fig. 12) in the form of a half-handkerchief, A B being parallel to, or straight with C D. The pattern sleeve is laid with the long straight end upon the crease, so as to lie crosswise. Cut through the folded muslin carefully by the pattern, so that the *pair* of sleeves is cut at once. The part which forms the bottom of the sleeve is straight, and should be gathered into the band. The sloped side is gathered or whipped into the shoulder-strap.

PLATE 4. FIG. 14.

The Scale is the same as Fig. 13 and 8.

This sleeve is the most favourite shape, and is cut out exactly like Fig. 13; after which the part, A B, is sloped off at 1 nail from the end, C. A triangular piece of worked muslin is hemmed round; the sleeve is then neatly put into the arm-hole, with mantua-maker's hem, or run and felled, after which the rest of the sleeve is whipped and sewed on to the triangular piece. These sleeves are generally made with a little frill very much fulled, which forms a cape behind, and also in front; the frill is therefore sewed on the sleeve neatly at the edge of the triangular bit.

PLATE 4. FIG. 9, 11.

This is another variety of sleeve, and is very pretty for a young child. It is cut out, in the first instance, exactly like Fig. 14; after which it is sloped off in the shape of a triangle below, so that the sleeve requires a triangular bit below, as well as on the shoulder, for the sleeve to be fulled to. The bottom triangle should be cut with the band, into which the sleeve is confined.

LONG SLEEVES.
PLATE 4. FIG. 15, 16, 17.

Long sleeves, if for bed-gowns and under clothes, may be cut according to the bits of cloth left, to prevent waste, always remembering to cut selvage-wise. They are generally the shape of Fig. 15, Plate 4. The sleeve is sloped off from D to A, so as to cut about a nail off the stuff (see D C). Slope in the direction D E, to make the wrist about 1½ or 2 nails wide. The part, A B D, should be hollowed. Sometimes it is desirable to piece the sleeve when there are many bits; in which case it may be joined across from B to E of the under double, taking care that the muslin pieced on also runs selvage-wise. In cutting out long sleeves, take care to cut them a pair, so that the joinings shall lie outside, and the hollowed part towards the inside or front. From A to C is 3¼ nails.

Long sleeves, for dresses, spencers, &c., to be properly made, should be cut as follows (Plate 4, Fig. 16 and 17):—turn up the corner of your muslin to form such an angle as will just hold the sleeve, so as to make the one side of the long sleeve lie along the selvage, as in Fig. 16, where, the sleeve being small, but little of the corner is turned up, in which the sleeve, A B C D, exactly fits. The top corner, F, must be sloped off, and the corner, D C, also, to the proper width for the wrist, which is 1¼ nail.

Fig. 17 is a better sort of sleeve, and is here introduced, though it properly belongs to the table of sleeves in Plate 12, in which a description and pattern of each size is correctly given. The corner is turned up to a complete half-square, so that A and B are parallel to C D. From A to B is 6 nails; from B to D 5¼ nails. From A to H. and from B to C, are 1½ nail. Curve from H to E. From H to G are 5½ nails. From E to F are 3¼ nails. From F to G, 1¼ nail. This sleeve is called the gigot, or gigot de mouton sleeve, from its likeness to a leg of mutton. For further particulars, see Sleeves, Plate 12.

AN INFANT'S RECEIVER.

A receiver, or wrapper, in which an infant is put immediately on its birth, previous to its being washed and dressed, is composed of the finest Welsh flannel, with a soft warm nap upon it. This flannel should be a perfect square, and is generally made of 2 breadths of flannel; the width of the flannel must, therefore, determine the size of the square, which should not be less than 24 nails, or more than 2 yards. A soft piece of fine calico, linen, or cambric muslin, is taken, of the same size, and they are bound together with flannel binding. This receiver is frequently used afterwards by the poor in the double capacity of coverlet and shawl, to carry the infant about in.

INFANT'S SHAWL.

For the first three months, infants should be carried about in a shawl, not only on account of the warmth, but as a matter of security to their tender heads and limbs, which cannot bear the hard pressure of the nurse's arm or hand.

These shawls for the nursery should be simply a square of flannel of 1½ breadth or 2 breadths. The best shawl, with which it is carried into sitting-rooms, should be made of merino, Indiana, kerseymere, or, what is better still, of the fine thick Saxony flannel. These are usually made with very deep hems, about 1¼ nail of the same material, braided with silk braid all round, and worked at the corners, or else the hem is formed of pearl-white satin or rich silk; but these last spoil so soon, that it is a great expense.

INFANT'S FLANNEL CLOAK.
PLATE 4. FIG. 19, 24.

It is recommended to all mothers to have a flannel cloak to wrap round their infants when carried about in their night clothes, and when up at night; and they will be found especially useful when the baby is old enough to be dipped in a cold bath, or obliged to be put in a warm one, as, on taking the child out of it, they can wrap it up entirely, and almost rub it dry with the cloak itself.

The first size here mentioned will last a child well from its birth until eighteen months or two years old.

SCALE.

	First size.	Child from 3 to 6 years.	Child from 6 to 9 years.
Number of breadths of 14 nails	3	3	4
Length of skirt	1 yd. 4 nls.	1 yd. 8 nls.	1 yd. 12 nls.
Distance of arm-hole from top	4 nails	5 nails	6 nails
Length of arm hole	2 do.	2¼ do.	3 do.
Collar (see Plate 13, Fig. 3)	column 4	column 2	column 2
Shoulder-piece (see Plate 13, Fig. 1)	—	—	—
Large cape, if wanted	2 breadths	2 breadths	2¼ breadths

The cloak requires two flannel shoulder-pieces to make it strong. Full the skirt very evenly all round to the proper size, and then laying the edge between the edges of the two shoulder-pieces, which should be held so as to fall back or down against the skirt, one on each side, sew, or rather backstitch them very firmly together. When this is done, turn up the shoulder-pieces on each side, so that the edges are completely hidden on both sides of the cloak. Sew the collar neatly on to the other two edges of the shoulder-pieces, and conceal the rough edges by means of a wide string-case of soft tape or calico.

The cloak is bound with flannel binding, and the arm-holes also; they are either opened in the seam, or if that would make them too far back, they should be cut in the flannel at once, at the proper distance. A deep cape might be added as the child grew older, or if it were sickly and required additional warmth.

CHILD'S BIB.
PLATE 4. FIG. 25.

This is often used by mothers for their children while cutting their teeth, to prevent the moisture from their mouths wetting their chests and the bosoms of their frocks. It is made of three or four folds of fine diaper, sewed together on the wrong side, and turned inside out, to conceal the edges, it is hollowed to fit under the chin, and made to tie with a ribbon round the neck.

INFANTS' PELISSES AND CLOAKS.
PLATE 4. FIG. 20.

Infant's first cloaks are generally made of some warm material, as cloth, merino, kerseymere, or wadded silk. The last-mentioned, though pretty, soon spoils, being easily injured by wet, and the colours of those parts near the baby's chin fly and look shabby; merino and kerseymere are decidedly the best for the purpose, and look equally neat and handsome. There is a kind of fine but thickly woven flannel, particularly strong and elastic, and well adapted for children's shawls and cloaks. It is called Saxony flannel, but is rarely to be procured at country shops, and seldom of any colour but white. It is about 1 and 1½ yard wide, and varies from 3s. 2d. to 5s. per yard: for the lower orders, cloth, stuff, nankeen, gingham, or print, are the most serviceable.

INFANT'S LONG PELISSE.
PLATE 4. FIG. 20, 21, 22, 23.

It must be made of two or more breadths, according to the material; as the widths vary exceedingly, it is impossible to lay down a definite rule further than this; that the whole width round the bottom should be from 30 to 33 nails; and at the top sloped off to 24 nails.

Supposing the material to be of wide width (say 20 nails), half one breadth would be wide enough for the back, and one whole breadth crossed according to Fig. 22, would form the two fronts. Observe that the two straight sides of the crossed pieces are set in front.

SCALE.

	First size.	Second size.	Third size.
	Yds. nls.	Yds. nls.	Nails.
Length of skirt	1 .. 3	1 .. 0	14
Width round the bottom, about	33	30	30
Sloped off at the top to reduce the width to	24	24	24
Length of shoulder	2	2¼	2¼
Sloped off from the shoulder	½	½	½
Length of arm-hole	2	2¼	3
Arm-hole curves into the skirt (see Fig. 28)	½	½	½
Length of sleeve down the selvage	5	6	7
Width of ditto	5	6	6
Double the sleeve selvage-wise, and slope off for the wrist to	1¼	2	2
Case for string sewed on inside	4	5	6
Whole length of band	10	11	12
Cape, according to Plate 13, Fig. 31	—	—	—
Collar, according to Plate 13, Fig. 13	—	—	—

The sleeves, collar, &c. should be cut from the remaining half breadth of the cloth.

If the material be but 10 or 12 nails wide, 3 breadths must be used, and the two front breadths sloped off to the proper width at the top.

In making up the pelisses, the front breadths are lined with silk or sarcenet, as also the top part or body, collar, cape, &c., but the back breadth should be lined with cambric muslin. The hem at the bottom of the skirt is about 1½ nail deep, while that up the sides and round the cape and collar are but ¾ of a nail. Take notice, in cutting your collar and cape, that allowance must be made for the hems.

The skirt seams are sewed up, as well as the lining, and joined together by means of the broad hem round the bottom; the shoulders, arm-holes, and sleeves are next completed, after which the neck is finished by making a hem at the top, and drawing a tape through it, which is fastened down at both ends after the skirt has been drawn up to the proper width which should be about 1 nail wider than is required to set round the neck. A strong case of ribbon or other soft material is next put round the neck inside, through which a ribbon is drawn and fastened in the middle. This ribbon, of course, ties in front.

For children's short pelisses, see Plate 14.

CLOAKS FOR SUMMER.
PLATE 4. FIG. 23.

This is a very simple and remarkably neat looking pattern for a second sized cloak. It looks well when made of twilled muslin, cloth, nankeen, print, and especially fine dimity. The material should be about 1 yard 3 nails wide, in which case one breadth and 14 nails is sufficient for the skirt, which should be one yard long.

SCALE.

	Yds. nls.
Quantity required for one at 19 nails wide	3 ..14
Width of cloak at the bottom	2 .. 1
Length of ditto	1 .. 0
Size of sleeves, both width and length	5
Length of wristband down the selvage	3
Width of ditto	2
Length of band	12
Width of ditto	2
Collar cut according to Plate 13, Fig. 3	column 2
Shoulder-piece (see Plate 13, Fig. 4)	column 1
Length of cape down the selvage	7
Whole width of ditto	2 .. 0

The remaining 5 nails off the second breadth of the skirt may be cut into collar, shoulder-piece, &c. The cloak has a broad hem laid on all round, which the cape and collar have also, to form which, strips should be cut selvage-wise of 1¼ nail, and sometimes worked muslin edging of a neat but open pattern is put on all round.

About 9 or 10 yards of the strips are required, and, as frequent joinings look ill, it would be better to cut off a piece of the material a yard long, from which all the strips can be taken off; 9 strips of this length will only take 11¼ nails out of the breadth ; therefore, if economy is a great object, 10 strips might be cut in the breadth of but 10 nails deep, which would cut up the breadth without waste.

	Yds. nls.
Material for Cloak and most of the et ceteras	2 .. 0
Ditto for long cape	14
Ditto for strips	1 .. 0
	3.14

If the strips are often joined, 3 yards 8 nails.

In making up the cloak, the shoulder-piece is piped all round, and the skirt fulled evenly into it. The collar is then sewn on, and a casing made at the top, to admit of a ribbon. The broad hem is next laid on all round, and the sleeves put in. At the waist, the casing is sewn on inside, and the band outside, the back may be confined to the band or not, at pleasure.

INFANT'S FIRST HOOD.
PLATE 4. FIG. 26, 27, 29, 30.

This is the most approved shape for infant's first hoods, whether they are boys or girls, owing to its warmth and softness, and also for the comfort with which an infant can rest its head on its nurse's shoulder. They are generally made of merino, Indiana, kerseymere, satin, silk, nankeen, or indeed of

PLATE 5.

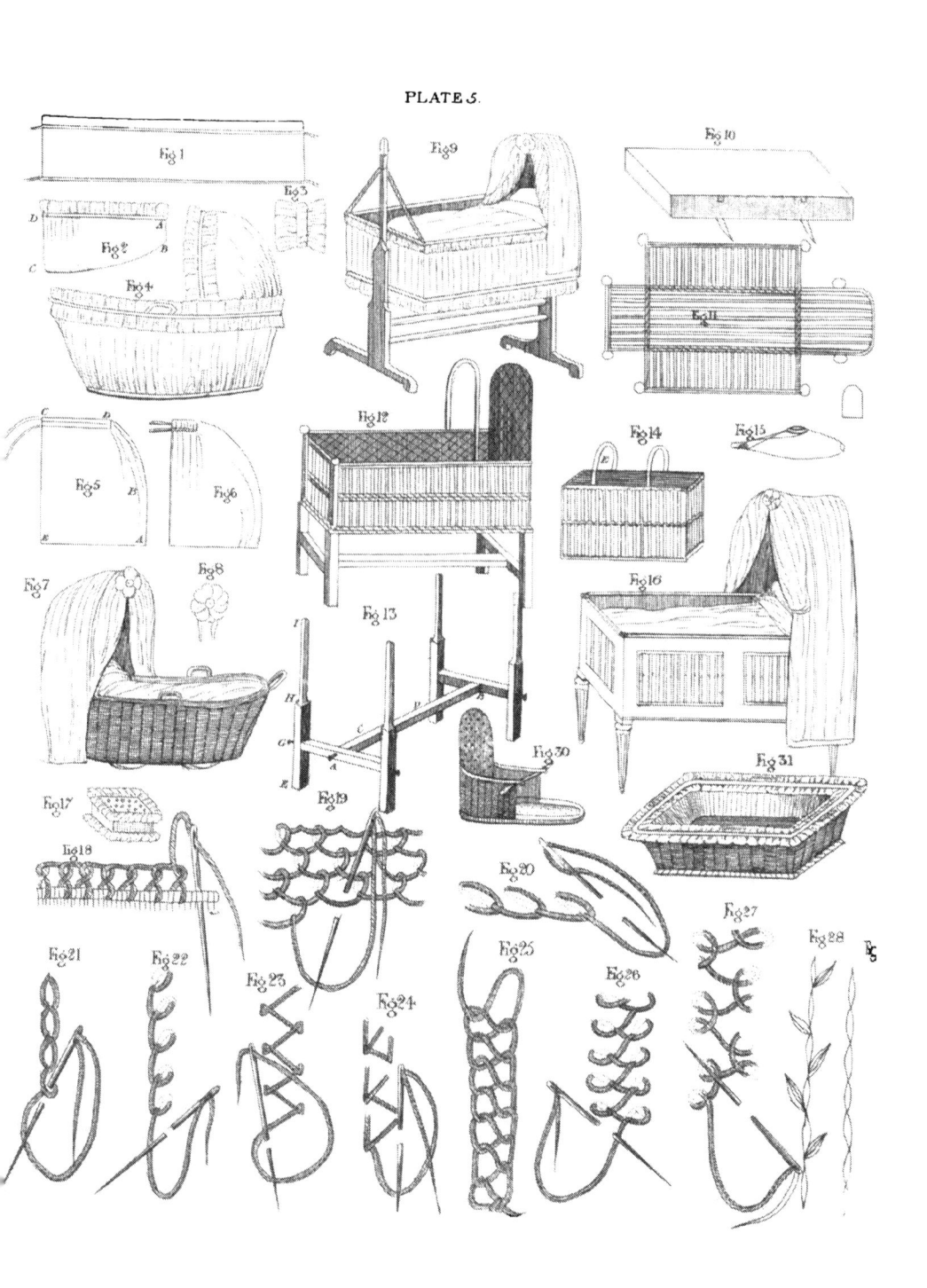

ON BABY-LINEN.

any material similar to the cloak. Kerseymere, lined with silk or satin of a pale colour is particularly pretty and suitable, from its simplicity.

Cut a piece along the selvage, 7 nails long, and three nails wide; double it in half its length, making it only 3½ nails. Let F A (see Fig. 27) be the doubled part, and on the opposite end, measure off one nail from C to B, and cut it off in a direct line from B to A. F D is the front of the hood. The horse-shoe crown (Fig. 26) must be cut next, for which take another piece of 2¼ nails long, down the selvage, and 2 nails wide. Fold it half the width, and slope off a third of a nail from the bottom, B to D, also round off the top. For the tippet or curtain, form a perfect circle, from a square of 8 nails, from which take out the triangular piece (see Fig. 30, A B C), the distance from B to C being 2 nails along the line. In making up the hood, cut a lining of silk or satin the same size; also one of fine flannel, wadding, or demet; then sew the crowns into the head pieces of each of the three materials separately. The merino hood may be piped with silk or satin, braided with silk braid or worked in chain-stitch, with netting silk, round the horse-shoe crown, after which, place the flannel lining between the merino and silk, and stitch them firmly together with small neat stitches, as close to the piping or braid as possible. Next run them all together at the edges, admitting a piece of chip or thin whalebone to give a little stiffness. Two runners are made three quarters of a nail from the edge, and from each other; these runners must be of sufficient width to admit the three-penny width ribbon. These ribbons are fastened at one side of the hood, and drawn up to the proper size, and then tacked down at the other, leaving sufficient ribbon to allow of the hood being undrawn entirely, when it is wanted; another ribbon is put behind. A rosette of satin ribbon is worn on the left side, if a boy, and in front, if a girl, and a small bow behind. The curtain is sewed on plainly along the horse-shoe, but fulled from thence to the ears.

These hoods will draw out to last a child twelve months after its birth, and will clean well, when of merino.

For children's hats and bonnets, see Plate 19.

COVER FOR A BASSINETTE.
PLATE 5. FIG. 1, 2, 3, 4.

A bassinette (see Fig. 4) is a very small cradle made of wicker-work, about 3 feet long, 18 inches wide, and 15 inches high. It is very useful for carrying about, and may be set upon a table, sofa, or bed, taken in a carriage, or even upon the lap with little inconvenience. For a delicate child, and in the winter, it is very desirable, being much warmer than a larger cradle.

Bassinettes are fitted up with a coloured lining under a thin dimity or muslin covering. The lining is sometimes made of white, blue or pink satin or silk, but more generally, and more sensibly, of glazed calico. It should be put on the outside of the wicker-work, and also very neatly fulled in regular folds inside it. The cover is made about half a yard deep down the selvage, and 4½ yards wide. When all the breadths are sewed together, a deep hem is made at the top, with a runner for a string (the hem and runner together to be about 1 nail). If the material is thick, it is better to sew to it, quite plainly, a deep frill, of a finer texture, to give it lightness, instead of having the frill made of the same; through the runner pass a tape, which will draw it all round to the proper size, to fit the body of the cradle; a second hem at the bottom will also be required for the same purpose (see Plate 5, Fig. 1). The head piece, Fig. 2, is made, so that when drawn up, it will fit the head of the bassinette. Cut a piece of ½ a yard down the selvage, and 1 yard 2 nails in width. As there must be no seam in the width, if the material be not wide enough, it would be better to cut the width down the selvage-way instead. It must be doubled in half the width (the 1 yard 2 nails), see Fig. 2, and sloped off from B to C in a very gradual curve, the space from A to B is 3 nails. Hem each of the two straight sides, and make a runner from B to C for a tape. Next full the straight part, D A, to the exact size round the front of the head; let the fulling lie towards the middle, and when ready, sew on the double frill, which is made of fine clear muslin. The frill, Fig. 3, is cut in strips width-way, of 3 nails each; sew these strips together till you have about 4 yards length of frilling; make a narrow hem on each side of the frill, and then begin to put it upon the front, or fulled part of the head-piece; for this purpose, double the frilling exactly in half, and while thus doubled, allow from the centre ¼ of a nail for the frilling, and make another even crease all along. Open the frills, and turning down at the one side, begin to run; and, dividing it, of course, into quarters, gather it evenly; when done, sew it firmly to the cover, at within ¼ of a nail from the edge; after which, turn down the other outer crease at the proper distance from the centre of the frill, and do the same with it; when ready, sew it on to the edge itself of the head-piece. This frilling should stand up well, and not lie flat against the cover; for this end, not quite so much as ¼ of a nail should be allowed between the two seams. A ribbon the same colour as the lining run through the puffing, and fastens the cover on in front, while the tape or ribbon, through the other runner, ties it at the bottom of the head, and draws it up to the right size.

CRADLE COVER.
PLATE 5. FIG. 5, 6, 7, 8.

A cradle merely requires a little drapery over the head, to form curtains, in order to guard the infant from the sun, or from draughts of air, while asleep, and to give an air of comfort and cleanliness.

The drapery should always be perfectly white, of dimity, twilled muslin, or other neat strong material. Some ladies put covers of thin muslin over a coloured lining, but nothing looks so well as perfectly white curtains. The dimity, &c. should be about 1 yard wide; take two breadths of the proper length from the head of the cradle to the floor, about 14 nails, pin them evenly together, and sew up the seam from A to B (Fig. 5), about the distance of ½ a yard, but this must be determined by the cradle, observing to sew up until it begins to curve. As the curve must be cut while the material is fitted on the cradle itself, the dimity should be pinned along the bottom of the cradle from A to E, and also from A to B at the back. Then fit it accurately by pinning the breadths exactly, though easily together, along the curve, allowing enough for shrinking in washing, and when nicely fitted on, cut off the superfluous part and stitch it along, while on the cradle; the rough edges may afterwards be turned over, and hemmed down. The remainder of the dimity in front, is intended to hang over the cradle top, to form little curtains; hem round each side, and connect them together with small stitches, by running a cord up one hem, and down the other (Fig. 5, C D), the piece is drawn up to a small compass. This drawn-up piece will require a bow or rosette of muslin (see Fig. 8); the whole piece may be trimmed with fringe, or turned up with a piping, which, if the cover be lined with glazed coloured calico, should be of the same. A loop of cord should come from underneath, and encircle the rosette (see Fig. 8).

For noblemen's families, these covers are sometimes edged with silk fringe, or turned up with silk or satin, to accord with a lining of the same.

CRIB COVERS.
PLATE 5. FIG. 16.

These are generally made with a horse-shoe back, reaching from the top to the bottom of the crib; it is piped all round, and a piece of the proper width to go from side to side over the hoops is cut selvage-way, and either sewn plainly or fulled on to the horse-shoe back. This piece may either be

ON BABY-LINEN.   43

finished in front like that over the cradle head, by drawing it up, and thus forming curtains; or two half breadths may be fulled evenly round to this head-piece. Crib covers are frequently lined with blue or other coloured calico, which is sometimes made larger than the cover, to admit of being turned up so as to form a little border outside.

INFANT'S HANGING COT.
PLATE 5. FIG. 9.

This is a convenient shape, as it easily takes to pieces when not in use. The sides are either made entirely of wood, when no drapery is necessary; but they are usually merely frames to which ticking or any other material is fixed.

If it is furnished with ticking, it is laid on plain, though almost any other material, which will not wash is laid in plaits or fulled. The material is bound all round, and nailed on at the inner side, after which, an inside lining of glazed calico, or other material is put.

If the material is a washing one, glaze dcalico, chintz, twill, or white dimity is used; and this last is particularly neat and nice, and in the country might be made to keep clean a long time; the pieces should be fulled into some strong binding, to which very small loops might be sewn, large enough to admit of the nail to confine it firmly to the crib, so that when the covering is removed for washing, the loops alone are torn by the nails, and they can be easily replaced. The head drapery is similar to that of Fig. 16. Cotton fringe and gimp set all round, both above and below, gives a pretty finish to the whole. The ropes of the cots should be often looked to, and frequently renewed, as they wear out quickly, and the child's safety depends on their strength.

THE TRAVELLING COT.
PLATE 5. FIG. 10, 11, 12, 13.

This is a most convenient crib for mothers to use when travelling with young children, as it is extremely light, and can be put up in two minutes, and if kept in a leathern case, with straps (see Fig. 10), it can easily be attached to the roof, or below a carriage, and be perfectly free from damp.

The stand (see Fig. 13) is made of strong beech-wood, and when taken to pieces, is in seven parts. The upright posts are fastened together two by two, by the short bits of wood, A and B, which are screwed tight into the legs by long iron screws, with brass heads. The long bar, C D, connects the two sides together also, by means of screws. These screws should be attached to the posts or bars they belong to, by a string, as the loss of one would render the crib unsafe. The lower parts of the four posts are much thicker than the upper, to give support to the crib. This is formed of five pieces of wicker-work (see Fig. 11), the bottom and four sides. The four sides are fastened firmly to the bottom, allowing, however, ample room to give full play for the sides to fold backwards or forwards. At each extreme corner is fastened a ring of iron, brass, or strong wicker-work. These rings are so placed, that when the sides are turned up to form the crib, the two rings at each corner shall slip over the top of each post of the stand, by which means all will remain firm.

The wicker crib should be 4 feet long, 2 feet 6 inches wide, and 15 inches deep. The one narrow end might be made deeper to give more protection to the head; and one or two hoops might be put into a ring or staple at the sides of the wicker-work, by which means a head piece is easily made.

The stand posts should be 30 inches high, letting from E to G be 13 inches, from G to H, 7 inches, and from H to J be 10 inches.

The head drapery might be made similar to Fig. 15. The lining should be very simple and easily put on; also very warm, on account of the open wicker-work sides. Wadding or flannel should be quilted well over, between two folds of Holland, coloured glazed calico, or chintz, and made to tie on inside. This lining should be very thin, else it will take room in packing. When the crib is packed up, the posts are unscrewed, and the basket is folded with the sides inwards, so as to require as small a case as possible. A pillow from any bed is all that would be required, as bedding for the crib.

A child's cradle or crib contains the following articles:—

A mattress, which should be 1 nail thick, made of ticking or Holland, and stuffed with wool or horse-hair.

Some ladies have their mattresses filled with finely cut chaff, others with sea-weed or with beech leaves. Chaff keeps particularly dry, and is cool and pleasant to lie on in the summer.

A bed, which should be very thin, and made either of best feathers or down.

A pillow, also thin, and made of down.

Three blankets, made of thick Welsh flannel, and bound round with flannel binding, or worked with coloured worsted.

One coverlet, of which some can be procured made for the purpose; or, if not, the material sold for toilette covers will answer as well, if it is light.

A head-piece, or drapery for the head.

To which may be added a pair of calico sheets, if the child is some months old; otherwise they are not sufficiently warm for them to lie upon: an Indian rubber or a leathern sheet, to prevent the feather bed from getting wet, and the ticking decayed; a foot flannel, or piece of flannel 2 breadths square, bound round, to wrap up the child's feet.

BABY'S BASKET.

PLATE 5. FIG. 31.

A baby's basket should be lined either with the finest dimity or cambric muslin; in the latter case, an inner lining of coloured glazed calico or silk is often added. The cover should be very full—about three times the length round the basket, or more. After cutting the strips width-way, and sewing together sufficient to form the length required, make a small hem or runner along one side; after which, another is made about ½ a nail or more from it, according to the exact width of the ledge at the top of the basket. Upon the outer of these two runners is sewed a double frill, and between this and the inner runner, slits are cut in the proper places to admit the four handles, which are neatly hemmed round. At the bottom, on the other side of the strip, there is also a runner, through which a cord is drawn. A piece of the dimity is next fitted to the bottom of the basket, after which, the strip that goes round it being drawn up evenly, it is sewed on very neatly and firmly to the bottom piece. To the four corner strings are sewed, which being passed through the straw-work of the basket, tie the cover firmly down to it.

The strings for the top are put in as follows:—four long pieces of cord are cut off, about 1½ yard each; they are doubled in two, so that one end is only a ¼ of a yard long: these cords are sewed firmly in the runner, each to the one side of each of the four handles, letting the short end of the cord be drawn through the runner at that shortest side next the corner, while the long cord has to be drawn past the handle and along to the furthest corner, where, on meeting the short end of another cord, it is tied firmly under the ledge of the basket. Of course these cords cannot be run in until the covering is actually upon the basket.

It may not be considered as out of place here, to state the usual contents of a basket, when prepared for an infant at its birth.

At the bottom, after putting in the bottle, with its leather or parchment suck, the other things are placed in the following order:—

The large flannel shawl, the calico bed-gown, night-flannel, night-cap, shirt, napkins, flannel cap and band, soft towels, sponge, hair-brush, powder-bag, or box. Quite at the top are the receiver, the pincushion, with large and small pins, large pair of scissors, and a ball of strong thread or fine twine.

THE PINCUSHION.
PLATE 5. FIG. 17.

"The satin cushion chequered o'er
With shining pins, this motto bore."—THE MOTHER.

One kind, out of the numerous sorts known to every body, is alone mentioned here, as being the best, on account of its steadiness and the depth, which renders it safer, should it chance to get into the hands of a young child.

It is rather longer than it is broad, being about 7 nails by 6 nails, and nearly 3 nails deep. This will hold the largest pins without danger of their pricking through to the other side. The top and bottom should be made alike, with a frill all round, as seen in the Plate. These pincushions are sometimes made of muslin over satin or silk, but, if intended to be useful, white dimity is by far the best.

THE LEATHER SUCK FOR BOTTLES.
PLATE 5. FIG. 15.

As most of the articles used by infants have been entered upon in turn, it is considered advisable to mention also the mode of making and fastening on the leather or parchment suck to the bottle. The suck is cut in the shape of the figure, so that when doubled down the middle, it resembles the upper part of the thumb of a glove. The two sides and the top are either joined together in the button-hole stitch or back-stitch; and if the latter, the suck must be turned inside out, that the smooth side may come in contact with the infant's mouth. If mothers follow the rather dangerous practice of putting a bit of sponge inside the suck, it should be first well tied round and fastened to the nose of the bottle, and the string brought round the ledge of the hole (see Fig. 15), and brought again to the nose of the bottle and fastened. The sucks are merely fastened on by a strong thread wound round the nose.

LINING FOR CHAIRS.
PLATE 5. FIG. 30.

These little chairs, without legs, which are so useful to set upon the table or floor, for those children to sit in who cannot support themselves safely, should be softly lined throughout. A piece of flannel and wadding, cut to fit the chair, should be quilted together with the material the chair is to be covered with, either Holland, chintz, or calico. The whole should be very neatly bound, and then sewn or tacked on to the chair. A little cushion, stuffed with bran or horse-hair, should be put for the seat. These chairs should have sticks, with large knobs to screw on at each end. They should also be made with the sides or arms to lay flat, or turn up and fasten at pleasure, as they can, when flat, be easily packed in a trunk or laid under the carriage seats; and these comforts, when travelling, are well worth attending to. These little chairs, when the child can walk, come in nicely for swings, when, of course, the sides require lacing up firmly. For the baby's night-chair should be made a flannel cushion to sit upon. Three or four doubles of flannel, cut to the size of the seat, with a hole stitched round in the centre, and run over in diamonds, is both neat and serviceable.

A child's travelling night-stool is so great a convenience in the carriage, during long journeys, that it is here mentioned, though there is little to be said as to its fitting up. The lid should be covered with cloth, stuffed well with horse-hair or wool, to make it soft as a seat. This cloth should be nailed all round with smooth brass-headed nails. The lid should open with a spring, and the seat inside be covered with soft quilted flannel or Indian rubber cloth. The pan, which is of block-tin or crockery, should have a lid made to fit it tightly. These little stools should be about 9 inches high, and 10 inches square.

CHAPTER VI.

WOMEN'S SHIFTS.

PLATE 6.

Shifts are generally made of fine Irish linen or calico, for the upper classes, and of stout linen, or strong but soft calico for poor children.

Shifts are cut out differently, according to the width of the cloth. If it is wide, the shift takes 2 breadths in the skirt, and gores are cut off from the top to sew on the bottom to widen the skirt.

If the cloth is still wider, so as to admit of only 1½ breadth in the shift, or else very narrow, so that 2 breadths are barely sufficient, the shift is crossed. The tops vary, as do also the shapes of the sleeves. The following are those generally worn.

SCALE FOR GORED SHIFTS.

——	Largest size.	Smaller size.	Second size.	First size.
	Yds. nls.	Yds. nls.	Yds. nls.	Yds. nls.
Width of material	14	14	13	12
Quantity required for one	3.. 2	2..14	2.. 7	1..15
Ditto ditto for six	18..12	17.. 4	13..11	9..11
Length of skirt, cut in one piece	2..12	2.. 8	2.. 2	1..10
Width of piece to gore off at the top	2½	2	2	1¾
Space to leave for the shoulders	1¾	1½	1¼	1
Depth to hollow the bosom	1¾	2½	2¼	2
Do. to hollow the back	2	2	1¾	1½
Do. of flaps, if preferred	3	3	2½	2
Length of sleeve down the selvage for Fig. 1	6	6	5	5
Depth of sleeve	3	3	2½	2¼
Size of gusset	3	3	2½	2¼

In goring a shift, the 2 breadths may be cut in one length, to prevent a seam on the shoulder. Fold your piece of cloth in two, and pin the sides very accurately together, or with long stitches tack them

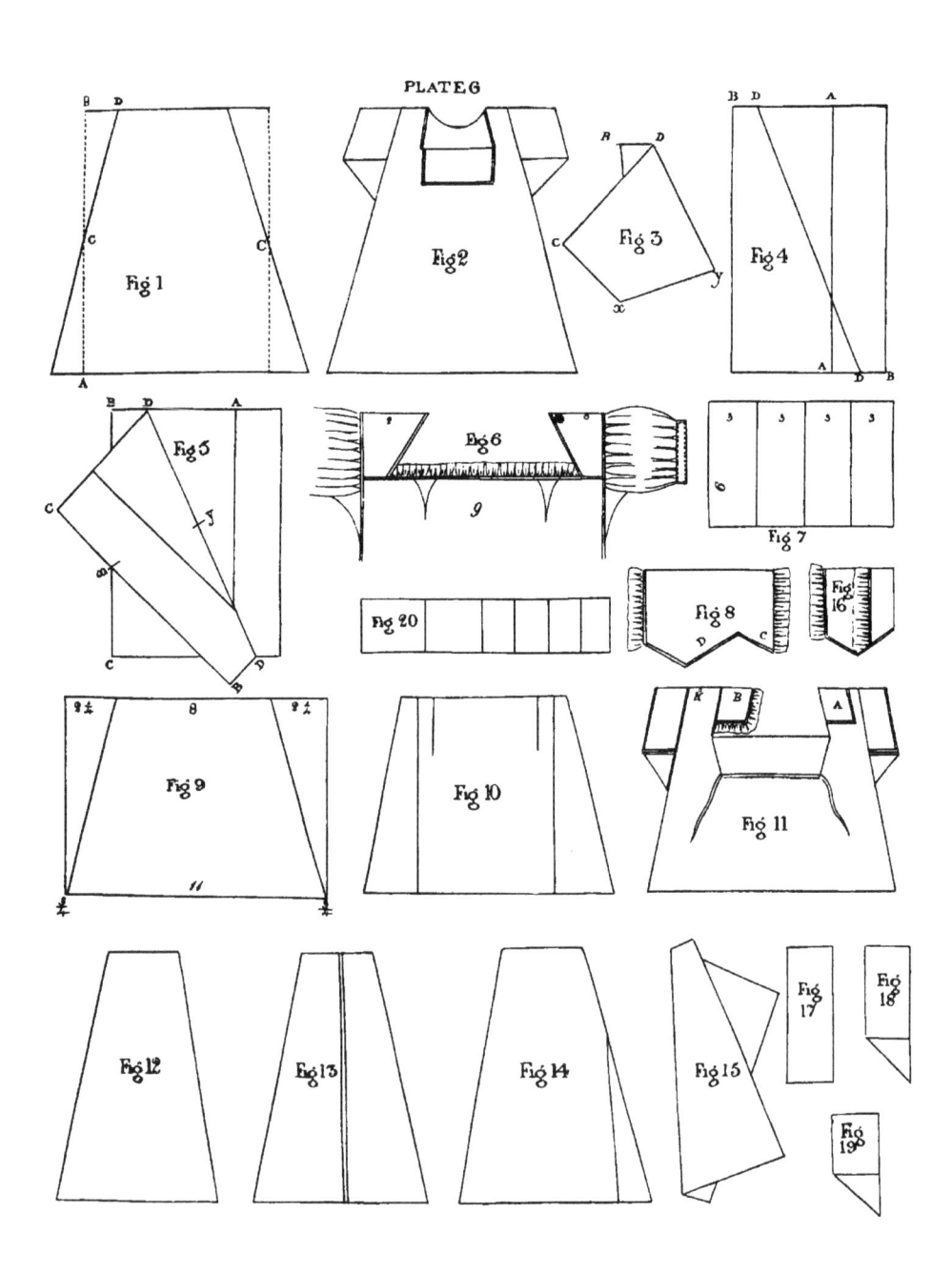

PLATE 6

up the selvages. Next double the shift in half its length, from A to B, and put in pins to mark the crease in the middle, C C. Unfold the shift and double it again very carefully the width way, so as to let the four selvages lie very evenly one upon another. Measure from the top, B, the space, B D, to be cut off, crease the linen in a straight line, from D to C, and cut it carefully off through the four thicknesses of cloth. The gores thus cut from off the top are reversed and sewed on to the bottom, to widen the skirt. The dotted lines in the Plate shew the width of the cloth, and the dark clear lines are intended to represent the shape of the shift. When the gores are sewed in, shifts are generally hollowed out at the back, and may either be also hollowed in front or have a flap cut, as seen in Fig. 2. The hollowing at the back is not so deep as in the front, therefore, great care must be taken in cutting the one not to injure the shape of the other; and in order to insure the two halves of each side being cut to correspond, it is advisable to cut the shape of the parts to be hollowed out in paper, to lay the paper on the linen, and cut by it. When the breadths are cut separately, as in some cases they must be, the seams on the shoulders should be sewed previously to the parts behind and before being hollowed. If the flap in front is preferred, it may either be cut straight down, as in Fig. 2, or in a slanting direction, as the shoulder in Fig. 6. This last plan is usually followed, and a button-hole is worked near the front of the shoulder-strap, which, being folded over to a button sewed on the shoulder-strap of the stays, neatly confines all straps, &c., in the fold.

SCALE FOR FIG. 6.

——	First size.	Second size.	Third size.
	Nails.	Nails.	Nails.
Length of shoulder-strap................	4	3½	3
Widest width of ditto	1¾	1½	1¼
Sloped off to..............................	¾	¾	⅝
Length of plaited sleeve	8	7	6
Depth of ditto	2½	2	1½
Size of gusset	2	1⅞	1½
Length of sleeve-band	4½	3¾	2¾
Width of ditto	½	½	½
Length of bosom gore	1 full nail	1	¾
Width of ditto at the top	1	1	1

There is another mode of cutting out the top of a shift, and, from its simplicity and economy, is preferable to any other. The shoulder-straps are cut separately from the skirt, which is, consequently, cut shorter, and is made quite straight at the top. The shift, after being gored or crossed, has little bosom gores put in front. The top is then hemmed, both before and behind, and the straps put on. A neat frill may be added, to give a finish to the whole.

The sleeves are sometimes cut out of the width of one of the breadths of the skirt, when the material is a little too wide; but unless you have linen of an awkward width by you, it is a wasteful plan, as the strip thus cut off is generally twice as long as the quantity required for the sleeves. Observe, if this plan be adopted, to cut off the length for the sleeves all in one piece, and not length by length from each separate breadth, as much waste would arise from so doing. If the sleeves are to be made as in Fig. 2, they may be cut in one length, sleeve and gusset together, down the selvage (see Fig. 17, 18, 19), and so many lengths in the width of the cloth. If they are to be made according to Fig. 6, an extra nail in length must be allowed for the plaiting. The gussets are reduced in size, according to the Scale, and a band to gather the sleeve into, at the bottom, is neatly stitched.

CROSSED SHIFTS.

PLATE 6. FIG. 3, 4, 5.

SCALE.

	Largest size.	Second size.	Third size.
	Yds. nls.	Yds. nls.	Yds. nls.
Width of material	1 .. 0	14	12
Quantity for one, not including sleeves	2 .. 12	2¼ .. 0	2 .. 0
Quantity for six, not including sleeves	16 .. 8	14¼ .. 0	12 .. 0
Length of skirt	1 .. 6	1¼ .. 0	1 .. 0
Width of skirt, when sewed up, should be	1 .. 0	14	12
Part to mark off at top and bottom, at opposite corners	10	9	8
Width of skirt at the top, when sewed up, and double	11	10	8
Width of ditto at the bottom, when sewed up, and double	1 4	1 .. 2	1 .. 0
Sleeves for one	6	6	5
Sleeves for six	1 .. 5	1¼ .. 0	15

Before crossing a shift, sew the 2 breadths or the 1½ breadth, whichever it happens to be, together, and next, after flattening the seams with your thumb nail, crease the skirt, so that these two seams shall lie exactly one upon the other, and tack or pin them firmly together; or, to give a neater effect, the seams are brought, one in front and the other behind, so as to divide it in exact thirds. Fig. 4 represents the skirt when sewn up, A A being intended for the seam. Measure off 1¼ nails at the left hand of the top B D, and on the right hand of the bottom B D of the skirt, and double it from D to D, as in Fig. 5; and that you may be sure your measurements are accurate, it is better to double it again upwards, at X and Y, so that B D at the bottom, should lie upon B D at the top, and the corner C upon C, as in Fig. 3. If they do not exactly correspond, the shift is not correctly folded. After pressing these creases with the hand, unfold C from C, as it was before (see Fig. 5), and cut evenly from D to D. The skirt must then be turned. The two wide ends are for the bottom—the two narrow ones for the top of the shift.

It is made up as follows:—After sewing and felling the seams, and hemming the bottom, the hem at the top must be turned down, as if for hemming, and then turned back again and sewed all round, which is much stronger than a common hem. The sleeves are generally set in plainly, excepting, of course, in those intended to be full, as in Fig. 6.

CHILD'S SHIFT.

PLATE 6. FIG. 9, 10, 11.

This is a particularly neat pattern for a child from five years up to any age, and is generally the first shift used after leaving off the little shirt which is seen in the baby-linen.

As these shifts consist of 1¼ breadth of 9 yards long, an even number, as 2, 4, or 6, should be cut out at the same time to prevent waste.

SCALE.

Width of Irish linen	12½ nails
Length of ditto	9 do.
Number of breadths	1½ breadth
Width of shift at the top, when gored, and double	8 nails
Width at the bottom, when double	11 do.
Space left for shoulders	1½ do.
Depth of slit for lappets	2 do.
Depth of arm-hole	2¾ do.
Whole length of sleeve, including gusset	4½ do.
Depth of sleeve	1½ do.
Length of shoulder-flap	3 do.
Width of ditto	1¼ do.
Length of lining	7 do.
Width of ditto	1¾ do.

Two gores, of 2¼ nails at the top, and ¾ of a nail at the bottom, are cut off the whole breadth (see Fig. 9), which reduces the body to 8 nails at the top, and 11 at the bottom, which is the proper width of the shift. These gores are sewn on to the half-breadth, which makes it exactly correspond with the other side. After sewing the two halves together, leaving 2¾ nails from the top for the arm-holes, cut down the slits for the bosom flaps 2 nails deep, leaving 1½ nail space for the shoulders. Next, cut out the sleeve flaps (see Fig. 11) of 1¼ nail deep, and 3 nails long, and, after hemming them all round, sew them with firm small stitches to the shoulder. At the edge, B, sew on a piece of tape, in which make a button-hole, which buttons over the shoulder to the button, K, and confines all straps, as seen in the sleeve marked A, in Fig. 11, where the flap is represented as turned back over the shoulder, as it is when worn; whereas in the sleeve, marked B, the flap is unturned. The sleeves are hemmed all round, and then one end is turned up to form the gusset, to one side of which the other end of the sleeve is sewn, as in Fig. 17, 18, 19; they are then put plainly into the arm-hole, which must be previously hemmed.

The lining is put in last, and is turned down once a deep fold, all round. It is neatly felled inside to the shift. The lining is 7 nails long, and 1¾ nail wide. It is sewn in a little below the arm-hole, and carried over the shoulder to the corresponding place on the other side of the shift. Strings are sewn to the points of the flaps, both before and behind. Children's sleeves are sometimes fulled on the shoulder. The work should be close and strong. The flaps are sometimes made of fine lawn, edged with a cambric frill or worked muslin, and allowed to lie over the shoulder, outside the dress, which has a clean and neat appearance.

A SECRET WORTH KNOWING.

HOW TO SAVE ONE SEAM AND TWO FELLS IN MAKING UP TWO SHIFTS.

PLATE 6. FIG. 12, 13, 14, 15.

This is a useful hint for those who make up much linen at home. It is done as follows:—

Take 3 breadths of the wide-width cloth, and sew them all together like a bag; then lay two of the seams very exactly one upon the other, and either pin or tack them firmly together; fold the whole piece in half, width-wise, so as to have four thicknesses of linen lying upon one another. Cross it like a common shift, Fig. 15, measuring it top and bottom to see if it is even, and it will cut into four pieces, one of which, Fig. 12, will have no seam at all; one, Fig. 13, will have a straight seam down the middle; the other two, Fig. 14, have each a piece like a gore on one side. These shifts, when neatly made, are just as serviceable and as good as those cut in the usual way, and it saves a great deal of work.

PLATE 6. FIG. 8, 16.

This is a pretty variety of sleeve, and is most suitable for young children. It is intended to fall over the frock. Fig. 8 represents the shape of the sleeve when cut out, and Fig. 16 when it is finished. The sleeve is cut all in one piece, taking care that the slope of the flap, C, when turned back, corresponds with the slope of the sleeve, D. The sleeve and flap are frilled with cambric, work, or lace. The advantage of this shape is, that both sleeve and flap are in one.

TROWSERS OR DRAWERS.
PLATE 7.

These are worn by men, women, and children of all classes, and almost all ages, under the different names of trowsers and drawers. They are made in a great variety of ways. Those mentioned here are the kinds most generally approved. Drawers for ladies and children are usually made of calico, twill, and cambric muslin. Those ladies who are invalids, or who ride much, frequently wear flannel or wash-leather drawers, with or without white calico leglets. For men, drawers are composed of very strong twill, calico, linen, flannel, and stockinet.

CHILD'S TROWSERS.
PLATE 7. FIG. 1, 2.

This is a child's first pair of trowsers, and should be made of fine twill or calico. Each leg is cut in one piece, and, when folded, is 4½ nails wide; therefore, to prevent waste, the material should be 9 nails in width.

Cut off the 2 breadths for the two legs, of the proper length, and observe the following directions:—

SCALE.

	Nails.
Width of material..............................	9
Length of each breadth	9
Fold the breadth in half its width	—
Measure from A to B, Fig. 2	4
From E to C....................................	2
From F to B....................................	4

Slope off from A to C, and cut from A to B, taking off ½ a nail from the width at the top.

In making, sew up the legs and join them at the seam in front, leaving them open behind, with a broad hem on each side, formed by laying a strip of the same material at each end, which is run at the edge on the wrong side, turned over to hide the stitches, and hemmed or back-stitched near the edge. The legs are then tucked, and the work or frill sewn on. The whole is next set into a band, ¾ of a nail deep when doubled, and 5 nails long, which buttons behind. Shoulder-straps, with button-holes, are attached to the trowsers by means of buttons before and behind. This plan is far more convenient than that of sewing on the straps, as, when they are only buttoned on, if it is necessary to change the trowsers in the course of the day, they may be simply unbuttoned without undressing the child, and the clean trowsers fastened to the shoulder-straps, which still remain over the shoulder.

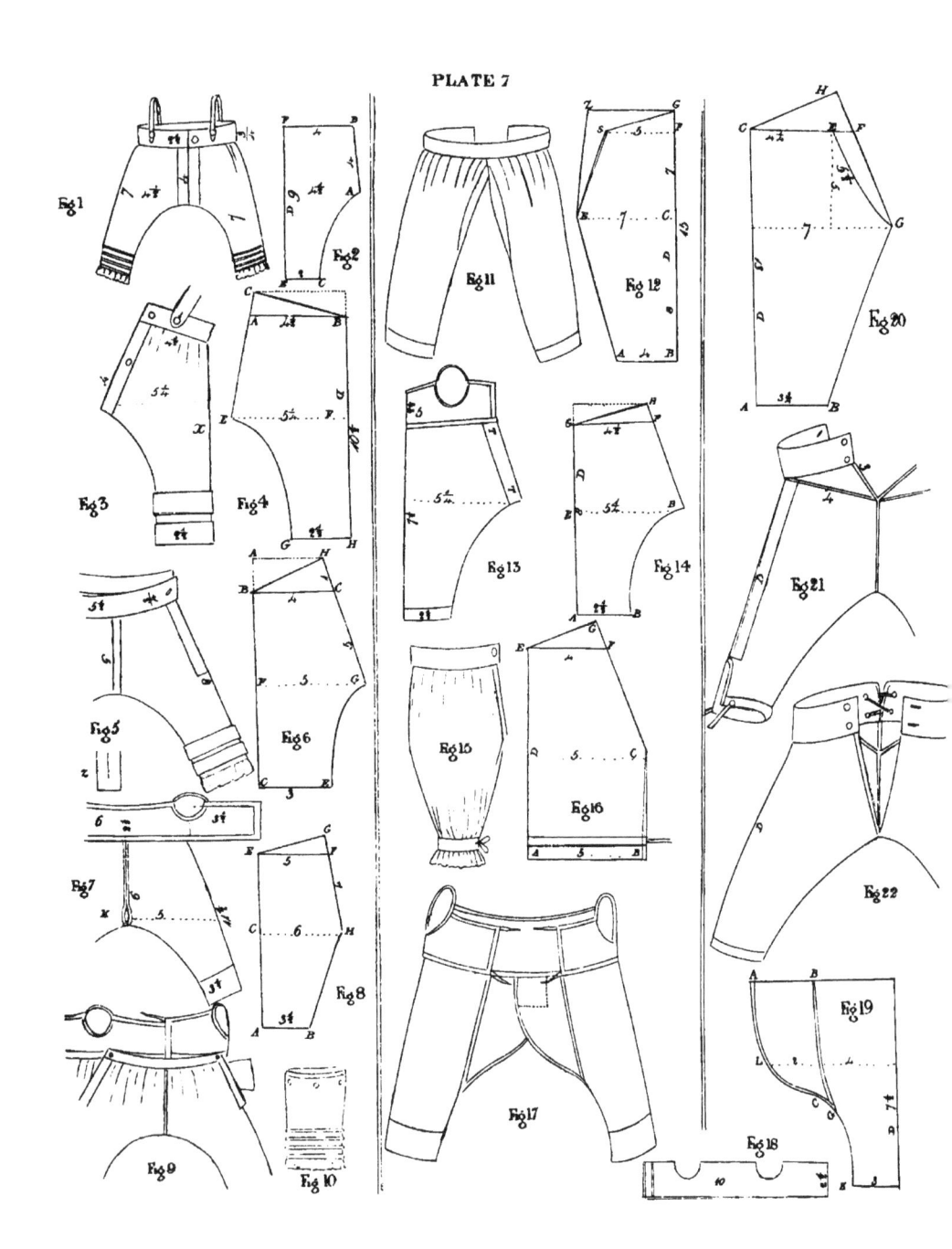

PLATE 7

A CHILD'S LARGER TROWSERS.
PLATE 7. FIG. 3, 4.

This resembles Fig. 1 and 2 in every respect, excepting that the top is sloped or hollowed at the back.

Procure your material 10¼ nails wide, to admit exactly of one leg being cut in the width.

SCALE.

	Nails.
Length of each breadth	10¼
Fold it in half, letting D be the double part	—
From the top to B	1
From B to A	4¼
From B to F	4
From F to E, or the half-breadth	5¼
From F to H	5¼

Slope from G to E, and again from E to C, through A; after which, cut at the top of one fold from A to B, and of the other from B to C. Take care to cut the pair to match, so that the outer, or hollowed parts of the legs should rise, the one towards the right, and the other towards the left side. These are made up in a similar manner to Fig. 1.

GIRL'S TROWSERS.
PLATE 7. FIG. 5, 6.

Each leg of these trowsers is also made in the entire breadth.

Procure your material 10 nails broad.

Cut each breadth 8 nails long, not including the tucks, which, if they are deep, will add about 2 nails more. Supposing it but 8 nails long, cut as follows, after folding the breadth in half its width.

SCALE.

	Nails.
From A to B	1
From B to C	4
From C to E	3
From F to G, or the entire half-breadth	5

Slope from E to G. Cut in a straight line from G, past C, to H. Cut one fold from C to B, and the other from H to B.

If the tucks require 2 nails length in addition to the above size, continue the width of the legs, the same as from C to E (3 nails), to the end.

In making up, sew the trowsers up before and behind, and cut two slits, one on each side, to the depth of 3 nails. These slits have broad hems laid on all round them; to form which, cut two strips of 4¼ nails long, and 2 nails broad; split each length down the middle, to within 1½ nail from the end (see Fig. 2). This strap is laid close to the edge and run all round the two sides of the slit, turned over, and hemmed down. This false hem greatly strengthens these slits.

The whole is then set into two bands, one for the front, and the other for the back of the trowsers. These bands are 5¼ nails long, and ¾ of a nail wide, when doubled. A button-hole is strongly worked, in a slanting direction, at each corner of the bands, by which they are fastened to two buttons sewed upon the stays.

TROWSERS FOR A BOY OR GIRL.
PLATE 7. FIG. 7, 8, 9.

This is a pretty body and trowsers, and is very suitable to little boys, especially if they are at all delicate, being particularly warm.

The body is composed of one middle piece, 6 nails long, and two side pieces, 3¼ nails long each. They are 2¼ nails deep, and, when sewed together, the middle is hollowed so as to make it only 2¼ nails.

The trowsers are made as follows:—

Width of material, 12 nails.
Length of each breadth, 11½ nails.
Fold each breadth in two (see Fig. 8).

SCALE.

	Nails.
From A to B	3¼
From A to C	4¼
From C to H, half the breadth, or	6
From C to E	6
From E to F	5

Slope from H to B; also from H, past F, to G, at the top of the breadth, whence it is cut to E, for the hollowed fold, while the under one is cut straight from E to F.

This trowser opens at the side; there is also a small opening in front (see K, Fig. 7). The body is hemmed all round, and sewed on plainly to the front band of the trowser, but it is left loose, as in Fig. 7, beyond the arm-holes on each side. The two bands button to each other at the sides, the body ties behind, and may, or may not be fastened also to the band of the trowsers at each side, having button-holes to correspond with the buttons. A little pocket should be sewed inside the slit down the sides, as in Fig. 9, where it is represented as if drawn out, or turned inside out.

LEGLETS.
PLATE 7. FIG. 10.

These are useful to put over the legs of children's trowsers, when they are soiled or tumbled, before it is necessary to put on an entirely clean pair. They are usually made of some finer material than the the trowser itself, and look well for an evening, when they are of fine cambric muslin, with open-work, or small tucks. They are fastened by three or four buttons and button-holes or loops, the buttons being sewed to the trowsers. Sometimes the trowser itself only reaches to the knee, and leglets are always attached to it, by means of small buttons; they should be put on pretty closely, to make the leglets fit well, say six or eight on each leg; button-holes are made to correspond in the leglets. They are especially advantageous for children who play a great deal out of doors, or who live in a town, they will sometimes soil one or two pair in a day.

WOMEN'S DRAWERS.

PLATE 7. FIG. 11, 12.

These are formed of two separate legs sewed into a band, which is made to button before or behind, at pleasure. For a moderate size, Fig. 12 will be a good guide.

Width of material, 14 nails.

Length of each breadth, 15 nails.

Fold each breadth in half its width, letting D be the doubled part, and measure as follows:—

SCALE.

	Nails.
From A to B is	4
From B to C	8
From C to G	7
From C to E	7
Cut in a straight line from A to E	—
From F to G	1
From F to S	5

Cut in a straight line from S to G; cut also from E to Z, the point Z being within $\frac{1}{4}$ a nail from the side. Hem the bottoms of the legs, after sewing up the seams, and hem round the slits, or open part; set them into the band, making them over-lap each other (see Fig. 11). The band is 11 nails long, and 3 nails wide.

ANOTHER SHAPE.

PLATE 7. FIG. 13, 14.

Some persons, both ladies and children, wear bodies attached to their drawers, as in the figure, which represents a child's size.

Procure your material 10½ nails wide.

Cut each breadth 9 nails long.

Let D be the doubled part, and mark as follows:—(Fig. 14.)

SCALE.

	Nails.
From A to B	2¼
From A to E	4
From E to B	5¼
Slope from B to B	—
From E to G	4
From the top to G	1

Cut from G to H, H being 4½ nails from the doubled side.

Cut from H to C.

Let the body be 2½ nails deep, and 10 nails long, fold it in four, cut out the arm-holes, and sew on the shoulder-straps.

In making up the trowsers, sew the legs together in front, after they have been run up, leaving them open behind, and laying on a broad tape (see T T, Fig. 13), sew on the body, and it is completed.

TURKISH TROWSERS.
PLATE 7. FIG. 15, 16.

These Turkish or full trowsers are often worn by little girls.
Procure your material 10 nails wide, to admit one leg exactly in the breadth.
Cut each breadth the proper length, say 9 nails long.
Fold each breadth in half, letting D be the doubled part (Fig. 16.)

SCALE.

	Nails.
From A to B, or the width of the doubled breadth......	5
From B to C	4
From the top to E	1
From E to F	4

Cut one fold from E to F, and the other from E to G. Cut from G to C in a straight line.

In making, sew up from B to C, and either gather the bottom, A B, into a band, to which a frill is set on, or else make a deep hem to admit of a ribbon, which draws it up to the proper size, and ties in a bow. To this hem is sewed a broad frill or handsome piece of work. The latter is the most convenient plan of the two for the washer-woman, as the leg will lie quite flatly to be ironed.

TROWSERS FOR A LITTLE BOY.
PLATE 7. FIG. 17, 18, 19.

This is a particularly good pattern, and very suitable for a boy.

Procure your material 10 nails wide, to admit of one leg in the breadth.

Cut each breadth 7½ nails long.

Double the leg so as to leave 2 nails unfolded, or rather, fold it to within two nails of the selvage. Let D, Fig. 19, be the doubled part. From A to B is 2 nails, and is not double. From B to C is 4 nails, the one fold being cut in a slight curve from B to C, and in a sweep from A to C. The bottom of the leg is 3 nails wide. Slope from G to C, G being nearly 2 nails from the bottom.

The body is 10 nails long, and 2½ nails deep; fold it in four, and cut out the arm-holes (see Fig. 18).

In making, sew up each leg from K to G, and hem round every other part; next, make the body, hemming it all round, after which, sew the legs firmly to the body, making the flap, A L C, of one leg, over-lap or lie across the flap of the other leg. These two flaps, after being firmly set into the band, are farther secured by back-stitching them together along the dotted line. Fig. 17.

MEN'S DRAWERS.
PLATE 7. FIG. 20, 21, 22.

These are men's strong drawers, made of coarse twill or calico.

Procure your material 14 nails wide.

Cut each breadth 13 nails long.

Fold the breadths in half, letting D, Fig. 20, be the doubled part. The drawers are quite straight at the top, the piece, C H F, being an extra bit put in (see Fig. 20).

PLATE 8

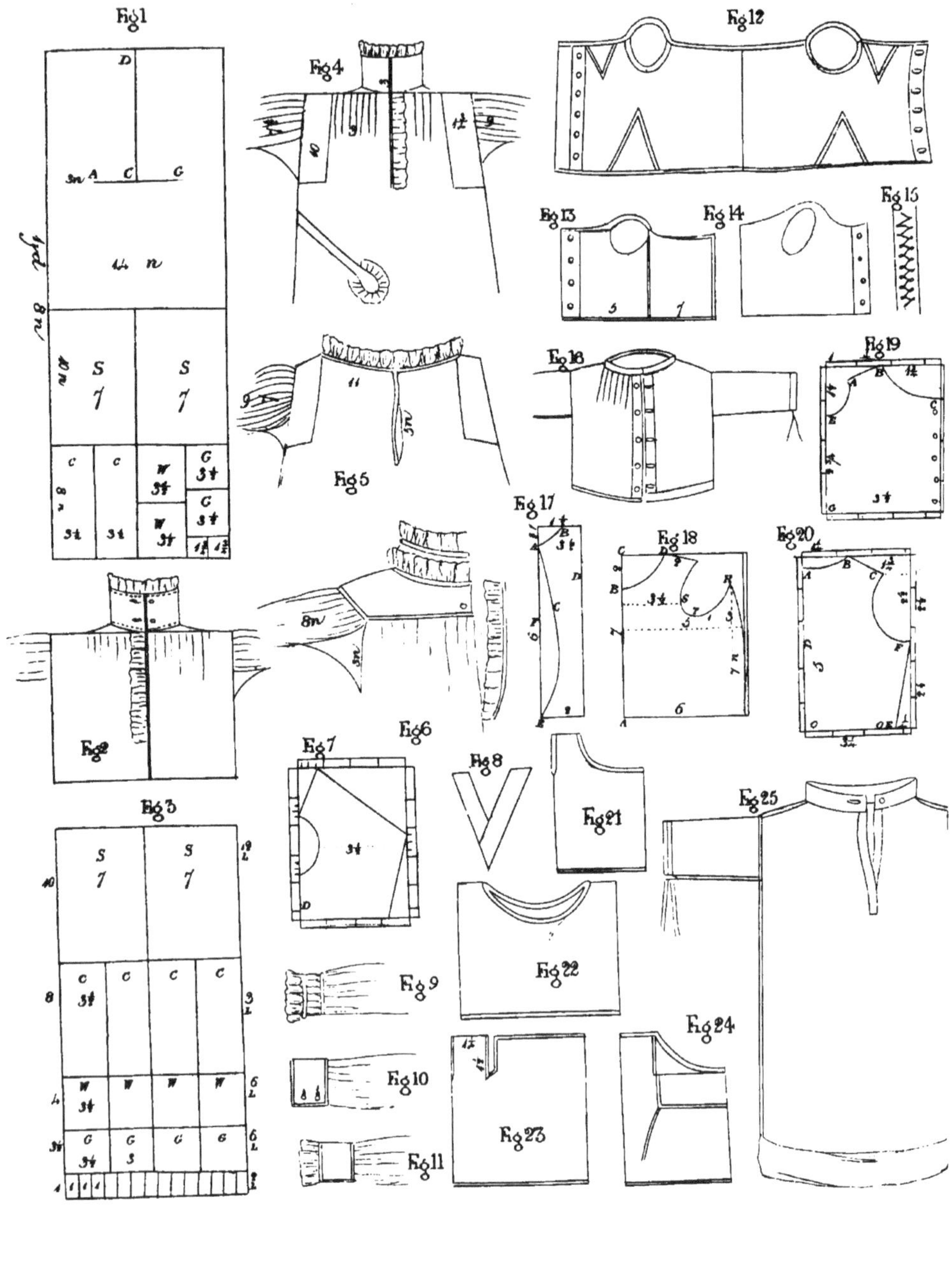

Fig 1
Fig 2
Fig 3
Fig 4
Fig 5
Fig 6
Fig 7
Fig 8
Fig 9
Fig 10
Fig 11
Fig 12
Fig 13
Fig 14
Fig 15
Fig 16
Fig 17
Fig 18
Fig 19
Fig 20
Fig 21
Fig 22
Fig 23
Fig 24
Fig 25

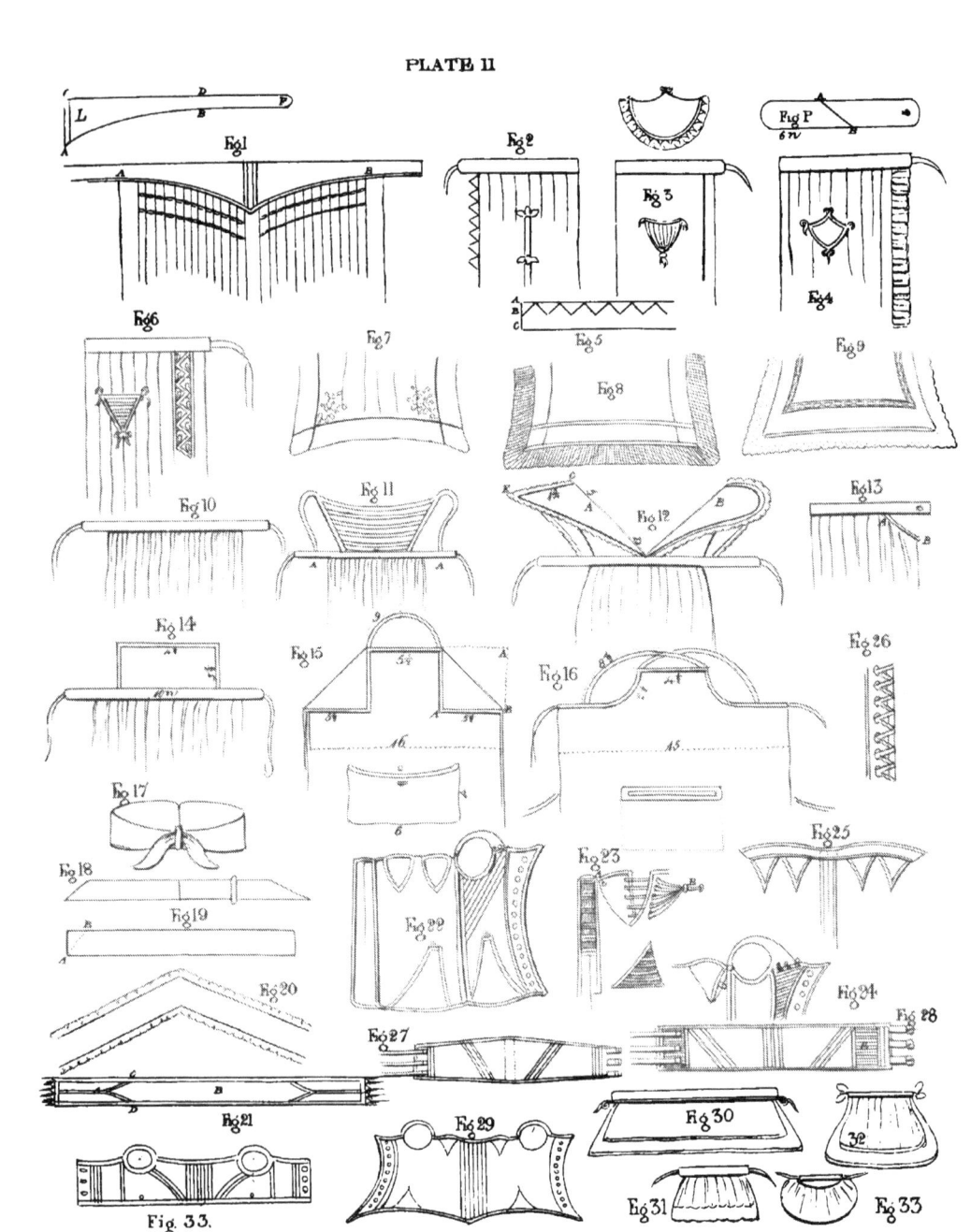

PLATE 11

SCALE.

	Nails.
From A to B....................................	3¾
From C to E....................................	4¼
From the top to G	5
From F to E....................................	½

Cut from G to B, and one fold from G to E; the other is from G to F.

A triangular piece is put in at the top of the back, of 3 nails in continuation from F to H.

The pair of drawers has two bands of about 7 nails long each, and 1½ nail deep, when doubled.

In making, sew up the legs, and put on the extra piece at the back. Sew the two legs together at the back, and hem the slit on each side in front. Set each leg into a separate band, leaving them open before and behind. Work four little oylet holes in the band behind, to admit tapes, which are laced through them and tie; in front, metal buttons are put, and button-holes made. Down each leg, in the front, a broad tape or piece of strong calico is laid, to strengthen it. A slit of about 2 nails long is made at the bottom of each leg. Broad tape is laid on round each leg at the bottom, forming a sort of hem, and oylet holes are worked on each side of the slit, for tape to come out at, which draws them to the proper size.

Fig. 20 represents the back of the drawers cut out.

Fig. 21 represents the back of the drawers made up.

Fig. 22 represents the front of the drawers made up.

WOMAN'S NIGHT JACKET.

PLATE 8. FIG. 1, 2, 3.

SCALE OF DIFFERENT SIZES.

———	Woman.	Girl of 18 yrs.	Girl of 12 yrs.
	Yds. nls.	Yds. nls.	Yds. nls.
Width of material	14	14	12
Quantity required for one	2..10	2.. 3	1..13
Quantity required for six	15.. 1	13.. 2	10..14
Quantity required for twelve	31.. 8	26.. 4	21..12
Whole length of body to be doubled............	1.. 8	1.. 4	1.. 0
Space to leave for shoulders	3	2¾	2½
Length of sleeves down the selvage	10	8	6½
Width of ditto, two in breadth	7	7	6
Length of collar down the selvage...............	8	7	6½
Width of ditto, or four in the width	3½	3½	3
Length of wristband down the selvage	4	3½	3¼
Width of ditto, or four in the breadth	3½	3½	3
Length of binder down the selvage	4½	3½	3
Width of ditto	1	1	1
Size of sleeve gusset................................	3	2¾	2½
Size of neck gusset	1½	1¼	1
Width of frill	1¼	1	¾

Night jackets for the higher classes are made of linen, lawn, cambric-muslin, and fine calico; also of dimity and twilled calico; and for the lower orders, of linen or calico. The calico should be soft and strong; and the unbleached or grey calico, as it is usually called by Linen Drapers, is warmer and often more durable than the white.

Fig. 1 represents the plan or picture of a piece of cloth of the proper width, on which all the parts for forming a woman's jacket are accurately marked, with the exception of the shoulder-straps, which, as they do not fit in, might be made of any extra bits.

Cut out the two breadths of the skirt in one length, to avoid a seam on the shoulder. Fold it very exactly in half, and, after leaving 3 nails at each end of the folded side, to allow for the shoulders, slit open the neck from A to G, after which, measure carefully and find the middle of the neck, C, and slit it down to the bottom, D, to form the opening in front of the jacket.

The sleeves, which are 10 nails long, and the two cut in the width, are either sloped off towards the wrist, fulled into a wristband, as in Fig. 10, or else neatly run, at a sufficient distance from the edge, to form a kind of frill (Fig. 9). This running is done in two rows, extended nearly all round the cuff, and neatly stretched upon a piece of tape, which is laid inside, and carried all round the cuff.

Fig. 3 represents a plan for cutting out twelve jackets, which is the most economical number, cut out at once, to avoid waste. The pieces in the Plate are marked with the initial letter for their use, and the width of the piece, thus, S 7, signifies sleeve 7 nails wide. On the left hand of the plan is marked the length of each piece, and on the right hand is set down the number of those lengths required to be cut to form the set complete, thus, 12 L means 12 lengths. The frills are generally of fine lawn or cambric, or else corded, jaconet, checked, or other muslins.

NIGHT-GOWN.

PLATE 8. FIG. 5.

SCALE.

——	Woman.	Girl of 18 yrs.	Girl of 14 yrs.
	Yds. nls.	Yds. nls.	Yds. nls.
Width of material, if gored	15	14	12
Width of gore to be cut off each side at the top	1¾	1¾	2
Width of the bottom will be	18½	17½	16
Width across the top will be	11½	10½	8
Quantity required for one	4 ..1	3 ..8	3.. 0
Quantity required for two	7..13	6 ..8	5..11
Length of skirt	1½..0	1¼..0	1.. 0
Depth of slit in front	6	6	5
Space to leave for shoulders	2½	2½	2
Slope of shoulders	1	1	¾
Width of binders	2	1¾	1½
Length of ditto down the selvage	8	8	8
Width of sleeves or two in the breadth	7½	7	6
Length of sleeves down the selvage	9	8	8
Width of wristband (if required)	2	2	2
Length of wristband down the selvage	4	3½	3
Size of sleeve gusset	3	2	3
Depth of frill	1½	1	¾

This shape is not so much worn as that of Fig. 4, nor perhaps has it so neat and finished an appearance, but on many accounts it is the most desirable, being in the first place, more economical; it also washes more easily, and above all, is particularly convenient in time of sickness, when it is very essential to a weak or suffering person to be able to draw open the gown at the neck and wrists, so as to have full play for the arms in changing her linen, or having blisters, leeches, &c. applied; whereas those night dresses confined at the neck in collars are very irksome, and cause much unnecessary suffering in being removed. The scale and plans so clearly explain the size, shape, &c. that nothing remains to be said, except that a band is sometimes worn round the waist, with a narrow frill sewn round the ends, which are sloped off, according to fancy.

It is better economy to cut three or six gowns together, as the gussets, binders, &c. take about the third of a breadth, so that in cutting out one, there is an unavoidable waste of the other two-thirds of a breadth. The two sleeves cut in the width, and are, for the largest size, 9 nails long.

ANOTHER NIGHT GOWN.

PLATE 8. FIG. 4.

It is more economical to buy your material of a sufficient width to merely gore it, if only one gown is to be cut out.

It is better to cross the skirt, and use 1½ breadth of very wide material, if six are to be cut.

SCALE FOR CROSSED SKIRT.

———	Woman.	Girl of 18 yrs.	Girl of 14 yrs.
	Yds. nls.	Yds. nls.	Yds. nls.
Width of material	18	16	14
Quantity required for six	18..14	16..15	15.. 0
Length of skirt	1½..0	1.. 6	1.. 3
Width of ditto	1½ breadth	1½ breadth	1½ breadth
Piece to mark off at top and bottom for crossing	7½ leaving 10½	7 leaving 9	6 leaving 8
Width of bottom when crossed	21	18	16
Width of top when crossed	15	14	12
Length of sleeve down the selvage	9	8	7
Width of sleeve	9	8	7
Length of binder down the selvage	10	8	7
Width of binder	1½	1½	1½
Length of collar down the selvage	8	6½	5
Width of collar	3	2½	2½
Length of wristband down the selvage	4	3½	3
Width of wristband	2	2	2
Size of sleeve-gusset	3	2	2
Size of neck-gusset	2	1	1
Depth of slit in front	6½	6	6
Space to leave for shoulders	3	2½	2
Width of frill	1¼	1	¾

SCALE FOR A GORED GOWN.

———	Woman.	Girl of 18 yrs.	Girl of 14 yrs.
	Yds. nls.	Yds. nls.	Yds. nls.
Width of material	15	15	14
Piece to be gored off at each end of the top	1¾	1¾	1¾
Length of skirt	1½..0	1 ..6	1.. 3
Width of sleeve	7½	7½	7
Width of binders	2	2	1½

All the other parts are the same as in the scale for the crossed gown.

In cutting out six crossed gowns, tear off the 9 breadths for the skirts, allowing 1½ breadth to each; after which, cut off the 6 lengths (9 nails long each) for the sleeves; two sleeves cut in the width. Next cut off a piece 10 nails long, which divide width-way into twelve binders of 1¼ nail wide each. Afterwards, cut off another breadth of 8 nails long, to divide width-way into six collars of 4 nails width. The gussets will require two breadths of 3 nails deep, to be divided width-way also, in six of 3 nails width.

The wristbands are 4 nails long; and as only nine of 2 nails width can be cut in 1 breadth, the remaining three must be cut off a second breadth, which will leave sufficient cloth over, exactly to cut the 12 neck-gussets, in two rows deep of 2 nails square. By this arrangement, no waste whatever is made.

The one gored gown is cut according to the scale; Fig. 8 is a bosom-bit, which adds much to the strength of the slit. It is impossible to cut out one of these gowns alone, without a little waste.

PLATE 8. FIG. 6.

This is an exceedingly neat looking night-dress, and for full size is cut according to the following dimensions. Cut two breadths of 1 yard wide, and 1½ yard long each, and sew up the seams, leaving 3 nails from the top for arm-holes. Cut out two shoulder-pieces according to Fig. 7, which represents half, the letter D being the doubled part. If it is made of calico, put a neat piping round the one shoulder-piece, as it materially strengthens the night-dress; and after fulling the skirt evenly round to the other, and setting in the sleeves, lay the upper shoulder-piece over the lower one. Pipe and frill it up the neck, and if preferred, a collar may be added, with a second frill above. If the night-dress is made of linen, it must be neatly stitched instead of piped. The sleeves are 8 nails square, and the wristband, as in Fig. 11, 4 nails square, to which a frill is added.

FLANNEL WAISTCOAT FOR A LADY.
PLATE 8. FIG. 12.

Cut a piece of flannel 12 nails wide, and 7 nails deep; fold it in two, and at 2 full nails from the middle or doubled part, cut the arm-holes, which are 2 full nails wide, and 1¼ nail deep, leaving 2 nails for half the back; hollow the front half a nail. At the bottom of the waistcoat, immediately under the arm-holes, cut a slit upwards to the distance of 3 nails, and put into these slits, gores of 3 nails wide at the bottom, sloped off to a point, being 3 nails long. These gores are differently cut to most others, being sloped equally on both sides, instead of having one side straight, so that the point is in a straight line with the middle of the gore at the bottom (see Fig. 12).

Cut two other slits to admit of bosom gores of similar shape, but smaller size, being 1¾ nail broad, and 1¼ nail long. They are put in 1 nail from the shoulder-strap.

In making up, herring-bone all round the waistcoat; the slits and gores, and the seams also, are herring-boned with strong thread, the seams being turned flatly back, and laid side by side on the finger, so that the one row of herring-boning shall join the two compactly together (see Fig. 15). Some persons lay a broad tape, say a nail wide, down the front, on which the buttons are sewed, and button-holes worked. Tape shoulder-straps complete the whole. This waistcoat buttons in the front.

A BOY'S WAISTCOAT.
PLATE 8. FIG. 13, 14.

The following size is suitable for a child of 12 years old:—

The waistcoat is made in three parts; the middle-piece should be 7 nails wide, and 6½ nails deep;

ON LINEN.

the side-pieces must be the same depth, and 5 nails wide. Sew up the seams, and fold the waistcoat in four, like a pinafore, then cut out the arm-holes, which, while thus doubled, are 1¼ nail in width, and the same in depth; the waistcoat is then opened, and hollowed out in the front (see Fig. 13).

In making up, tape is sewed all round the edge, at the inside, and broad tapes down the sides, in which the button-holes are cut. Straps are sewed on, and the whole is finished.

A WAISTCOAT FOR AN INVALID BOY OF THE WORKING CLASS.
PLATE 8. FIG. 16.

Take a breadth and a half of flannel, each 9 nails long, and sew them together, leaving them open in the front. Fold the waistcoat in four, and cut the shoulders, and slits for the arm-holes, as in a pinafore; the shoulders are 1½ nail deep, and the arm-holes 2½ nails long. Hollow it a little at the top, and after sewing up the shoulders, gather it at the top into a tape the proper length (say 5 nails). Put in sleeves without gussets, which are 7 nails long, and 4 nails wide before being sewed up; hem the fronts, and lay on a broad tape at the inside of the hem, in which the button-holes are made; herring-bone the bottom and sleeves.

A MAN'S UNDER WAISTCOAT.
PLATE 8. FIG. 17, 18.

This is generally made of fine calico, and is cut out according to the Plate.

For the back (Fig. 17), cut your paper pattern 9 nails long, and 7 nails wide: double it in half its width, and, as in the Plate, letting D be the doubled part, mark as follows:—

SCALE.

	Nails.
From A to the top	1¼
From B to the doubled side	1½
C is half way, and from C to the side F	1¼
From E to the doubled side	2

Curve from A to B, and from A through C to E.

The front is cut as follows:—Let your pattern be 11 nails long, and 8 nails wide (see Plate 8, Fig. 18).

SCALE.

	Nails.
From A to B is	9
From B to C	2
From C to D	2¼
The shoulder, from D, slopes	¼
Length of the shoulder	2

The arm-hole is sloped, and is rather difficult to manage, but by looking at the Plate, and following the directions, as nearly as possible, the same shape may be attained.

SCALE.

	Nails.
From the arm-hole, S, to the side	3½
From the bottom, T, to the side	5
From the point, R, to the top	2
From the side to R	1

Curve from R to the bottom, also from D to B, and cut out the arm-hole.

In making up, sew the pieces together, lay on a broad piece of calico all down the front, lay a tape round the neck, and set on your buttons down the front, with button-holes to correspond.

This shape, but varying of course in size, will do for boys of all ages.

BOY'S VEST OR UPPER WAISTCOAT.
PLATE 8. FIG. 19, 20.

This is made of cloth, jean, or nankeen. The size here given, would suit a boy ten or eleven years old.

The vest is in three parts, viz.—one back and two fronts. To cut out the front (Fig. 19), let your paper pattern be 3½ nails wide, by 4¼ nails long.

SCALE.

	Nails.
From the corner to E is	2¼
From the top to A	½
From the side to A	½
From B to each side	1¾
From C to the top	1

Curve in for the arm-hole, from E to A, cut from A to B, and curve from B to C.

For the back (Fig. 20), let your paper be 5 nails long, by 3¼ nails wide.

SCALE.

	Nails.
From the top to A	½
From the corner to B	1¼
From the side to C	1
From the top to C	¾
From the top to F	2¼
From the corner to E	½

Curve slightly from A to B, cut in a straight line from B to C, hollow for the arm-hole from C to F, cutting into the cloth about 1¼ nail, slope from F to E.

In making up, join the two shoulders together, then sew E G, Fig. 19, to F E, Fig. 20; line it, bind with galloon or tape round the neck, arm-holes, waist, and up the fronts, put on buttons, and make button-holes to correspond in front. Buttons are also put on round the waist, to which the trowsers are to button, as no braces are worn with this vest.

CHILD'S NIGHT VEST.
PLATE 8. FIG. 21, 22.

Some children are in the habit (when in bed) of kicking off their sheets; and it is very desirable for such to wear fine flannel or demet waistcoats under their night-gowns in winter, and calico ones in summer, to prevent their catching cold. These waistcoats or vests, if for children under five or six, may be cut two in the width of the flannel, and about 8, 10, or 12 nails long, according to the size of the child. After cutting off the pieces required, fold each in half its length, and sew up the side-seams, leaving 1½ nail from the top on each side, to form the arm-holes, which are neatly herring-boned round. The top is hollowed thus: leave about 1¼ nail on each folded side for the shoulders, and hollow down to 1½ nail in front, for the bosom, and to 1 nail behind, for the back. Herring-bone flatly all round, and the vest is completed.

CHILD'S DAY VEST.
PLATE 8. FIG. 23, 24.

Delicate children are often recommended to wear flannel shirts or vests next their skin. They should be of the finest flannel, with plenty of nap, which should be next the skin. These are cut much in the same shape as babies' second shirts (see Plate 2, Fig. 30), excepting that the back is hollowed out, and it has no sleeves. Two shirts might be cut in the width, of 8 or 10 nails long. When folded in two, and sewed up at the seams, leaving 1½ nail for the arm-hole, the front should be cut. Leave 1¼ nail in each folded side for the shoulders, cut down nearly straight to 1½ nail for a front flap, and slope down behind to the same depth.

BATHING GOWN.
PLATE 8. FIG. 25 -

Bathing gowns are made of blue or white flannel, stuff, calimanco, or blue linen. As it is especially desirable that the water should have free access to the person, and yet that the dress should not cling to, or weigh down the bather, stuff or calimanco are preferred to most other materials: the dark coloured gowns are the best for several reasons, but chiefly because they do not shew the figure, and make the bather less conspicuous than she would be in a white dress.

As the width of the materials, of which a bathing gown is made, varies, it is impossible to say of how many breadths it should consist. The width at the bottom, when the gown is doubled, should be about 15 nails: fold it like a pinafore, slope 3½ nails for the shoulders, cut or open slits of 3½ nails long for the arm-holes; set in plain sleeves 4½ nails long, 3½ nails wide, and make a slit in front 5 nails long.

In making up, delicacy is the great object to be attended to. Hem the gown at the bottom, gather it into a band at the top, and run in strings; hem the opening and the bottom of the sleeves, and put in strings. A broad band should be sewed in about half a yard from the top, to button round the waist.

WOMEN'S CAPS.

Women's caps are generally made of checked, spotted, clear, or twilled muslin, widow's lawn, and if for night caps for the poor, sometimes of soft fine calico. The borders are of corded, cambric, jaconet, or clear muslin, and are sometimes, for ladies' caps, edged with narrow lace, or are made entirely of hemmed net.

WOMAN'S DAY OR NIGHT-CAP.

PLATE 9. FIG. 1, 2.

This is a favourite shape for a day-cap among the poor.

SCALE.

	Yds. nls.
Width of checked muslin	1¼ . . 0
Width of crown to cap, four in the width of material, or	6
Length of crown down the selvage...	6¼
Width of puffing or head-piece, twenty-four in width of material, or	1
Length of ditto down the selvage	14
Width of bands to confine the puffing, 48 in the width, or.....................	¼
Length of bands down the selvage..	7
Width of strings, forty-eight in the breadth...	¼
Length of strings down the selvage	7
Quantity of material for one cap	14
Quantity of material for twenty-four..	4 . . 3
Length of bordering to each, three breadths of.....................................	16
Depth of bordering down the selvage	1¼

Observe, that in the Plates the letter D always stands for the doubled part of the muslin.

In cutting out these caps, it is by far the most economical to cut out 24 at a time, as, if half that number is cut, half the width of the length of cloth from which the puffing is cut, is wasted, whereas the 24 exactly fit in.

The crown must be rounded off at the top, for which purpose, double it in half its width, and at 2 nails from the top corner each way, round, or slope off the piece from A to B (see Plate 9, Fig. 1).

The cap is made up as follows:—

Double the bands in two, and turn down the edges as if for sewing. Hem the crown-piece with a very narrow hem up each side, to the distance of half a nail, and sew it firmly to each end of one of the bands; after which, whip and stroke evenly the remaining part of the crown, and sew it to the rest of the band in the middle. To the other side of the band, full on the head-piece or puffing, which is afterwards confined on the other side by being whipped and sewed to the second band. The double border is sewed on in front, and a single one behind, where previously there has been a pretty deep hem made, to admit of strings to draw behind. These strings are sewed into the cap, each at the opposite end of the hem to that on which it comes out. The strings are hemmed at the end, being either pointed or rounded, according to taste. Some ladies prefer their being 1 nail wide and rounded at the end, with a narrow frill or edging sewed on to the distance of 3 or 4 nails round the ends.

A VERY NEAT NIGHT-CAP.

PLATE 9. FIG. 3, 4, 5, 6.

This, when made of checked muslin, with a border of corded muslin, has a very pretty appearance, and is particularly comfortable for a night-cap, as it sets close to the head.

PLATE 9

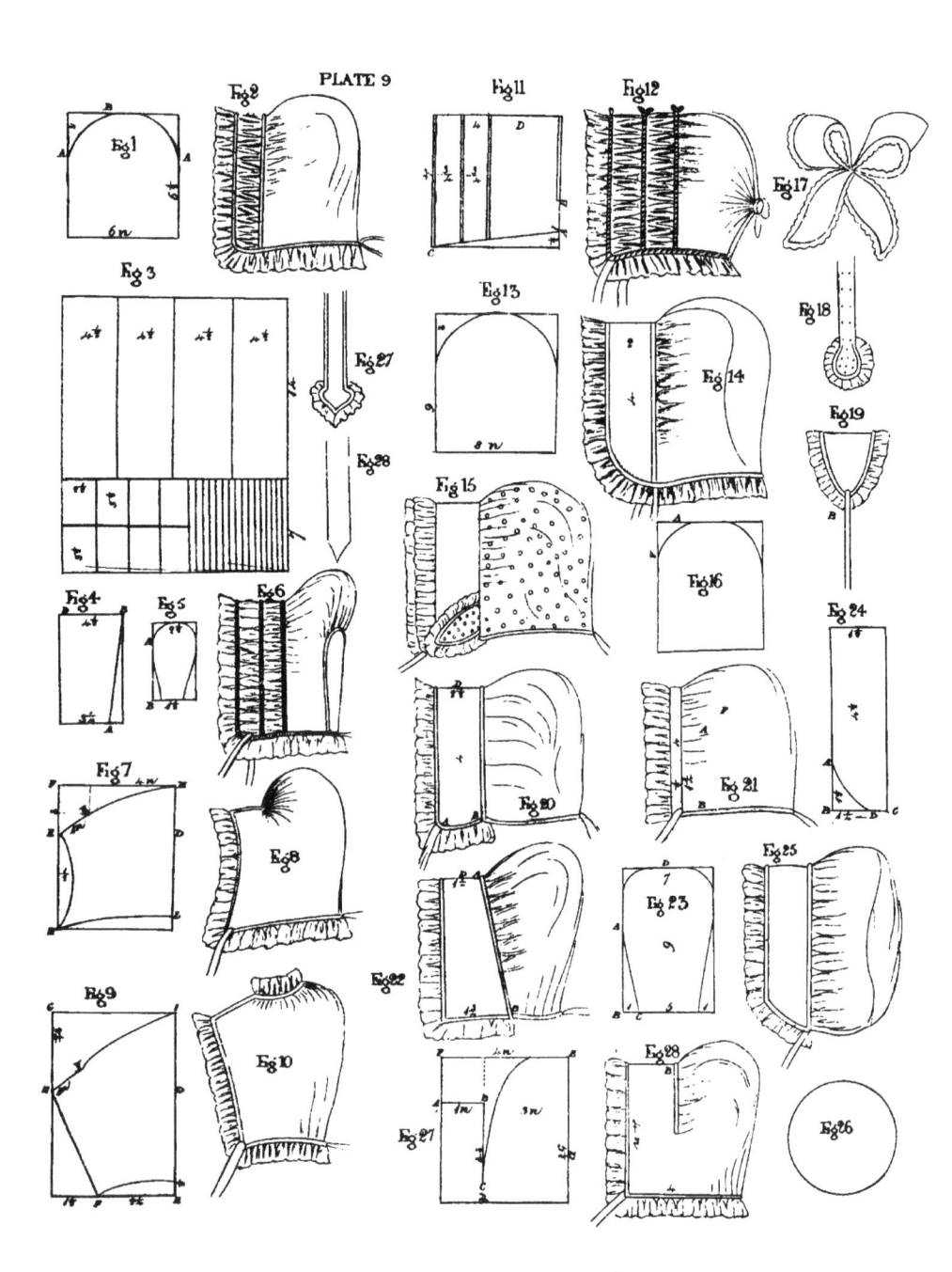

ON LINEN.

SCALE.

	Yds. nls.
Best width of material..	18
Length of head-piece down the selvage	14
Width of ditto..	4¼
Length of horse-shoe down the selvage............................	3¼
Width of ditto	2¼
Length of strings down the selvage	7
Width of ditto	¼
Quantity of material for eight	2..3
Quantity of bordering, 3 breadths of muslin in width.........	16
Depth of ditto	1¼

The most economical number of caps of this pattern to cut at once, is eight, and should be done as follows, to prevent waste (see Fig. 3). Tear off two lengths of 14 nails, which, when torn each in four, will form the eight head-pieces. The horse-shoe crowns must be cut in two rows deep, four in each row, of 2½ nails wide, which will require 10 nails of the breadth, leaving a piece 8 nails wide and 7 nails long. This piece will cut the eight pairs of strings, which are each half a nail wide, and 7 nails long. After cutting out the cap, shape the head-pieces according to Fig. 4 in the Plate, by which it will be seen that 1¼ nail is taken off in a direct line from A to B. The piece for the horse-shoe crown must be folded, and rounded carefully at the top, and then sloped off in a direct line, thus cutting off half a nail from each side.

In making up the cap, place the straight part of the head-piece in front, and put two runners, besides hem, at equal distances from each other in front, say ¾ of a nail. Whip the back neatly, and after hemming the horse-shoe crown, sew the head-piece firmly to it. Some people hem a cord round the horse-shoe which gives it a greater firmness, and looks like a piping when the head-piece is sewed in, as it ought to be, to the bottom, instead of the top of the hem. A hem is made at the bottom of the cap for a string to draw. Double borders in front, a single one behind, and the strings sewed on, complete the cap.

A YOUNG SERVANT'S NEAT DAY-CAP.

PLATE 9. FIG. 7, 8.

This shape is generally made of clear muslin, widow's lawn, or jaconet, and is particularly adapted for girls on first going to service, from its neat simplicity.

SCALE.

	Nails.
Best width of material...	16 or 24
Width of cap	8
Length down the selvage......................................	5
Quantity required for four caps, if yard wide	10

The cap is folded in half the width, and cut according to Fig. 7. The side marked D is the doubled part. Mark on the opposite side 2 nails from the top, E, and slope or hollow out a piece from E to H very gradually, letting the greater width of the piece thus hollowed out not exceed half a nail.

Next slope off gradually from H to L at the distance of ½ a nail from the bottom; after which, cut the straight line E K, which is 1 nail in length, the letter K being situated about ¾ of a nail from the side and 1¼ from the top, and then slope gradually to M. In making up the cap, sew from E to K, and gather in the top from K to M, as in Fig. 8. A single or double border is put in front. This is a small size.

Fig. 18, 19, 27, and 28 are different shaped strings for caps.

ANOTHER NEAT CAP FOR SERVANTS.
PLATE 9. FIG. 9, 10.

This shape is particularly liked by the poor, from the ease with which it is made up and washed, as, upon undrawing the string, it opens readily at the top, and lies quite flat to be ironed.

As the shape is peculiar, if many are to be cut at once, it would be the least wasteful plan to cut out on a doubled piece of paper, the pattern of the cap, according to Fig. 9; open it out and lay it on the material in such directions as to cut to most advantage. If only one is to be cut, procure a piece of muslin 8 nails wide and 5½ nails long; which, when folded evenly in half its width, shape as follows, according to the Plate. The side marked D is the doubled part; from E at the bottom to F is 2¼ nails. From the top, G to H, measure 2¼ nails, and cut off in a sloping line from I, at the top of the doubled corner, to H, again cut from H to F, after which cut off from F to about ½ a nail above E, and then the shape of the cap is formed.

Strings of the usual size, ½ nail wide and 7 nails long, complete the cap.

In making it up, sew from H to Y, and then hem all round the open part along Y to I, and sew on a full frill of ¾ nail deep, and about 18 nails long. Afterwards hem the front and back of the cap, put double borders in front, and a single one behind, of 1 nail deep, and 3 breadths of 16 or 18 nails wide.

ANOTHER SHAPE.
PLATE 9. FIG. 11, 12.

This is a very simple shape, and for washing and making up is equally convenient with Fig 10. It answers well for a bonnet cap for ladies, in which case it might be made of net or tulle, with a quilling or lace border.

SCALE.

	Yds. nls.
Best width of material............................	1 .. 2
Width of cap without runners......	4
Length of cap down the selvage................	9
Sloped off at the bottom from C to A	¼

Fold the cap in half its length, making D the doubled part (see Fig. 11). Sew and fell from A to B, to the depth of 1 nail, and hem round the rest of the opening behind, to admit of a ribbon. Let there be two runners besides the hem in front, to admit of tape or narrow ribbon. The border must depend upon the purpose for which the cap is intended: if for a night-cap, a double border in front and single behind will be required: if for a bonnet-cap, a double border or quilling only, in front will be sufficient. It may be as well also to remark, that if it is meant for a night-cap, the length of the cap down the selvage should be greater, say 11 or 12 nails; and the width of the material, to cut to the best advantage, must, of course, be either exactly the same, or double.

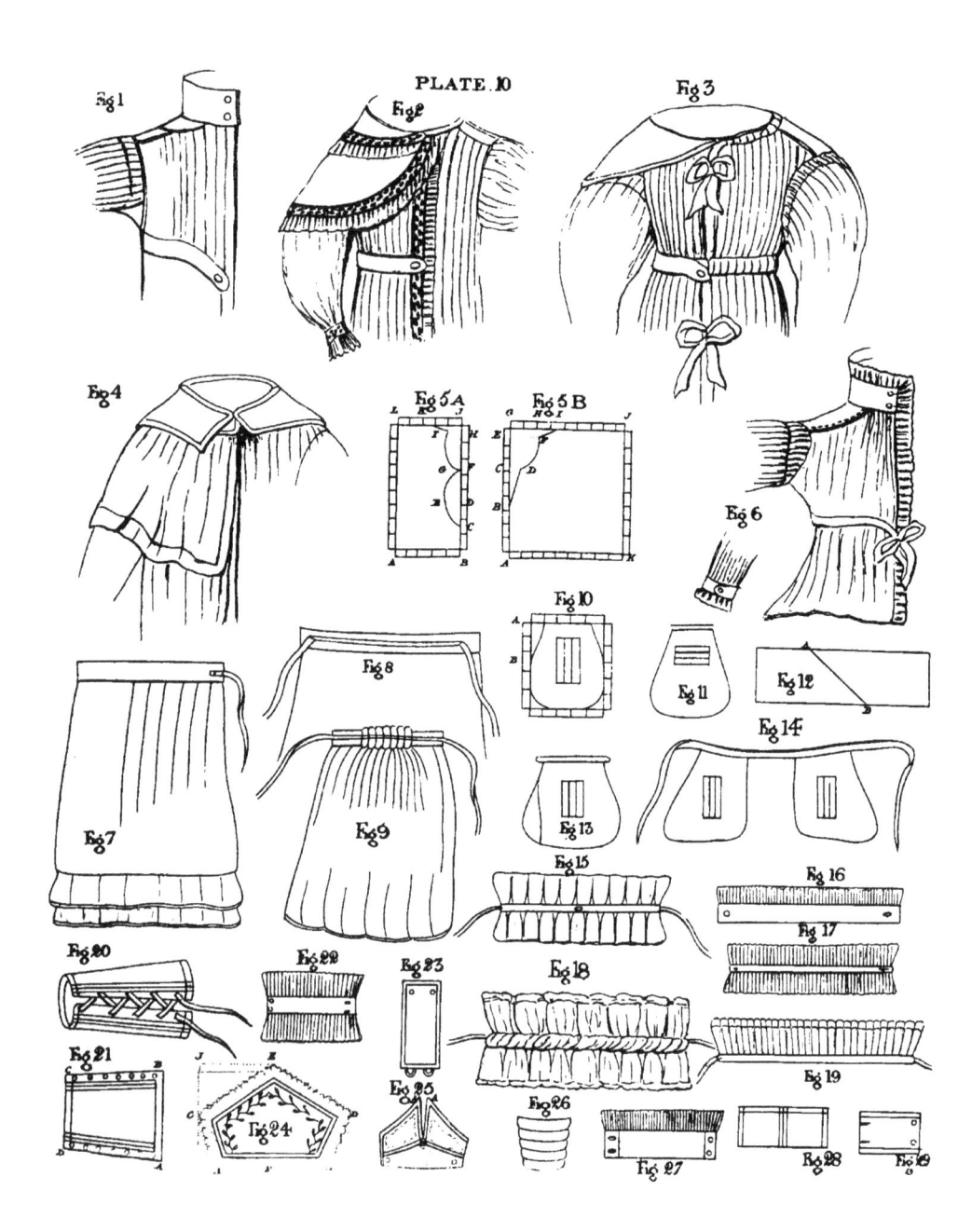

PLATE 10

ON LINEN.

A NEAT SCHOOL-GIRL'S CAP.
PLATE 9. FIG. 13, 14.

SCALE.

	Yds. nls.
Best width of material	1..8
Length of the crown down the selvage	6
Width of the crown, or three in the breadth	8
Length of the head-piece down the selvage	8
Width of the head-piece, or twelve in the breadth	2
Quantity required for twelve caps without strings	2..0
Quantity required for twelve caps with strings	2.12

This pattern needs little further explanation, the shape and size are so clearly given in the Plate. The head-piece is sloped off at the ears, beginning to cut at 1 nail above the corner, to 1 nail beyond the corner, at the bottom of the cap.

This cap is for school-girls, and is particularly neat if of checked muslin with corded muslin frills.

A FAVOURITE CAP FOR LADIES AND POOR WOMEN.
PLATE 9. FIG. 15, 16, 17, 18, 19.

SCALE.

	Yds. nls.
Best width of material	1..8
Width of crown-piece, three in the width	8
Length of ditto down the selvage	6½
Width of head-piece, twelve in the breadth	2
Length of ditto down the selvage	8
Length of weepers (if wanted) down the selvage	2½
Width of ditto, sixteen in the breadth	1½
Length of bands down the selvage (if wanted)	1.14
Width of ditto, twelve in the width	2
Quantity required for twelve caps, without extras	2..2
Quantity for twelve, if with weepers	2..5
Quantity for twelve, if complete with bands	4..3
Width of bordering	1
Length of ditto, two breadths width	1..8

This cap is pretty and not expensive if made without the band and weepers, which, of course, add much to the cost; twelve is the best number to cut out at once. They are generally made for ladies of sprigged muslin, when the head-piece should be of strong muslin or fine calico. The borders are cambric, muslin, or net, edged with Valenciennes lace, or other neat trimming. The weepers are also frilled and edged, as also the rounded ends of the band. The crown is sloped off a little at the corner, as seen in Fig. 16, at A, which is about 2 nails from the corner. The weepers are also shaped to a point, as in Fig. 19 (see B). The band (Fig. 18) is gathered in at about 1½ nail from the end, which is rounded, with edging sewed on. The middle of the band is plaited, and sewed firmly on to the middle of the head-piece, in front.

A NEAT COMFORTABLE DAY OR NIGHT-CAP.
PLATE 9. FIG. 20.

This is a shape particularly suitable for day-caps for young servants, or night-caps for any age or station. If intended for day-caps, they should be made of clear or jaconet muslin; if for night-caps, of check or calico.

SCALE.

	Yds. nls.
Best width of material..	1.. 0
Length of head-piece down the selvage..................	8
Width of ditto, or four in the width	4
Length of crown down the selvage........................	6
Width of ditto, or four in the width	4
Quantity required for four caps without strings	14
Quantity required for twelve caps without strings ...	2..10

⁎ Cap strings, for any number of caps not exceeding sixteen, require seven additional nails, as sixteen pairs exactly cut in the width, so that sixteen caps would be the most economical number to cut.

The head-piece is a little sloped off at the ear from A to B, and is made up double, so as to be only 2 nails deep, when the cap is completed.

ANOTHER CAP.
PLATE 9. FIG. 21.

This shape is very suitable for a servant's day or bonnet-cap; it is simple and pretty in appearance, and not expensive.

SCALE.

	Yds. nls.
Best width of material..	1¼.. 0
Length of crown down the selvage........................	7
Width of ditto, or four in the width	6
Length of band down the selvage	8
Width of band*	1
Quantity required for twelve caps with strings.........	1.. 13

* The remainder of the breadth from which the bands are cut will make strings.

In making it up, the band is doubled in half, the crown whipped and sewed to it, leaving it plain from A to B, for the space of 1¾ nail. A double border is sewn on in front.

AN OLD WOMAN'S CAP.
PLATE 9. FIG. 22, 23.

This shape is generally preferred by old women, as it sets comfortably over the ears.

ON LINEN.

SCALE.

	Yds. nls.
Best width of material	21
Length of head-piece down the selvage	7
Width of ditto, or twelve in the breadth	1¼
Length of crown down the selvage	9
Width of ditto at the widest part, or three in the width	7
Width of ditto when sloped off at the bottom	5
Quantity required for twelve caps without strings	2..11
Additional quantity for strings	7

It is almost impossible to cut out a number of these caps without a little waste.

The head-pieces, when torn off, are 7 nails long, and 1¼ wide; double them in half their length, and then slope off from A to B, one nail. The straight part is the front, to which a border is sewed. The crown is next shaped, according to Fig. 23, for which purpose, double the piece in half its width, and from the corner, B, measure 7 nails on the side to A, and 1 nail on the bottom, to C, and cut off in a straight line from A to C. Round off the corner at the top, from A to D. The crown is sewed on plain for the space of 1½ nail from the bottom, and then evenly fulled into the remainder of the head-piece.

A POOR WOMAN'S NIGHT-CAP.
PLATE 9. FIG. 24, 25, 26.

This shape is sometimes made of linen, but generally of strong calico or check.

SCALE.

	Yds. nls.
Best width of material	18
Length of head-piece down the selvage	9
Width of ditto, or twelve in the breadth	1¼
Size of squares in which to cut out the circular crown, or two in the breadth	9
Quantity required for twelve caps without strings	3..15
Additional quantity for twelve pair of strings	7

The head-piece is sloped off, as in Fig. 24, from A, which is 1½ nail above the corner, B, to C.

The crown, after being rounded, is evenly fulled into the head-piece, which latter is sewed neatly together behind, at the opening, D C.

ANOTHER CAP.
PLATE. 9. FIG. 27, 28.

This is a pretty shape for almost any purpose, and in any thin material; it is cut out in front very much in the same manner that a baby's cap is cut behind, which will be seen if the Plate is turned round, so as to place the doubled part, D, at the top.

SCALE.

	Yds. nls.
Best width of material..	1..8
Length of cap down the selvage..	5¼
Width of ditto, or three in the breadth.....................................	8
Depth from F to A..	1¼
Space from A to B, to be cut..	1
Length to be cut from B to C	2
Then slope gradually, in a circular direction, from E to C..........	

In making up the cap, sew neatly from A to B, and then full in the part from E to C, evenly to the part between C and B; a hem in the front and at the back, is next made for a ribbon or tape, and a small bow, either of the same material (see Fig. 17), or white or coloured ribbon may be put at B (Fig. 28).

BATHING CAP.

These are made of oil-silk, and are worn, when bathing, by ladies who have long hair. Cut a piece of oil-silk, 4 nails long and 8 nails wide; double it so as to make a square; let the doubled part be the back of the cap, and slope off the corner at the top, towards the back, in a curve, so as to shape it to the form of the back of the head. Sew up along the top of the bathing cap, binding it with tape at the seam, both at the top and in the front Lay on a tape behind to form a hem, making oylet-holes at the ears, and passing a string through each oylet-hole, which is fastened down at the opposite side; these strings draw up the cap, when worn, to the size required.

It is advisable, however, for those who have not long hair, to bathe in plain linen caps, so as to admit the water without the sand or grit, and thus the bather, unless prohibited on account of health, enjoys all the benefit of the shock without injuring the hair.

These caps are often worn by children when the head is shaved, if subject to diseases in the head, as ring-worm, scald-head, &c.

DRESSING-GOWNS.
PLATE 10.

Dressing-gowns are generally made of warm materials, for the winter, as flannels, either printed or plain, merino, shawl, either the real or imitation, and for gentlemen, of cloth or jean. For summer, they are of dimity, calico, twilled muslin, and sometimes, though rarely, of silk. There are various ways of making them; only a few of the most approved shapes will be here mentioned.

PLATE 10. FIG. 1.
A PLAIN USEFUL SHAPE, ESPECIALLY FOR MEN.

This gown is made with a deep hem turned up, and a strong piping at the top of it. It is divided into four, and the arm-holes left in the two front seams, sloping the flannel 1 nail deep, and 2½ nails long, for the shoulders. The neck-gusset is put in double, and the shoulder-strap laid over it. The gown must be neatly plaited behind and in front, set firmly into the double collar, and stitched with strong thread near the edge. Some people pipe every seam of a dressing gown with white or coloured muslin, linen, or glazed calico. The back is drawn up by means of a string-case, over which a band should button. A large button is put on the band, and on the collar, and the button-holes should be very firmly sewed round, either with tape or with button-hole stitch. After putting in the sleeves, run or backstitch the plaits firmly down again, at about ½ nail below the gathering, to make them lie flat.

SCALE.

———	Man's size.	Woman's size.	Girl's large size.
	Yds. nls.	Yds. nls.	Yds. nls.
Width of flannel	14	14	14
Quantity required for one	10.. 5	8 ..10	6 ..0
Length of skirts	2.. 0	1¾.. 0	1½..0
Number of breadths..........................	4.. 0	4 .. 0	4 ..0
Length of sleeve down the selvage.........	12	10	8
Width of ditto	9	8	7
Length of shoulder-strap.....................	4½	4	3½
Width of ditto	1½	1½	1
Size of double neck-gusset	2½	2	2
Size of sleeve-gusset.........................	3	3	2¼
Width of collar..............................	5	6	4
Length down the selvage.....................	10	8	8
Width of wristband	2½	2	2
Length of ditto down the selvage	4¼	4	4
Width of band	2½	2	2
Length of ditto down the selvage	20	12	12
Space to cut for the shoulders	2½	2	2
Depth for the shoulders to slope	1	1	¾

PLATE 10. FIG. 2.

This figure represents a dressing-gown made of dimity. A deep hem of 3 or 4 nails is made at the bottom, insertion-work is sewed up the fronts, and round the cape, collar, and wrists, at the edge of the work a frill is put on. The gown is fulled in evenly to the shoulder-strap and neck-gusset at the top, and may be confined or not, at the waist behind, according to pleasure. The front is generally left unconfined, so that the band alone arranges it in folds.

FIG. 2, 3.

SCALE.

———	Woman's large size.	Woman's small size.
	Yds. nls.	Yds. nls.
Width of material	14	14
Number of breadths.................................	3 breadths	3 breadths
The one breadth crossed off at the top	5	5½
Length of breadths	1¾..0	1½..0
Length of shoulder-strap...........................	3¼	3¼
Width of ditto	1½	1½
Length of neck-band or case	10	9
Space for shoulder	3½	3½
Length of arm-hole	3	2½
Arm-hole curved into the cloth	1¼	1
Length of waist	5	4½
Length of string-case	10	8
Sleeve cut according to Plate 12, Fig. 5 and 6 ...	Fig. 5 & 6.	Fig. 5 & 6
Collar cut according to Plate 13, Fig. 7	Fig. 7.	Fig. 7
Cape cut according to Plate 13, Fig. 6	Fig. 6.	Fig. 6

PLATE 10. FIG. 3.

This gown, made of flannel, either plain or printed, is plaited in small regular folds at the neck, where a string-case of muslin or white ribbon is put for a string to pass through. The gown is again plaited in the same folds at the waist, in two rows, to which another string-case is sewed all round the waist. A deep hem is made at the bottom, and turned up with a piping of white; or if it is a printed flannel, of some coloured glazed calico or muslin; the ribbons in front are the same colour, and a flannel band is piped with it, as well as the wristbands and every seam on the shoulders, round the sleeves, &c. The sleeves should be stitched down about 1 nail below the shoulder, to make the fulness lie close and flat. If made of printed flannel, it is useful to wear at the sea-side, as a walking dress, to and from bathing.

CLOAK DRESSING-GOWN.
PLATE 10. FIG. 4.

This is a comfortable simple pattern; it can be made either of flannel or lighter material, and is equally suitable for men, women, and children; it is very convenient for the latter when taken out of a bath, or for sitting up in bed.

SCALE.

	Man.	Woman.	Girl of 16 yrs.	Girl of 10 yrs.	Child of 5 yrs.
	Yds. nls.	Yds. nls.	Yds. nls.	Yds. nls.	Yds. nls.
Length of skirt	2 ..0	1¾..0	1¼..0	1¼..0	1¼..0
Number of breadths	4 ..0	4 ...0	4 ..0	3 ..0	3 ..0
Space for shoulder	2	1	1	¾	¾
Depth of arm-holes	5	4	3¼	3¼	3
Length of string-case	12	10	9	8	7
Length of band	16	14	12	10	8
Shoulder-piece (see Plate 13)	Fig. 1	Fig. 1	Fig. 1	Fig. 4	Fig. 4
Collar (see Plate 13)	Fig. 7	Fig. 7	Fig. 7	Fig. 31	Fig. 13
Cape (see Plate 13)	Fig. 6	Fig. 6	Fig. 6	Fig. 6	Fig. 6
Sleeves (see Plate 12)	Fig. 16	Fig. 16	Fig. 16	Fig. 16 cut smaller	Fig. 16 cut smaller

After the seams have been herring-boned up, the cloak is folded in four, to find the shoulders, which are cut in a gentle slope to the proper width, and sewed up. The arm-holes having been left, the sleeves are next put in, after which, the gown is fulled evenly into the double shoulder-piece; the collar and cape are next put on; the hem at the bottom should be deep, and turned up with a flannel or tape piping; down the sides and round the cape, collar, &c., should be bound with flannel binding, to give a finish. Some persons omit the sleeves, having merely slits for the arms.

A DRESSING JACKET.
PLATE 10. FIG. 5, 6.

Some persons merely wear a little flannel, calico, or twilled muslin dressing jacket, and as it is usually made to fit the figure, the breadths are much gored; for the purpose, therefore, of better explaining the shape, a figure is made of the breadth when cut out. Fig. 5 A, is half of the back breadth, which is doubled in two, and Fig. 5 B is the whole of one of the front breadths.

SCALE.

———	Woman's large size.	Woman's small size.	Girl's large size.	Girl's small size.
Number of breadths..............	3	3	3	3
Width of material..................	12 nls.	11 nls.	11 nls.	11 nls.
Length of each breadth	14 —	12 —	10 —	8 —
Length of sleeve	12 —	10 —	8 —	8 —
Width of ditto	10 —	8 —	8 —	8 —
Length of collar.....................	8 —	6¾ —	6 —	5½ —
Width of ditto	3 —	3 —	2 —	2 —
Size of neck-gusset	2 —	1¾ —	1½ —	1¼ —
Length of arm-hole	4 —	4 —	3½ —	3 —
Length of string-case	4 —	3½ —	3½ —	3 —
Space for shoulder	3¾ —	3½ —	3 —	2½ —
Length of skirt-gusset	4 —	3 —	3 —	2½ —
Breadth of ditto	2 —	1½ —	1½ —	1½ —

FIG. 5 A.

Or half the back of the jacket when cut out, supposing the breadth to be folded exactly in two. Let A L be the folded side.

SCALE.

	Nails.
Space from A to B	5½
Do. do. B to C	2½
Do. do. C to D	3½
Do. do. D to E	1¾
Do. do. D to F	2¾
Do. do. F to G	¾
Do. do. F to H	3
Do. do. H to I	1½
Do. do. H to J	½
Do. do. J to K	3
Do. do. K to L	2½

FIG. 5 B.

Or the whole of one of the front breadths.

SCALE.

	Nails.
Space from A to B	4
Do. do. B to C	4½
Do. do. C to D	1
Do. do. C to E	2½
Do. do. E to F	2¾
Do. do. E to G	1
Do. do. G to H	2¾
Do. do. H to I	2¼
Do. do. I to J	6
Do. do. J to K	12

In making up this jacket, sew the 3 breadths together, putting in at the bottom two gussets or triangular pieces. Make a narrow hem at the bottom, sew up the shoulders, and put in the sleeves. Set the back breadth plainly into the collar, but full it at each end into the neck gusset, and also in front. Put the string-case about a nail lower than the arm-holes.

FLANNEL PETTICOATS.
PLATE 10. FIG. 7.

The breadths of flannel are cut according to the height of the person, allowing a good tuck besides, to be let down after the petticoat has been washed.

SCALE.

First or largest size, for a full grown woman:—3 breadths of flannel sewed simply together; slit behind 6 nails deep, and opened in a seam.

Second size, for a middle sized woman, 2½ breadths; the half is crossed off 5 nails, and the two gores are sewed, one on each side, between the two plain breadths; slit behind 5 nails; it is made in the middle of one of the plain breadths. It is more economical to cut two petticoats at once, as 5 breadths will make two, but it requires 3 to cut one out, and there must be waste.

Third size, for a girl of fourteen or sixteen, 2 breadths. From 1 breadth is cut a gore of 5 nails at the top, sloped off to 1 nail; this gore is sewed at the opposite side of the same breadth, placing the 1 nail width at the narrow end of the breadth. The slit behind must be determined by doubling the petticoat exactly in half, letting it be about 4 nails long.

Another way of cutting this petticoat, is by crossing it like a shift, and then putting the two broader ends to the bottom, while the narrow part is at the top; by this method there is no waste, and it saves both time and trouble.

Fourth size, 2 breadths: 1 breadth is cut in half, and 1 half is gored 5 nails; the two gores are sewed, one on each side of the whole breadth, in front, and the half breadth is put in behind. The slit is torn down the middle of the half breadth, and is 4 nails long.

Fifth size, for a girl eight or ten, 1½ breadth. The ½ breadth is gored, and the whole breadth torn in half; a gore is sewed on each side between the two half breadths. Slit behind 3 nails deep, in the middle of the ½ breadth, behind.

Sixth size, for a child five or six, 1½ or 2 breadths, sewed simply together without goring. Slit 3 nails long behind.

Petticoats are variously made up. The most usual way is plaiting the top in regular folds on each side, letting it be quite plain, or nearly so, in front; it is then set firmly into a linen, calico, or jean band, of the proper width to encircle the waist, and of 1 nail deep when doubled and turned in. Strong tapes are sewed to the ends of the band, and sometimes a large button-hole is made in the band, about 2 nails from the end, through which the tape of the opposite end is drawn, which makes the petticoat set neatly to the figure.

Another manner is to make the petticoat up without any slit behind, so as to be a round skirt; a band of the same size is set on quite plainly, without plait or fulness (see Fig. 8). A runner is made all round in the middle of the band, and two button-holes for the strings to come out of, are made at the two sides of the petticoat under the arm; one tape is sewed firmly down at the end of one of the button-holes, carried all round the petticoat, and drawn out again at the same hole; the other tape, in a similar manner, is sewed down at the other button-hole: when the petticoat is on, and the tapes drawn and tied in front, the fulled part lies behind, forming a sort of bustle to set off the dress properly (see Fig. 9).

ON LINEN.

The tops for children's petticoats are generally a kind of stay, to which the skirt is either sewed or fastened by means of buttons, and to which the drawers button also. For children's stays, see Plate 11.

POCKETS.
PLATE 10.

Pockets are either worn tied round the waist, fastened into the petticoat, or buttoned upon the stays. When fastened into the petticoat, they are made of the same material, otherwise of dimity, calico, jean, twilled muslin, and sometimes of nankeen or brown jean.

Take a doubled piece of six nails width-way, and seven nails selvage-way when doubled, and cut according to Fig. 10. For this purpose, double the folded piece in half width-way, and slope off from A to B one nail. The hole in the pocket is slit down about four nails, beginning at three-quarters of a nail from the top. Cut the slit in the shape of an I, in order to allow of a deep hem being made on each side. The two pieces of the pocket are run firmly together all round, at a little distance from the edge, on the wrong side. It is then turned inside out, the seam well flattened, and back-stitched all round with white silk, about a quarter of an inch from the edge. The top is set into a broad piece of tape, which is doubled over it and forms the strings also. The slit is hemmed or back-stitched neatly down. Sometimes an inner pocket or pockets are made for a watch, &c., and this is done by sewing a square piece of the material inside the pocket. The top is left open, but the sides and bottom of it are firmly sewed down.

ANOTHER POCKET.
PLATE 10. FIG. 11.

This differs from the other merely in having the slit cut the contrary way, so as to open width, instead of lengthwise.

ANOTHER POCKET.
PLATE 10. FIG. 13, 14.

This shape is preferred by some persons, as it sets better to the figure than the others. The straight side is worn in front; and, in cutting out a pair of pockets, care must be taken to make them for the right and left side. The shape is exactly the same as Fig. 10, excepting that, after they are cut out, a gore is taken off from the one side and sewed on to the other, by which means the one is straight and the other, in consequence of the addition, is very much sloped. When pockets are fastened into gowns and petticoats, they are a little fulled at the top, and the slit of the pocket is sewed to the corresponding slit of the petticoat. Some people cut out the slit for the pocket differently, as they are considered to lie flatter to the person than the usual shaped pocket. It is formed by making an oblong bag or pocket, about eight nails long and five nails wide, and cutting at one end, in a slanting direction, so as to take off a triangular piece. To save waste, it is better to make two pockets at once, letting the oblong piece be still five nails wide, when doubled, but fifteen nails long (see Fig. 12); crease it in half its length, and then cut, in a slanting direction, across from A to B. The part cut forms the slit or opening to the pocket, which is sewed all round to the slit in the petticoat or gown.

ANOTHER METHOD.

This is simply a lining or square piece of calico, about ten nails wide and eight nails deep, sewed to the inside of the petticoat quite plainly. The petticoat has a slit of four nails deep.

FRILLS.

Frills are in use when high gowns are worn, and are made of cambric, muslin, net, lace, tulle, crape, &c.

A SIMPLE FRILL.

This is merely a strip of muslin, about fourteen nails long and three nails wide, more or less, according to pleasure. It is merely hemmed all round, and simply plaited up, in regular folds, to the proper size.

A PARTICULARLY NEAT FRILL.
PLATE 10. FIG. 15.

This is made of net or clear muslin, and is neatly fulled to the band. The edge, instead of being hemmed, is rolled over a bobbin to stiffen it. The band is about half a nail wide, and doubled, and is nine nails long. The frill on each side is fourteen nails long, and two nails wide. A button-hole is put in the middle to fasten it to the gown, and it ties at the ends with ribbons.

A CRIMPED FRILL.
PLATE 10. FIG. 16.

This is very suitable for young children, especially boys, and is generally made of lawn or cambric. The frill should be double the length of the size round the neck, and about one nail wide. A neat hem at one edge, and the other is sewed to a band of the proper length, say about five nails, and of half a nail in depth. These frills should be crimped very neatly.

PLATE 10. FIG. 17.

This frill is to be made like Fig. 15, excepting that the muslin is only one nail deep, and crimped in the same manner as Fig. 16. It is very suitable for young children.

PLATE 10. FIG. 18.

Another and more ornamental frill, made of muslin or net, with edging sewed on it.

The muslin or net must be about four nails wide, and fourteen or sixteen nails long. The frill is creased down the middle, and on each side of the crease, at a quarter of a nail distance, it is neatly run with a long thread, and drawn up to the proper width, forming a puffing in the centre of the frill. This puffing is first stroked with the needle into an even fulness, and then sewed at each side close to the gatherings, to a band of a quarter of a nail wide only, or still narrower, so as to raise the puffing sufficiently to look well, and yet not too much to admit of a ribbon being drawn smoothly through it. This ribbon ties the frill round the neck.

PLATE 10. FIG. 19.

This is a very simple frill, and, when well made, looks remarkably neat. The net of which it is composed must be about two nails and a quarter wide, creased in the middle, and finely plaited in small neat plaits. It is then doubled, and bound on the outside down the folded centre with a narrow ribbon, so that the two sides of the frill lie close together, instead of being open, like Fig. 18.

ANOTHER FRILL.

This kind, which is sometimes called a Ruche, is made exactly contrary to the usual mode. The frill, instead of being run down the middle, is joined down the sides, and confined at the joining into

ON LINEN. 75

a ribbon, so that the top of the frill is double; and as it is usually made of tulle, or some rather stiff material, it stands out stiffly from the neck. Pelerines have sometimes a double frill or Ruche, of the same material that they are made of, sewed to them.

CUFFS.
PLATE 10.

There are various kinds of cuffs, for different purposes, of which the most useful only are here explained.

TIDY CUFFS.
PLATE 10. FIG. 20, 21.

Tidy cuffs are much worn by persons whose employments are apt to injure the sleeve of the gown, either by wearing it out, staining, or greasing it. They are very valuable whilst drawing, writing, pasting, or when in the kitchen; and in these cases are generally made of Holland or nankeen, and when braided with dark blue, green, crimson, brown, or any other suitable colour, with ribbons to lace up of the same, they have a particularly neat effect. The cuff is cut out as follows (Fig. 21):—Procure a piece of Holland four nails down the selvage, and five nails wide; double it in half its width, and slope down by the selvage from A to D, and from B to C, cutting off half a nail in a direct slope, so that, when open, the end, C D, is but four nails wide, while A B is five. Turn down a deep hem along each of the sloped sides half a nail deep, and over the stitches put a braid, with two other rows of the same close together on the hem, leaving sufficient space between to insert a thin whalebone to support the cuff, and keep it from wrinkling when on the arm. The lace holes are worked with silk the same colour as the ribbon. Fig. 20 represents the cuff when laced up.

PLATE 10. FIG. 22.

This is a neat cuff to lay on the dress, and is either made of plain net, of lace, or of muslin, with or without edging, and sometimes of satin ribbon. If for mourning, the net should have a broad hem. It is gathered and sewed into a band about one nail deep, and three or three and a half wide, according to the size of the wrist. There should be two pearl buttons set on one end, and buttonholes made to correspond.

PLATE 10. FIG. 23.

This is a plain band, to be made to fit the wrist exactly, of silk, satin, or velvet, to be laid on a thin evening sleeve. It may be one nail broad or more. A rouleau is sometimes laid on round it, or a narrow piping. If it is made of silk the colour of the dress, or of white silk embroidered, it has a very pretty effect.

PLATE 10. FIG. 24.

This is a dress cuff, to wear with lace or tulle sleeves, and may be made of any rich material, with a piping of satin and an edging of blonde or lace. The inside is sometimes embroidered in floss silk. In cutting it out, procure a piece of paper about two nails and a half deep, and four nails long; double it in half its length, and measure up the side from A to C, one nail and a quarter, leaving from C to the upper edge, J, one nail and a quarter also. Cut off the corner from E to C, curving it a little inwards, and again, from C to A, cut off in a direct line one quarter of a nail. Open it, and it will resemble Fig. 24 exactly.

PLATE 10. FIG. 25.

This cuff resembles the preceding one, but has, in addition, a small second cuff laid on the lower part of it, and a slit cut down from the top to about one nail and a quarter depth from A to B. The top of the second cuff comes just below the slit, and it is a little sloped away at the sides.

PLATE 10. FIG. 26.

A cuff worn in deep mourning, especially by widows, and made either of clear muslin or black crape. It consists of fold lying upon fold, and is either sewed upon the sleeve or made to slip over the hand. The folds are four or five in number, and lie just one above the other, each being about a quarter of a nail deep.

PLATE 10. FIG. 27.

This is to be worn as a trimming or edging, below the sleeve, upon the hand: the band buttons inside the sleeve. The frill is of muslin, cambric, net, or lace. It should be very full, and got up in puffs, or very finely crimped. The ends of the bands should have deep hems, in which the button-holes are worked. The band is about three-quarters of a nail deep, and three or three nails and a half wide.

PLATE 10. FIG. 28.

This is a neat simple little cuff, and suits the collar, Plate 13, Fig. 26. It is well adapted for mourning. Cut two pieces of muslin, net, lawn, or cambric, of two nails square, and hem each round with a broad hem; sew the two together to the depth of about one nail; the parts sewed together form a sort of band inside, while the others, being unattached, fall backwards over the sleeve.

PLATE 10. FIG. 29.

A simple, plain, mourning cuff, with a broad hem above and below. The cuff to be about two nails deep, and three and a half or four nails long, according to the size of the wrist.

APRONS.
PLATE 11.

If for common use, aprons are made of white, brown, blue, black, or checked linen, of black stuff, calico, Holland, leather, nankeen, print, or long cloth; if for better purposes, of cambric muslin, clear, mulled, or jaconet muslin, silk, satinette, satin, &c. The length of the apron is, of course, generally determined by the height of the wearer, and the width, by that of the material, and by the purpose for which it is intended. For working aprons, the width is generally one breadth of a yard wide; for dress aprons, two breadths, one of which is cut in half, and these halves put one on each side of the whole breadth. If the material should be wide enough, one breadth, of from fourteen to twenty nails, will answer very well.

DRESS APRON.
PLATE 11. FIG. 1.

This is made of satinette, or thick satin silk, and consists of two breadths, one in front, and a half breadth sewed on each side of it. None of them are to be at all sloped. The length is regulated by the pleasure of the wearer, and a broad hem of three-quarters of a nail deep is made all round. The length of the band must vary according to the size of the waist, and must be cut by Fig. L, which represents it when doubled. The part from A to B, or that to which the apron is fulled, is five nails and a half; from A to C is one nail and a half; and from B to D is one full nail. The remainder of the band, from B D, onwards to F, is determined by the size of the waist. A piece of whalebone is stitched into the centre of the band, A C, and on each side of it a little chain-stitch is worked, in thick silk, of the same colour as the apron. The folds are exactly according to the Plate, beginning within the hem, and laid evenly along until below the whalebone, when a space is left. The chain-stitch is next worked in two rows, parallel with the curved shape of the band, allowing little more than a quarter of a nail between the rows. By this means the folds are neatly confined, and it prevents the bustling effect they might otherwise have. These folds are very small and close. The band has a small piping below, but is plain at the top, and fastens behind with hooks and eyes.

PLATE 11. FIG. 2.

This apron is generally made of silk, but looks well also in muslin. It requires care in the making as well as in the washing. The vandykes are formed by turning the edge of the apron down once, all round, to about three-quarters of a nail deep; and, after tacking it firmly down, vandykes are neatly run, in very small stitches (Fig. 5), from the edge of the apron to pretty near the rough edge of the silk, leaving sufficient to turn in well afterwards:—thus, let the vandykes be run to the depth of from A to B, leaving a small space all the way from B to C. When finished turn each vandyke inside out, and smooth all the wrinkles at the corners and points with a stiletto or scissors. When it is well and evenly pulled out, turn in the rough edge and hem it neatly down. Sometimes a little braid, or a row of chain-stitch, is put over the stitches on the right side. The plaits are regularly laid, those on each side being folded towards the middle. The band is frequently lined with buckram or stiff muslin, and is made with or without piping. Scollops are sometimes substituted for vandykes.

PLATE 11. FIG. 3.

This apron is of muslin, either clear or otherwise. A broad hem is made all round, of the proper width to admit a coloured or white ribbon of the half or three-quarter nail breadth. Some fine work or edging may be sewed to the hem all round. The band should be open at the ends to admit of the ribbon that ties it being drawn out when the apron is washed. The hem all round should also be kept open at the ends for the same purpose, and merely tacked up when the ribbon is put in.

PLATE 11. FIG. 4.

This is an apron with a broad hem all round, and a full frill of any fine material.

PLATE 11. FIG. 6.

A clear muslin apron, with a broad hem of three-quarters of a nail deep, and a shawl bordering laid all round within the hem, either half or three-quarters of a nail deep. This is a pretty apron for a young person. The bordering must be taken off before the apron is washed.

PLATE 11. FIG. 7.

This represents the bottom of an apron when hollowed out. It has a simple broad hem, turned up with a piping.

PLATE 11. FIG. 8.

The broad hem here is surrounded by a deep crimped frill of about a nail broad. These aprons are generally made of jaconet or cambric muslin, and the frill of cambric or lawn. They are very suitable for ladies to wear in a morning when cutting out, or in the housekeeper's room.

PLATE 11. FIG. 9.

This is a pretty evening apron, made with a broad hem, and muslin insertion-work let in all round, inside which, coloured ribbon may or may not be run. Edging, either of lace or worked muslin, is put on all round.

APRON POCKETS.

These vary very much, some being laid on the apron as in Fig. 3, 4, and 6; others put on at the back, a slit being made in the apron to correspond with the place of the pockets. These last are made as in Fig. P, from a long double piece, which, being sewed up, is cut diagonally or crosswise, from A to B, and forms two pockets, the part cut being sewed to the slit of the apron. The whole length of the narrow piece, before it is cut, is six nails, and the width, when double, two nails. The slit in the apron is neatly hemmed, and a trimming of ribbon or silk put round it, with a bow at the bottom, or a fringe and tassels.

In Fig. 3 the pocket is a piece of two nails and a half deep and five nails wide. This piece is plaited in regular folds at the top to a lining of only two nails and a half deep, and the same width. The bottom is fulled nearly to a point in small folds, and the lining, being turned in to the same shape, is sewed to it with a piping. The pocket is then stitched firmly on to the apron, and trimmed according to fancy. One or three small bows are put on the pocket.

In Fig. 4 the pocket is cut in the shape of a heart, and put plainly on the apron. It is about two nails and three-quarters wide, and two nails and a half deep. The pocket is piped or trimmed with edging.

In Fig. 6 the pocket is particularly neat and pretty, being made of folds of the same material as the apron, with a coloured piping all round it, and three bows the same colour as the piping.

COMMON APRONS.

The simplest kind, and that generally worn by working men, is a yard wide or more, hemmed at the bottom and at the top, with a string run through to tie round the waist. It is thus worn by brewers, &c.

PLATE 11. FIG. 10.

This is a simple shape, and the one most in use. It is either plaited or gathered into the band, which is about a nail deep. These aprons are usually worn by all servants and women while at work. Blue, check, and brown linen are most used for scouring and cleaning; white linen, Holland, and print, for less dirty employments. Ladies wear them of silk or muslin, with or without pockets.

PLATE 11. FIG. 11.

This is a pretty apron, often worn by girls from eight to sixteen or eighteen years of age. The bib is made of the proper size to fit in front, between the shoulders of the wearer, coming down in a slope to the waist. These bibs may be plain, or they are ornamented with tucks or folds, either upright or length-wise. The shoulder-strap may be of the same material, or of tape or ribbon. The apron is gathered evenly, or plaited so as to reach to A on each side, which is situated exactly between the bottom of the bib and the shoulder-strap behind.

PLATE 11. FIG. 12.

May be worn either as a common or as a pretty dress apron, according to the material and trimming. It may be made of silk, coloured muslin, or print. After being properly gathered into the band, two shoulder-straps, in the form of four lappets, are cut out, either pointed, as in A, or rounded, as in B. These lappets may be piped, and either edged with lace or fringe, or left plain. For a full size, the lappet is five nails along the selvage, from D to C, and one nail and three-quarters from C to B. The two straps are sewed together at C, and fastened with a bow of ribbon. The lappet is piped all round with a strong cord, to make it wear well.

PLATE 11. FIG. 13.

This shape is much worn by men servants, apothecaries, grocers, &c., and is simply gathered into a band, leaving a piece of two nails unattached to it, A B, which is hemmed at the top, and falls negligently down.

A COOKING APRON.
PLATE 11. FIG. 14.

This is a neat pattern for a housekeeper, cook, or kitchen-maid. The bib is quite plain, and pins to the gown at the corners. The size given in the Plate is suitable for a girl, but the bib should be cut to suit the wearer at once, and not made by guess. The apron is made of check or strong linen.

A PANTRY APRON.
PLATE 11. FIG. 15.

A very good shape for men servants to wear when trimming lamps, cleaning shoes and knives, &c. The apron is about a yard and a quarter long, and it is made of strong linen or calico. The tape for the neck should be nine or ten nails long. A pocket may be added in front. The corners of the apron are simply turned down to the distance of five nails and a half from the top (see A A), the letters, A A, being each exactly five nails and a half from B. These corners are either sewed or strongly hemmed down.

GENTLEMEN'S WORKSHOP APRON.
PLATE 11. FIG. 16.

This is very useful for gentlemen when turning, or using tools, and is generally made of Holland or strong white or brown linen. The width is fifteen or sixteen nails; the part for the neck four and a half, five, or more, according to the width across the shoulders of the wearer. The depth of this part two nails and a half or more. The straps, about eight nails and a half long, cross each other from the neck to the half of the shoulder part of the apron; which plan holds it up neatly in front, and makes it set more comfortably. A pocket may be added, according to pleasure, in front, or two at the sides. A slit in the apron, bound round with tape, and a square piece put on behind it, looks the neatest as a pocket.

SENTIMENT, FIANCÉE, OR NECK-TIE.
PLATE 11. FIG. 17, 18.

This is made of velvet, satin, or silk, and is worn for the purpose of keeping the neck warm, and as a finish to the dress. It is made of two colours, which are joined in the middle and lined with sarsenet: the silk or other material is cut cross-wise and pointed at the ends. The sentiment is six or seven nails long from point to point, when made up, and within one nail and a half of the point at one end, is fastened with strong stitches or a silk ring. When the tie is worn, the other point is passed through the ring and drawn close. Sometimes the neck-tie is of a dark-coloured silk in the middle with two coloured ends.

A DRESS SCARF OR CAPRICE.
PLATE 11. FIG. 19, 20.

This is made of the broadest satin ribbon that can be procured, say two nails and a half wide, and is two yards and three quarters long. Double the ribbon on the wrong side exactly in two, and, while so doubled, run across the width of the ribbon in a slanting direction (Fig. 19, A B), and when opened, the scarf will set to the form of the neck. An edging of swansdown is sewed all round, and the ends may be either embroidered, braided, or left plain, according to the taste of the wearer.

A CACHEMIRE OR INDIANA SCARF.
PLATE 11. FIG. 21.

This is a kind of scarf which is easily made, and is a pretty finish to a walking dress, or may be worn in an evening at home: it is formed of three colours, say black, scarlet, and light blue. To make one scarf, you will want one yard and six nails in length and four nails and a half in width, of the black cachemire.

Sometimes the length of the scarf will lie in the width of the material, in which case it will be a great saving of expense. Procure a piece of each of the other two colours, seven nails long, and of the same width as the black, viz., four nails and a half. Find the middle of each end of the black strip, and slope off one nail and a half from the middle to each side (see Fig. 21, A C A D): next, slope one end of the blue, and one end of the scarlet strip, to accord exactly with the black strip, cutting the nail and a half from the middle to the ends. After this, split the blue and the scarlet pieces down the middle, sew half the blue and half the scarlet very accurately, first together, and then to the black strip, making the points fit in as neatly as possible to the half strips: do the same at the other end, arranging the colours so as to be at cross corners with each other. Observe that the pieces are sewed flatly together, and herring-boned all round on the right side. A narrow silk gymp, one-third of a nail wide, is laid at the edge and upon all the joinings; this gymp should be of some clear bright colour, as yellow and deep brown or gold colour, and at the ends is a silk fringe of blue and scarlet, to match the two half strips.

A SIMPLE SCARF.

This is made of plain net or tulle, the whole width of the material, say three quarters of a yard, and three yards long. A broad hem is made all round, wide enough to admit of a satin ribbon of a three-penny breadth.

STAYS OR CORSETS.
PLATE 11.

It is impossible to give any particular patterns or sizes of stays, as they must, of course, be cut differently, according to the figure, and be variously supported with more or less bones or runners of cotton, according to the age, strength, or constitution of the wearer; we shall, therefore, confine ourselves to a few observations on the making up: and with respect to the cutting out, it is recommended to those who make their own stays, to purchase a pair from an experienced stay-maker that fit perfectly well, and also a pair cut out, but not made up, so as to be a good pattern for the home-made stays.

WOMEN'S STAYS.
PLATE 11. FIG. 22.

If for ladies, they are made of sattine, or best French jean, which is half a yard wide, and about 20d. or 2s. per yard: if of an inferior quality, they are made of white, brown, grey, or nankeen jean, at 8d. or 10d. per yard, and lined with calico between the doubles. The stay is generally lined between the two pieces of jean with union cloth or Irish linen in every part excepting the gores. Stays are usually cut in four parts, all of which are generally upon the cross, as this assists materially in making them set better to the figure. Two of the pieces reach from each side of the back, nearly to the hips, and the other two from thence to the middle of the busk or steel. There are two gores on each side for the bosom, and two larger ones on each side below, for the hips.

The necessary bones are as follows:

A steel in the middle, which should be narrower at the top than at the bottom, and confined in a strong wash leather, before being put into the stay-case.

Two bones at the extreme ends, to prevent the holes from bursting beyond the edge.

We may also add, as they are in common use, a second bone down each back, on the other side of the lace-holes.

Bones between the front bosom gores, on each side; but these should be very thin and elastic, and are seldom wanted unless the wearer requires much additional support.

Two other bones, one on each side, from about a nail below each arm-hole to the bottom of the stay.

A few slight rib or cross-bones are sometimes put in.

It is as well to observe that unless particularly feeble, or otherwise an invalid, it is most desirable to wear as few bones as possible; and that for healthy persons, the two back bones, with the steel in front, are quite sufficient. The casing of the steel in front is sometimes made elastic to the depth of four nails from the top, by means of Indian rubber runners; which adds much to the comfort of asthmatic or delicate persons. (See Fig. 23.)

On each side of the steel is a cotton runner, and these are also put in various other parts of the stays, according to fancy.

ON MAKING UP.

The needles used for making stays are called the *between* needles. Strong sewing silk, called stay-silk, is used for the best corsets, and strong waxed cotton for the common ones. In sewing the seams, take great care to turn in the work properly, so as to have all the rough edges within the stay: for this purpose, first turn down the outside and inside piece of jean lying on one side of the seam, with the rough edges and the lining prepared as if for common sewing; do the same with the other side of the seam, placing the two seams, thus prepared, side by side, and sew them firmly together. It will have the effect of a double ordinary seam, when held between the finger and thumb. The mode of sewing these four thicknesses so as to make them lie flatly when opened, is rather peculiar. Take up with your needle, three of the thicknesses, leaving the fourth unsewed. The next stitch, take again three folds, leaving the other outside one unsewed: continue alternately taking up one outside and omitting the other, letting the stitches lie close together: when completed, open the seam, and flatten it with the finger and thumb.

The gores are next laid between the doubles of jean, and neatly back-stitched all round; the narrow parts at the top being worked in button-hole stitch.

The bone-cases are then made, and the cotton runners back-stitched.

The oylet or lace-holes are next worked, and after the stay-bones are put in, the top and bottom of the stays, with the shoulder-straps, are neatly bound with stay-binding.

As there are many varieties in the shapes of the different parts of stays, they will be described in detail, under their respective heads.

GORES.

These are sometimes made of elastic wires, as in Fig. 23, sometimes of Indian rubber, and sometimes of a kind of elastic twill.

SHOULDER-STRAPS

Are made of the same material as the stays, and back-stitched to the front and back of the shoulder. Sometimes they are buttoned down in the front, which enables the wearer, by unbuttoning them, to dress her hair in an evening with perfect ease. (See Fig. 22.)

Others have oylet-holes to admit of bobbins, which lace them to corresponding holes in the stays. (See Fig. 24.)

A piece of Indian rubber or elastic wire, of about one nail in length, is frequently sewed to the end of the strap, and this is considered the most convenient, as it will lengthen or contract at pleasure.

LACE-HOLES

Are generally worked round in button-hole stitch; sometimes tape is laced from the outside through these holes, being drawn through every other hole till they reach the top, and then brought down again, drawing it round the edge, through the intermediate holes; this preserves them from being worn. (See Fig. 26.) Others insert in every hole a ring, called a patent lace-hole. These are very durable, but are said to destroy the laces.

MODESTY-PIECE.

To the top of the stay is sometimes attached a small modesty-piece, which for some people is an excellent contrivance, as it makes it set more closely and delicately in front. This extra piece is all in one, and is the cross-way; it is carried along the whole of the front of the stay: it is about half a nail deep over the bosom, and sloped off to a quarter of a nail over the stay-bone; at the top of this additional strip, which is bound all round, a bobbin is run to draw it up. When drawn properly, this modesty lies over the bosom so as to shade it delicately, whereas if it were cut all in one piece with the stay it would make it higher, but it would stand out, and not answer the desired end. (See Fig. 25.)

NURSING STAYS.

It is essential to open the front of nursing stays, so as to give the mother the greatest ease while feeding her infant; for this purpose, care should be taken that no stay-bones or hard buttons should come in contact with the child's face: the two or three best modes of opening them are the following:

Leave open that side of the bosom gore which is next to the shoulder-strap, to the depth of a full nail and a half; neatly bind the side of the gore, and after back-stitching the opposite side, sew on very firmly two buttons, one at the top and the other lower down. To the gore is attached two loops, by which it can be buttoned or unbuttoned at pleasure. (See Fig. 24.)

Another mode is that of leaving open the outer sides of those gores nearest the steel or middle of the stays.

These sides, and the parts with which they accord, have oylet-holes worked down them, exactly opposite to each other. Through each oylet-hole in the gore, pass a bobbin of about two nails and a quarter long, which is fastened at one end firmly to the wrong side, just behind the oylet-hole. The other end of each bobbin is drawn across to the inner side of the corresponding hole, and pulled through. By this arrangement all the ends of the bobbins lace up the whole gore. The bobbins are sewed together at the ends, forming a loop to attach it to a button on each side of the steel (see Fig. 23, A B).

These bobbins should be carefully cut and joined, so as to pull the gores properly in their places. When it is unbuttoned the whole front lets down comfortably. It is advisable to sew a little fold or oblong piece to the stay on the inside, which forms a flap to lie between the shift and the opening, as a guard from cold.

MEN'S STAYS, OR BELTS.
PLATE 11. FIG. 27, 28.

These are worn by gentlemen in the army, hunters, or by those using violent exercise.

They are made of strong jean, duck, leather, or webbing.

Sometimes the stay is merely a strip or belt, as Fig. 28; at others it is a little shaped or peaked, as Fig. 27. Towards the ends is sewed a piece of elastic work (see Fig. 28 E). Runners of cotton are made in various places to strengthen the whole. Long webbing straps are sewed three on each end. These straps are sewed on with pieces of leather over them, and are about three nails deep. The length is, of course, determined by the size of the wearer.

BELT FOR A HUNTER OR COACHMAN.

This is often merely a simple leather belt, with three tongues and buckles.

CHILD'S LITTLE STAY.
PLATE 11. FIG. 33.

This is made of fine jean, doubled, of three nails depth, and of the width required by the child. Cord runners are made in front, and at the backs, and buttons are put on, before and behind, for the drawers and flannels to be attached to.

AN OLDER CHILD'S STAY.
PLATE 11. FIG. 29.

This is formed of double jean, and may be lined between with Irish linen. If it is preferred, all the runners may have cotton drawn through them, so as to admit of no bones.

BUSTLES.
PLATE 11. FIG. 30, 32.

Bustles are worn by those whose shape requires something to set off the skirt of the gown. They should not be too large, or they look indelicate, and in bad taste. They are made of jean, strong calico, and sometimes of glazed calico.

Fig. 30 represents a simple bustle of strong calico. It is composed of one piece the width of the calico, say a yard, and eight nails deep. This piece is doubled in two, so as to make two flounces, the one four nails and a half long, and the other three and a half. At one nail from the doubled top make a narrow case to admit of tapes. The bottoms of the flounces are hemmed with a very thick cord in them. When worn, the bustle is turned inside out, by which means the frill falls between the two flounces (see Fig. 32).

Fig. 31 is merely two flounces of jean, one four nails deep and the other three nails, gathered into a tape at the top and vandyked at the bottom.

Some persons wear down bustles (see Fig. 33), which are made of glazed lining muslin. A flat half circle or oval is cut out, about two nails and a half wide by two nails deep, and another piece, of an oblong shape, rounded at the corners, much longer and deeper, say three-quarters of a yard long by four nails and a half deep, is fulled into the smaller piece on one side, and into a tape on the other or top, thus making a bag to contain the down, which should be either swan's or the best goose down.

VEILS.

The subject of veils is one that may soon be dismissed, as a few words on the materials of which they are composed, together with the usual sizes, comprises all that can be said upon them.

Veils for ordinary wear may be of a kind of soft tulle, made on purpose, of net, gauze, or crape. The size for a grown-up person is from thirteen nails to a yard long, and about twenty nails wide; for a child, eleven nails long, and the width is determined by that of the material. Demi-voiles are about four nails deep, and the width is regulated by that of the bonnet to which they are attached.

A pretty way of making a net or tulle veil is by hemming a satin ribbon half a nail deep all round it, either the same colour, or, if the veil is white, of some pale shade to suit the bonnet or the dress. This, by strengthening the edges, makes the veil wear better than it would otherwise do.

A crape or gauze veil is simply hemmed all round, the hem being deeper at the bottom to give it a little weight. A ribbon is run in at the top.

Mourning veils are of black crape. They should be made of what is termed the best, or jet black crape, as the blue-black soon wears whitish, and looks shabby. The other, though the most expensive at first, is the best economy in the end. They are made quite plainly, with a broad hem all round—say three-quarters of a nail deep.

Demi-voiles, when not of blonde, Chantilly, or worked lace, are of tulle, with ribbon run in. They should be set on the bonnet slightly, fulled all round the brim, but much more so at the ears, to make them hang well. A demi-voile should also be a little taken up at the ears, so as not to be the full depth, which is apt to give a slovenly appearance.

Riding veils are much shorter than any other kind except demi-voiles, and sufficiently wide to draw nearly all round the hat. They are made either of black lace, worked on purpose, or of brown or green crape. It is a good plan to run a string through a riding-veil, both at the top and bottom, taking care that the ribbon at the bottom is only just as long as the veil is wide, so that it is not seen when not in use. The advantage of this second string is, that in hot weather, and under a glaring sun, the wearer may tie both ribbons round her hat, thus forming a double veil for the protection of her eyes, whilst the lower part of the face has all the benefit of the cool air.

SLEEVES.
PLATE 12.

Sleeves should, when it is possible, be cut upon the cross; for which purpose a corner of the material should be turned up, until the doubled part, which is the cross way, is large enough to admit of the length and width of the sleeve.

Silk is sometimes too narrow for a very large sleeve to be made without joining, when care should be taken to join together two selvages. The joinings must be so contrived as to set either under, or at the back of the sleeves.

In order to make sleeves set well, they are hollowed out, as it is called, which is nothing more than

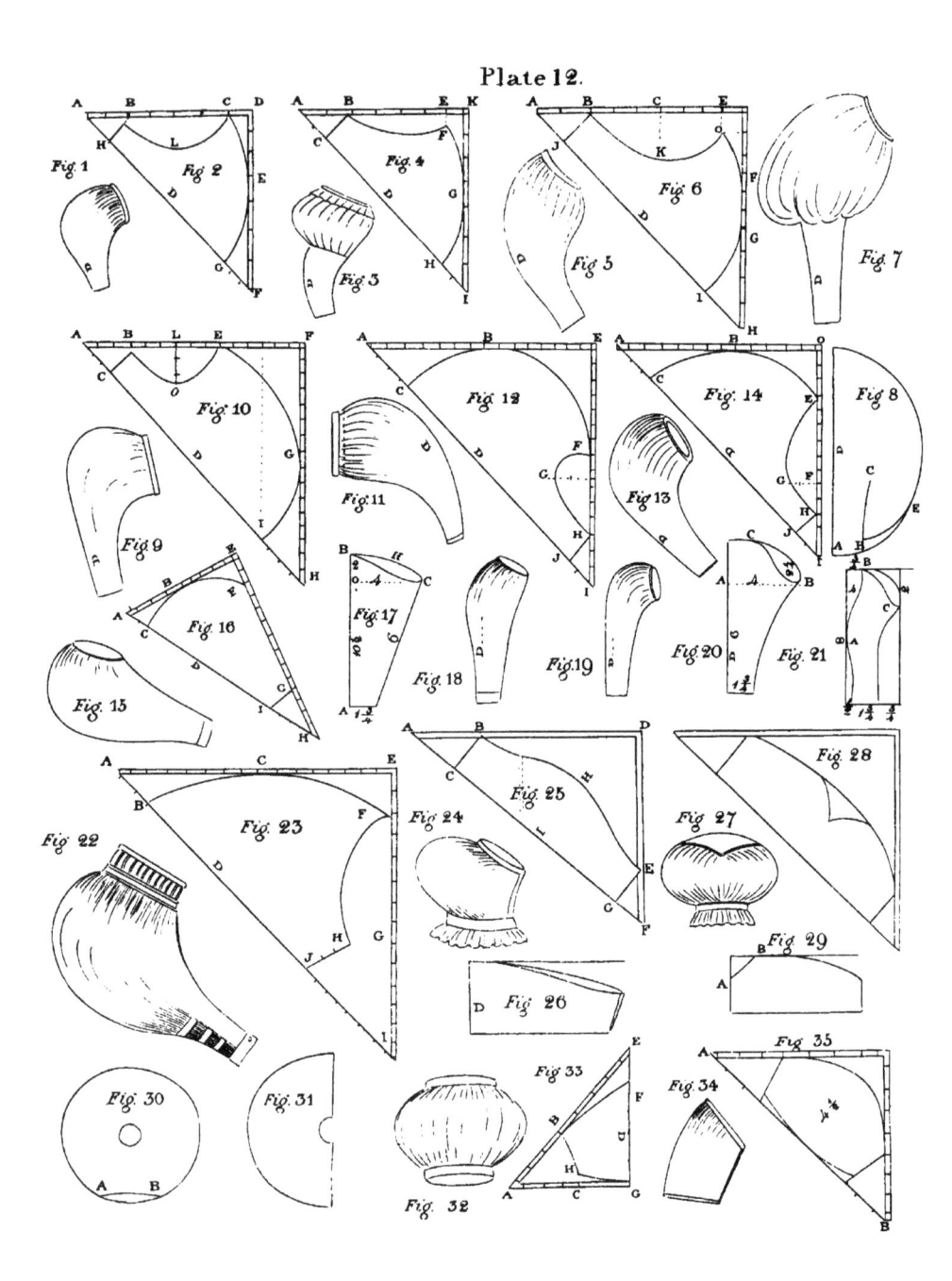

Plate 12.

cutting away a little of the front, at the top, so as to make it less deep than the back, observing always that it is straight in the front, the crosswise part of the sleeve falling behind. This is of great importance, as the set of the sleeve depends upon it. Of course attention must be paid to make them in pairs.

There are so many ways of finishing sleeves, and so many fancies about them, that to describe them all would be equally impossible and useless. A few rows of biassing, both at the top and bottom, or small plaits, confined once or twice by narrow bands, or by back-stitching, give a very neat appearance when the sleeve is at all a full one.

For lining sleeves, see the description in Chapter I.

A CHILD'S FIRST SLEEVE.
PLATE 12. FIG. 1, 2.

This is a neat shape for a child of a year old, before which time their sleeves are generally cut straight, and merely sloped down to the cuff.

Turn up your material seven nails, and, after cutting a pattern according to the figure, lay it on the piece and cut by it.

The pattern is cut as follows (see Fig. 2) :—Take half a square of seven nails each way, and from A to B measure two nails; the same from A to H, and mark across, letting the wrist be one nail and three-quarters wide. From B to C is four nails, between which, measure downwards, one nail and a half, and curve from B, by L, to C, which is one nail from D. Measure next to E, three nails, and curve from C to E, and again from E to G, which is two nails from F.

The part marked D in all the sleeves is double. When made up it resembles Fig. 1.

AN OLDER CHILD'S SLEEVE.
PLATE 12. FIG. 3, 4.

Turn up seven nails crosswise, and cut as follows, see Fig, 4) :—

SCALE.

	Nails.
From A to B	1¾
From A to C	1½

Cut across one nail and a quarter for the wrist.

SCALE.

	Nails.
From A to E is	6
From E to F	1

Slope gradually from B to F.

SCALE.

	Nails.
From the corner, K to G	3¼
From the corner, I to H	1¼

Slope from F to G, and from G to H.

In making up Fig. 3, after joining the seams, and hemming or piping it at the bottom, gather it into the arm-hole at the top, and make a string-case just above the elbow to confine it as in the Plate. If preferred, it may be gathered above the elbow, and a narrow band put on.

LONG SLEEVE FOR A GROWN-UP PERSON.
PLATE 12. FIG. 5, 6.

This is cut as follows:—Turn up your paper pattern, or material, nine nails upon the cross (see Fig. 6).

SCALE.

	Nails.
From A to B is	2
From A to J is.............................	2

Cut straight from J to B for the wrist.

SCALE.

	Nails.
From B to C	3
From C to E..................................	3
From E to the corner	1

Cut straight from B to K, which is two nails below C. Cut in a sweep from K to the point, O, which is a quarter of a nail below E.

SCALE.

	Nails.
From the corner to F	3¼
From F to G	2¼
From G to H	3
From H to I.................................	2

Cut in a sweep from O to F, and from G to I.

The making up is perfectly simple. It is for a small-sized person.

THE CIRCULAR LONG SLEEVE.
PLATE 12. FIG. 7, 8.

This takes rather more of the material than the other shapes, but it is so easily cut out, and looks so well when made up, that it is allowed a place here.

For the full size it is a perfect circle, in a square of about fifteen nails.

After the circle is formed, double it in half (see Fig. 8); measure at A B a sufficient width to admit of the wrist, and slit up, in a slightly curving line, from B to C for about four nails, to form the arm of the sleeve. A little of the circle, from E towards B, is then sloped off to form the hollowing.

When made up, this part, E, is all taken up and gathered into the shoulder-strap. It is considered to hang particularly well, falling over the tight part of the sleeve (see Fig. 7.)

ON LINEN.

A PLAIN LONG SLEEVE.
PLATE 12. FIG. 9, 10.

Turn up your material a yard or fifteen nails. If it will not permit of this being done without joining, add a straight piece along the dotted line, running the two selvages together. Cut out as follows:

SCALE.

	Nails.
From A to B is	3
From A to C	2
From B to L	3
From L to E	3
From E to F	6
From F to G	8
From G to H	8
From H to I	4

Cut from C to within half a nail below B for the wrist. Cut nearly straight from B to O, which is two nails and a half below L, and in a sweep from O to E.

Sweep well from E to G, and from G to I.

The making up is perfectly simple.

A FULL SLEEVE.
PLATE 12. FIG. 11, 12.

Turn up fifteen nails of your material, and mark as follows:—

SCALE.

	Nails.
From A to B	8
From B to E	7
From E to F	7
From F to H	5
From the side to G	1¾
From H to I	3
From I to J	2
From A to C	3¼

Curve from C to B; from B to F. Hollow from F to G, and cut nearly straight from G to H.

It is made up either quite simply, or with one or two rows of biassing below the gathers at the top.

ANOTHER FULL SLEEVE.
PLATE 12. FIG. 13, 14.

Turn up thirteen nails of your material, and mark as follows:—

SCALE.

	Nails.
From A to B	8
From A to C	2¼
From B to O	5
From O to E	3
From E to F	6
From F to G	2
From F to H	2
From H to I	3
From I to J	2

Slope in a regular curve from C, by B, to E. Curve easily from E to G, and cut nearly straight from G to H. Cut from H to I for the wrist.

A SMALL SLEEVE.
PLATE 12. FIG. 15, 16.

Turn up your material so that the cross part, is seventeen nails long. Cut as follows (Fig. 16):

SCALE.

	Nails.
From A to B	3¼
From A to C	2
From B to E	5¾
From E to F	3
From F to G	8
From G to H	3¼
From H to I	3¼

Slope, in an equal and full curve, from C, by B, to F. Cut straight from G to I.

AN OLD WOMAN'S SLEEVE.
PLATE 12. FIG. 17, 18.

This is an economical kind of sleeve, worn much by the working classes.

Double your material either on the cross or nearly straight, according to taste and economy. From A to B, the doubled part, is ten nails and a half. C is the point opposite O, which is two nails below B. Slope, in an outward curve, from B to C, and then, taking but one fold of the silk, cut the inward curve from B to C, which forms the hollowing or inside of the sleeve.

A BOY'S SLEEVE.
PLATE 12. FIG. 19, 20.

This is for a boy of about six years old, who wears tunics of cloth. The sleeve, when doubled, is six nails long, four nails wide at the top, and one nail and three-quarters at the wrist. A is three nails from the top, opposite to which is B.

Curve from C to B, hollowing out one fold. Fig. 20 represents the sleeve made up.

A BOY'S SLEEVE.
PLATE 12. FIG. 21.

This sleeve is for a boy's coat or tunic, and has two seams in it, like a man's coat sleeve.

Take two pieces of cloth eight nails long and three wide. A is half way down the length. Curve from A to the bottom, to within half a nail from the corner. Curve from B to C at two nails from the top, and from A to B at three-quarters of a nail from the side, which forms the elbow. Curve from C to the bottom, at three-quarters of a nail from the side.

A WOMAN'S LARGE SLEEVE.
PLATE 12. FIG. 22, 23.

Turn up your material fourteen nails, and double it so as to be sixteen nails long at the top, A C E.

SCALE.

	Nails.
From A to B is	2
From A to C...	8
From C to E...	8
From E to F...	2
From F to G...	6
From G to H	3
From G to I	6
From I to J	7

Sweep gradually from B, past C, to F. Curve again from F to H. Cut in a straight line from H to J.

In making up, the sleeve may be biassed one nail from the top, and a piped band laid on, and again three or four times at the wrist, or it may be confined above the elbow; in which case it must be made a little longer than would otherwise be necessary.

This is a pattern that can only be used when large sleeves are worn; but, being a good shape, it is hoped it may prove acceptable.

SHORT SLEEVES.

PLATE 12. FIG. 24, 25, 26.

These are for dresses, frocks, or even petticoats, when full sleeves are worn and liked.

Cut the pattern of the whole sleeve in paper; and then, turning up your material to a sufficient size crosswise, lay the sleeve open upon it, placing the long side of the pattern upon the cross or doubled part of the material. Both sleeves may thus be cut out at once.

SCALE OF DIFFERENT SIZES.

——	Large size.	Second size.	Third size.	Girl's size.	Small girl's size.	Child's size.
	Nails.	Nails.	Nails.	Nails.	Nails.	Nails.
Turn up the material at the side	17	13	12	9	6½	5½
From A to B................................	3	2	3	2	1	1
From A to C................................	3	2	3	2	1	1
From C to B................................	2	1½	2	1½	¾	¾
From B to D................................	14	10	8	7½	5	4½
From D to E................................	15	11	9½	7	5	4½
From E to F................................	2	2	3	2	1½	1
From F to G................................	2	3	2½	2	1½	1
From H to I................................	6	5	4½	3½	2½	2
From C to G................................	20	14	12	9	7	6
Length of band, say.........................	5½	5	4½	4	3½	3¼

When cut out, fold each sleeve in half (see Fig. 26), and hollow one fold out to form the inside.

Take care to hollow the sleeves properly, so as to make a pair, the straight part of the sleeve being in front, which is to be hollowed. If the sleeve should require joining, sew two selvages together (see the dotted line, Fig. 25).

N

In making up, the bottom of the sleeve may be either set into a band, as in the Plate, or into a piping; at the top it is gathered, and frequently a piping is put round it, which gives it a neat finish: it is set into the dress quite plainly under the arms; the fulness is thrown a little back, for if brought too forward, it is very unbecoming to the figure.

SHORT SLEEVE.

PLATE 12. FIG. 27, 28, 29.

These are cut out exactly like Fig. 25, excepting that after the sleeve is simply cut out, a triangular piece is taken from the top of the doubled part of it, and a triangle of worked muslin inserted. To cut out this piece, double the sleeve, as in Fig. 29, and cut off from A to B: when opened again, it will resemble Fig. 28, and when made up, it will be like Fig. 27.

In making up, after setting the sleeve into a band or piping at the bottom, gather it at the top and sew it to the triangular piece, throwing the fulness pretty equally at the sides, and making it very full at the point of the triangle. Sometimes the triangle is piped to make it firmer.

CIRCULAR SHORT SLEEVE.

PLATE 12. FIG. 30, 31, 32.

This is another kind of short sleeve, being cut out of a circle. It is hollowed a little (see Fig. 30), A B, for the inside of the arm. A circular hole is cut in the centre, a little larger than the width of the arm; this inner circle is gathered and set into the band, and the outer one, also gathered, is sewed into the arm-hole of the dress.

The following are good sizes for circular sleeves, all of which must be cut out of squares.

SCALE.

——	Full size.	Second size.	Third size.	Girl's size.	Child's size.	Baby's size.
	Nails.	Nails.	Nails.	Nails.	Nails.	Nails.
Size of the square........................	18	15	$13\frac{1}{2}$	11	9	7
Size of the hole across..................	$3\frac{1}{2}$	$3\frac{1}{4}$	$3\frac{1}{4}$	$2\frac{1}{2}$	2	$1\frac{3}{4}$
Length of the band	$5\frac{1}{2}$	5	$4\frac{1}{2}$	4	$3\frac{1}{2}$	$3\frac{1}{4}$

TIGHT SLEEVE.

PLATE 12. FIG. 33, 34, 35.

This sleeve may be used either for petticoats, or, when tight sleeves are worn, for evening dresses, and children's frocks, in which case it is ornamented in different ways.

Turn up the material on the perfect cross, and for the better cutting it out, double it again, as in Fig. 33, on which four folds lay your pattern, D being the doubled part.

Turn up your material eight nails, then fold it from A to B, Fig. 35, and cut as follows, see Fig. 33:

SCALE.

	Nails.
From A to B..............................	3
From A to C..............................	3
From B to E..............................	$4\frac{1}{2}$
From E to F..............................	2
From F to G..............................	$3\frac{1}{2}$
From C to H..............................	$\frac{1}{2}$

Cut from B to C, sweep from B to F, and then cut from H, which is half a nail above C, to G.

PLATE 13

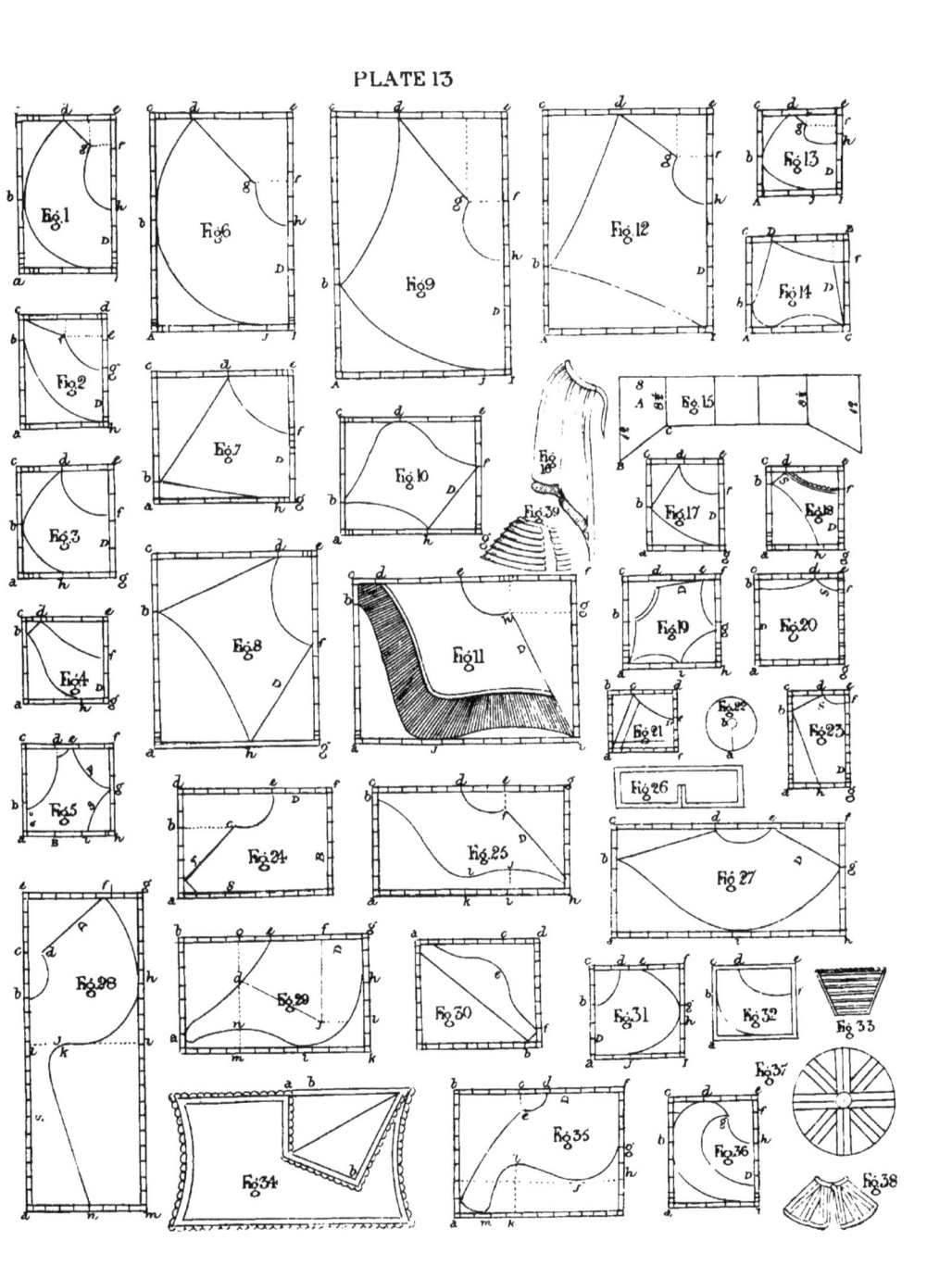

SHOULDER-PIECES, COLLARS, CAPES, &c.
PLATE 13.

As the above articles, together with pelerines, tippets, and collarets, are required for cloaks, gowns, pelisses, frocks, and dressing-gowns, it is advisable to class them under a head by themselves, by which means they can be more readily explained, without confusion or repetition, and the pattern wanted for any particular dress, referred to.

Patterns of the prettiest and most varied forms are selected, together with a few scales for different sizes.

OBSERVE that the Plates represent but half of the pattern, which is supposed to be double at the end marked D; also NOTICE, that they are drawn to a scale of the exact size of the pattern when *made up*, so that about a quarter of a nail must be allowed all round, for the turnings in. It is a good plan, when cutting out any difficult shape, to make a pattern on paper, very accurately, first; and then to lay it on the material and cut by it.

As it would be impossible to describe any intricate shape clearly, without putting it into some regular form, it is deemed necessary to enclose each pattern within an oblong or a square, on the sides of which are marked distinctly the nails, so that by making a figure on paper to a scale of real nails in the same proportion, and marking with great accuracy the parts, which the extreme points of the irregular pattern within, touch, the shape may be easily obtained by curving inwardly or outwardly from point to point, according to the shape to be represented in the drawing. It is always preferable to cut the above articles crosswise, both before and behind, as they set much better to the shape, especially behind; for the sake of economy, they are sometimes cut straight-wise with one end placed against the selvage; sometimes the collar or cape is joined behind with a neat piping, in which case the back of the pattern is frequently laid against the selvage and the points made to lie crosswise. The Plate represents the patterns as cut on the most economical plan, shewing whether the front or back should be straight-wise. Observe that if one side of the back be cut across, the other side must be so likewise, and if one side of the back be cut selvage-wise, so must the corresponding; whereas, with regard to the front ends, one side may be straight, while the other is on the cross.

IN CUTTING CROSSWISE.

Turn up a sufficient quantity of the corner of the material, like a half-handkerchief, and laying the pattern with the part marked D on the doubled part of the material, cut it out, allowing a quarter of a nail all round for the turning in.

IN CUTTING STRAIGHT-WISE.

Double the material selvage-wise to the proper width, and cut out according to the paper pattern, still placing D on the folded part of the muslin.

SHOULDER-PIECES.

Are generally employed in dressing-gowns, cloaks, and capes, also in boys' high dresses. It is the part to which the skirt or deep cape is fulled, and should be made to set particularly well to the figure, else the whole dress will have an awkward appearance.

In making up, the shoulder-pieces are generally lined, unless they are intended for any light article of dress. If they are meant for a cloak or warm cape, a piece of fine flannel or demet, is often put between the material of which the cloak is made and the lining, with a piping round the edge.

A NEAT SHOULDER-PIECE FOR A WOMAN'S CLOAK.

PLATE 13. FIG. 1.

SCALE.

	Nails.
Width of square when doubled	3⅛
Length of square	5¾
Space from A to B	2¾
Space from B to C	3
Space from C to D	1⅛
Space from D to E	2
Space from E to F	1
Space from F to G	1
Space from F to H	2⅛
Space from H to I	2¼

Shape off in a gradual curve from D to B, from B to I. Cut in a straight line from D to G. Slope from G to H.

SHOULDER-PIECE FOR A CHILD'S CLOAK.

PLATE 13. FIG. 2.

SCALE.

	Nails.
Length of square	4¼
Width of square when folded	3¼
Space from A to B	3
Space from B to C	1¼
Space from D to E	½
Space from E to F	1¾
Space from E to G	1¾
Space from G to H	2

Cut in a straight line from C to J. Curve gradually from F to G, and from B to H.

A VERY NEAT SHOULDER-PIECE FOR A WOMAN'S CLOAK.

PLATE 13. FIG. 3

SCALE.

———	Shoulder-piece.	Collar for a baby's cloak.
	Nails.	Nails.
Length of square	4¼	4
Width of square when double	3¾	3½
Space from A to B	2¼	1½
Space from B to C	2	2½
Space from C to D	1¾	1½
Space from D to E	2	2
Space from E to F	1¾	2
Space from F to G	2½	2
Space from G to H	1½	2

ON LINEN. 93

Form the curve from B to H, so as to end without abruptness, and be lost in the straight line. Round well from B to D.

SHOULDER-PIECE FOR A BABY'S CLOAK.
PLATE 13. FIG. 4.

SCALE.

	Nails.
Length of square	3
Width of square when doubled	3
Space from A to B	2¼
Space from B to C	¾
Space from C to D	¾
Space from D to E	2¼
Space from E to F	1¼
Space from F to G	1¼
Space from G to H	1

SHOULDER-PIECE TO A CHILD'S PELISSE.
PLATE 13. FIG. 5.

This shape is much in use for spencers, pelisses, and boys' high dresses. The part marked S sets over the shoulder when the sleeve is fulled on at the top. The parts marked B and F lie in the middle, exactly behind, and in front; thus the pattern shows half the shoulder-piece, the curve being for half-round the neck. The other half is piped and sewed on to it in front, and is fastened behind by buttons. The fulness of the body is then sewed on to this shoulder-piece, which is piped all round.

SCALE.

	Nails.
Length of square	3
Width of square	3¼
Space from A to B	¾
Space from B to C	2¼
Space from C to D	1¼
Space from D to E	¾
Space from E to F	1¼
Space from F to G	1¼
Space from G to H, and from H to L	1

VARIOUS SIZES FOR CAPES AND TIPPETS FOR WOMEN AND CHILDREN.
PLATE 13. FIG. 6.

Column 1. A woman's large cape for walking in.
Column 2. A woman's large cape for morning dress.
Column 3. A child's large cape for walking in.
Column 4. A woman's collar.
Column 5. A child's pretty cape for morning dress.
Column 6. A child's cape for a pelisse.
Column 7. Pretty cape for the morning dress of a child of four or five years old.
 The Plate represents the pattern in the fourth column.

THE WORKWOMAN'S GUIDE.

SCALE.

	No. 1.	No. 2.	No. 3.	No. 4.	No. 5.	No. 6.	No. 7.
	Nails.	Nails.	Nails.	Nails.	Nails.	Nails.	Nails.
Length of square	12¼	9¾	8½	7½	8	7¼	6¼
Width of square doubled	8¾	7¾	5½	5½	5	4¾	4¼
Width from A to B	6¼	4½	4½	4½	5	3	3
Width from B to C	6	5¼	4	3	3	4½	3¼
Width from C to D	3¾	2¼	1½	1½	2¼	2¾	1
Width from D to E	5	5½	4	3½	2¼	2	3¼
Width from E to F	2¾	1¼	2¼	1¼	2½	2	1
Width from F to G	1½	1¾	1¼	1¾	½	¾	1
Width from F to H	2¼	2	1¾	1¾	1½	1¾	3¼
Width from H to I	7	5¼	4½	4½	4	3¼	3¼
Width from I to J	3¼	3	¾	½	1	¾	

PLATE 13. FIG. 7.

Column 1. A neat collar for a woman's cloak or dressing gown.
Column 2. Rather smaller pattern of the above.
Column 3. A very neat collar for a girl of fourteen.
Column 4. A collar for a baby's flannel cloak.
   The Plate represents column 2.

SCALE.

	No. 1.	No. 2.	No. 3.	No. 4.
	Nails.	Nails.	Nails.	Nails.
Length of square	5½	5	4½	4
Width of square when doubled	5¾	5¼	5¼	5
Space from A to B	1¾	1	corner rounded	½
Space from B to C	3¾	4	4	3¼
Space from C to D	3¼	3	2	2
Space from D to E	2¼	2¼	3¼	3
Space from E to F	2¼	2¼	1¼	1
Space from F to G	3	2¾	3¼	3
Space from G to H	½	½		

In column 3, mark one quarter of a nail above the corner, G, and slope off in a direct line from the mark to the opposite corner, A, which is merely rounded off at the corner, about a quarter of a nail on each side.

PLATE 13. FIG. 8.

A pretty collar to put on a silk mourning shawl, or for a dress or cloak. Both the back and front must be on the cross.

ON LINEN.

SCALE.

	Nails.
Length of square	7¼
Width of square	6¼
Space from A to B	5¼
Space from B to C	2
Space from C to D	5
Space from D to E	1¼
Space from E to F	3½
Space from F to G	4
Space from G to H	2½

A PARTICULARLY NEAT AND WELL-SETTING CAPE.

PLATE 13. FIG. 9.

SCALE.

	Nails.
Length of square	12
Width of square when doubled	8
Space from A to B	4
Space from B to C	8
Space from C to D	3
Space from D to E	5
Space from E to F	3¼
Space from F to G	2
Space from F to H	3
Space from H to I	5¼
Space from I to J	1½

PLATE 13. FIG. 10, 11.

Fig. 11 is a very pretty pattern for a walking cape, and is often worn in mourning, with black crape gaufiered round the edge a nail deep, as in the Plate. Fig. 10 is a simple collaret, which is sewed on the cape to give it a finish.

SCALE TO FIG. 10.

	Nails.
Length of square	4¼
Width of square when doubled	5½
Space from A to B	1
Space from B to C	3¼
Space from C to D	2¼
Space from D to E	3
Space from E to F	2
Space from F to G	2¼
Space from G to H	2

SCALE TO FIG. 11.

	Nails.
Length of square	7½
Width of square when doubled	10½
Space from A to B	6½
Space from B to C	1
Space from C to D	1
Space from D to E	4
Space from E to F	5¼
Space from F to G	1¼
Space from G to H	3
Space from G to I	6
Space from I to J	7

A REMARKABLY NEAT MORNING COLLAR.

PLATE 13. FIG. 12.

SCALE.

	Nails.
Length of square	10
Width of square when doubled	7½
Space from A to B	2¾
Space from B to C	7¼
Space from C to D	3½
Space from D to E	4
Space from E to F	2
Space from F to G	1½
Space from F to H	2¼
Space from H to I	5¼

A PRETTY LITTLE CAPE FOR A BABY'S CLOAK OR PELISSE.

PLATE 13. FIG. 13

SCALE.

	Nails.
Length of square	3¼
Width of square when doubled	3
Space from A to B	1¼
Space from B to C	2
Space from C to D	1¼
Space from D to E	1¾
Space from E to F	½
Space from F to G	1
Space from F to H	¾
Space from H to I	2

SMALL COLLAR TO BE SEWED TO A HABIT-SHIRT.

PLATE 13. FIG. 14.

SCALE.

	Nails.
Length of square	4
Width of square when doubled	4¼
Space from A to B	1
Space from B to C	3
Space from C to D	1
Space from D to E	3¼
Space from E to F	1
Space from F to G	3

PLATE 13. FIG. 15, 16.

Fig. 15, is the pattern of a very handsome long pointed cape, commonly worn to rich silk cloaks, and sometimes alone; when that is the case, they are frequently made of velvet or fine cloth, and trimmed with fur or swan's down.

The cape is made as follows:—Sew together three breadths of the material, eight nails and a half long and about eight nails wide (of course a less number of breadths will be required, if the material be much wider, as merinos, &c.), to each end of the three breadths thus sewed in one length, add another breadth, which, as in Fig. 15 (see A), is eight and a half nails deep at one end, and twelve nails deep at the other, the material being cut in a straight line from B to C.

A GOOD SHAPE FOR A LADY'S RIDING COLLAR, TO BE SEWED TO A HABIT SHIRT.

PLATE 13. FIG. 17.

SCALE.

	Nails.
Length of square	4
Width of square when doubled	4
Space from A to B	2
Space from B to C	2
Space from C to D	1¼
Space from D to E	2¼
Space from E to F	1¾
Space from F to G	2¼

These collars are made of a doubled piece of lawn, which being run together and turned inside out, are neatly stitched near the edge like gentlemen's collars.

A CHEMISETTE DE VIERGE, MODESTY, OR TUCKER.

PLATE 13. FIG. 18.

This is but a quarter of the article, and when the paper pattern is made from the drawing, it should be doubled, so that when cut, it forms half the chemisette, which if it is again laid on a piece of muslin or net doubled, the two sides may be cut at once.

Chemisettes are worn under evening dresses, and are trimmed with blonde, lace, or muslin edging, which should just be seen above the gown. The part marked S is the shoulder. The chemisette is put on over the head and draws round the waist by a tape.

SCALE.

	Nails.
Length of square	4¾
Width of square	4¼
Space from A to B	3¾
Space from B to C	1
Space from C to D	1
Space from D to E	3¼
Space from E to F	1½
Space from F to G	3¾

A BABY'S COLLERETTE.

PLATE 13. FIG. 19.

This is particularly neat for a baby's pelisse, and may be sewed on to the shoulder-piece. (Fig. 5.)

SCALE.

	Nails.
Length of square	3¾
Width of square when doubled	4
Space from A to B	2¼
Space from B to C	1½
Space from C to D	1¼
Space from D to E	2
Space from E to F	¾
Space from F to G	2½
Space from G to H	1¼
Space from H to I	1½

This collerette should be piped all round, and edged with work, excepting the curve, which goes half round the neck. Two half collerettes must be cut, one for the right, and one for the left side of the neck.

A HABIT SHIRT.

PLATE 13. FIG. 20, 23.

Fig. 23 represents half of the back of a habit shirt. Fig. 20, one of the two fronts which are sewed on to the back at the shoulder, the parts marked in each figure, S, being the corresponding pieces.

SCALE TO FIG. 23.

	Nails.
Length of the square	8½
Width of the square when doubled	4
Space from A to B	6½
Space from B to C	2
Space from C to D	2¼
Space from D to E	1¼
Space from E to F	1

This back, which, of course is cut in the whole piece, has a tape passed through a hem at the bottom, which tape also passes through the hems at the bottom of the two fronts, and ties before.

SCALE TO FIG. 20.

	Nails.
Length of the square	6¼
Width of the square	6
Space from A to B	5¼
Space from B to C	1
Space from C to D	4
Space from D to E	2
Space from E to F	1¼
Space from F to G	5

This figure represents one of the fronts of the habit-shirt; the part marked D is the front, S is the shoulder; where the two fronts meet they may be fastened by small buttons, and sometimes work is let in, or narrow tucks made, which have a neat effect. Below the shoulder, and down the front, it is finished with a narrow hem. A collar may be sewed to it at the neck, by a mantua-maker's hem.

A MOURNING COLLAR.
PLATE 13. FIG. 21.

Made of clear muslin, white crape, widow's lawn, net or tulle, with a broad hem one nail deep all round.

SCALE.

	Nails.
Length of square	5¼
Width of square	6
From A to B	5¼
From B to C	2¼
From C to D	3¼
From D to E	2¼
From E to F	3

The hems to these collars are generally laid on, by being run at the edge, and then turned back and hemmed, this is a much neater plan than any other. Sometimes two collars with deep hems are worn one above the other.

For mourning collars of net with either a broad hem, frills with deep hems, or gaufiered frills are used. If the mourning is very deep, the muslin collar is covered with black crape.

A ROUND CAPE OR TIPPET.
PLATE 13. FIG. 22.

No scale can be made to this tippet, as the size is only determined according to the purpose for which it is to be used. Form a perfect circle, and slit from the outer edge of the circle A to the centre B, after which cut out a piece for the neck. This is a very good shape for school-girls, it also makes a useful dressing or combing tippet.

100   THE WORKWOMAN'S GUIDE.

A HABIT SHIRT.
PLATE 13. FIG. 94.

This is a very simple neat shape for a habit shirt. T is the front, and D the middle of the back. It is all cut in one piece, and the part marked B may be laid against the selvage; S is the shoulder.

SCALE.

	Nails.
Length of square	6
Width of square	10
Space from A to B	4
Space from B to C	3
Space from B to D	2
Space from D to E	6
Space from E to F	4

Cut in a straight line from C to A, and square the corner off at A.

A PELERINE.
PLATE 13. FIG. 95.

The back is on the cross and the front is straight.

SCALE.

	Nails.
Length of oblong	7
Width of oblong when doubled	13
Space from A to B	6¼
Space from B to C	¼
Space from C to D	6
Space from D to E	3
Space from E to F	1
Space from E to G	4
Space from H to I	4
Space from I to J	1¼
Space from I to K	3
Space from K to L	¼

PLATE 13. FIG. 96.

This is a very simple collar, and much worn by persons of quiet unassuming habits. It is composed of two oblong strips of muslin, hemmed all round with rather a broad hem, and sewed together at the ends half the way up. Each oblong is four nails long and about three nails deep.

A REMARKABLY PRETTY PELERINE FOR A MORNING DRESS.
PLATE 13. FIG. 27.

SCALE.

	Nails.
Length of square	5
Width of square	11
Space from A to B	3½
Space from B to C	1½
Space from C to D	5
Space from D to E	2¼
Space from E to F	3½
Space from F to G	2
Space from F to H	3
Space from H to I	5

ON LINEN.

PLATE 13. FIG. 28.

This is the pattern of a very handsome long pelerine. The part marked S must be laid along the selvage. Of course this is in two parts, both of which will nearly lie side by side on the opposite selvages of the same breadth.

SCALE.

	Nails.
Length of the square	21
Width of the square	8
Space from A to B	14
Space from B to C	3
Space from C to D	1
Space from D to E	4
Space from E to F	5¼
Space from F to G	2¼
Space from G to H	6
Space from H to I	4
Space from I to J	5¼
Space from I to K	1
Space from K to L	1¼
Space from I to M	11
Space from M to N	4

A HANDSOME SHAPE FOR A PELERINE WITH A SQUARE COLLAR.

PLATE 13. FIG. 29.

SCALE.

	Nails.
Length of square	7
Width of square when doubled	12
Space from A to B	6¼
Space from B to C	4
Space from C to D	2¼
Space from C to E	2
Space from E to F	3
Space from F to G	3
Space from G to H	4
Space from H to I	1
Space from I to J	3
Space from I to K	2
Space from K to L	4
Space from L to M	4¼
Space from M to N	2

The letters E, F, J, and D, point out the shape of the upper collar.

PLATE 13. FIG. 30.

This is a frill to go over each shoulder of a cape or pelerine, as a finish, and is peculiarly adapted to Fig. 25, 27.

SCALE TO FIG. 30.

	Nails.
Length of the square	8
Width of the square	10

Draw a straight line across from A to B, which are situated one nail within the corners of the square.

SCALE.

	Nails.
Space from the corner to C	7
Space from C to E	2
Space from C to D	3¼
Space from F to the corner	1

Curve, according to the pattern, from the corner to E. The cross part is then fulled on to the pelerine, leaving about two nails from the front and back points.

A CAPE FOR A BABY'S PELISSE.
PLATE 13. FIG. 31.

SCALE.

	Nails.
Length of square	5
Width of square when doubled	5
Space from A to B	3
Space from B to C	2
Space from C to D	1¼
Space from D to E	1
Space from E to F	2¼
Space from F to G	1¼
Space from G to H	1
Space from H to I	2¼
Space from I to J	3

ANOTHER SHOULDER-PIECE, OR NEAT COLLAR.
PLATE 13. FIG. 32.

If used for the latter, it may be made with a hem all round, through which a coloured or white satin ribbon may be drawn of about twopenny width. A single or double frill of net should be sewed round it, with a corresponding hem for ribbon. This frill, after the hem is made, should be a full nail deep.

SCALE.

	Nails.
Length of square	4
Width of square when doubled	4
Space from A to B	2
Space from B to C	2
Space from C to D	1¼
Space from D to E	2¼
Space from E to F	1¼

A MODESTY, OR TUCKER.
PLATE 13. FIG. 33.

This little front, or modesty, is to put inside a low dress, and may be made very prettily. The materials most in use for them are cambric, lawn, muslin, net, tulle, satin, or crape. They are generally

ON LINEN.

tucked, or in folds, or frilled into strips of insertion-work, either the length or the width-way, and always trimmed with a little work or edging on the top. When made, they are about three nails deep, and five nails wide at the top, and tapering to three nails at the waist. They are almost always made the straight way, particularly when they are intended to wash.

A SIMPLE COLLAR.
PLATE 13. FIG. 34.

This is a particularly simple pretty collar, and is frequently made of net or muslin, trimmed with narrow work or muslin. It has a broad hem all round, through which satin ribbon is passed. The collar is merely a straight piece, eight nails deep and fourteen nails wide. Double it in half lengthwise, and also width-wise to find the centre, and then cut in a straight line from A B, at the top, to the centre. The points, A B, each fall over, as seen in the Plate, and give the appearance of a second collar. The ends should be a little hollowed out, to make the whole set better.

ANOTHER HANDSOME PELERINE.
PLATE 13. FIG. 35.

SCALE.

	Nails.
Length of square	8
Width of square	11
Space from A to B	8
Space from B to C	4
Space from C to D	1¼
Space from C to E	2
Space from D to F	5
Space from F to G	4
Space from G to H	2
Space from H to I	2¼
Space from H to J	2
Space from J to K	7
Space from K to L	3
Space from K to M	2

The corner or tip to be rounded off, beginning at two nails from A, at the bottom, to one nail above A, at the side.

A ROUND COLLAR.
PLATE 13. FIG. 36.

This is a small and simple shape for a round collar, with a smaller one upon it. When the larger is cut, the lesser one may be cut by the eye, only taking notice to shape it off more abruptly in front than the other.

SCALE.

	Nails.
Length of square	6¼
Width of square	5¼
Space from A to B	3¼
Space from B to C	3
Space from C to D	1¼
Space from D to E	3¼
Space from E to F	¾
Space from F to G	1¼
Space from F to H	2¼
Space from H to I	3¼

A SCHOOL-GIRL'S TIPPET.
PLATE 16. FIG. 37, 38.

This is an economical mode of making tippets for poor children, or charity schools, of remnants of cloth, print, &c. Cut a circle in paper, of the right size, and pin it on the carpet or table cloth, whilst you arrange strips of your material on it, in regular lines, as in the Fig.; two or three strips may cross each other at right angles; between them should be other straight pieces, and then triangular bits will fill up the circle. Black, orange, crimson, blue, and brown cloth, look very well.

ANOTHER SCHOOL-GIRL'S TIPPET.
PLATE 16. FIG. 39. (Near to FIG. 10, 16.)

This is made of the list of flannel, the selvage of cloth, or any other warm material, and is sewed on to calico; cut a lining in the shape required, and beginning at the bottom, place layer above layer, or strip above strip, something in the way that the many capes of a coachman's great coat are done: the list or cloth is not put on quite flat, but is a very little fulled. It is then lined with flannel or cloth, and is a most comfortable and strong tippet.

PETTICOATS.
PLATE 14.

Petticoats are made of calico, twill, dimity, cambric, and jaconet muslin, sometimes for mourning, or for wearing under thin dresses of silk and satin: for the middling and lower classes, they are of calico, strong dimity, calimanco, stuff, and bombazine: they are made in various ways, which will be described in the following pages, and the patterns given: the figures and sizes of persons differ so essentially that scales will not be attempted.

Petticoats are in three distinct parts—the skirt, the body, and the sleeves, the varieties of each will be treated of in their turn.

SKIRTS.

Skirts have generally from two, to two and a half breadths in them, according to the width of the material of which they are made: they are sometimes finished at the bottom with a deep hem, three nails broad, tucks, or worked muslin. Sometimes they are bought with cotton runners, woven in them at the bottom, six or eight nails deep, which make the dress stand out, and if the gown is of a clinging material, causes it to hang better. Skirts are generally made with the opening behind, but for elderly persons or servants, it is at the sides, the seams being left unsewed for about four nails from the top; sometimes they are furnished with pockets on one or both sides; for a description of which, see Pockets. Skirts may be set on to the body, either equally full all round, plain under the arms, and full at the front and back, or with all the fulness behind. Servants frequently wear their petticoats merely set into a tape round the waist, without any body, and with or without tape shoulder-straps, to keep them up. Under or middle petticoats are also made in this manner.

BODIES OR WAISTS.

These are made either full or tight to the figure.

Tight or plain bodies consist of five parts: the front, two side-pieces, and two backs (see Fig. 1). The front is always cut on the cross, and reaches from below one arm to the other: the side-pieces are also cut crosswise on one side, and straight on the other, the straight side being joined to the front, and that which is cross being stitched to the backs, which are straight behind. Fig. 1 represents a tight

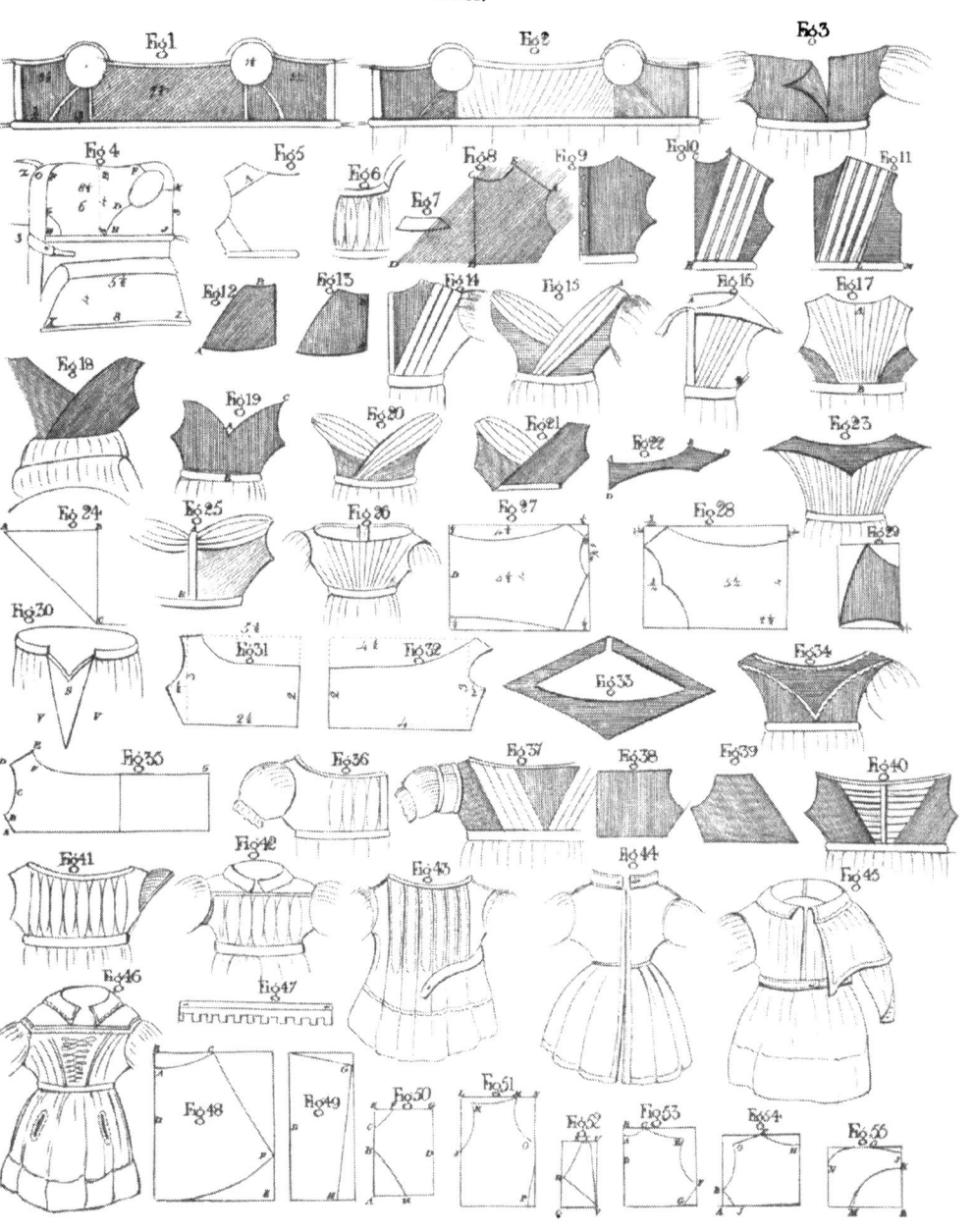

PLATE 14.

ON LINEN.

body made up, for a small person. Observe that the various directions of the lines drawn on the engravings, represents the selvage-way of the material, as a better guide for the inexperienced. In making up, all the parts should be back-stitched together; the band ought to be very strong; it is often made of webbing or stout tape. Petticoat bodies may be made with or without sleeves, according to the taste of the wearer.

Full bodies are made in a similar manner to tight ones, excepting that two nails more are added in width to the front, so that when laid open it is ten nails and a half at its greatest extent, instead of only seven and a half, like the plain body, and half a nail is also given to each back. The front is cut straight instead of cross, in the full bodies. (See Plate 14, Fig. 2.)

SLEEVES.

For figures of sleeves, see Plate 12 and the descriptions annexed.

NURSING PETTICOATS.

PLATE 14.

For the convenience of those mothers who nurse their infants, the petticoat body in front may be opened in various ways.

PLATE 14. FIG. 3.

The most general mode is simply to have the front of the body in two pieces, so as to open in the middle before, hemming it on each side, and letting the parts tie or button together at the top: it is as well to set the two sides of the front into the band, so that they may over-lap each other, in order to guard against cold. This petticoat fastens behind in the usual manner.

PLATE 14. FIG. 4.

Another approved method is that of having the petticoat open on each side in front, so as to be close at the back. This petticoat body is made in four parts: one back, two side pieces, one front. The back piece is cut the straight way, so as to let A B, Fig. 4, lie selvage-wise.

SCALE.

	Nails.
Depth from A to B	4
Width from G to D	6
Width from F to F	8¼
Slope it down to H H	1¼
Side-piece from below the arm to the waist	2¼
From H to J	4
From J to K cut straight-wise	3
Length of shoulder-straps	2
Breadth of shoulder-straps	1

The shoulder-straps connect the top of the side-piece with the top of the back. The front of the body is in one piece, being eight nails wide at the top, sloped down to five nails and a half at the bottom; it is four nails deep in the middle, but being hollowed out, is half a nail deeper at the sides. This front has a broad hem all round it, and is set into a band, which is attached to the front breadth of the skirt, the seam on each side of this breadth being open for the space of four nails. Tapes are attached to the band of the back breadth, and tie in front; buttons are set on, to within a nail of the end of the band below the side pieces, to which the band of the front buttons on each side, and by this means overlaps the opening: button-holes are also made at the two corners of the front (see X Z), which correspond with the buttons on the shoulder-strap, Z. The left hand side of Fig. 4 represents the petticoat with the body drawn forward, as if for the purpose of tying it, while the opposite side shows it as if thrown back, ready to put the arm into the sleeve. The front is unfastened and has fallen down.

GOWNS.
PLATE 14.

Gowns being a part of dress much influenced by the fashion or custom of the day, will not be fully entered on in this work, as it would be impossible to give the variety of form and size which is seen in them, and equally impossible, were a selection attempted, to please all tastes, or suit all figures: a few simple patterns for those kinds which are independent of fashion, and especially for those worn by servants, and persons engaged in laborious employments, with a very few other plain ones, will alone come within the limits of the work.

Those commonly worn by servants, and the working classes, are of print, linen, stuff, and for best, light ginghams, merino, or bombazine; ladies wear muslin, gingham, silk, merino, and for dress, either lighter or richer materials, as satins, velvets, gauzes, &c.

GENERAL OBSERVATIONS.

The bodies of working gowns should be lined with strong linen, which is preferable to calico, as it does not shrink in the washing; they should be of dark and good washing colours, deep blue and lilac are the best for wear.

It is a good plan to line silk and merino, or stuff gown bodies, with strong linen or brown Holland, as it keeps them in shape, by preventing them from stretching.

In buying striped dresses, be careful that the stripes run selvage-wise, otherwise they are very unbecoming. In making up the bodies, the stripes should lie in the same direction, and not cross-wise from shoulder to shoulder.

Checks or plaids are rarely becoming when they are large: for children they should be particularly small and narrow, the colours should not be too bright or gay, but sufficiently contrasted and decided, to give a clear clean effect; plaids of which the colours are pale and indistinct never look very well; and after wearing a short time appear faded and shabby.

Checks are becoming to tall people, and stripes to short ones, as the former rather diminish, while the latter give an appearance of greater length to the figure than is natural to it, in the same way that a striped paper makes a room look higher, than one which is checked, or of which the pattern goes round instead of from top to bottom.

Broad hems and deep flounces also tend to lessen the height, it may therefore be taken as a general rule that tall persons should endeavour to add to their width, by making all the accompaniments to their dress as full and wide, as is consistent with the reigning taste, while those who are short, should let all theirs be as moderate as possible.

The same observations will also apply to stout and thin persons; for the former, all trimmings of the bodies in front, such as rouleaux, folds, and straps, should, generally speaking, be carried from the shoulder to the waist, in preference to being laid on cross-wise; while with those who are of a slighter make, it is merely a matter of fancy, only remarking that every advantage of fulness should be given them.

If the trimming of a dress does not exactly match it, care should be taken to select it darker than the dress itself. Waistbands, when shaded, or of two colours, should be always worn with the darkest shade or colour at the bottom of the waist.

The complexion should determine the choice of colours. Persons of a sallow or muddy complexion should carefully avoid bright and glaring, or on the other hand, undecided colours; such as yellow, cherry colour, light green, buff, or drab; clear tints are more suitable to them, as white, light blue, violet, or black.

Those with pale but clear complexions, may wear all the shades of rose colour, primrose, apricot, buff, light green, lilac, brown, and violet.

Fair persons with a colour, will find few shades decidedly unbecoming; perhaps it will be as well for them not to wear buff.

Dark olive or brown complexions should avoid either very dark or very light colours, but they should be careful to select clear tints: pink, geranium, and violet are the most decidedly suitable to them.

On all occasions let the old saying be kept in mind,

"Gaudy colours strike the eye,
And magnify deformity."

These remarks may seem superfluous to some, but as attention to the minutiæ of dress adds much to a lady-like and refined appearance, and as an endeavour to please by an agreeable exterior, does not necessarily involve a disposition to vanity and frivolity, it is hoped that they will not be hastily condemned.

GENERAL OBSERVATIONS ON CUTTING OUT DRESSES.

It would be useless to form scales for the different kinds of dresses, as shapes vary so much, therefore none will be introduced, excepting for children and young persons; as, however, this article of dress forms one of the most important parts of a person's wardrobe, all general observations for cutting out, that can be reduced to rule, will be given as clearly as the subject will admit of, at the same time, it is strongly recommended to all those who can afford it, to have their best dresses invariably made by a mantua-maker, as those which are cut out at home seldom fit so comfortably, or look so well, as when made by persons in constant practice. To those who have large families or limited means, it certainly is a great saving of expense having them made at home, and to such, the following rules may be useful. It would be very advisable, *as a practice*, for persons little acquainted with cutting out, to purchase cheap print for poor children's dress and by fitting them on, much experience and nicety might be acquired at little waste or expense.

In making a dress for any body, the following measurements should be taken with a piece of common tape.

From the waist to the bottom of the skirt.
From the nape of the neck to the waist behind.
Round the waist.
Round the wrist.
From the shoulder to the wrist, with the arm bent.

In sending to London or elsewhere for a dress or riding habit, of which the exact measure is required, observe the following directions for transmitting measure in inches:—

1. Height of the person, observing if they stand upright.
2. The length of the arm from the centre of the back to the elbow, and thence to the knuckles.
3. The circumference of the body, over the full part of the chest.
4. The circumference of the smallest part of the waist.
5. Length of the nape of the neck to the waist, and thence to the ground.
6. From the front of the armpit to the centre of the bosom, thence to the chest.
7. From the nape of the neck, over the shoulder, to the centre of the bosom, and thence to the waist immediately under it.

PLATE 14.

The bodies of dresses contain various parts, called the fronts, the backs, the side-pieces, the shoulder-straps, the shoulder-pieces, collars, &c., &c. These parts are variously employed and differently cut out, according to the style of the dress, sometimes being on the cross, and sometimes on the straight-way.

Observe that the lines in the engravings denote, by their direction, which way the selvage side of the material runs. For the purpose of making this quite clear, let it be supposed that these lines represent stripes which run along or down the selvage.

Linings should always be cut to lie the same direction as the material of the gown.

In cutting out a dress, it is usual to fit the lining upon the figure, and cut out the gown from it, though, with an inexperienced person, it would be advisable to fit on the gown also, if the dress is to be full, or in folds.

Gowns are high, low, three-quartered, plain, or full, open before or behind, all of which sorts will be treated of in their proper order.

SIDE-PIECES.
PLATE 14. FIG. 12, 13.

Most dresses have side-pieces or bits under the arm, to join the backs to the fronts. These side-pieces are cut variously. For stout persons, the selvage-way or stripe should run from the extreme point at the bottom of the back of the side-piece, A, towards the middle of the top, B, of Fig. 12. For slight figures, the selvage-way or stripe should run along, or nearly along the front of the side-piece, thus A B, in Fig. 13.

The size of a side-piece depends much upon the figure and fashion. It should never, however, be brought much forwarder than under the middle of the arm-hole. It varies very much at the back, sometimes being brought but just behind the arm-hole, at others to within a nail of the middle of the back. The side-piece is sometimes cut straight at the back, and at others in a kind of half-arch; the latter is required for stout persons.

BACK SHOULDER PIECES.
PLATE 14. FIG. 5.

These are not necessary to the set of the gown, and are seldom introduced, unless it is the reigning fashion, or for the better cutting up of the material. When these are used, of course shoulder-straps are unnecessary, as they connect the backs with the fronts. A represents a back shoulder-piece.

SHOULDER-STRAPS.
PLATE 14. FIG. 6, 7.

These are mere straps to connect the fronts and backs, and lie over the shoulder. The straps are always double and are generally sloped at each end, so as to be wider next the sleeve than at the shoulder or neck (see Fig. 7).

SKIRTS.

These vary very much as to the number of breadths, according to fashion and material. Thin clinging materials, as muslin, require more breadths than thick or standing out articles of dress, as silk-gauze, velvet, &c.; six, seven, or eight breadths are worn now for full dresses, but formerly four breadths were deemed sufficient. They are usually lined with thin glazed muslin, unless the dress is very heavy as stuff, merino, &c., it is economical to line the skirt, as it keeps the dress cleaner and makes it look better if turned.

A PLAIN HIGH BODY.
PLATE 14. FIG. 8.

For stout persons, indeed for the generality of figures, it is preferable to have the fronts of the body in two pieces, with a piping up the middle. In cutting out a high plain body, lay the material upon the person as follows:—

Let the selvage-way or stripe of the cloth lie in the direction from the extreme point of the shoulder, A (see Fig. 8), to the middle of the waist, B. In doing this, pin it at a sufficient distance from the selvage of the material to allow of plenty to cover the front. Thus, pin the material on at A B, which is some distance from the selvage, C D. Stroke the material up to the neck in front and hollow out at the neck, putting pins at C E. The front is thus thrown quite on the cross, up the middle. Do the same on the opposite side. Hollow out towards the arm, and cut off where it meets the side-piece. The back pieces, Fig. 9, always have the selvage up the middle, and are properly fitted to the figure till they meet the side-pieces.

In making up, a piping is laid along each seam, and the edges of the lining, and the dress should be well overcast. The sleeves have piping also round them. The backs should have broad hems, and, together with the waist, be lined with a strong tape or calico.

A FULL FRENCH HIGH BODY.
PLATE 14. FIG. 10, 11, 14.

This body is also in two parts in front. The material is pinned for the selvage-way, or stripe to run from the side of the neck or collar bone, A, to the middle of the waist, B (in Fig. 10), so as to throw the part up the front but slightly on the cross. Put strong pins in at A B C, to keep the material firm, and then commence laying the material in plaits (see Fig. 11), slanting from the shoulder towards the waist, folding them much deeper at the waist than at the top; five, six, or seven of these plaits are sufficient. In laying them along they should be arranged so that when the last plait is formed, and the plain part of the body pinned under the arm, the selvage-way or stripe should lie almost parallel with, or along with, the waist (see L M, in Fig. 11).

The backs, Fig. 14, are always selvage-way up the middle; the plaits, about three in number, should lie from the shoulder to the middle of the waist in a fan-like direction. They will almost form themselves properly at the top on the shoulder, if first properly pinned on the waist, and the material held up, and slightly pulled or shaken above the shoulder, with one hand, while the other arranges them. They will naturally fall in deeper folds below than above.

A WRAP HIGH DRESS.
PLATE 14. FIG. 15.

This has two fronts, to be cut out as follows:—

Lay the merino, or other material, selvage or stripe-wise from the top of the shoulder, A, to a little beyond the middle of the waist, so as to throw the body a little on the cross up the middle.

The plaits must be formed, while on the person, one after another, slanting from the shoulder, across the middle, to the opposite side of the waist. These plaits should be so folded, as to make the plain part, under the arm, fall selvage-wise along the band.

The back is made to correspond, the selvage is straight up the back, and the material being held tightly above the shoulder at the top, with one hand, the three or four plaits are the more easily arranged by the other, and should be folded over more deeply at the bottom than upon the shoulder. These plaits should exactly meet the others on the shoulder.

The backs and fronts join under the arm without side-pieces. In making up, the plaits should be secured on the shoulder, with a pipe or strap, and again secured about half a nail on each side of the shoulder. The fronts cross, or wrap over, and are well secured to the waistband.

A HIGH FULL GOWN, TO OPEN IN FRONT.
PLATE 14. FIG. 16, 17.

These are particularly suitable for house-maids, dairy or kitchen-maids, chair and washerwomen; they should be made of the strongest print, at 8*d.* or 1*s.* per yard. It is bad economy to buy a cheap poor material for a working dress, under the idea that it will do very well for common purposes, when it is of importance that they should stand a good deal of wear and tear.

For a young person, the skirt is in three breadths of extra-width print, of about eighteen nails; the seams must be sewed up, making one come in the front, which must overlap half a nail down the whole length of the skirt, leaving the hem or seam open for about four nails below the waist. The body is six pieces, having one back, two fronts, two side-pieces, and one collar.

The two fronts are selvage-wise up the middle, and are cut as follows:—Pin the material selvage-wise at A, and at the bottom, lay it in plaits or fullings along the shoulder, to lie towards the waist, and smooth the plain part to fit the shape, till it meets the side-piece, cut it off, and hollow it under the arm. The back piece, Fig. 17, is in one piece with the selvage, to lie up the middle; therefore, pin it firmly at the middle of the top, A, and at the waist just below, B. Lay the material on each side in fullings or plaits, pinning them down here and there, and, after arranging them at the top, along the back and shoulders, smooth down the plain part, hollow out at the arm-holes, and cut along the shoulders. Cut the side-piece next, and then make a neat simple collar; one like Fig. 7, in Plate 13, would be very suitable. In making up, after cutting out your tight lining, lay each part of the gown upon each piece of the lining, and begin to stitch strongly together all the pieces, laying a piping up every seam, and over-casting the rough edges inside, to make them wear well and look neat. The sleeves are short (see Fig. 24, in Plate 12). The collar and arm-holes are also piped.

Make a broad hem up each side of the front, and put the body into the band; let the fulness be pretty even along the piping on the shoulder, but bring it rather towards the middle of the waist-band, in front.

The fulness behind is regular along the shoulders and collar, but drawn towards the centre of the back, at the band. Sew the body on the skirt, put strings or bands, of the same material, of about one nail wide, to tie the dress at the throat. The waist-band is one nail deep and about eleven nails long, and can either button or fasten with a strong hook and eye in front.

A HIGH BODY, TO OPEN IN FRONT.
PLATE 14. FIG. 18.

This shape is often worn by elderly ladies, sometimes by servants, and is convenient, as it enables the wearer to dress herself without the assistance of a maid. The gown is open down the two seams at the sides for about four or five nails, so that the front ties round the waist like an apron, being of course well fulled in front into a band, to which strings are attached. The slits at the sides form pocket holes.

The body is sewed on to the skirt behind and opens in front. It has one back, which, if full, is cut with the selvage-way or stripe to lie straight down from the neck to the waist, but if plain, it should be on the cross. The fronts are generally on the cross with the material cut to lie with the stripe or selvage-way, from the extreme point of the shoulder to the middle of the waist. The fronts are continued so as to pin down at the waist, one across the other, over which the front breadth or apron ties.

PLAIN LOW BODY.

Pin the material with the selvage-way or stripe, to lie from the extreme point of the shoulder to the middle of the waist, so as to throw the body quite on the cross up the middle, which is joined with a piping. The backs are always selvage-wise up the middle. Join the backs and fronts with a piping on the shoulder, also at the seams, for the side-pieces. Stitch up the plaits that are made at the bosoms.

ANOTHER FRENCH LOW PLAIN FRONT.
PLATE 14. FIG. 19.

This is in five pieces, two backs, one front, and two side-pieces. The front is all in one piece, and in cutting it out, the material is pinned with the selvage-way or stripe up the middle. Pin it firmly at A and B, at the top and bottom of the middle of the body. Lay the material along to the shoulders, and pin it down again at C. Slope with the scissors from the point of the shoulder to a peak down at the front. The backs are likewise cut selvage-wise up the middle, and peaked from the back to the shoulders: the side-pieces are joined to the front and back by a piping. Make the bosom plaits and stitch them up.

VARIOUS MODES OF TRIMMING LOW BODIES WHEN TIGHT TO THE FIGURE.
PLATE 14.

Tight or plain bodies require some ornament or finish to set them off, a few neat methods of putting on folds, &c., will therefore be explained.

Plate 14, Fig. 20, represents a plain body with the folds sewed on. These folds are in two parts one for each side of the body in front. They are cut crosswise and are only suitable to those gowns which are not of a washing material, they should be from nine to ten nails wide, and as long as will reach from the shoulder to the middle of the waist. In making them up stitch them firmly down on the shoulder in regular plaits, and again about a nail in front of the shoulder. Arrange them as regularly at the waist, sewing them firmly into the middle of the band, exactly to meet or correspond with the folds of the other side.

Plate 14, Fig. 21, represents a plain body with loose folds upon it, the body is made exactly like that of a petticoat, the front may or may not be in two parts, according to pleasure, and convenience;

if there is a joining, a piping should be laid between the two parts. If the dress is of a washing material, the folds should be the stright-way, and the cross-way if it is not.

The straight folds are merely a piece of muslin or print, six and a half or seven nails long and about seven nails wide, gathered at the top, and neatly biassed two or three times at intervals of half a nail; the upper gathering is then sewed very strongly on the shoulder, where the front joins the shoulder-strap; the bottom is simply hemmed. When worn, this piece is folded in large or small plaits, according to the taste of the wearer, and neatly pinned across under the waist ribbon. This method of making muslin, gingham, or print dresses, is very convenient for the washerwoman.

The loose cross-way folds are very similar. The piece of silk, or other material, must be six nails and a half or seven nails long, and nine nails wide. It is secured, both at the top and bottom, in the proper folds, as in this instance no advantage can accrue from the piece being left unconfined at the bottom, as in the washing gowns. The top is sewed on the shoulder, and, when worn, the folds are pinned under the waist ribbon, as in the kind described above.

Other modes of ornamenting plain bodies are so various, it would be endless to have plates to illustrate each—suffice it to say that bands or rouleaux of satin, silk, gauze, &c., are often laid in various forms. For white gowns, straps, with a neat piping at one or both sides, are generally made; also puffings, frillings, and flouncings. For silks, merinos, &c., satin, silk, or velvet pipings, to straps of the same material as the gown, look well. Sometimes gaufiered or quilled ribbon or lace is employed. For children, braid, bobbin, or coarse netting-silk is laid or worked on, in every variety of pattern.

A FRENCH FULL LOW BODY.
PLATE 14. FIG. 22, 23.

This dress is composed of a kind of plain shoulder-piece round the top, to which the body is fulled all round. This piece is cut as follows:—

Lay the material with the selvage-way or stripe down the middle of the top, in front (see A, Fig. 22), to the extreme point of the shoulder, B, and pin it firmly down. Begin to cut at E, which is at a little distance within B, and slope it along to the middle, A, making it a little on the cross. Cut again, according to taste, either in a peak or slope, from B to D. The backs, which are made to accord with the fronts, are quite straight at the bottom, but a little sloped or hollowed at the top. The fulling for the body is cut variously, according to the texture of the dress. Cotton, muslin, or other thin dresses should have the fulness set in with the selvage-way up the middle; but silk, merino, and other thick dresses are made otherwise. This body is sometimes set in plaits, and is exceedingly pretty. In this case, the width-way of the material lies up the middle.

A GRECIAN LOW BODY.
PLATE 14. FIG. 24. 25.

This is a remarkably pretty shape, but requires great nicety in arranging it, to make it fit well.

Turn up the corner of your material half-handkerchief way until sufficiently wide, A to B, to reach amply from the middle of the top of the body in front, across the bosom, to the shoulder. The folded part, A C, must next be laid down the middle of the front. Pin A to the top of the middle, and B to the shoulder, and begin to make four or five plaits to lie in the same direction, making them swell more in the middle than at the ends. In arranging these plaits fold in plenty of the material, or they will not set well. Smooth the remainder to the figure, and hollow out under the arm. As the material is double, both sides are thus cut at once. The plaits should be secured twice or three times on the shoulder. The backs, as usual, selvage-wise down the middle, and a few plaits may or may not be added along the top.

A SIMPLE FULL BODY.

Let the width-way of the material lie up the middle in front, and plait it in straight regular folds from top to bottom, letting the last fold be rather deeper, in order to throw the plain part of the body more on the cross. These plaits or fullings should slant a little towards the middle in a fan-like shape.

FULL LOW BODY.
PLATE 14. FIG. 26, 27, 28, 29.

This is only worn by very young persons and children. It is made nearly like a full petticoat body. The front is in one piece, and may be either the straight or the cross-way, according to pleasure. That in the Plate is a good average size for a girl of ten years old.

The pattern should be cut first in paper. Fig. 27 is the front, D being the doubled part. The measurements need not be repeated, as they are quite accurately given in the Plate. The reason why the front is so much sloped at the lower part, is to make it set better than it would do if left straight; and it is considered preferable to slope the bottom rather than the top of the body: of course it is gathered and sewed to the band in the usual manner. Fig. 28 is one back, and Fig. 29 a side-piece. In making up, if the top of the body is set into a narrow band, instead of having a string-case, the fulness should be pretty equal all round, only making it a little plainer towards the shoulders, but at the bottom of the waist the gathers should be drawn towards the centre, both in front and at the back, which gives a becoming fan-like appearance to it.

VELVET DRESSES.
PLATE 14. FIG. 30.

Velvet dresses have frequently a breadth of satin put in behind, as velvet injures by being sat upon. The great object is to put in the satin so that it shall not be seen when the person who wears it is standing or walking. There are various methods of doing this. The following is one of the best.

The piece of satin is sewed in at the back, in addition to the full number of breadths of velvet. After joining the breadths together, and lining the whole skirt, the two back breadths of velvet are sewed together at the bottom for the depth of about half a yard, the satin being plaited up within them, and not seen at all.

At the top the opening or pocket-hole behind is made in the satin, but not in the velvet, as the two back breadths of velvet are left open all the way up from the half-yard at the bottom, previously mentioned, having the satin between them. The gathers of velvet are sewed in the usual manner into the band, but the satin is sewed back on each side within it, so that when the gown is unfastened the pocket-hole gapes open, and the dress has the appearance given in Fig. 30. S, in the Plate, means the satin, and the V, velvet breadths of the skirt. Instead of putting in a satin breadth, some persons have the back breadth of velvet wadded, which is said to answer well.

NURSING GOWNS.

These must vary according to the pattern of the gown. In a body with folds laid on, the openings must be made in the bosom-gore on each side, which button up, having a fold or flap of silk behind, to prevent any danger of taking cold.

114   THE WORKWOMAN'S GUIDE.

Sometimes a tight body may be made cut in a point from the shoulders to one nail above the waist: over this, full loose folds, confined at the shoulder, may be pinned over at the waist.

A third may be made like a pelisse body, open in the middle of the front.

CHILDREN'S FROCKS AND TUNICS.
PLATE 14.

These should be made of strong and washing materials, as children should be allowed to have full exercise, and not be restrained from running and rolling about, both in doors and out: for this purpose (unless from its extreme delicacy a child requires much additional warmth) cloth, merino, and stuffs are not good or suitable for them; neither are silk, velvet, or gauze, as they soon become dirty and look tumbled, and the child cannot play with ease or comfort.

Jeans, twills, prints, Holland, and nankeen are most proper for the morning dress, and white or coloured muslin, or fine twill, and sometimes washing silks, for an evening.

For children's simple frocks, refer to the Scales belonging to the description of baby's frocks.

CHILDREN'S SIMPLE PLAIN FROCKS.
PLATE 14. FIG. 31, 32, 33, 34.

This is the most simple body that can be made, and equally suited to boys and girls.

The body is in three parts—namely, two backs and one front.

The front is cut along the width of the material, and joins the backs on the top of the shoulders and below the arms, so as to require neither side-pieces nor shoulder-straps. This front lies quite plain to the figure, but the backs are made to have two plaits and a broad hem. This body can be ornamented in various ways, either with braid sewed on, or by capes. A very pretty cape is made by cutting a diamond (see Fig. 33), and hollowing it out on the inside exactly to correspond with the neck of the frock.

Fig. 31 represents half the body in front.

Fig. 32 represents half the body behind, when cut out.

Fig. 33 represents the diamond for the cape.

Fig. 34 represents the front, when made up.

The sleeves may be plain, like petticoat sleeves, having three frills laid upon them, and braided at the edge. The skirt to a frock of this size would be about nine nails, including the deep hem of two nails, and about two and a half breadths wide, each breadth being thirteen nails wide. If there are pockets in front, the slits may be braided round, and are two nails and a half deep. In making up, the body and cape are sewed firmly together to a band at the top, which is ornamented by two lines of braid. The skirt is evenly gathered behind, the gathers lying close together. The remainder is laid in regular plaits all round.

The band round the neck is ten nails long, cut crosswise, and the waistband ten nails long, cut selvage-wise.

A CHILD'S FULL FROCK.
PLATE 14. FIG. 35, 36.

This body is also in three parts, the front and two backs. They are very much fulled, and are both cut the width-way of the material, so that the selvage-way goes up the middle, both before and behind.

For a child of three, four, or five years old, cut the body as follows:—

Cut for each back a piece of six nails along the width-way, and two nails and three-quarters down the selvage-way of the material. Cut for the front a piece of thirteen nails along the width-way, and two nails and three-quarters down the selvage-way of the material. Fold the front in two, very evenly, and lay the two backs upon the two ends of the double front, and pin the four thicknesses together, so as to lie quite firmly and evenly one upon the other, as in Fig. 35. Then with the scissors, after sloping one nail for below the arm, A B, begin to cut, B D, for the arm-hole, cutting into the cloth about half a nail at C. Slope from D, which is half a nail from the top, to E, for the shoulder, letting the part, D E, be three-quarters of a nail. Hollow down from E to F one nail, letting F to G be quite straight, for the bosoms and backs; from G to the bottom is one nail and three-quarters deep.

In making up, after sewing the backs to the front and putting in the sleeves, begin to full in the body to the band round the neck, leaving it plain both before and behind, for about one nail and a quarter from the sleeve.

This band is about eleven nails long, and should be cut on the cross; being doubled in quarters, mark the points for the middle behind and before, and for the two shoulders.

The waistband is also eleven nails selvage-way, and one nail and a quarter wide. The body is gathered at the waist, exactly to correspond with the top.

The skirt of two and a half breadths, of thirteen nails width, is gathered (not plaited) all round quite evenly. The sleeves are the usual shape (see Plate 12, Fig. 27 or 32). A braid may be laid along the top and band, round the sleeves and the broad hem, and the whole is completed.

CHILD'S SIMPLE THREE-QUARTERS DRESS.
PLATE 14. FIG. 37.

The body has one front and two backs.

For the front, cut a piece of thirteen nails width-way, and two nails and three-quarters selvage-way of the material; and the back pieces each six nails width-way, and two nails and three-quarters selvage-way of the material.

In cutting the arm-holes, leave one nail and three-quarters under the arm, and cut into the cloth three-quarters of a nail. Leave nearly three-quarters of a nail for the shoulders. In making up the frock, prepare a piping of ten nails and a half long, and a waist-band of eleven nails and a half. Divide the piping into four parts, and then begin laying the plaits to go from the shoulders rather towards the middle of the waist, as in Fig. 10, sewing them firmly with piping at the top. The back is similar to the front. The skirt is laid in regular plaits all round. The sleeves are fulled or plaited evenly at the shoulder, and confined by a strap a little below it. A frill may be put round the sleeve.

A CHILD'S PLAIN DRESS.
PLATE 14. FIG. 38, 39, 40.

This frock has two backs, two side front-pieces, and one centre front-piece.

The backs, Fig. 38, are cut with the selvage-way up the middle; they are first fitted on the figure to set plainly, afterwards, allowing two extra nails in width for the fulness, they are hollowed out for the arm-hole, leaving one nail and a half under the arm. The side fronts, Fig. 39, are cut a little on the cross, so that the selvage-way or stripe leans in the same direction with the strap or piping which joins the centre-piece. The centre-piece, Fig. 40, is cut quite on the cross, for which purpose, turn up a piece of material half-handkerchief way, and lay it in fourteen or fifteen regular plaits. This centre-piece, when plaited up, should form a triangular piece of two nails deep, three nails and a half at it greatest width, and half a nail at its narrowest. Put a band from each side of the triangle to the back, to confine the gathers. The front requires no band.

A CHILD'S FULL FROCK.
PLATE 14. FIG. 41.

This frock has body and skirt all cut in one piece.

For a child's frock, of two, four, or five years old, cut two breadths and a half of the proper length, from the shoulder to the bottom of the skirt. Double it in four, like a pinafore, slope for the shoulder, and hollow it out for the arm-holes. Cut a band crosswise of the proper length, from ten to twelve nails, and pipe it on each side; after which, confine the top into it in regular gathers. After marking a proper depth for the body, gather the skirt again in two rows, upon which lay a waist-band piped on each side. To this dress may be worn long sleeves, which are piped round the arm-hole, and plaited evenly with a strap a little below, to confine the plaits. This dress is very pretty, when made in spotted or figured muslins or prints. The piping should be matched with the darkest shade on the dress. Sometimes three buttons, covered with the same as the piping, are worn on the shoulders.

CHILD'S MORNING DRESS.
PLATE 14. FIG. 42.

This looks very neat when made of Holland, and is a useful dress to put on, for keeping the under clothes clean; it also looks well in any other material. The skirt and body, all in one, is doubled in four, and the arm-holes cut from the top, without sloping any for the shoulders. A shoulder-piece is made of the proper size (see Plate 13), to which the skirt is fulled, with a piping, in regular plaits. Set on the sleeves also to the shoulder-piece, and full the skirt again in two rows, on which lay the waist-band, also piped. A collar or neck-band is put on, to finish it at the neck. The sleeves are strongly biassed, or confined by a strap, laid on regular plaits, a little below the shoulder.

DRESS FOR A BOY OF FOUR YEARS OLD.
PLATE 14. FIG. 43.

This little frock may be worn with or without trowsers.

The width must be regulated of course by that of the material; if nankeen is preferred, it being only six nails wide, six breadths must be put in. Divide it into four, cut the arm-holes and a slit behind, put in the sleeves, and then set it in double plaits all round, behind, and before, to a band the proper width to fit the child's neck. On the edge of each plait, lay a piece of silk braid, which reaches to the waist and then turns and is brought up at the other side (see the Plate). A runner or string-case is made inside, at the bottom of the waist, for strings to draw, and a deep hem at the bottom of the frock.

A BOY'S JEAN TUNIC.
PLATE 14. FIG. 46, 47.

This is worn by boys of five and six years old, with trowsers of white or some material to match the dress, which is of coloured jean or gingham cloth.

Cut a shoulder-piece similar to Fig. 5, Plate 13.

The skirt is in three breadths, and when they are sewed together, it is doubled like a pinafore, to cut out the arm-holes. It is then gathered before and behind to the shoulder-piece, which has previously been piped all round. The sleeves are also fulled into the shoulder-piece, leaving sufficient plain of them to sew into the arm-hole of the skirt, which is about one nail and a half deep. A robing is put on in the front. The dress is braided in front, and round the shoulder-piece and collar. The bottom of the skirt is turned up two nails and a half, and braided above the hem. The dress is open behind

A belt is cut out, as in Fig. 47, which is braided round each square, and fastens behind with hooks and eyes, or buttons. The sleeve is finished with braiding.

SURTOUT FOR A BOY OF FIVE OR SIX YEARS OLD.

PLATE 14. FIG. 44, 48, 49, 50, 51, 52.

This is made of cloth, lined with silk or net, according to pleasure, and trimmed with flat black braid.

The body is separate from the skirt. The former is in five parts; viz. the back, two side-pieces, and two fronts.

For the back, Fig. 50, let your paper be four nails long, and five nails and a half wide. Fold it in half its width, letting D be the doubled part or middle of the back. Mark as follows:—

SCALE.

	Nails.
From A to B..................................	2¼
From B to C..................................	¾
From C to E..................................	1
From E to F..................................	1¼
From F to G..................................	1½
From A to H	1½

Cut from H to B, and from C to F.

For the front, Fig. 51, cut your paper three nails and three-quarters wide and five nails and a quarter long.

SCALE.

	Nails.
From the bottom to J	1¾
From K to the side	1
From K to the top	½
From L to M	2¾
From M to N	1¼
From N to O	2¼
From P to the side	¼

Slope from J to K for the arm-hole. Cut from K to M for the shoulder. From M to O for the neck. Slope from O to P.

For the side-piece, Fig. 52, cut your paper one nail and a half wide and three nails long.

SCALE.

	Nails.
From Q to R..........................	1½
From the side to S	¾
From the top to S	½
From T to U..........................	½

Cut from V to R, and again from R to S. Curve from S to T. The small collar, or band, is attached to O M, Fig. 51, and F G, Fig. 50. Of course the other side of the body is made up in a similar manner.

The skirt must be next put together, and the back-piece, Fig. 48, being opened, the two fronts, Fig. 49, being also opened out, C F, Fig. 48, is sewed to G H, Fig. 49, it is then set on to the body in regular plaits, and left open in the front.

The body should be lined entirely with tailors' twilled silk, and part of the front breadths with the same, each with half a breadth of silk. The parts should all be strongly and neatly back-stitched together, and braid laid on all the seams of the body. The hooks and eyes are put on between the lining and the cloth. The skirt is hemmed and braided in front.

The dress is worn with a broad black band. Trowsers made to button at the side, and an under waistcoat, are worn with this surtout.

CHILD'S FIRST PELISSE.

PLATE 17. FIG. 45, 53, 54, 55.

These are made of gingham, jean, cloth, merino, or silk. The former are the best for the summer, and cloth for the winter.

For the skirt, take three breadths of about eleven nails wide and nine nails long. Sew up the seams, make a deep hem of one nail and a half, on which is sewed a broad flat braid. The opening behind or pocket-hole, should be made in one of the seams.

The body is in three parts, besides the collar; viz. one front and two back pieces. For the front piece, Fig. 53, cut your paper seven nails wide and three nails and a half long. Fold it in half its width, making it a perfect square, and letting D be the doubled part, as in Fig. 53.

SCALE.

	Nails.
From A to B	¼
From the corner, B, to C......................	1¼
From the side to E	¾
From the top to E	⅛
From the lower corner to F	1¼
From the corner to G	2

Curve from A to C. Cut straight from C to E. Curve, for the arm-hole, from E to F. Cut in a line from F to G.

For the back, Fig. 54, cut your paper three nails and a half square.

SCALE.

	Nails.
From A to B..	¾
From B to the top	2½
From the top to O	¾
From the side to O	¾
From the corner to F	1¾
From the corner to H	½
From A to J...	⅛

Cut from J to B. Curve from B to O. Cut in a straight line from O to F. Curve gently from F to H.

The collar is in two parts. For each part let your paper pattern be three nails wide and two nails and a half long.

SCALE.

	Nails.
From N to the bottom	1¼
From O to the corner	1
From J to the top	¾
From J to K	½
Leaving from K to L	1¾
From the corner to M	1

Slope from O to N, and from O to J. Curve from K to M.

In making up, sew O F, Fig. 54, to E C, Fig. 53, for the shoulder. F G, Fig. 53, is placed against B J, Fig. 54.

The skirt is fulled on evenly all round. The collar, cuffs, and top of the hem may have a bordering of braid or work, and a trimming of the same may be put down the front of the skirt.

A cape, or tippet, is added to it, which is made separate.

CARE OF THE LADY'S WARDROBE.
"Order is the best economy of time."

It is of great consequence that dresses should be carefully and neatly put away, as their preservation depends much on the attention paid to this: a gown smoothly folded, and laid by directly it is taken off, will last half as long again as one that is thrown about upon dirty chairs, or tumbled and creased in the wrapping up. The dresses that are in constant use may be hung up in a closet; but those that are only occasionally worn, should be folded up and wrapped either in a linen cloth, or covered with the coarsest brown paper; the latter is particularly good for white silk or satin dresses, as the turpentine in it excludes the air, and thus preserves the colour more effectually than any thing else.

The best way to fold up a dress, either when put away or packed up, is as follows:—

Place your gown upon a bed, so that the front and back breadths, lay one upon the other quite flatly, the back breadth being uppermost, and the slit behind in the centre, then fold the two outer sides over, so as to make them meet down the middle of the back; take hold at the bottom of the skirt, and double it underneath the gown for about a quarter of a yard deep, then fold the upper part of the skirt forwards, to lie above it, turn back the body and arrange it and the sleeves neatly, so as not to crush them or the trimming, turning the sleeves in towards the middle; then take hold of the upper two folds of the gown, and by lifting them up, the tail falls down again without displacing the upper part of the dress: this tail or bottom of the gown is then turned up over the sleeves and body: a pin is put in at each end, and thus the dress may be carried about, or packed up, without tumbling it in the least. It may be well to mention that the reason the bottom of the skirt is turned up in the first instance, is to determine the size to which the body is to be folded, and the reason why it is let down in the second, is, that it may preserve the body, &c., from being crushed. The dress may be folded to fit any drawer or trunk by wrapping the sides more or less over each other in the middle. This is called the French method of folding; it may appear rather complicated at first, but by exactly following the directions here given, and a little practice, it will soon become easy.

To wrap up a child's frock, place it on a bed, so that the front and back breadths lie one upon the other quite flatly, the back being uppermost; fold the skirt once or twice, according to the length, letting the body lie upon the skirt, and turn the two ends over the centre.

After travelling, dresses are apt to be creased, they should therefore be hung up, either in a closet, or on hooks fixed in the wall; they should never be pinned to bed or window curtains, as this very bad practice is apt to tear the chintz.

Care should be taken to separate mourning from coloured dresses, winter clothing from that worn in the summer, perfectly white articles from those of a dark colour, as they are liable to be soiled and injured by coming in contact with each other.

Stains, grease spots, &c., &c., should always be taken out as soon as possible, or they may become fixed in the silk or other material (see Receipts). After walking in dusty or dirty weather, the dress should be carefully wiped with a clean towel or handkerchief: if splashed with mire, it should be dried first, and then rubbed clean with the hand and a cloth.

Caps or bonnets should be put on cap poles when they are laid by, but as these take a great deal of room, it is a good plan to have hooks or branches fixed in the wardrobe for the purpose.

After being out in the damp, wadding or tissue paper should be put in the bows of a bonnet, until they are quite dry, and then removed, lest from its weight it should pull the ribbon out of shape.

Veils should be stretched out on a bed to dry after having been worn in the damp: if this be not done, they will dry tumbled and creased.

Shawls should never be put away whilst they are at all damp, nor left folded as worn, but wrapped up properly.

For those persons who have not ample space for the number of drawers, &c., requisite to contain their clothes, it is a good plan to have a long narrow ottoman, settee, or sofa, without backs or ends, which is made hollow, and to open: it might be the proper length to stand at the foot of a bed, in a window, &c., &c. These are useful to contain bonnets, furs, or for putting away winter or summer clothing. Plate 21, Fig. 2, 4.

A dressing stool might also be contrived hollow, which would hold soiled linen, &c. Plate 21, Fig. 2.

An exact inventory of the linen should be kept in the wardrobe or drawers.

Plate 21, Fig. 1, represents a very convenient wardrobe for ladies' dresses, heavy linen, bonnets, caps, furs, sleeves, &c., and is contrived as follows. The centre is divided into two compartments, the upper is enclosed with doors, and contains sliding shelves or trays for dresses, collars, &c., the rest, consisting of drawers, contains the heavy linen. The left hand wing has one door from top to bottom, in which a mirror is fixed. This closet is intended for dresses to be hung in, and the drawers below to put away furs, &c. The closet on the other side holds bonnets in the upper part, and shoes in the lower, each part having a door to itself.

GENERAL OBSERVATIONS ON PACKING.

Arrange so that your heavy linen, books, &c., shall go in strong trunks, whilst the lighter articles may be put in boxes.

Every leather trunk or portmanteau, should have the name and residence of the owner engraved on a brass plate, in the middle, at the top: these trunks should have leather or sacking cases (for the latter, see Plate 24), to fit them: the cases are made to have an opening just above the plate, so that if going home the person needs no other direction, but in case he is travelling elsewhere, holes are made in the cover all round the edge of the aperture, to which a card may be fixed, with the address.

ON LINEN.

The keys should each be labelled with the name of the trunk, or box, as Imperial Portmanteau, No. 1., &c.

No trunk should be filled so as to strain the hinges.

Every trunk or portmanteau should have straps fixed in the inside half-way up, in order to strap down when the linen is packed over the three flat sticks joined together with webbing, which it is usual to lay at the top of trunks. These sticks are of great use in keeping the linen flat and in its place. Tapes should be nailed across the top of the trunk in the inside, for inventories, &c., to be slipped into.

Carpet bags should be purchased with large gores at the sides, as when thus made, they contain many more articles, and more conveniently than when they are only two plain pieces of carpet. They should also have a brass plate.

When gentlemen travel much between two places, it is well to have the brass plate moveable, and engraved with one address on each side, so that nothing is necessary but to turn it, thereby preventing the necessity of constantly renewing the written directions: this plate is fastened at one end by a pivot, which is secured between the two locks (every bag should have two locks), at the mouth of the bag, and at the other end of the plate is a brass loop, which is fastened to the lock at either side.

In packing for a large family it is a good plan to keep the linen separate by putting a towel between the layers of linen, letting each layer consist only of the clothes of one person, so that on unpacking, the towel containing the linen of each individual is simply lifted out, without the trouble of looking at the marks.

When the party sleep several nights on the road, it is advisable to have a large carpet bag containing the night-dress of each individual packed up in night-gown bags, dressing tidies (see plate 24), marked with the initials of the person; by this means much trouble is saved.

It is a good plan to sew a camphor bag to the night-gown to prevent the attack of fleas and bugs.

In packing, observe the following general rules:—

First, divide the light things from the heavy ones; lay drawings, portfolios, books, desks, boxes, shoes, and all hard flat things at the bottom of your trunk, taking great care to fit them together, so as to be perfectly even at the top, putting paper, or any small soft things in the crevices; then put in a packing cloth, and on this lay flannels, linen, &c., &c.: these things should be opened to their full extent, and laid quite flat; in the corners, stockings, rolls of ribbon, &c., may be put; silk or any thick dresses, folded as described above, may be laid at the top, and the whole carefully covered with the packing sheet tightly pinned down, and strong brown paper to prevent the possibility of rain getting in.

Bonnets, caps, muslin, or gauze dresses, and collars, should be put in a box by themselves: tapes may be nailed across the box and the bonnets or caps pinned to them to keep them steady.

In packing a carpet bag, it is well to roll every thing *possible* in small compact parcels, and to put them in, very close together, especially at the corners and ends, keeping the bag as flat as it can be, and stretched out to its full extent, width-wise at the same time.

CARE OF THE GENTLEMAN'S WARDROBE.

Above all things in a gentleman's wardrobe, it is necessary that the linen should be kept perfectly separate from the cloth clothes, because the dark colour of coats, &c. comes off slightly, and would soil the linen.

The following is the best method of folding a coat for travelling, or for putting away in a wardrobe, where there is not much room:—

Lay the coat at its full length upon a table, with the collar towards the left hand; pull out the collar, so as to make it lie quite straight; turn up the coat towards the collar, letting the crease be just at the elbow; let the lapel or breast on one side, be turned smoothly back on the arm and sleeves. Turn the

R

skirt over the lapel, so that the end of the skirt will reach to the collar, and the crease or folding will be just where the skirts part at the bottom of the waist; when you have done one side, do the same with the other. Turn the collar towards the right hand, fold one skirt over the other, observing to let the fold be in the middle of the collar.

It is advisable to have about a yard and a half of brown Holland in which to wrap the coat, trowsers, and waistcoat; this will keep them clean and free from dust.

If a coat is new, sponge it the way the nap lies; a silk handkerchief is a good thing to wipe cloth with, when spotted with drops of wet.

When a hat gets wet, it should be gently brushed till dry, so as not to crack the felt.

Boot-stands should always be made so that the legs of the boots hang downwards.

When boots are packed up, they should always be put into cases (see Plate 24), which cases should be marked in pairs.

An exact inventory should be kept, and pasted on one of the doors of the wardrobe.

MOURNING.

It shows the best taste to make mourning as plain and as little fanciful as possible.

The deepest mourning is bombazine trimmed with crape; and entirely crape, or silk and crape bonnet.

The next is black silk trimmed with crape: silk and crape bonnet. There is a peculiar kind of very rich silk worn only by widows, and called "Widow's silk."

A third or slighter mourning, is a plain silk dress, with either black or white silk, or even a straw bonnet.

Half-mourning is grey or lavender silk in a morning, and the same or white with black ornaments in an evening: bonnet either white or lavender silk, or straw.

Bombazine and black silk dresses have broad hems at the bottom, or are turned up with crape from five to eight nails deep; this is cut the crossway, and is put on with a crape piping at the top. The crape should be put on double, or if economy is an object, should be lined with black book muslin, which makes it wear much better, than it would do if put on single.

The cape or collar of the dress should be either of silk covered with crape, or of plain silk, edged with hemmed or gaufiered crape, and the cuffs to suit.

In very deep mourning, the collar and cuffs are made of white muslin, covered with crape.

Frills and caps, either for the bonnet or to wear in the morning, should have the borders of white crape lisse, tulle, or net, with broad hems.

The peculiar kind of ribbon worn in mourning is called love ribbon, and may be had either white or black; it is very plain gauze ribbon, without any pattern on it but stripes.

Young persons, or those who are in mourning for young persons, frequently wear a good deal of white, as for instance, white ribbons, handkerchiefs, and white gloves sewed with black: very young children, only wear white frocks and black ribbons.

For caps, collars, veils, see under their respective heads.

It is the wisest economy in the end to buy the best or jet black crape, it is more highly curled or craped than the blue black, which makes it more expensive, but it wears well to the last, whereas the other, even when new, does not look handsome.

The following observations may be found useful in some cases, though they should be received with allowance, according to the circumstances in which the individuals are placed.

Mourning is worn for a husband or wife, from one to two years.

For a parent, six months or a year.

For children, if above ten years old, from six months to a year; below that age, from three to six months; for an infant, six weeks and upwards.

For brothers and sisters, six to eight months.

For uncles and aunts, three to six months.

For cousins, or uncles and aunts, related by marriage, from six weeks to three months.

For more distant relations or friends, from three weeks upwards.

It is usual for persons of large fortune to put their servants in mourning on the following occasions:—

At the death of the heads of the family, their parents or children, the deepest mourning is given, as follows:—

For women servants, one stuff or bombazine gown for best, and two black print or working gowns, a bonnet made of silk and trimmed with crape, muslin for collars and caps, a black silk handkerchief, black stockings and gloves.

For men servants, a complete suit of dress and common livery, with hat-bands and shoulder-knots, gloves and stockings.

For the brothers and sisters of the master and mistress of the family, the mourning is slighter, consisting of one best and one common gown, and no crape on the bonnet: collar, caps, handkerchief, stockings and gloves, as above.

In less affluent families, of course, a difference is made, as it is a great expense to put a whole establishment into mourning, and frequently only one suit is given.

For infants or very young children, the nurse or immediate attendant alone receives mourning.

Hat-bands, scarfs, and gloves, are given to those who attend a funeral, including servants; and also, in some counties, are sent, as well as cake and gloves, to the intimate acquaintance and friends.

HAT-BANDS,
PLATE 20. FIG. 36,

Are worn of black or white silk by all those who attend a funeral; the latter only, if the deceased is a young girl. They are made of the whole width of the silk, and two yards and a quarter long; they are laid in plaits, and then doubled in half the length, and tied together with ribbon, so as to fit the hat, leaving long ends: these silk are replaced by crape during the rest of the mourning. Crape hat-bands are generally put on the best, at the mercer's shop: they are the whole width of the crape, which goes round the hat, and are sometimes put on plainly, and sometimes folded in several folds. When made up, a hat-band is from one nail and a half to three nails deep, according to the relationship of the person to the deceased.

Scarfs are made the whole width of the silk, and three yards long, tied under the arm with a piece of narrow love ribbon. A scarf is worn over the right shoulder, so that the bow comes below the left arm. Plate 20, Fig. 37.

Military men merely wear a piece of crape, two or three nails deep, folded round the left arm, below the elbow.

HOODS.
PLATE 20. FIG. 38.

The hood which is worn by female mourners at a funeral, is composed of black or white silk, book muslin, or cambric; it is the whole width of the silk, and is three yards long; it is made as follows:—

Double the silk in half, making three folds in the front or part near the face, all the way down; the back is plaited or gathered up, and the two sides sewed together for half a yard from the top, so as to form a kind of cap with long lappets; a bow is put on at the gathered part, another in the middle in front, and a third on one side near the ear. These hoods are made in pairs, because those who wear them walk two and two; that is, the bow above the ear is put on the right side of one, and the left side of the other.

A SHROUD,
PLATE 20. FIG. 39,

Is composed of a peculiar kind of flannel, woven on purpose, and called shrouding flannel; it is made of a breadth and a half, full length, so as to cover the feet; one seam is sewed up, leaving the other open behind, like a pinafore; slits are cut for arm-holes, and plain long sleeves, without gussets set in; the front is gathered at the waist, and drawn up into a narrow piece; this is twice repeated, at intervals of three nails down the skirt, upon each of these gatherings, round the neck and at the wrists, a kind of border of the same flannel, punched at the edge in a pattern, is plaited, and an edging of the same is made at the bottom.

For men, the shroud is made exactly the same as the above for women, excepting that there is no gathering in the front.

CAP.

If the usual cap is not put on, the following is made for a man:—it is of flannel, cut exactly like an infant's foundling cap (see Fig. 40). A quilling of the punched flannel is put round the face, and a band of it laid on behind, and across the top of the head, strings of the same, are also sewed on.

CAP FOR A WOMAN.

This is of flannel, cut in the shape of Fig. 41: the round part is plaited up to form the front, and a quilling of the bordering put on, a band of the same laid on at the back, and strings (see Fig. 42).

DAY CAPS.
PLATE 15.

Caps are made of worked muslin, lace, tulle, or blonde, and are usually formed upon chip or wire ribbon, either silk or cotton, which gives a firmness, and causes the cap to set better to the head. A few of the simplest shapes are given in the Plate, and a separate description of each is annexed; in the mean while, a few words on the general manner of making up caps, equally applicable to all, may be found useful by the inexperienced.

After collecting your materials, and spreading a clean cloth upon the table, begin to make your cap, by sewing wire ribbon on such parts as require it, generally all round the head-piece; the crown is then put in; if a round one, it may be either gathered or plaited—the latter looks the best; the fulness is usually put quite in the front, letting the part at the side of the face be plain: horse-shoe crowns are sometimes fulled a little at the top. The joinings of caps are covered or concealed by a narrow piping or rouleau of satin.

When you buy stiff satin ribbon, before trimming your cap, pull it obliquely across all the length, first one way and then the other, to take out the dressing.

Bonnet or other caps, made of a washing material, should have white lambs' wool run in the string-cases, when they are sent to the laundress, it does not take the starch so much as the net itself, and thus the ribbons are easily run in again, on drawing the lambs' wool out.

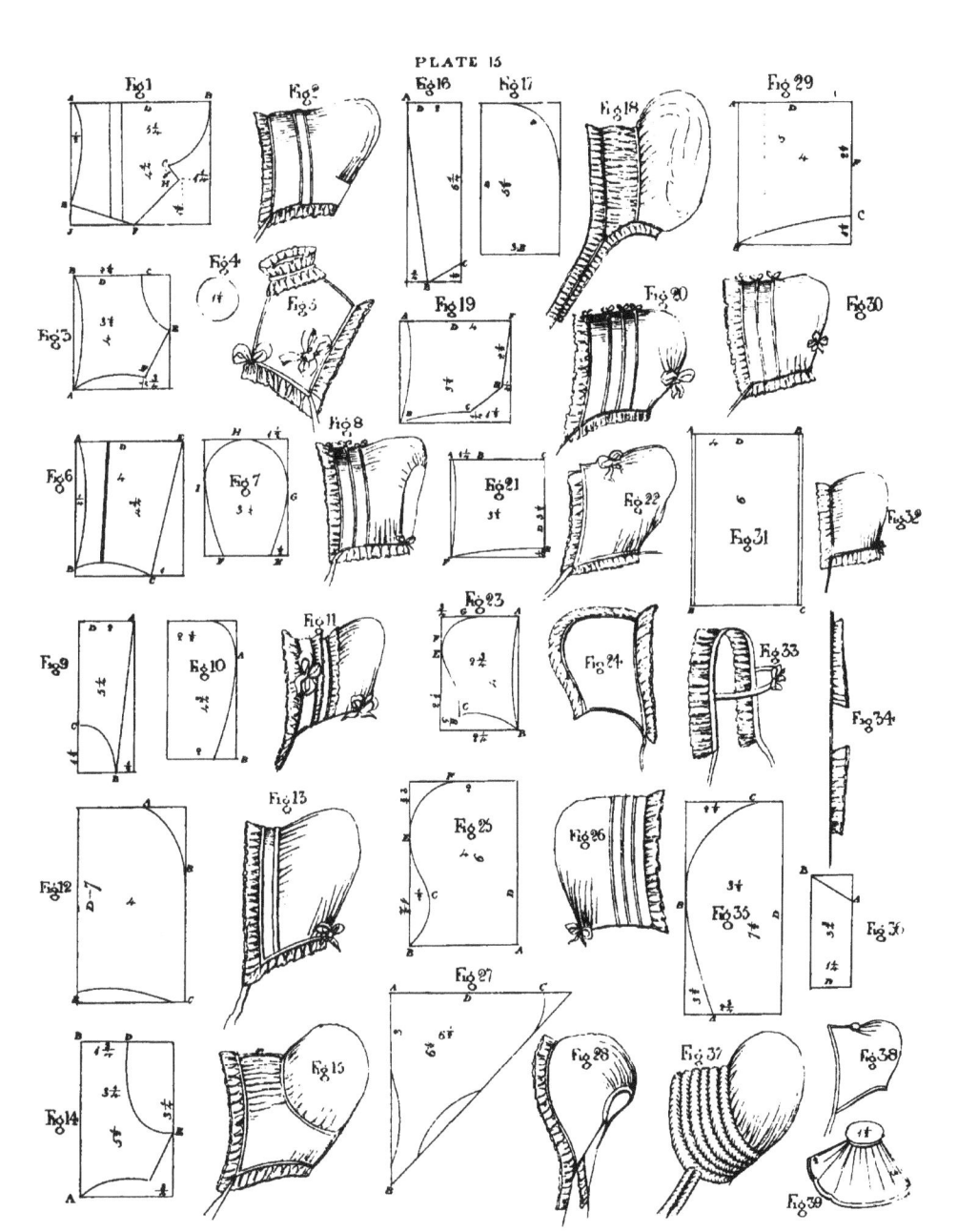

PLATE 15

CAP FOR A YOUNG LADY.
PLATE 14. FIG. 1, 2.

This is a pretty simple cap for a young lady or invalid, as it is not liable to be crushed by lying on a sofa.

Take a piece of paper, four nails and a quarter long, and five nails and a quarter wide, curve out nearly half a nail from the top, A, to within half a nail of the bottom, E, to form the part that is to set round the face; from the corner, J to F, is two nails and a half, cut in a straight line from E to F, and from F to H, in a slanting direction, the point H being one nail and a half from the bottom, and one nail and a quarter from the side; cut into the cap from H to C, also sloping a quarter of a nail, and then round it gradually up to B. When you cut out your cap, be careful that the net is doubled at D.

In making up this cap, join it neatly from F to H, and then gather the crown, B C, into the small piece, H C. Hem it from E to F, and run a coloured ribbon into the string-case: hem or bind it in the front, and make one broad runner, to contain a ribbon, which sets it off. A small bow may be put at H: and any simple trimming of loops or bows between the borders.

A MORNING CAP.
PLATE 15. FIG. 3. 4, 5.

This is easily made, takes very little material, and has a pretty effect. The head-piece is cut all in one.

For the pattern, take a piece of paper four nails long by three nails and a half broad. The front, A B, is four nails; from B to C two nails and a half. Curve from C to E, E being two nails from the top. Cut in a straight line from E to F, at a quarter of a nail from the bottom, and curve from F to A. The net must be doubled at D. The small circular crown is one nail and a half across.

This cap is made up as follows:—Wire the head-piece all round, and put a wire also from B to C, up the front, and from E to F, up the back, to keep it in shape. The round crown is put in quite plainly, the part into which it fits having been previously wired. The border may then be sewed on, and a double quilling of blonde or tulle put round the crown at the top. Lay a piece of ribbon in the middle of the quilling, and cover the wires up the back and front; bind it with the same behind, and put a ribbon, which forms the strings, across the border in front. A bow at the side, and two behind, at the top and bottom, will be found sufficient trimming.

A SIMPLE UNDRESS, OR BONNET CAP.
PLATE 15. FIG. 6, 7, 8.

This cap is in two parts, a head-piece and a horse-shoe. To cut the pattern of the former, Fig. 6, let your paper be four nails broad by four nails and three-quarters long. A to B is the front of the cap. Curve it slightly about a quarter of a nail to B, which is a quarter of a nail from the bottom; then curve to E one nail from the side, and from C to E is a gradual slope, D being the doubled part. For the horse-shoe, let your paper be three nails broad by four nails long. F and K are each half a nail from the side. Slope from F to I, which is two nails and a half from the bottom, and then round to H, which is in the centre.

In making up, hem or bind the front, and put one or more runners, according to fancy. The size here given is only measured for one. Whip from E to C, and sew it to the horse-shoe, keeping the fulness at the top of the cap. Hem or bind it behind, and put on the border.

DRESS MORNING CAP.
PLATE 15. FIG. 9, 10, 11.

This cap is in two parts. For half the front-piece, Fig. 9, cut a piece of paper five nails and a quarter long and two nails wide. D is the doubled part of the net, cut in a straight line from A to B, which is half a nail from the side. Slope from B to C, which is one nail and a half from the bottom.

For half the crown, cut a piece four nails and three-quarters long and two nails and a half wide. Slope off from the top, A to B, cutting off half a nail. D is the doubled, or middle part of the crown.

In making up, the head-piece is wired all round, and the crown then set in quite plainly for two nails above the ear, and the rest plaited in small neat plaits quite in the front: then take two pieces of wire, rather shorter than the front of the cap, and quill upon them tulle, blonde, or lace, similar to that of which the border is made. This quilling should be narrower than the border, and only moderately full. A ribbon must be laid upon the edge to conceal the stitches and the wire. When these bands are put upon the cap, one of them is laid on close to the crown, and the other between it and the front. The cap is plaited a little behind to make it fit, and a small bow is put on in the middle of the back. A ribbon, forming also the strings, is passed over the front, and a small bow put on one side, close to the border.

In making up this cap more simply, or as a bonnet cap, the two trimmed bands may be omitted, and a satin or gauze ribbon merely put across the crown and in front, with two or three loops between the borders.

PLAIN CAP FOR AN ELDERLY LADY.
PLATE 15. FIG. 12, 13.

Cut your pattern four nails wide by seven nails long. Slope off at the top from A to B, D being the back or doubled part of the cap, and hollow it a little at the bottom.

In making up, run two string cases, to admit ribbon in the front, hem it behind and pass a ribbon through, sew on the border, put a small bow at one side, close to the front, and with strings it is complete.

CAP FOR A YOUNG MEMBER OF THE SOCIETY OF FRIENDS.
PLATE 15. FIG. 14, 15.

This cap is in two pieces. For the pattern of the head-piece, let your paper be five nails and a half long, and three nails and a quarter wide. A B is the front of the cap. From B to D is one nail and three-quarters, and is the top or doubled part of it. Curve from D to E, the point, E, being three nails and a half from the top. F is three-quarters of a nail from the side and half a nail from the bottom. Cut in a straight line from E to F, and curve from F to A.

For the crown, cut a circle of six nails across.

In making up, join the head-piece behind, and hem it all round with a narrow hem, so as only to admit a bobbin, which draws it to the proper size. The front is quite plain for one nail and a half above the ear, on each side, and then drawn equally in the middle. The crown is gathered regularly all round, and set in. The single border, about one nail broad, is of the same material as the cap. A narrow hem is made at the edge, and it is set on rather scantily. White ribbon strings are sewed on at the ears.

CAP FOR AN ELDERLY MEMBER OF THE SOCIETY OF FRIENDS.
PLATE 15. FIG. 16, 17, 18.

This cap is also in two pieces. The paper pattern should be six nails and a quarter long and two nails wide. Slope from A to B, B being three-quarters of a nail from the corner. Slope again from B to C, cutting off half a nail.

For the crown, D, which is the doubled part, is five nails and a half long. E, or the bottom of the cap, is three nails wide. Round off the corner at the top, F.

The front border of this cap is in one with the head-piece. The first thing to be done in making it up, is to join a piece of the same material, six nails long, and double the width of the border, say one nail and a half, to the corner or ear of the cap. This is neatly hemmed on both sides, together with the front edge of the head-piece, which is to form the border. A frill the same breadth is sewed to each end of the head-piece, and is joined to the long chin-pieces at one end, and at the other end to the lower part of the crown, which is to be the border behind. A narrow string-case is made in front, one nail and a half from the edge, and a bobbin run in along the front to the ends of the chin-piece. A similar string-case is also made at the lower part of the crown, and two bobbins run in, fastened at one end, and brought out at the opposite one, so that when drawn up they make the cap set to the head. The crown is set in equally full along the head-piece, the straight part being behind.

A BONNET CAP.
PLATE 15. FIG. 19, 20.

This cap is in one piece. Let your paper be four nails wide by three nails and a half long. The front, A B, is a little hollowed, say a quarter of a nail. D is the doubled part. E is two nails and a half from the top, and a quarter of a nail from the side. Slope from F to E, and from E to C, which is one nail and a half from the side, and a quarter of a nail from the bottom. Curve a little to B.

In making up, hem it in the front, and make three or four runners to admit a coloured ribbon, the number and breadth of these depending on fancy. They must be allowed for in cutting out, as the pattern here given is not measured for any at all. Join it from E to C, either plainly or with a piece of insertion-lace, and at the back, C B, make another string-case. The upper part, from F to E, is gathered and drawn together, and a bow put on to conceal the gathering.

A BONNET CAP.
PLATE 15. FIG. 21, 22.

The pattern of this cap is a square of three nails and a half. D is the doubled part at the back. It is slightly hollowed, as in the Plate.

In making up, hem the front, A F, and the back, F E; join it up neatly from A to B, either with a piece of insertion-lace, with a satin rouleau, or with a ribbon, and gather the rest, B C, up to the point, B, where a bow of ribbon finishes it. Sometimes, as in the Plate, the border is not carried on in the front, but, leaving about one nail from the top of the cap, is carried back again to the ear, forming a second frilling.

HELMET CAP.
PLATE 15. FIG. 23, 24.

This is a remarkably pretty little morning or bonnet cap, and is generally made of tulle or lisse, as the shape is not so suitable to a washing material. It is in three parts, the two sides and a piece let in between them.

128   THE WORKWOMAN'S GUIDE.

To cut the pattern of the sides, Fig. 23, let your paper be four nails long by two nails and three-quarters broad. A B is the front, which is a little sloped.

SCALE.

	Nails.
From B to C	2¼
From C to the bottom	¾
From E to the bottom	2½
From F to the top	1
From G to the corner	¾

Curve from B to C. Slope upwards from C to E, and round from F to G.

The piece let in between these two sides is about three-quarters of a yard long, two nails broad in the front, and one nail and a quarter behind, gradually sloped.

In making up, the long narrow strip is gathered on both sides and sewed to the other pieces, Fig. 23, at A, G, F, E, C, equally full all the way. The stitches are concealed by a small satin rouleau laid on. The front and back are then wired and bound with ribbon. The border and any simple trimming complete it.

BONNET CAP.
PLATE 15. FIG. 25, 26.

To cut the pattern of half this neat and simple bonnet cap, let your paper be six nails long and four nails broad. A B is the front. Curve from B, past C to E, C being one nail and three-quarters from the bottom and half a nail from the side, and E being two nails and a half from the top. D is the part where the net is to be doubled.

In making up, plait it behind in the centre, or rather large folds, seven on each side of the middle, and wrapping the folds over each other, so as to keep them all quite behind. Ribbon is laid on in two or three rows in front, either simply upon the cap, or covered with net. Bind it behind, and put on a border and some light trimming.

HANDKERCHIEF BONNET CAP.
PLATE 15. FIG. 27, 28.

This cap is formed of a half-handkerchief, cut from a square of six nails and a half. D is the doubled part. The front is from A to B. Shape it a little, beginning about three nails from the top, to make it set better to the face. The extreme point, C, is rounded off.

In making up, hem it all round, and run in a tape or ribbon behind.

BONNET CAP.
PLATE 15. FIG. 29, 30.

The pattern of half this cap is cut from a paper five nails long by four nails broad. A B is the front, D the doubled part of the net. Slope from B to C, cutting off one nail and a half. Allow for runners, according to your taste.

In making up, hem the front and back, run the string-case, join it up the back from C to F, and hem the rest from F to the top. Run a ribbon in this hem, which draws it up into a crown, and ties with a bow behind at F. This cap looks very like Fig. 20, but the chief advantage of it is, that it can be very easily ironed, as, when the ribbon is drawn out of the crown, it is a flat piece.

BONNET CAP FOR A CHILD.
PLATE 15. FIG. 31, 32.

This is an oblong, seven nails long by four nails wide. Hem it all round. A E is the front. a ribbon is run through the hems, both in front and at the back, B C, which draws up the cap as much as is necessary to make it fit.

A CAPETTE.
PLATE 15. FIG. 33.

A capette is a sort of half-cap worn by young ladies, as a preservation from cold; it is also useful as a pretty kind of evening head dress; they are not expensive and are easily made.

Take a piece of silk or satin ribbon, the proper length for the front of a cap, and about two-thirds of a nail broad, along each edge hem in a wire ribbon so as to reduce the width to half a nail, putting three ribs or stays of wire across, to keep the ribbon its full breadth; one should be in the middle, and one at each end: then take another piece of wire ribbon, which is to go at the back of the head, and which is covered with ribbon similar to the front; the length of this must be regulated by the size of the wearer's head, and it should be very accurately fitted, as all the comfort, and much of the neat appearance of the capette depends upon it setting well and closely to the shape of the head; this back piece should be sewed very firmly to the front, a little above the ears. A border of net, tulle, or blonde is then plaited on to the front, and a gauze or satin ribbon folded, and laid upon the edge of it, so as to cover the stitches, and the foundation; this ribbon is long enough to form strings. On the back-strap is also laid a similar piece of ribbon, and sometimes a small bow is put in the centre of it. The front is trimmed according to fancy, the most simple mode generally looking the best.

Some persons wear capettes under their bonnets, and then they are usually made without wire, and merely bound with ribbon.

LAPPETS.
PLATE 15. FIG. 34.

Lappets are merely a double border of net, tulle, or blonde, three nails on each side, leaving a space in the middle; sometimes they are plaited all round, or made with a plain piece of blonde over the forehead. The edge is bound with ribbon, the ends of which form the strings.

WIDOW'S CAP.
PLATE 15. FIG. 35, 36, 37.

A widow's cap is a very difficult thing to make well, and looks particularly slovenly when ill put together; it is, therefore, often the best economy to buy one ready made, as there are persons who do little or nothing else; however, as there may be some cases in which this plan is not advisable, a pattern is given of a full sized one, and a few words on the manner of making it up.

These caps should be of book muslin (not of the thinnest kind) or of white crape.

In the Plate, half of the crown, Fig. 35, and half of the head-piece, Fig. 36, are represented. To cut out the former, let your paper be seven nails and a half long, and three nails and a half wide; from the side to A is two nails and three quarters, from the bottom to B is three nails and three quarters, and from the corner to C, two nails and a half. The doubled part of the muslin is to be laid upon D.

For the head-piece, Fig. 36, your paper must be three nails and three-quarters long, by one nail and a quarter broad. From A to the corner is three-quarters of a nail, slope gradually to B. D is the doubled part.

In making up, after setting the crown into the head-piece, with the fulness chiefly in the front, and hemming it behind and all round the face, sew on the borders: these are made of the same muslin, about a quarter of a nail deep, they are double in front, and put on very full: after the muslin is hemmed, a short round stick is run through, which gives a crimped appearance, and makes the hem hollow; to keep the border in its place, a fine tape is passed through each hem, which is tied up to the proper size; a sort or binder is then laid upon the head-piece and meets behind; it is thus made:—take a piece of muslin, one nail and a half broad and two yards long, make a hem at each edge and a tuck in the middle, the same width as the hem of the borders, pass the stick through all these hems, and run in a fine tape or bobbin, to draw it up to the proper size. A piece is then prepared to fasten under the chin which is three quarters of a yard long, and broad enough to admit of a hem, one quarter of a nail deep at each edge, no plain muslin being left between; the stick is passed through these hems, and a tape run in. When worn, the ends are pinned on each side at the ears of the cap.

VELVET OR WADDED SILK CAP.
PLATE 15. FIG. 38.

This cap is very useful to wear under a bonnet, especially in travelling. It is four nails long in the front, when folded in two, and three nails and a half wide, it is sloped behind one nail, and rounded about half a nail at the top.

In making up, a lining is put into it, and a piece of wadding laid between it and the cap: they are neatly run together down the front and behind: a string-case is made at the back, for about half a nail on each side of the middle, and a ribbon run in to draw it up to the proper size. It is neatly joined for one nail and a half, and the rest is gathered up, the stitches being concealed by a large button, covered with the same silk.

SILK CAP.
PLATE 15. FIG. 39.

These are often worn by elderly or invalid ladies, under their caps and bonnets. Fig. 39 is an approved shape, to wear under a cap; it is made of silk that approaches the nearest in colour to the shade of the hair. It is in two pieces, the one a strip ten nails long, three nails deep, and sloped off at the ends to two nails; and the other a round cushion, one nail and a half across, and half a nail high: the strip is joined up at the ends, which part fits to the front of the head, hemmed all round, and strings run in to draw it up to the proper size. The cushion is made and filled with light sheep's wool, and the strip or head-piece gathered regularly to it. The use of it is to make the crown of the cap stand up.

PINAFORES, SACCARINES, &c.
PLATE 16.

Pinafores and saccarines are worn chiefly by children of both sexes, and of every age, also by house-maids, while making beds, or persons engaged in particularly dusty or dirty employments. For children's pinafores during their earliest years, look in Plate 3, where two or three patterns are entered, among other articles of baby linen, and where scales are affixed for children of various ages. The following are the other shapes most in use.

CHILDS' SURTOUT PINAFORE.
PLATE 16. FIG. 1.

This is a neat and simple pinafore for a young child, and is made of diaper, Holland or print.

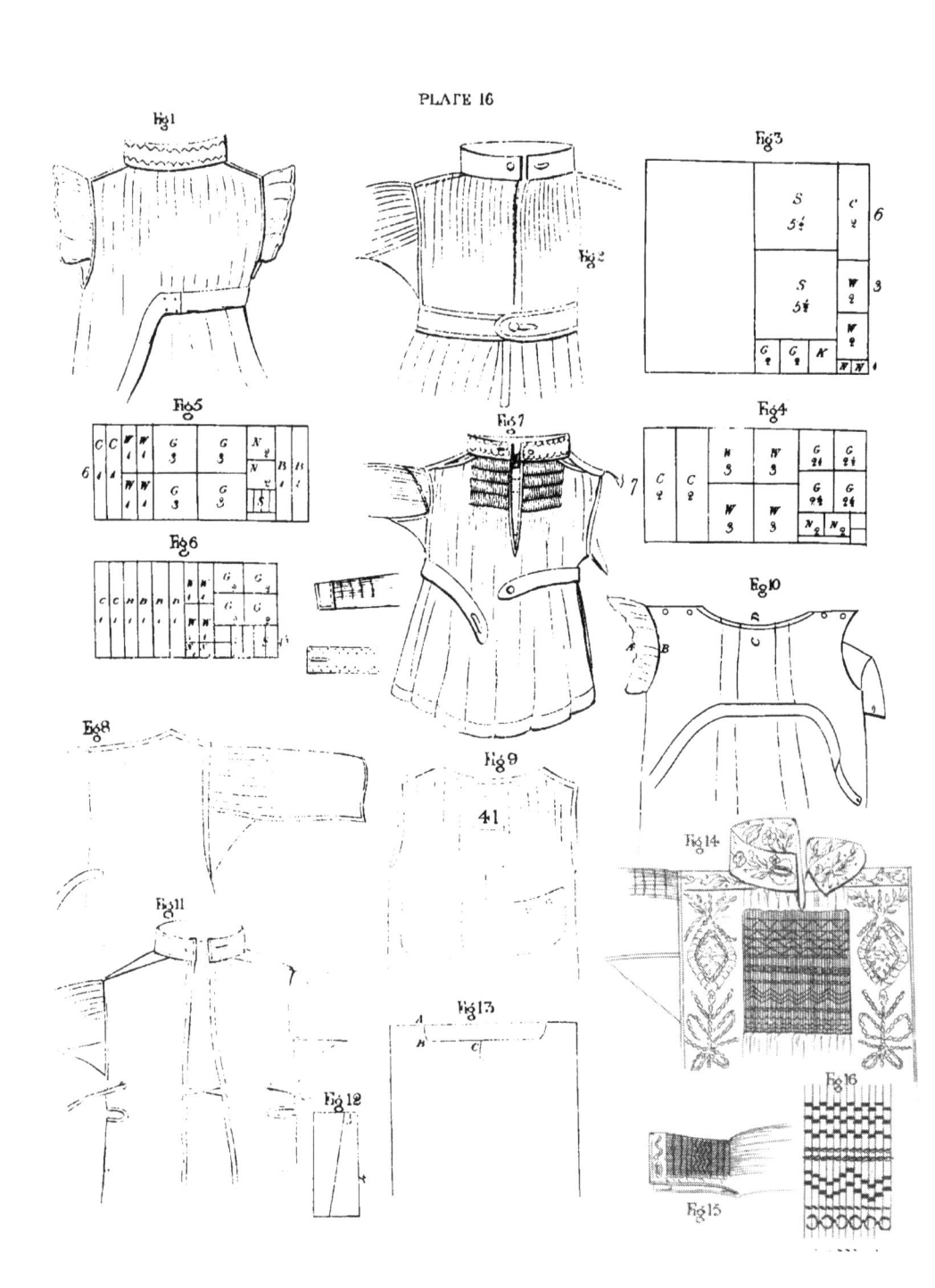

PLATE 16

SCALE.

	Child of 1 yr.	Child of 3 yrs.
	Nails.	Nails.
Width of cloth	12	14
Length of cloth	6¼	8
Depth of shoulder	1	1¼
Slope of shoulder	¼	¼
Length of arm-hole	2¼	2¼
Depth of lappet or shoulder	1	1¼
Length of lappet or shoulder	8	10
Depth of neck-band when open	¾	1
Length of neck-band when open	5	6
Depth of band round the waist	1	1

The pinafore is folded in half, and again in two, to find the situation of the arm-holes at the quarters: after sloping the shoulders, hollow out the neck about a quarter of a nail; the shoulders must then be sewed up, and the pinafore set into the neck-band, which is first doubled exactly in half; this neck-band buttons behind. The sleeve lappets are gathered near the edge, and neatly set on to the arm-hole before it is hemmed, so that when the hem is turned down, no stitches are seen on the right side; the lappet is then fulled at the edge a second time, which being also firmly sewed down, makes it lie flat upon the hem. The other edge of the lappet is hemmed, and silk washing braid put on, to hide the stitches. The lappet should be set on to within half a nail of the bottom of the slit of the arm-hole on each side; little gussets may be put in at the bottom of the slit, to make it stronger. A band is sewed on in front, of the proper length to button behind, its proper situation is in the centre in front, and a little below the level of the bottom of the arm-hole. Boys often wear a band of patent leather instead, with a buckle. This pinafore is quite open behind, being only fastened by the neck-button and the band.

A CHILD'S SMOCK-FROCK, OR CLOSE PINAFORE.
PLATE 16. FIG. 2, 3.

If for gentlemen's children, they are made of Holland, either black or brown, or diaper, but for the lower classes, of blue check, dark blue linen, brown and black linen, or coloured prints. These close pinafores are very suitable for children playing in a garden, or for going to school in, and preserve clean frocks, or hide soiled ones effectually. It would be well if at most large charity schools, children attended with these kind of pinafores, which at once give them a neat respectable appearance.

The number of breadths is not mentioned in the scale, as the widths of the material differ so much; but it is advisable, if possible, to obtain it of such a width as will agree with the width of the pinafore, to admit of their being but one, one and a half, or exactly two breadths in it. The sleeves, collar, bands, and gussets, may be made to cut to little or no waste, by fitting them well, one with another, especially if the band be made in two pieces, instead of one length. The pinafore is easily made up; after putting in the neck gussets, the collar is set on, the skirt being regularly fulled into it. The sleeves, &c., are all put on as in a shirt, excepting that the wristbands are sewed up so as to form cuffs.

Metal or bone buttons are those in general use to fasten them. The two nails by one and a half that are over (see K), serve for covering buttons, or make a small gusset for the slit behind, and also for the bottom of the sleeves, if the wristband is made open.

SCALE.

———	First size.	Second size.	Third size.
	Nails.	Nails.	Nails.
Width of skirt when sewed up	9	10	12
Length of skirt	9	11	13
Length of shoulder	1¼	1½	1¾
Slope of shoulder to	¼	½	½
Length of arm-hole	2½	3	3½
Size of neck-gusset	1	1½	1¾
Size of sleeve-gusset	2	2¼	2½
Length of collar	6	6½	7
Depth of collar before doubled	1	2	2
Depth of slit behind	3	3½	4
Length of sleeve down the selvage	4½	5¼	6
Width of sleeve	4	5½	6½
Depth of wristband	1	1¼	1½
Length of wristband down selvage	3	3½	3¾
Depth of band	1	1½	1½
Length of band down selvage	11	12	13

LARGE SIZED PINAFORE.

PLATE 16. FIG. 4.

To prevent waste, it would be advisable to cut out two at once, as the collars, &c., will cut for both pinafores in one width. Cut two breadths for each pinafore, and from one breadth of each, cut the sleeves. For the collars, &c., cut off a piece of Holland, seven nails long, and divide it according to the Figure in the Plate, first taking off the two collars, C C, the whole length selvage-wise, and each two nails wide; next, the four wristbands, W W, of which two cut in the length, of three and a half nails long, and three nails wide; afterwards the four gussets, G G, two and a half nails square, leaving a strip, two nails long, and five nails wide, out of which cut the two neck gussets, each two nails square, to be afterwards cut cross-wise in half; also little gussets for the slit behind, and the sleeves, if the wristbands are made open.

These pinafores are made up like those before mentioned.

PINAFORES FOR BOYS, OF STRONG BLACK GLAZED CALICO, OR HOLLAND, AT 1s. PER YARD.

PLATE 16. FIG. 2, 3,

Represents the width of the cloth on which the pieces composing the pinafore of the smallest size are marked.

Cut two breadths and divide one in half, from the half cut all the et cetera according to the figure.

S S are the two sleeves, five and a half nails square.

C is the collar, two nails by six long.

W W are the two wristbands, two nails by three long.

G G are the two sleeve gussets, two nails square.

N N are the two neck gussets, one nail square.

SCALE.

—	Boy of 8 years.	Boy of 10 years.
	Yds. nls.	Yds. nls.
Width of material	15	15
Quantity for one	1..10	2..0
Number of breadths in each pinafore	2 bdths.	2 bdths.
Length of breadths	13	15
Length of sleeve down selvage	5½	7
Width of sleeve	5½	6
Length of wristband down selvage	3	3½
Width of wristband	2	2
Neck-gusset cut in half	1	1½
Sleeve-gusset	2	3
Length of collar	6	7
Width of collar	2	2

CHILDREN'S SACCARINES.

PLATE 16. FIG. 7.

These are exceedingly pretty, if finished neatly with braid or silk, and are generally made of Holland, either brown, or the light grey called French Holland. They answer well as morning dresses, in which children can run about, and work in the garden, with less danger of tearing or dirtying their under clothes, than with frocks of lighter materials.

SCALE.

—	Child from 2 to 4 yrs.	Child from 4 to 6 yrs.
	Yds. nls.	Yds. nls.
Quantity for one	1..14	2..2½
Width of material	12	14
Number of breadths	2 bdths.	2 bdths.
Length of skirt	9	11
Length of shoulder	1¼	1½
Slope of shoulder	¼	¼
Length of arm-hole	2¾	3
Length of slit behind	4	4½
Length of sleeve down the selvage	6	6½
Width of sleeve	6	6
Length of collar down the selvage	6	6
Width of collar	1	1
Length of shoulder-strap	1½	1¾
Width of shoulder-strap	½	¾
Sleeve-gussets	2	3
Neck-gussets	¾	¾
Length of wristband down the selvage	2½	3
Width of wristband	1	1¼
Length of band down the selvage	11	12
Depth of band	1	1

In making up these saccarines, the work must be very good and strong. The hem at the bottom should be about one nail and a half deep. The shoulder-straps and neck-gussets being put on, the slit hemmed, and everything ready for biassing the pinafore, prepare some strong netting silk of a colour that will wash well—black, purple, or white are the best—and then bias the front and back in four rows below the collar. Small spots worked on the gathers, between the rows of biassing, in the same coloured silk, have a finished and neat effect. The sleeve is also biassed at about a quarter of a nail below the shoulder, and at the wrist. For a description of biassing, see Part I., Chapter I. Some persons put coloured worsted braid over the biassing, and, if chosen of a colour that washes well, and sewed on with crewel, it looks pretty, and stands washing better than most kinds of netting silk. Little pockets of Holland should be put in front, being particularly useful to children for their handkerchiefs, &c. The wristbands, collar, and band should have some little ornamental work, either in silk or braid, to correspond with the rest.

FIG. 5

Represents the width of the Holland on which the pieces are marked for the largest saccarine, supposing two of them cut out together, which is by far the most economical way.

After cutting out the skirts, mark off and cut in one piece the two breadths for the two pairs of sleeves, and, before dividing the breadths, cut selvage-wise the whole length a strip two nails wide, which will be twelve long, and form one of the bands. The two sleeves exactly fit in the remainder of the width. Cut next another breadth of the cloth of six nails long, and from it take, according to the Plate—

Two collars, C C, the whole length, and one nail wide each.
Four wristbands, W W, two in the length, and one nail wide each.
Four gussets, G G, three nails square, two in the length.
Two half bands, B B, to be sewed together to make one, each one nail wide, and the whole length. (The other band is already cut off.)
Two neck-gussets, N N, of two nails square, to be afterwards cut cross-wise to form the pair.
Four shoulder-straps, S S S S, of half a nail wide and one nail and three-quarters long, and one piece over, which will form a slit-gusset.

FIG. 6

Represents the smaller saccarine on cloth of the proper width. In this case, also, it is necessary to cut two at once, to prevent waste.

After cutting the two skirts and two pairs of sleeves, of which two sleeves exactly fit in the width, cut off a breadth six nails down the selvage, and divide it as follows, according to the Plate :—

Two collars, C C, one nail wide each, and the whole depth.
Four half bands, B B B B, one nail wide each, of the whole length of two nails and a half, leaving one nail over.
Four sleeve-gussets, G G G G, of two nails square, underneath which lie
Four shoulder-straps, S S, of three-quarters of a nail wide and one nail and a half long, and two other gussets.
A strip of Holland, half a nail by three nails, remains to bind round the slit behind, which makes it firm and durable.

HOUSEMAID'S PINAFORE.

PLATE 16. FIG. 8.

House-maids have, or ought to have, a calico pinafore to put on when making beds, as, after cleaning grates and emptying slops, their clothes should not come in contact with clean bed-linen and counterpanes, lest they should soil them.

ON LINEN.

SCALE.

	Yds. nls.
Quantity for one	3..5¼
Number of breadths	2 bdths.
Width of calico	1..0
Length of pinafore	1¼ 0
Length of shoulder	2¼
Shoulder sloped to	¼
Length of arm-hole	5¼
Length of sleeve down selvage	9¼
Width of sleeve	9
Size of sleeve-gusset	4

The sleeves should be left large and loose, so as to admit of the pinafore being easily put on and off, over the gown. It is more economical to cut out two pinafores than one, as otherwise two gussets are wasted.

SCHOOL GIRL'S PINAFORE.
PLATE 16. FIG. 9.

Pinafores for the national and other schools are generally made of strong blue linen check, with one or two pockets at the front and sides, in which their knitting and needle-work are put. These pinafores, after buttoning up the pockets, are carefully taken off when school hours are over, folded, and locked up at the school-house. In front, near the top of the pinafore, is sewed a square patch of the linen, on which is marked, in red or other tape, the number of the child to whom it belongs. The child is generally called by her companions by the number of the pinafore, instead of being addressed by her name, which is, in many ways, a great saving of memory, time, and trouble.

SCALE.

	Girl from 6 to 8 yrs.	Girl from 8 to 10 yrs.	Girl from 10 to 13 yrs.	Girl from 13 to 18 yrs.
	Nails.	Nails.	Yds. nls.	Yds. nls.
Width of material	12	14	1..0	1..0
Length of pinafore	10	12	14	1..0
Piece for shoulder	1¼	1½	1¾	2
Sloped to	½	½	¾	1
Slit for arm-hole	2½	3	3½	4
Hollowed in front	¼	¼	¼	¼
Length of pocket	3½	3½	4	4
Width of pocket	4	4	4¼	4¼

A CHILD'S PINAFORE.
PLATE 16. FIG. 10.

This is made of brown Holland, or any other neat material, and trimmed with braid or an edging, or simply piped, to give a sort of finish to it. Take two breadths of the proper length (say twelve nails), and sew them together up the seams, leaving two nails and a half from the top for the arm-holes. When thus sewed, fold the skirt in half the width, and hollow out the arm-holes, cutting into the cloth, from A to B, half a nail. The neck is also hollowed to about one nail, from C to D, leaving one nail and a quarter for the shoulders, which are not sewed up, but neatly hemmed and made to button together.

There is no slit behind, but the back is made exactly like the front, either with large plaits, as in the figure, biassed, or gathered. A band, sewed on in front, buttons round the waist. When the pinafore is taken off, the shoulders are merely unbuttoned, and it falls down, as seen on the right hand side of the figure. Lappets or frills may be added with advantage round the arm-holes, taking care to divide them at top, to allow of the shoulders separating.

A SURGEON'S DISSECTING PINAFORE.
PLATE 16. FIG. 11.

These pinafores are worn by surgeons over the coat, and are made high up to the neck and down to the waist, to prevent anything soiling the dress while dissecting and performing operations. The pinafores are generally of black, but sometimes of grey Holland. They have two pockets, in which to put the instruments, cloths, &c. &c.

SCALE.

	Yds. nls.
Width of material	1..0
Number of breadths	1¼ bdth.
Length of pinafore	1..6
Length of sleeve down the selvage	10
Width of sleeve, or two in the breadth	8
Length of collar down the selvage	9
Width of collar	2¼
Length of wristband down the selvage	4
Width of wristband	1
Length of shoulder-strap down the selvage	4
Width of the two together before being cut	2
Size of sleeve-gusset	3
Length of arm-hole	5¼
Size of square pocket	5
Distance from under the arm to the pocket-hole	3¼
Slit width-way for the pocket-hole	3

The breadth and half are sewed together, the pinafore doubled as usual, and the slits for the arms cut; after which the shoulder-straps are sewed between, and not upon the parts forming the shoulder, taking care to put the wide end of the shoulder-straps (which are sloped as seen below), towards the neck. Put in the sleeves, and set the neck into the collar. Find the situation of the pocket-hole, letting the middle of it fall in a straight line, exactly under the arm. The slit is cut width-way, and a piece of narrow tape is sewed round it at the edge, and hemmed down. The pocket is *sewed* on (but not *hemmed*) at the inside with small stitches, and, when done, well flattened with the finger and thumb.

The piece for the shoulder-straps is crossed, making the narrow end about one-third of a nail, as in Fig. 12.

A strong case is sewed round the pinafore inside, made of 2d. or 3d. tape. Two large oylet-holes are made at the sides, and a very long piece of tape is first drawn all round the string-case coming out behind, and secured in front. These strings cross behind, and are carried through the opposite string-

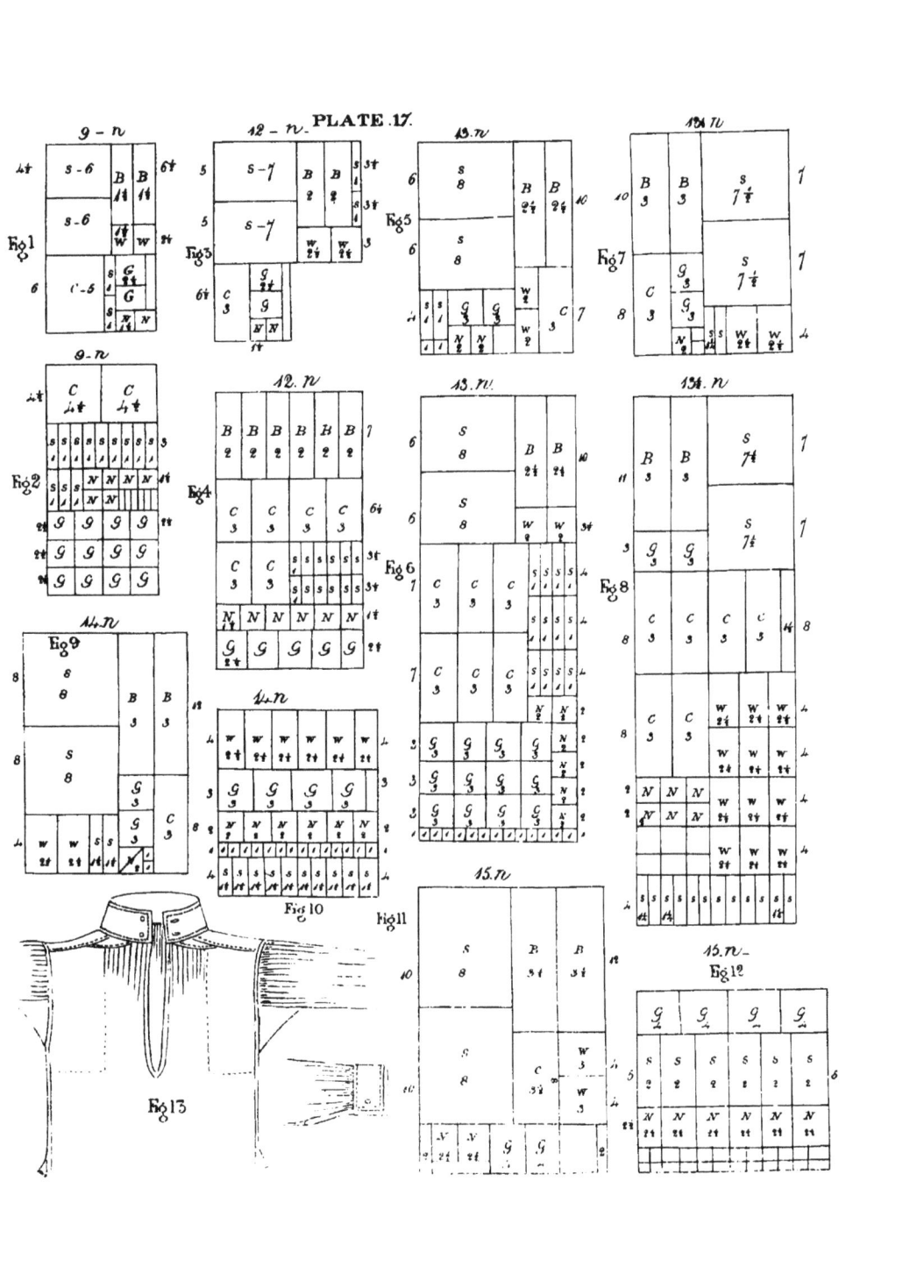

PLATE 17.

case, as far as the oylet-holes, at which they are brought out. The pinafore is generally put on over the head. The strings draw round and tie in front.

WAGGONER'S SMOCK FROCK.
PLATE 16. FIG. 13, 14, 15, 16.

It is made of strong linen, similar to that used for sheeting, and the biassing upon it is worked with the strongest glazed thread or cotton that can be procured. This work must be firmly and regularly done, as the price of these frocks depends on the quantity and quality of work in them.

SCALE.

	Yds. nls.
Width of the material	1 .. 0
Length of the body, both breadths being cut in one piece	2 .. 14
Length of each half collar down the selvage	6
Width of each half collar	4
Length of shoulder-binding	3
Width of shoulder-binding	1¼
Length of sleeve down the selvage	10
Width of sleeve	8
Length of wristband down the selvage	5½
Size of gusset	1
Length of slit behind and before	1¼
Length of worked part in front	5
Wrist biassed up to about	1¼

The two breadths are cut in one piece, and hollowed out at the neck to the depth of one nail, making the hollowing, Fig. 13, from A to B, as abruptly as possible, so that from B to C is quite straight by a thread. After the body is gathered to the proper size, so as to correspond with the two half collars, set them on so that the divisions shall come behind and in front, at which places the frock itself is cut down one nail and a quarter deep.

The shoulders and wrists, as well as the front and back, are biassed with strong glazed thread, in various patterns, and stitched as in Fig. 16. The plain part, between the biassing and arm-hole, is worked in chain-stitch, as also the collar, in various patterns.

These frocks are to be met with at clothing warehouses, and cost from 9s. to 18s. each, the price depending upon the quantity and quality of work put on.

SHIRTS FOR THE LABOURING CLASSES.
PLATE 17.

Shirts for labouring men are generally made of the stout linen called shirting-linen, at from 9d. to 1s. per yard. Shirts for men of lighter occupations are sometimes of calico, with linen collars and wristbands. Blue checks, unbleached, and striped calicoes, or prints, are used for that purpose.

Linen for shirts should be chosen of exactly the proper width, according to the size wanted; and as it is an expensive article, especially when cut to waste, six Scales are drawn upon the Plate for six different sizes of shirts, by which the most economical plan for cutting the shirt is seen.

Each Scale is drawn upon the width of cloth suitable to the sized shirt. Scales are also affixed for cutting out a set of six of the same sized shirts, as, by a little management, and occasionally reducing or enlarging a sleeve a quarter of a nail, or making some such immaterial difference, the various parts of a set, take much less cloth by being cut together.

If shirts are made of linen, they should always be cut by a thread; but if they are of calico, they may be torn: still, however, the smaller parts, as gussets, straps, &c., should be cut, in preference to tearing, as they are apt to pull out of shape. In preparing a set of shirts, time is saved by cutting out all the pieces of the same size together, instead of cutting first a sleeve, then a wristband, &c. It also saves cloth to cut strips all in one length, and then sub-divide it: for instance, when binders and sleeves are cut in the breadth, as one is longer than the other, it is necessary to mark off the width of the sleeve, and then cut down the whole length of the set of sleeves, leaving the strip in one length, to be sub-divided afterwards. The bodies should be cut each in one piece, and not in two separate breadths. The neck-gussets are generally single, therefore, one gusset, cut cross-wise in half, forms the pair.

Before cutting the bosom, slit, &c., of the body, observe that the shirt should be folded in two, so as to let the front breadth be one nail shorter than the back breadth. When thus folded, crease it by a thread, and, after leaving the proper distance for the shoulders, proceed to cut the slit for the neck, and down for the bosom. Next measure the length of opening for the flaps, and for the arm-holes, and put in pins as marks.

A FEW GENERAL OBSERVATIONS ON SHIRTS.

There are nineteen useful parts to a shirt, which are cut out pretty nearly by the following rough proportions; but as the figures of men differ materially, no exact rule can be laid down.

    1st. The SKIRT or BODY, which is cut, with the two breadths in one piece, and should be long enough to reach from the shoulder to the knee of the wearer.

    2nd and 3rd. The SLEEVES, which are generally about half the length of the skirt when sewed up, and the breadth the same.

    4th. The COLLAR, which is the same length as the sleeve.

    5th and 6th. The WRISTBANDS, each of which is half the length of the collar.

    7th and 8th. The BINDERS, the length of a sleeve and a quarter.

    9th and 10th. The SHOULDER-STRAPS, the same length as the wristbands.

    11th and 12th. Two SLEEVE-GUSSETS.

    13th and 14th. Two NECK-GUSSETS.

    15th and 16th. Two HIP, or SIDE-GUSSETS.

    17th and 18th. Two WRIST-GUSSETS.

    19th. One BOSOM-GUSSET.

ON LINEN.

PLATE 17.

SCALE OF SHIRTS OF VARIOUS SIZES.

	Fig. 1, 2. Child from 8 to 10 yrs.	Fig. 3, 4. Child from 11 to 14 yrs.	Fig. 5, 6 Child from 15 to 18 yrs.	Fig. 7, 8. Man's small size.	Fig. 9, 10. Man's larger size.	Fig. 11, 12. Man's largest size.
	Yds. nls.	Yds. nls.	Yds. nls.	Yds. nls.	Yds. nls.	Yds. nls.
Quantity required for one	2..8	2..11¼	3..1	3..4	3..8	3..14
Quantity required for six	13.14	14..8	18..0	19.12	21..1	23..0
Proper width of cloth	9	12	13	13¼	14	15
Whole length of skirt	1..9	1..11	2..0	2..2	2..4	2..5
Space to leave for shoulders	2	2	2¼	2¼	2¼	3
The space for the neck will then be	5	8	8	8¼	9	9
Slit downwards for bosom	3¼	3¾	4	4¼	5	5¼
Length of arm-holes	3	3¼	4	5	5¼	5¼
Slit at the bottom for flaps	3	3¼	4	5	5	5
Width of sleeve	6	7	8	7¼	8	8
Length down the selvage	4¼	5	6	7	8	10
Width of binders or linings	1¼	2	2¼	3	3	3¼
Length down the selvage	6¼	7	10	11	12	12
Width of collar	5	3	3	3	3	3¼
Length down the selvage	6	6¼	7	8	8	8
Width of wristband	1¼	2¼	2	2¼	2¼	3
Length down the selvage	2¼	3	3¼	4	4	4
Width of shoulder-strap	1	1	1	1¼	1¼	2
Length down the selvage	3	3¼	4	4	4	5
Size of sleeve-gussets	2¼	2¼	3	3	3	4
Size of neck-gussets	1¼	1¼	2	2	2	2¼
Size of bosom-gussets	½	¾	¾	¾	¾	¾
Size of flap-gussets	¾	¾	1	1	1	1

PLATE 17. FIG. 2,

Represents the best mode of cutting out six shirts of the same size as Fig. 1.

Cut off the bodies or skirts.

Cut off from the breadth the strip for the twelve sleeves, being in all three yards six nails in length, and six nails in width.

Cut from the remainder of the breadth the twelve linings, two in the breadth, six nails and a half long, and the twelve wristbands, two in the breadth, of two nails and a half long, thus using up all the strip.

Cut the other pieces as follows:—

    Two collars in the breadth, C C, six nails long, three breadths.

    Nine shoulder-straps, S S, three nails long, one breadth.

    Three shoulder-straps and six neck-gussets, N N, three nails long, one breadth.

    Four sleeve-gussets, G G, two nails and a half long, three breadths.

    The collar is very wide, and intended to turn over.

PLATE 17. FIG. 4.

The most economical plan of cutting six shirts, the size of Fig. 3:—

    Two sleeves in the breadth, five nails long, six breadths.

    Six linings, B B, seven nails long, two breadths.

Four collars, C C, six nails and a half long, one breadth.
Two collars and twelve straps, S S, six nails and a half long, one breadth.
Six sleeve-gussets, G G, two nails long, two breadths.
Four wristbands (leaving two nails over), three nails long, three breadths.

The remainder, two nails wide, and nine nails long, to be cut up into six neck-gussets, N N, one nail and a half square, leaving a piece, half a nail wide and nine long, to form the remainder of the gussets.

PLATE 17. FIG. 6,

Is the most economical plan of cutting six shirts of the same size, as Fig. 5.

Take off twelve sleeves, eight nails wide, and six long, twelve lengths.
From the long strip cut two binders, in width eight nails and a half, six lengths.
And two wristbands in the width, W W, three nails and a quarter long, six lengths.

The whole strip is thus exactly used up.

Three collars, C C, to be three nails wide and a piece over, seven nails long, two lengths.

The piece left over of the breadth to be cut into

Twelve shoulder-straps, S S, four in the width, four nails long, three breadths.
Also two neck-gussets, N N, two nails square.
Four leeve-gussets, G, three nails square, and one neck-gusset, N, in the width, three nails square, three breadths.
Thirteen flap and bosom-gussets, one nail square, one breadth.

PLATE 17. FIG. 8,

Represents the best plan of cutting six shirts, similar in size to Fig. 7.

Cut twelve sleeves, S S, seven nails and a half wide, seven nails long, twelve lengths.

In the remainder of the breadth, two binders in the width, of

Eleven nails long, six lengths.
Twelve sleeve-gussets, G G, three nails square, six lengths.

After which, cut as follows:—

Four collars, C C, three nails wide and eight nails long, leaving a strip one nail and a half wide for little gussets, one length.
Two collars and six wristbands, W W, eight nails long, one length.
Three wristbands, and six neck-gussets, N N, four nails long, two lengths.
Twelve shoulder-straps, S S, four nails long, one length.

A PLAN FOR CUTTING SIX SHIRTS OF THE SAME SIZE AS FIG. 9.

PLATE 17. FIG. 10.

Measure off the whole length for sleeves, eight nails square, twelve lengths.
From the remainder of the breadth cut

Two linings, B B, in the width, of twelve nails long, six lengths.
Two collars, C C, in the width, of eight nails long, three lengths.

The strip is thus exactly made up ;—

Cut six wristbands, W W, in the width, four nails long, two lengths.
Four gussets, of three nails square and two nails over, three lengths.
From the piece over, cut two shoulder-straps, four nails long, and a piece over.

Six neck-gussets, two nails square in the breadth, one length.
Ten shoulder-straps in the width, four nails long, one length.
Fourteen gussets in the breadth, one nail square, one length.

A PLAN FOR CUTTING SIX SHIRTS SIMILAR IN SIZE TO FIG. 11.
PLATE 17. FIG. 12.

Measure off the twelve sleeves, eight nails wide, and ten long, twelve lengths.
Two binders in the width, twelve nails long, six lengths.
Two collars in the width, eight nails long, three lengths.
Two wristbands in the width, four nails long, six lengths.

The strip is thus exactly used up, after which,
Cut four sleeve-gussets in the width, three lengths.
Six shoulder-straps, five nails long, two lengths.
Six neck-gussets in the width, one length.
Twelve flap-gussets in the width, two lengths.

EXPLANATION OF MAKING UP SHIRTS.

Double the long piece for the skirt in two, making the front breadth one nail shorter than the back breadth.

Measure the proper distance from the top for the arm-holes, and the proper distance from the bottom for flaps, and put in pins for marks.

The skirt is usually simply sewed up, but it is preferable, especially with gentlemen's shirts, to make a hem the whole length of the skirt, on each side, and then sew up between the arm-holes and flaps, firmly, with thick even stitches.

Proceed next to stitch the collar and wristbands. Let the stitching be made about six threads from the edge, and carried all round both the wristbands and collar; taking care not to pass the stitches through both folds of them, at the opening or part, in which the fulness of the sleeve or shirt is to be gathered.

Next prepare the straps by turning them in, and drawing the threads; do the same with the neck and other gussets.

Now sew up the sleeves, putting in the large gussets, the little wrist-gussets and gathering them into the wristbands, to prepare them for putting into the shirts. Then put in the side-gussets, and hem the flaps and bottom of the shirt. These gussets are fixed by sewing them on at the wrong side of the shirt to within a quarter of an inch less than the square, and felling the other side nearly over. The neck gussets are next managed in the same manner, taking care to put the stitched part on the right side.

The shoulder-strap is then doubled in half, and slightly tacked on the middle of the shoulder in the inside; then place each side flat on the shirt, and stitch it in the lines that have been prepared for it.

The bosom is then stitched; and the button-holes made, or if, as in gentlemen's shirts, a piece is let into the front, it must be arranged according to the taste of the wearer.

The lining is now neatly felled on, and the neck gathered, and set into the collar, after which the sleeves are gathered and put in. The bosom-bit may then be sewed in, and when the buttons are put on the whole is completed.

The shirt is marked about an inch below the left hip or gusset.

GENTLEMEN'S SHIRTS.

PLATE 18.

Gentlemen's shirts are usually made of fine Irish linen or lawn, and sometimes of long cloth. Some gentlemen wear striped calico, but seldom, unless engaged in sporting, boating, or fishing. Gentlemen's sons, up to ten or eleven years of age, or persons going into hot climates, wear strong calico, it being considered more healthful than linen, the latter is, however, the best wearing of the two, but more expensive. Care should be taken to procure the proper width, according to the size wanted; and the proper quantity, according to the number required. The Suffolk hemp is considered the best for shirting.

Gentlemen's shirts are cut much on the same principle, but upon a more liberal plan than those mentioned for the labouring classes, with a few exceptions: such as some varieties in the pattern and size of binders, collars, shoulder-straps, &c. In most of them also, a piece of the linen is cut out in the front or bosom, and two pieces of cambric, or fine lawn, either plaited, or fulled in the place, to form the two sides or half fronts to the shirt. A scale is first given of different sizes, and then the best of the various patterns will be explained.

SCALE.

——	6 Years.	8 Years.	10 Years.	12 Years.	16 Years.	Men's Small.	Men's Large.
	Yds. nls.	Yds. nls.	Yds. nls.	Yds. nls.	Yds. nls.	Yds. nls.	Yds. nls.
Quantity of cloth required for 1, about	2...7	2.15	3...3	2.14	3...5	3...9½	3.15
Quantity required for six, about	14.10	16...4	20.10	18...9	18...9	20.11	22 7½
Proper width of cloth	9	9	10	12	14	14½	16
Whole length of shirt	1...8	1...9	1.12	1.13	2...0	2...2	2...4
Space to leave for shoulders...........	2	2¼	3	3¼	3½	3½	3½
Length of arm-holes	3	3¼	3¾	4½	4½	5	5
Slit at the bottom for flaps	3	4	4	4½	4½	4½	4½
Width of sleeve..........................	4½	6½ or 7 nls	6	6 or 7 nls.	7	7½	8
Length of sleeve down the selvage ...	6½	7	8	9	9	9	11
Width of binders or linings	1½	1½	1½	2	3	3½	4
Length of ditto down the selvage......	6½	8	8	12	9	11	11
Width of collar..........................	4 or 5 nls	2	5 or 6 nls.	2 or 2½ nls	2½	2 or 3 nls.	4
Length down the selvage	6	6	7	8	8	8	8
Width of wristband	1½	2	2	3	3	4	4
Length down the selvage	2½	3 or 3½ nls	3½	4	4	4	4
Width of shoulder-straps	1	1		2	2	1½	1½
Length down the selvage	3	3	4	6	4½	4½	5
Size of sleeve-gussets	2	2	3	3	3½	3½	3½
Size of neck-gusset	1½	1½	1¾	1¾	1¾	2	2
Length of piece to cut for bosom ...		5	5	6	6	6	6
Width of ditto		3	3½	4	5	5	5
Width of cambric to put in each side		4	4	4	6	6	6
Width of shoulder-strap, if gored......	1½	2	2	2¼	2½	2½	2½
Widest width to be gored to	1	1½	1½	1¾	2	2	2
Width of frills if used		½	¾	¾	1	1	1¼
Bosom flap and wrist-gussets	½	½	½	½	½	½	½
Slit for bosom............................	4	5	5	6	6	6	6

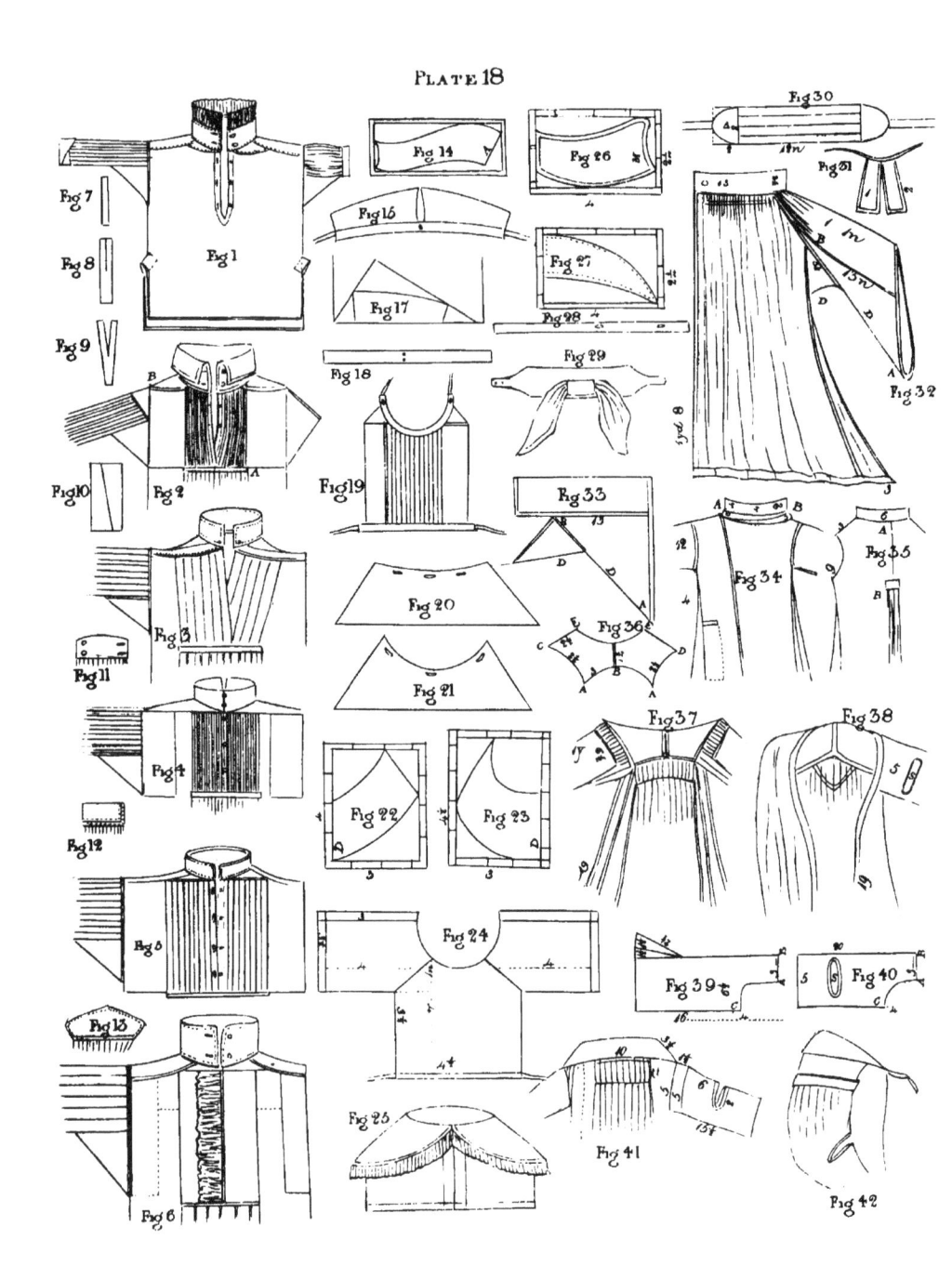

PLATE 18

GENTLEMEN'S SHIRT FRONTS.
PLATE 18.

There are various modes of making up fronts, dependant on the age and taste of the wearer, as well as upon the changes of fashion. The material of which the front is made, should be of a width as to allow of the two half fronts being cut in the breadth; the length is measured from the top of the shoulder to the bottom of the opening prepared for it, allowing plenty to turn in at each end. The two halves having been made up according to fancy, are put into the front, making them overlap each other a full nail, exactly in the middle (see Fig. 2), which prevents the slit opening and exposing the skin. The most approved fronts, and those in general use, are the following:—

A YOUNG CHILD'S FRONT,
PLATE 18. FIG. 1.

Is generally quite plain, with a broad hem and small pearl buttons; it should overlap half a nail.

A BOY'S FRONT.
PLATE 18. FIG. 2.

This is neatly gathered in, and at the end marked A, the fulling is set into a band of calico or linen, according to the material of the shirt, into which the shirt itself is also gathered.

AN OLDER BOY'S FRONT.
PLATE 18. FIG. 3.

These are usually secured in broad or narrow plaits, according to taste, at both ends, but not stitched down the whole way. The advantage of this is to permit of the first being pulled over when washed and ironed, at the same time that it naturally arranges itself in regular plaits whilst worn. The hem is sometimes made to project from the collar to half its depth at the top, where a little corner is left, attached to which is a button-hole which buttons it over to the other side of the collar.

ANOTHER BOY'S FRONT.
PLATE 18. FIG. 4.

This is arranged in small neat tucks, and is more adapted to young boys than the last. The make of this shirt differs from the others in most particulars. The front is entire, but with false buttons, and it opens behind, where there is a slit for the purpose in both shirt and collar. Many boys have their shirts made in this manner, but the washerwomen complain much of the trouble of ironing these closed fronts.

A GENTLEMAN'S SHIRT.
PLATE 18. FIG. 5.

This front is stitched down with the greatest neatness, in the most perfectly regular plaits, either broad or narrow, according to the fashion. The distance of the spaces between the plaits also varies much; sometimes an equal distance with the width of the plait is observed, at others only a half or a quarter, and sometimes the plaits are made to over-lap one another: this last mode looks heavy and common. Either buttons or two sets of button-holes are put, to admit of shirt studs, in which case, the buttons of one side are straight down the hem, and the corresponding button-holes on the other side are cut width-wise.

ANOTHER GENTLEMAN'S FRONT.
PLATE 18. FIG. 6.

This is fulled evenly at the top and bottom, and a frill of the finest cambric, sewed on to both sides. Sometimes the front is sewed in plain, and two frills sewed on one side, without any on the other, but this is rather an old fashioned shirt.

SHOULDER-STRAPS.

The shoulder-straps to gentlemen's shirts vary also a little, but the plain long strap, Fig. 1 and 7, is the one most usually approved of, nevertheless the few following shapes will be explained, for the benefit of those who may like to adopt them.

A CHILD'S SHOULDER-STRAP.
PLATE 18. FIG. 2.

The skirt of this shirt is carried straight up to the neck-gusset, which alone forms the strap, while an extra neck-gusset, the same size, is sewed on to the skirt at B, to lengthen the shoulder; this gusset must be cut in two parts, to admit of the fulling of the sleeve between the pieces. All the sleeve is fulled into this gusset, and the sleeve-gusset below, forms the rest of the arm-holes.

A SHOULDER-STRAP FOR ANY SIZED SHIRT.
PLATE 18. FIG. 3, 8, 9.

Some straps, instead of being continued over the neck gusset, are divided, or split into two parts, for about half their length, and are made to be laid along, the one on each side of the neck-gusset. The piece is cut in a straight length, and merely slit far enough to admit of the neck-gusset between.

ANOTHER SHOULDER-STRAP.
PLATE 18. FIG. 4, 10.

This forms shoulder-strap and neck-gusset at once, and has a neat appearance. The strip of cloth must be of the proper length and width for straps when gored, as mentioned in the Scale: after being gored, this piece of cloth is set on the shoulder, with, of course, the wide end towards the collar.

SLEEVES FOR LITTLE SHIRTS.

Young boys often have short sleeves confined into a band, as in the right hand sleeve of the shirt marked Fig. 1.

ANOTHER SLEEVE.
PLATE 18. FIG. 2.

This is often worn by children of the working classes, and is merely a large gusset doubled, and sewed on double (see the right hand sleeve of Fig. 2).

AN OLDER BOY'S SLEEVE.
PLATE 18. FIG 3.

This is made similar to those of a regular shirt, excepting that sometimes half a gusset only is sewed on to the sleeve instead of a square. This is less clumsy, and with a thin arm is more comfortable, though, generally speaking, the square gusset is the best, both for wear and for appearance.

ON LINEN.

VARIOUS WAYS OF PLAITING THE SKIRT IN FRONT.

When the part is cut out in front, a piece of cambric that is not so wide is put in for the front, so that the skirt below the slit is full and requires confining; this is done in various ways:—

Sometimes in regular fulling, as in Fig. 2.
Sometimes in regular plaits, as in Fig. 3.
Sometimes in gathers, brought much in front, as Fig. 4.
Sometimes in double plaits.
Sometimes in plaits, stitched down, as in Fig 5.

VARIOUS SHAPES OF WRISTBANDS.

The most common shaped wristband, and one of the neatest, is that which is perfectly straight, and stitched neatly all round.

ANOTHER SHAPE.
PLATE 18. FIG. 1, 13.

Fig. 13 is a favourite shape, especially for boys. It is pointed; care must be taken in stitching it, to make the right side lie on the outside, when turned back, as in Fig. 1 (see the wristband attached to the sleeve).

ANOTHER SHAPE.
PLATE 18. FIG. 11.

This is a very neat shape, and accords with the collar of the shirt, Fig. 6. It is stitched all round, neat button-holes made, and buttons sewed on.

ANOTHER SHAPE.
PLATE 18. FIG. 12.

This is remarkably pretty, and is much worn. The wristband when unturned is nearly as wide again as its proper width, not including the stitched hems.

BINDERS AND LININGS.

Shirts should always have binders or linings, and these vary in a few particulars. The binder is intended to strengthen that part of the shirt brought most into play by the movement of the arms, especially at the back, and also prevent the wear and tear of the braces.

Gentlemens's shirts have usually the binders very narrow, so as to leave a pretty wide space between each binder and the front, as in Fig. 4. It is however thought preferable by prudent wives, either to increase the width of the binder, so as to join the front, as in Fig. 5, or else to have a second binder or lining smaller than the first, between the regular lining and the front (see A, Fig. 6).

GENTLEMEN'S AND BOYS' COLLARS.

These vary so very much, according to the make of the neck and chin, as also the taste of the wearer, that only a few general patterns will be introduced as guides.

Many gentlemen prefer, having a narrow band sewed on to the shirt, as in Fig. 5, about three-quarters of a nail deep, on which they fasten the collar, by letting the shirt button slip through a button-hole made in the middle of the collar.

Collars are always of double lawn or linen.

A LITTLE BOY'S COLLAR,
PLATE 18. FIG. 1,

Is a neat finish to a shirt, being a simple broad band back-stitched, and a fine cambric or lawn frill crimped and sewed at the top. The band should be one nail deep, when made up.

AN OLDER BOY'S COLLAR.
PLATE 18. FIG. 2.

This is a very pretty collar also for the children of friends, being particularly simple. It is, when made up, about two nails and a half deep. As it falls over the jacket, observe to stitch it properly. It would suit the wristbands in Fig. 12.

OTHER COLLARS FOR OLDER BOYS.
PLATE 18. FIG. 3,

Is merely a straight band about one nail deep, and Fig. 4 is the same a little curved, so as to be deeper and more pointed in front than at the back, which gives a light appearance.

A MAN'S COLLAR.
PLATE 18. FIG. 6.

See Fig. 6. This is a very neat collar, for an elderly gentleman especially, and when made up, is about two nails and a quarter deep. The front is curved, and rather deeper than the back (say half a nail): to this collar should be worn wristbands, Fig. 11.

ANOTHER COLLAR.
PLATE 18. FIG. 14.

This is a neat shape, but, as it is doubtful whether it would suit every one, it should be cut in paper, and tried on. The Plate only represents one half, the letter A being the centre. It should be sewed into a band.

A NEAT GENTLEMAN'S COLLAR.
PLATE 18. FIG. 15.

This is the most approved sort, and may be sewed to the shirt, or to a loose band. The half or gills, are cut cross-wise of the cloth, and four of them make one collar, as they are double; in sewing them on the band, two places are left to form a kind of long button-hole, through which the strings are put when tying it on. A button-hole in the middle of the collar, enables it to be firmly fastened to the shirt, as also do the two strings sewed to the band. Fig. 17 is one gill, and Fig. 18, the band.

ANOTHER GENTLEMAN'S COLLAR.
PLATE 18. FIG. 27.

This is also sewed upon a band, and is a remarkably pretty shape, if cut according to the plan of the drawing, on which the measurements of the nails are marked. The band, Fig. 28, has in it two button-holes; it is about one nail deep, and eight nails long. The collar is cut all in one length, and slit down in the middle to within half a nail of the bottom, thus making the slit one nail deep.

A LITTLE BOY'S COLLAR.
PLATE 18. FIG. 20, 21.

These are particularly pretty collars for little boys of from six to eight or nine. They are made of double Irish linen stitched round, and made to fall over the dress. Frills are sometimes attached to them, and suit young children very well; two or three button-holes are made in them, to attach them to the shirt. A broad black ribbon is generally worn with them round the neck.

A MAN'S FRONT.
PLATE 18. FIG. 19.

These are worn by men and boys, to put on over a soiled or tumbled shirt, to give a neat appearance; they are, however, seldom used, it being much better to put on a clean shirt at once. It has two sides of fine lawn, with a front of cambric, which is plaited or gathered, according to pleasure, with a false hem down the middle, and buttons, so as to appear to open. This is hollowed under the neck, to the depth of a nail; two neck-gussets are attached, of one nail and a half square.

The gussets and front are sewed to a band or collar eight nails long, and about one nail and a half in depth before it is made up.

A BOYS CHEAT OR FRONT.
PLATE 18. FIG. 23, 24, 25.

This is a kind of habit shirt, to which a collar with a frill is attached. Fig. 23 is the collar, which should be neatly stitched, and a frill of fine lawn or cambric, half a nail in the whole depth, set on round it. Fig. 24 is the habit-shirt of the dimensions marked on the Plate, and Fig. 5 is the cheat completed, when sewed together.

A GENTLEMAN'S STOCK.
PLATE 18. FIG. 26.

Gentlemen's stocks are worn round the neck over the collar, and are made of stuff, muslin, horsehair or buckram: the Figure is the shape of half of one. The halves are sewed, firmly together up the centre (see M); they are bound round the edge with leather, and covered with satin, mode, or rich twilled silk. They are sometimes made, as in Fig. 29, with a fold of silk in the middle, through which two ends are passed; these are of one piece of silk, cut the cross way, and are four nails broad, and seven nails long, rounded a little at the ends.

CRAVATS.

They are generally made of fine muslin, and are the shape of a half handkerchief, being cut from a square of eighteen nails.

CLERGYMAN'S DRESS.

The cassock, the gown, the surplice, the badge or sash, the scarf or hood, and the bands, constitute the chief.

THE CASSOCK.
PLATE 18. FIG. 34, 35.

It is made sometimes of stuff, sometimes of rich black silk, in the following manner:—

Cut four breadths of silk, one yard and a half long each. Two breadths form the front, and are sewed together; after which, a gore is cut from each outer side, the width of half the breadth at the top, sloped to a point at the bottom, by which means, when reversed and the seams are sown, the front is increased at the bottom to three breadths, while at the top it is reduced to one.

The other two breadths form the back; they are gored in the same manner, excepting that the gore is only a quarter of a breadth wide at the bottom.

The shoulder is hollowed down two nails.

The shoulder is two and a half or three nails long.

The arm-hole is three nails deep.

The arm-hole is cut into the stuff one nail.

The collar is six nails long, four nails wide behind, and two nails wide in front.

The sleeve is shaped like a coat-sleeve, with two seams down it, three-quarters of a yard long, and the whole width of the silk, which just admits of its being shaped off in the width. The wristband is four nails long, and about two nails wide. The pocket is six nails long, and just the width of the breadth of silk, which, when doubled, forms it.

In making up, run and fell the seams very neatly, making the two gores fall together between the front and back breadths.

The hem down the opening in front, is half a nail broad.

The back has a piece of sufficient width cut out from the top, A, to the waist, B (Fig. 35), to admit of its setting plain to the figure, and from the waist the skirt is left open; the extra fulness may be confined in two large plaits behind.

The top of the front is cut on each side to a point, and on each point is a little loop or button-hole; one loop fastens to a button inside near the collar, see A (Fig. 34), and the other outside, to a button at the opposite side of the neck (see B).

The collar is sewed on to the back of the cassock, so as to leave off on each side, just at the turn in front, thus allowing plenty of space for the bands. The pocket is put in straight, under the right arm, about four nails below the arm-hole (see the dotted line, Fig. 34).

The sleeves are lined with black twilled cotton, the wristbands are also lined and turned up.

A cross-way piece of silk is laid on at the bottom of the collar of the cassock inside, and also in front at A B (Fig. 34).

THE GOWN.
PLATE 18. FIG. 36, 37, 38, 39, 40.

This is made of fine bombazine, and contains four breadths, of nineteen nails long, and four gores of the same length, and three nails and a half wide at the bottom, sloped to a point at the top.

Two of these breadths fall behind, next are sewed the two gores, one on each side, and then the one breadth to hang in front on each side.

The sleeves are one yard long, and, when open, thirteen nails wide. At the end they are shaped according to Fig. 39, 40: the end, A B, being but three nails wide, and a piece cut out at C, at four nails from A. At five nails from the shoulder, a slit is made in front (see S), through which the arms appear, whilst the remainder of the sleeve is sewed up all round. At the back of the sleeve, two gores of one nail and a half wide, and two nails and a half long, are put in.

The shoulder-piece is cut according to Fig. 36.

The distance from A to B being three nails, and the depth of the sides, C to E, D to E two nails and a half, while that in the middle is only one nail and a quarter.

In making up, after sewing the seams, &c. together, and making a hem of about one nail broad all round, the two back breadths of the skirt should be fulled into the middle of the shoulder-piece. This fulling is biassed down at about the distance of one nail and a half below the first gathering. The two gores are set in on each side into the sleeve, which is set into the shoulder-piece, and also biassed; the other breadth comes in front.

The shoulder-piece is lined with buckram and silk, or black glazed calico, to make it more durable.

THE SURPLICE.
PLATE 18. FIG. 32, 33.

This is made of fine Irish linen, yard wide, and has in it four breadths of one yard and a half long; two breadths being behind, and one on each side of the opening in front. Besides these four breadths, a gore, three nails wide and carried up to a point, is put between the front and back breadths, up to below the arm.

The straight part of the gore comes in front.

The sleeve, Fig. 33, is one yard and one nail long, and the whole width of the linen in the breadth.

The sleeve has two gussets in it; that in front of the sleeve, or nearest the wrist, is thirteen nails square; the other gusset, which also forms part of the arm-hole, is five nails and a half square.

The collar is thirteen nails long, and five nails and a half in its whole width.

In making up, run and fell the seams, letting in the gores, observing to put the straight part in front. Hem down the fronts half a nail deep, and at the bottom one nail. The sleeve is very peculiar, and requires attention in making up (see Fig. 32, 33). The large gusset is put into the sleeve towards the wrist, so as to hang down very low below the arms. This gusset is rounded off at the corner, A; and form the other corner of the gusset, B, along the doubled part, B A, cut open a piece large enough to admit of the small gusset being sewed into it; D is the doubled part of each gusset. The whole of the top of the sleeve is gathered up into the neck at the collar, while part of the side of the sleeve and the small gusset form the part that fits into the arm-hole of the surplice; the skirt is all fulled into the collar, together with the top of the two sleeves, and then nicely biassed down in two rows below the collar.

The collar is stitched all round like that of a shirt.

THE SASH OR BADGE.
PLATE 18. FIG. 30.

It is made of rich black silk or satin.

It is the whole breadth of the silk in depth, and three quarters of a yard long. It is folded in three or four regular plaits until it is about two nails broad; these plaits are confined at the ends by sewing them to double pieces of silk (see A), which are cut out two nails square, and rounded off at the outer ends, to a half circular form. Strings of ribbon of 3d. width, are sewed to these ends, which tie round the waist.

THE SCARF OR HOOD.

This is made of silk, but of such various forms, depending on the degree of the wearer, and the college where he has been educated, that it is needless to enter upon the subject in detail.

THE BANDS.
PLATE 18. FIG. 31.

They are made of the finest cambric, and are about two nails deep, and one nail wide when hemmed.

The hem being a quarter of a nail deep. They should be a little hollowed at the top, to fit the neck. The two bands are sewed to a tape in the inside, which ties round the neck.

THE CLERK'S GOWN.
PLATE 18. FIG. 41, 42.

The clerk's gown is made of black stuff or calimanco.

Cut four breadths of about one yard and a half long; these breadths when sewed together, leaving one open for the front, are biassed behind, from the middle of the second to the middle of the third breadth; this biassing is in three rows from the collar, the first row being one quarter of a nail below it, and the two others at one nail distant from each other.

The shoulders are next sloped from the remainder, like those of a pinafore, being three nails and a half long, and sewed up. The arm-hole is cut into the front breadth at the distance of one nail beyond the first seam, and is five nails long. The shoulder-flaps are one nail and a half deep, by five long.

The sleeve is the whole width of the breadth, about six nails wide when doubled, and is fifteen or sixteen nails long; at six nails from the top, the slit is cut in the sleeves of two nails deep on each side of the top of the arm. The bottom of the sleeve is sewed up together, and when done, instead of sewing them as the sleeve would naturally lie, the stuff at the bottom is differently folded, so as to make the two creases lie together, and thus distorts or twists the sleeve.

Strings are put to the collar, which is cut like Fig. 13, Plate 16. A broad hem is made in front, and at the bottom.

CHILDREN'S BONNETS.
PLATE 19.

The first bonnet for infants after the hood (see Chap. 4, in baby-linen), should be soft and warm, and till they are two or three years old, children should wear them of cloth, merino, silk, satin, print, or calico, in preference to straw, or pasteboard. Bonnets should be light but warm, and for young children especially, should have little trimming or ornament. A few pretty and simple shapes for both the upper and lower classes are here given and explained.

SOFT BONNET FOR A CHILD SIX YEARS OLD.
PLATE 19. FIG. 1, 2, 3.

This may be made of cloth, merino, chintz, or nankeen, with cotton runners. It is in three parts, the brim, front or poke, the crown, and the round patch.

Cut first a paper pattern the whole size of each part of the bonnet, the Plate represents but half, therefore double the paper and cut it by the figure. Your paper must be five nails wide by four long, for the poke, Fig. 2.

Measure along the top, A B, two and three-quarter nails, the point, C, is exactly half-way down the side, two nails from the top and bottom; the point, G, is two nails from the side, and one and a half nails from the top; curve along B G C. E is two and a half nails from the corner; from C to E, must be gradually sloped or rounded: go on, sloping it easily, up to F, which is one and a half nails from the top; from F to A, is quite straight.

The crown comes next; your paper must be four nails square, when doubled at D. From the corner to H, is half a nail, from H to I, two nails, slope gradually to K, which is two and a quarter nails from the top: cut in a straight line from K to L, which is situated two nails from the corner, and again in a straight line from L to M, one and a quarter nail from the bottom. From M to H, is slightly curved. The patch is made to fit the crown.

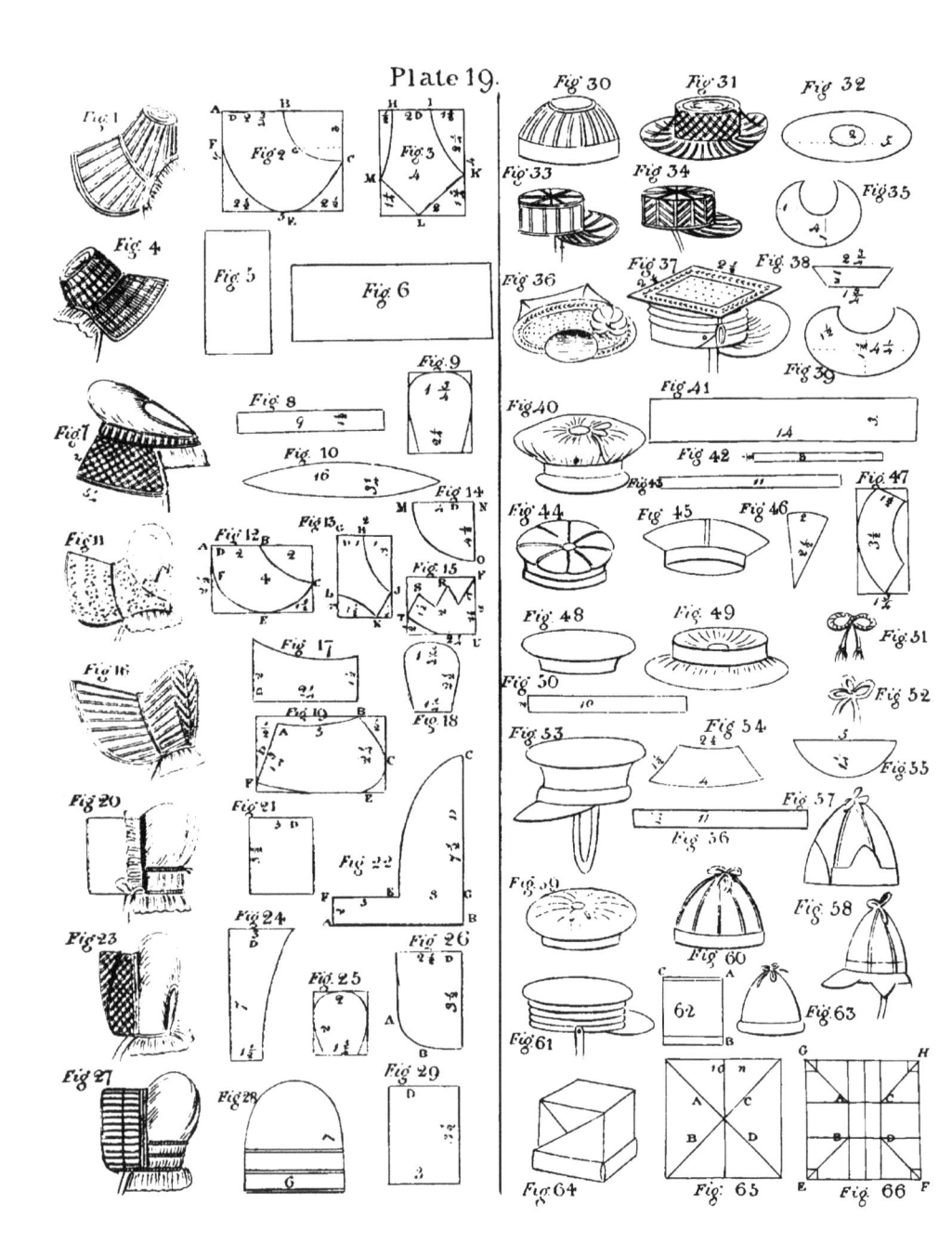

Plate 19.

In making up, a lining is cut out exactly the size of the outside, run the two together on the wrong side, at the edge of the brim, and turn them; then run cotton cords between the lining and the outside, as in the Plate, and two or three are put round the edge to give it firmness: runners are also made in the crown and the patch, the latter having a cord all round it, and they are then sewed strongly together, the part, H M, fitting into B G C, and the patch into I K. A curtain, one nail and a half in depth, is put on rather full behind, and strings of the chintz, or calico neatly hemmed, or of ribbon will complete it. The size here given is for a child five years old, but it is a useful kind of bonnet for those much younger.

CHILD'S DRAWN BONNET.
PLATE 19. FIG. 4, 5, 6.

This is usually made of silk, satin, or glazed calico.

The poke or front (Fig. 5), is an oblong, which is cut two or more nails down the selvage, according to the depth desired, and of such a length (cut width-way of the material), as will be two and a half times the length from ear to ear. This oblong is hemmed at each side, and bobbins put in to draw it up: two runners are made at equal distances between to draw up. The crown or head-piece, Fig. 6, is in one piece, and is also an oblong, about one nail deeper than the poke, and a fourth longer. Make runners down each side, and three or four equal distances between.

In making up the bonnet, the poke is drawn up to the proper size, and a double piping laid round it. The crown is then formed by drawing up the first runner as close as possible, and the second sufficiently so to make it flat and circular. The remainder is drawn to the proper shape to form the head-piece, being less drawn at each succeeding runner to make it wider at the bottom. Lay on a band of silk piped at each end, and sew it firmly round, and then attach the poke to it. Next make a soft lining to the head-piece, and a circular piece of wool in muslin may be attached to the crown, to keep it in shape. A curtain and strings complete the bonnet. A quilling of ribbon round the edge, and a rosette at the side, give a greater finish.

SOFT BONNET FOR A CHILD SEVEN OR EIGHT YEARS OLD.
PLATE 19. FIG. 7, 8, 9, 10.

This is a remarkably neat little bonnet; it is in four parts. The poke is a plain piece two nails and a half deep, by ten nails and a half long, sloped off at the outer edge one nail and a half at each end, it is ornamented with cotton runners, quilted or braided; cut a strip, Fig. 8, nine nails long by one nail and a half wide, which must have a runner at each edge, and the same in rows across, to give it firmness, if it is not quilted or braided; the third part is another strip sixteen nails long, and three nails and a quarter wide at the widest part, sloped off nearly to a point at each end, Fig. 10; the horse-shoe, two nails and a quarter long, and one nail and three quarters broad at the top, is lined and has a cord run all round the edge. The curtain is one nail and a half deep, put on rather full.

In making up, sew the quilted poke or front strongly to the straight strip, Fig. 8; gather the sloped strip, Fig. 10, at each edge, set it on one side into the straight piece, and on the other into the horse-shoe, fulling it more in front than at the sides. Put on the curtain, and the bonnet is finished. It draws up behind to the side of the head; here it is represented as undrawn.

SOFT BONNET FOR A CHILD TWO YEARS OLD.
PLATE 19. FIG. 11, 12, 13, 14, 15.

This is well adapted for a child's first or second bonnet, and looks well, made of coloured kerseymere or Indiana braided or worked in chain-stitch.

To cut out the poke, take a piece of paper, which when doubled is four nails long by two and a half nails wide (see Fig. 12), the doubled part from D to B, is two nails long; slope off gradually from A to E, beginning the greatest sloping at F, which is about half way down the side; the point E is one nail and a half from the corner, continue sloping to C, which is about one nail above the bottom of your paper; the curve, B C, is parallel to, or even with the curve, A F E. The head-piece, Fig. 13, is cut from a paper, which when folded is three nails long and two broad; from G to H, the doubled part, is one nail, from G to L, two nails and a quarter; cut a slightly curved line from L to K, the point K, being half a nail from the corner, next cut quite straight to J, being three quarters of a nail above the angle or corner, sweep gradually from J to H. Fig. 14 represents half the crown; D is the doubled part, and is four nails long from M to N; the part from N to O is four and a half nails, the rest from O to M, is cut like a quarter of a circle. Fig. 15 is the part that supports or holds up the crown behind, the doubled part, U P, is two nails and a half long, from U to T is two nails and a quarter, curve it gently about half a nail; from the corner to T is half a nail; from T to S is one nail and a half, S being half a nail from the side of the square; the top of R, the next vandyke is two nails in a straight line from the bottom. These vandykes are about one nail deep.

The Plate shows sufficiently clearly how this bonnet is made up, to dispense with any further description, except to say that the crown, Fig. 14, is evenly gathered into the head-piece, Fig. 13, and the back-piece, Fig. 15. The curtain is put on, strings and a small bow may be added behind.

SOFT BONNET FOR A CHILD THREE YEARS OLD.
PLATE 19. FIG. 16. 17, 18, 19.

This bonnet is very generally worn; the one represented in the Plate is for a little girl about three years old, though older and younger children would find it both suitable and comfortable; it is made of cloth, print, or nankeen, lined, and with runners in every part. It is in three pieces; to cut out the poke, Fig. 19, take a piece of paper, which, when folded in two, is four nails long and two nails and a quarter broad; D is the doubled part; from A to B is three nails, it is slightly curved; A being about one quarter of a nail from the top and half a nail from the side, next cut in nearly a straight line to C, and continue the curving to E, which is half a nail from the corner; from B to E, in a straight line, is two nails and a quarter; cut in a straight direction from E to F, the latter being one quarter of a nail above the corner; from A to F is one nail and three quarters.

The head-piece, Fig. 17, when doubled (D being the folded part), is two nails and a half long, and two nails at the deepest part, which is to go in the front, sloped off to one nail and a half for the back. The crown is merely a horse-shoe; Fig. 18 is two nails and a half long, one nail and three quarters at the top, and sloped off one quarter of a nail on each side, so as to make it only one nail and a quarter at the bottom.

In making up, the runners may be put in simply as in the Plate, or arranged in a pattern, or the bonnet may be quilted, but there must be two or three runners round the edge, and inner part of the poke, at the top and bottom of the head-piece, and all round the horse-shoe.

Put on a full curtain of one nail and a half deep.

BONNET FOR A CHILD FOUR YEARS OLD.
PLATE 19. FIG. 20, 21, 22.

This is a neat little bonnet with a stiff front, and is cut out as follows:—

For the pattern of the front, Fig. 20, let your paper, when folded in two, be three nails and a half long, by three nails broad, it may be rounded or left square at the ends, according to fancy, D being the doubled part; this front or poke is made of stiff pasteboard.

The crown, Fig. 22, is seven nails long at the doubled part, D, and six nails long at the bottom, A B, cut in a straight line, A F, for two nails, and again straight, F E, for three nails, then round it gradually up to C.

Before making up, cut out two pieces of calico, print, silk, or other material, the size of the poke, Fig. 21, then run them neatly together at the edge, and up the ends, and slip the pasteboard in; hem the bottom of the crown, Fig. 22, A B, and up the ends, A F, for the curtain. Hem from F to E, and make a runner about half a nail within the edge up to C, through which a bobbin must be passed, and drawn up to the width of the poke; it must be sewed strongly to the outside of the front, letting the little frill lie over it, as in the Plate, forming a sort of trimming; the lining of the poke must be only turned in, and slightly tacked down, so that the pasteboard may be easily taken out when the bonnet is washed. A runner is made across the back of the crown, about two nails above F E G, through which tapes are passed: the ends of the lower ones are sewed a little way along the poke, and when the bonnet is fitted to the head, these runners are drawn to the proper size. Put on hemmed strings of the same material.

SOFT BONNET FOR A CHILD, THREE, FOUR, OR FIVE YEARS OLD.
PLATE 19. FIG. 23, 24, 25, 26.

This is a school child's common bonnet, it may be made of print, gingham, or nankeen, and is in three parts. The head-piece, Fig. 24, when folded in two, is seven nails long, and three nails wide at the doubled and widest part, D, sloped off to one nail and a half at the bottom. The poke, Fig. 26, when doubled, is two nails and a half broad, by three nails and a half long, and a little rounded from A to B. Fig. 25 is the horse-shoe, two nails long, and two nails broad at the top, sloped off to one nail and three quarters at the bottom.

In making up, the front is wadded or quilted, with a cotton runner at the outer edge, and two or three at the inner edge, to give it firmness; a runner is also put in round the horse-shoe. The front of the crown is gathered evenly to the poke, the horse-shoe set in, and a curtain set on behind.

When worn, the front of the bonnet is turned up, as in the Plate.

ANOTHER SOFT BONNET FOR A YOUNG CHILD.
PLATE 19. FIG. 27, 28, 29.

This is also a school child's bonnet, and may be made of any soft or washing material.

Fig. 29 represents the poke, which, when doubled at D, is three nails and a half long, by three nails wide. The crown, Fig. 28, is six nails wide at the bottom, and seven nails at its longest part, rounded off on each side; three runners are made at the bottom of it, about a nail apart.

The poke is quilted, wadded, or run with cotton, and the crown sewed to it, rather fuller in the centre in front, than at the sides; the runners are drawn up, and tied at the proper size, and upon the lower one a curtain, one nail and a half or two nails deep, is set, and extends a little on each side upon the ends of the front or brim.

HATS AND CAPS.
PLATE 19.

Hats and caps for young boys should be made of soft materials, similar to bonnets for little girls; as they become older, their hats must of course be stronger and stiffer; some of both sorts will here be described, as well as travelling and other caps for grown up persons.

w

PORRINGER CLOTH CAP.
PLATE 19. FIG. 30.

This is an extremely simple cap for young boys; it is made of cloth or merino, and consists of three pieces. The band, which is merely a piece of cloth half a nail deep, and sufficiently long to go round the child's head, say, eight nails and a half, or nine nails long; the head-piece, which is also about nine nails long, before being joined up, and one nail and a half deep, is made with runners in an upright direction or across the cloth at regular distances, which give a degree of firmness to the cap; the round patch or crown is about one nail and a half across, with a runner made round the edge of it. When made up, it should be lined with demet or flannel and soft calico.

SOFT HAT FOR A YOUNG CHILD.
PLATE 19. FIG. 31, 32.

This little hat looks very pretty made of glazed cambric muslin or of calico, either white or coloured; if wanted for winter wear, it may be made of merino, cloth, or kerseymere, plain or braided.

For the brim, Fig. 32, cut a circle five nails across, with a hole in the centre of it two nails across, for the head, a little may be sloped off from the back, or not, according to pleasure; the crown is one nail and a quarter deep, and nine nails long before it is joined up, and the circle or patch is made to fit exactly. When the hat is made of glazed calico, it is lined with the same, and runners of cotton put in, either simply or in a pattern. A strap or ribbon is attached on each side, from about half way up the crown to about half the breadth of the brim, to keep it up and in its place. Strings are sewed at the inside.

SOFT CAP FOR A YOUNG BOY.
PLATE 19. FIG. 33.

This cap is made of glazed calico, white or coloured, or of any other soft light material, with runners in it; the brim is cut in the shape of Fig. 39, it is four nails and a quarter long, one nail and a half broad at the deepest part, sloped off as in the Plate; the crown is one nail and a quarter deep, and from eight to nine nails long before being sewed up; the circle of course is made to fit it.

ANOTHER CAP.
PLATE 19. FIG. 34.

This is only a variety of the preceding cap; the brim is cut like Fig. 35, and is four nails long, and one nail deep, at the broadest part in front, sloped off at the ends; the Plate shews the way in which the runners are put in.

CAP FOR AN INFANT BOY.
PLATE 19. FIG. 36, 37, 38, 39.

This is a remarkably pretty cap for an infant, after he has left off his hood; it is made of white or coloured satin, kerseymere, or merino.

The brim, Fig. 39, is four nails and a quarter long, one nail and a half deep, and sloped as in the Plate, the head-piece is a full nail deep when folded in small plaits, and eight nails and three quarters long before it is sewed up; the little flap or piece behind, Fig. 38, is about one nail deep; the longest part of it, or that to be turned up, is two nails and three quarters long; that fastened to the hat is one nail and three quarters; it is sloped at each end. The square or top of the hat, is two nails and a half every way; four other pieces must be cut one nail deep, and two nails and three quarters wide at the top, sloped at each side down to two nails at the bottom.

In making up, take a piece of buckram of the size of the head-piece, lay it upon a demet or thin wadding, and flute the kerseymere upon it, putting a fine silk cord, or a piece of coarse stay or netting silk between the flutes.

The crown must next be prepared; ornament the square according to fancy, working the pattern in spots, either in braid, or in stay or netting silk; line this also with buckram, demet, and silk, to each side of the square, sew the widest side of each of the four pieces above described, these pieces having previously been lined, as before mentioned, sew the corners of the four firmly together, inlaying a piping; the head-piece is then put on, next set on the back-piece, Fig. 38, this is lined with silk or satin, in the following manner:—After the buckram is put in, the lining is sewed to it, and not being sloped at the narrow end of the kerseymere, it allows of being fulled or plaited at the part nearest the hat. The brim is finished in the same manner, the satin lining being plain at the edge, and gathered to the head-piece; it has also demet and buckram within the lining, and is worked in a similar manner to the square, upon the front or turned up part, which is of kerseymere. Put a silk, calico, or muslin lining into the head, and a silk tassel at the left corner of the square; a satin rosette in front, and strings complete the cap.

BOY'S CAP OF FIVE OR SIX YEARS OLD.
PLATE 19. FIG. 40, 41, 42, 43.

This cap is made of cloth or Holland; the crown, Fig. 41, is fourteen nails long, and three nails deep; the band, Fig. 42, is eight nails long, and half a nail broad; the brim or edge, Fig. 43, is eleven nails long, and one nail deep.

In making up, the crown, Fig. 41, is wadded and lined, it is then gathered evenly into the band on one side, and into the small circular patch or button on the other; the band, Fig. 42, is lined with flannel as well as calico; the brim, which is wadded and lined, has a piece of buckram put within the lining, it is sewed on so as to turn up and set rather round. A tassel or bow of ribbon may or may not be added at the top, according to pleasure.

CAP FOR A BOY SEVEN OR EIGHT YEARS OLD.
PLATE 19. FIG. 44, 45, 46, 47.

This looks neat made of Holland, with a piping of dark blue, green, or the same colour.

The top of the crown is in eight pieces, cut out of a circle, five nails across; this will make each division two nails and a half long, and two nails at the broadest part, sloped to a point, and the shape of Fig. 46. The side of the crown is in four pieces, Fig. 47; to cut these, make another circle the same size as the top, and in the centre of it cut a smaller one, two nails across, then divide the circle into four parts. The band is about one nail broad, when made up, and nine nails long, before it is joined at the ends.

In making up, sew the eight pieces together, laying a coloured piping between them, and putting a button at the top; the four sides, Fig. 47, being previously lined with buckram, demet, and glazed calico, are then each sewed to the circle thus formed, one of the sides fitting to two of the smaller pieces at the top; they must be sewed on the wrong side very firmly, and turned down, so that the stitches are not seen on the outside, the ends of these four pieces being piped, are then sewed together. The cap is now ready for the band, which, after being wadded, is stitched on, and the whole is finished.

CAP FOR A BOY, SIX OR EIGHT YEARS OLD.
PLATE 19. FIG. 48, 49, 50.

This is a simple cap and easily made; it consists merely of two pieces.

The crown is a circle of eight nails across, lined and wadded, which is equally gathered all round, and set into a band, which is one nail and a half deep, and nine or ten nails long before it is joined up, Fig. 50: this band is also wadded, and a bow of ribbon may be put on one side.

CAP FOR AN OLDER BOY.
PLATE 19. FIG. 53, 54, 55, 56.

This is a remarkably neat cap, and may be worn by either a boy or a man; it is generally made of cloth.

The circle at the top is five nails across, the side part is cut out of a circle in the same manner as that of Fig. 45, the outer circle being five nails across, and the inner one two nails; this circle is divided into four pieces; the band, Fig. 56, is one nail and a quarter broad, and eleven nails long before it is sewed up; the peak, Fig 55, is generally made of patent leather; it is part of a circle, five nails across, and is one nail and a quarter deep at the broadest part.

In making up, the circle is first lined with flannel and then with silk; it is stretched over a strong but not very thick wire at the edge, to keep it in shape, and a piping of cloth put on all round: the sides, Fig. 54, are then lined with soft leather, and sewed to the circle on the wrong side, before being joined together; the seams are next sewed up, and a thin hoop of whalebone put at the bottom of these sides, just where the band is to be joined on, round the head; the band is firmly stitched to it, which band is also lined with thin, but not very pliable leather: the peak is then put on; a lining of leather one nail and a quarter deep is sewed in the inside, to the inner part of which, a piece of silk is attached, with a string-case and cord to draw it up to the size of the head. Sometimes a band of black velvet, or of silver or gold lace is laid upon the cloth one, sometimes it is left quite plain. The strap under the chin is of patent leather, fastened at the side with a small buckle.

GENTLEMEN'S TRAVELLING CAP.
PLATE 19. FIG. 57, 58.

This is a particularly comfortable cap, and is easily made. It is composed of fine cloth of any dark colour, trimmed with fur.

Make a circle, seven nails across, and cut it into six parts; the brim is made either of patent leather, or of cloth, it must be three nails and a half long at the straight part or bottom of it, one and three-quarters of a nail deep at the broadest part, and rounded off at each end: the flaps or pieces for the ears are also one and three-quarters of a nail deep at the broadest part; they are cut in one length with the band, which goes behind the cap, and is one nail deep; the whole length, including the ear-flaps, is seven nails.

In making up, first join with a piping of the same, all the six divisions of the crown, fastening them at the top with a round button, and put in a lining of wadding, stiffened muslin, and any dark coloured silk; sew all these round the edge, and then put on the brim or peak: this, when of cloth, is made of two pieces the same size and shape; run them together at the edge on the wrong side, with a piping between them, turn them to the right side, put in a piece of stiff muslin, and a thin wadding, sew it on to the front of the cap at the edge, and again half a nail above, so that, though it can be pulled down over the eyes, it usually remains turned up, as in Fig. 57: the band behind, with the ear-flaps, is then sewed on; this is a piece of cloth, with a strip of dark fur or velvet laid on it, so that when the strings of the ear-flaps are tied under the chin, the fur lies against the throat and ears, and when not required, the strings are tied on the top of the head, the velvet or fur forming a kind of trimming to the cap.

A LADY'S RIDING CAP.
PLATE 19. FIG. 59.

This is made of velvet, and is simply a straight piece, a yard long and about eight nails deep, lined with flannel or wadding, buckram and silk, which is joined up at the two ends, and gathered on the one side, under a small flat silk or gold button, and on the other, into a velvet band, one nail deep, and made to fit the head. A silk bow and tassel (see Fig. 51) are put on at the top, and ribbon strings fasten under the chin, or not, according to pleasure.

A TRAVELLING CAP.
PLATE 19. FIG. 60.

This is a soft cap, and is generally made of cloth. It is formed of a circle, eight nails across, cut in eight parts, which are joined with pipings of the same, and fastened at the top with a knot or tassel. The crown is lined in a similar manner to Fig. 58, and the band, which must have buckram within the lining of silk or soft leather, is firmly stitched to it.

A NEAT BOY'S CAP.
PLATE 19. FIG. 61.

This is made of cloth or Holland. The top is a circle of five nails across, the head-piece is nine nails long, and one nail and a half deep when made up, it is plaited in very small exact folds, and therefore before it is made up, it must be four nails and a half broad: the brim or peak is of patent leather, and the strap under the chin of the same.

In making up, the top or crown must be wadded, stiffened with buckram, and lined: the head-piece is then prepared, by being folded, and the folds stitched upon a piece of stiff buckram, the proper length: the crown is sewed to it, the peak and strap put on, as in the Plate.

A TRAVELLING CAP FOR GENTLEMEN OR LADIES.
PLATE 19. FIG. 62, 63.

This is a very simple, and at the same time, a very good looking cap: it is made either of velvet, or of fine cloth, and when doubled, as in Fig. 62, forms nearly a square.

To make it, put in a wadding and lining, join it up behind, A B, make a string-case, A C, through which a silk cord must be run, which draws it up to the shape of a cap, and trim it round the edge or brim with some rich fur. The advantage of the string-case at the top is, that when not in use, it will pack quite flatly and take up little room.

THE WORKING MAN'S CAP.
PLATE 19. FIG. 64. 65, 66.

Fold a sheet of common brown paper to make a workman's cap, as follows:—

Let it be a square of ten nails, double it across like a half-handkerchief, and crease it well; open it and cross it again the other way, open it again, double down the middle one way, and crease it well;

on spreading it out, it will be marked according to the lines in Fig. 65. Measure from the centre on the cross lines, about one nail and three-quarters (see A B C D), next crease the paper from side to side through these points, thus:—one line through A B, another through C D, and again C A, and D B; this will form a square in the middle. Cut out a nail square at every corner, as in Fig. 66.

In folding it up, the square, A B C D, in the centre, forms the top of the cap, and the points, E F, are doubled according to the cross-wise plait, and crossed in front towards each other, the other points, G H, are likewise crossed behind towards their opposite ends. The cap is then formed by merely turning up a piece all round to make it stand firmly. (Fig. 64.)

WOMEN'S BONNETS.
PLATE 20.

Bonnets being, like gowns, dependent in a great measure on the fancy and whim of the day, will only be treated of as to the general modes of making them up, and a few of the very plainest shapes given.

Bonnets are made of velvet, plush, satin, silk, crape, book-muslin, chip, gingham, and glazed calico. The foundations are either pasteboard, buckram, stiff muslin, or willow.

Bonnets are kept in shape by means of wire, chip, or whalebone.

They are lined either with the material of which the bonnet is made, or with some other, lighter or warmer, according to taste, and the time of the year; but care must be taken that the colours either harmonize or decidedly contrast. When the lining is white, a sheet of tissue paper is put between it and the bonnet, whether it be of silk, or only of straw; this makes the white material, whatever it may be, look a much purer colour than it otherwise would do. A piece of demet or of thin wadding should always be laid between the foundation and the silk, or other material of which it is made, unless that material is very thick.

Bonnets may be lined with ribbon in the following manner:—

Take a piece similar to the trimming, and long enough to be run plainly to the outer edge of the bonnet all round, the other side of the ribbon is finely gathered, and being drawn up to the size of the inside of the bonnet, it is neatly sewed to it, forming a kind of border or trimming.

When a bonnet is lined plainly, or the cross-way, it takes half a yard cut cross-wise. If a curtain is required in addition, three quarters of a yard, cut the straight-way, must be purchased.

In fitting your lining, lay it across the bonnet, so that as little as possible is wasted or cut off at the corner; put small pins all round the edge, and the inside also, so as to keep it in its place, cutting off the superfluous quantity and then sew it, concealing your stitches as much as possible between the lining and the bonnet.

To line a bonnet the straight way, so that, though plain at the edge, it is a little fulled or plaited into the crown, about three quarters of a yard is required, influenced of course in some degree, both by the depth of the poke and its width. This lining is very easily put in; sew it round the edge on the wrong side as far as the ears or rounded part of the bonnet, by which means the stitches are quite concealed, then turn it, and sew the rest as neatly as you can; the lining looks the best plaited into the crown; to do this equally, begin in the middle, making a perfectly straight fold, the rest on each side should incline a little to the centre, and be very small and regular.

Bonnets may be trimmed in a great variety of ways with the material of which they are made, cut cross-wise and either hemmed or lined, so as to form a kind of ribbon, with velvet, plush, satin, silk, crape, gauze, muslin, or ribbon.

Plate 20.

Bows to be worn in front, or at the side, are generally made up and sewed upon a piece of wire ribbon, which gives them firmness, and makes them keep in their place and shape.

Velvet or plush trimmings are generally lined with satin or silk of the same shade. The colour of the ribbon, if not an exact match with that of the bonnet, should be darker.

Curtains may be made either of the material that lines the bonnet or ribbon. For the former, the silk or satin is cut the cross-way, and is from one nail and a half to two nails deep; it is hemmed at the edge, and sometimes a straw plait or silk cord is laid on above the hem; they may be either plaited on to the bonnet in large full plaits, or hemmed, and a piece of ribbon, exactly the length that the curtain is to be, run in; this looks better than the plaiting, and does not so soon become flattened.

Ribbon curtains are made in two ways, the one by merely plaiting or gathering a straight piece of ribbon, and hemming the ends; the other, and much the prettiest method, is also the most complicated. Fold the end of your ribbon down like a half handkerchief, Fig. 13, and cut it off, thus leaving a cross-way end; fold it again, straight down the ribbon, measuring it so as to be doubled the same depth top and bottom, thus forming a piece like Fig. 14: cut off a number of these pieces, which must then be run very flatly together, so that the cross-way parts of the ribbon are at the top and bottom, and the border or edge lies in oblique or slanting lines across the curtain, Fig. 15, 16; one end will be pointed or sloped outwards, in order to make the other like it, the half square cut off at first, must be joined to it. The number of pieces of course must depend on the breadth of the ribbon, the whole curtain should be about three quarters of a yard long; when the parts are joined together, hem your curtain top and bottom, running a ribbon in at the top, in order to full it properly to the bonnet.

OLD WOMAN'S BONNET.
PLATE 20. FIG. 1, 2, 3.

This is a comfortable shape for an old woman, and is very easily made. It is in two pieces, the front or poke is made of pasteboard, covered with silk or any dark coloured material. To cut the pattern of it, take a piece of paper, four nails and a half square when folded (see Fig. 2), let D be the doubled part, and round it off gradually at the corner, A. The crown is cut out according to Fig. 3.

SCALE.

	Nails.
From B to C the doubled part	8
From B to G	8¼
From G to F	2
From F to E	4
Then slope gradually to C from E	

In making up, having previously cut out two pieces the proper size to cover the poke, one for the outside, and one for the lining, run them together on the wrong side, round that part which is to form the edge of the bonnet, leaving open that which is to be sewed to the crown, and slip the pasteboard into it: then begin the crown, Fig. 3, hem it at the bottom and make a runner from F E to H, and another, one nail or one nail and half above it, and put in a string; set the front of the crown, C E, on to the poke, either in gathers or small plaits, draw up the runners behind to the proper size to fit the head, and fasten them; sew each end of the curtain a little way on the ends of the poke as in the Plate; put a ribbon on across the front, and strings, with a bow at the top; one may be added behind, at pleasure.

BONNET FOR A MEMBER OF THE SOCIETY OF FRIENDS.
PLATE 20. FIG. 4, 5, 6.

These bonnets are made of black, white, grey, or fawn coloured silk. They are cut out as follows:—

For the pattern of the poke, Fig. 6, let your paper be doubled at D, which part must be four nails and a half long; from A to B is three nails and three quarters; slope off the front at the corner. For the crown, Fig. 5, let the doubled part, D, be eight nails long, and from C to E is four nails and a half; it is gradually sloped from F, as in the Plate.

In making up, run the pieces cut for the outside and lining together at the edge, on the wrong side, and having turned them, slip in the pasteboard; plait the front of the crown into the poke in very small exact folds, leaving it quite plain for some distance above the ears; make a narrow runner behind of one nail and a half in depth, to form a curtain, and put on ribbon strings the same colour as the bonnet.

A NEAT BONNET FOR A SERVANT.
PLATE 20. FIG. 7, 8, 9.

To cut out the poke of this bonnet, Fig. 8, which is of pasteboard, take a doubled piece of paper, five nails wide, by four nails and a half long, letting D be the doubled part.

SCALE.

	Nails.
From A to B............................	2
From A to F............................	1
From the corner to E	3
Above the corner to C................	$2\frac{1}{4}$

Curve from B to C, slope from C to E, round from E to F.

The foundation of the crown, Fig. 9, is of buckram, or willow; let your doubled paper be three nails and a half wide, by four nails and a quarter long; D is the doubled part.

SCALE.

	Nails.
From the corner to C	$2\frac{1}{4}$
From the corner to H	$2\frac{1}{4}$
From the corner to I	$1\frac{1}{4}$
J above the corner	1

Curve from G to H, cut from H to I, and from I to J.

The circular top or patch, is cut to fit the bonnet.

In making up, cover each part with silk, laying a thin piece of wadding between the silk and the foundation, then sew them very firmly together, with strong silk or waxed thread, and put a Persian or muslin lining in the crown. Silk cut the cross-way and laid in moderate sized plaits may be folded round the crown of the bonnet, which has a very neat appearance. The more simply it is trimmed, the better it looks; a ribbon across, to form strings, and one bow behind or at the side, is quite sufficient.

A SCHOOL GIRL'S BONNET.
PLATE 20. FIG. 10, 11, 12.

To cut out the poke, Fig. 11, when laid open, let your paper be eight nails wide, by seven long.

SCALE.

	Nails.
From A to S is	3¼
From S to B..	2¼
From T to C..	4
Above the corner to E.....................................	1¼
From the side to F	1
From the top to F	2¼
From Z to Y..	3¼

Cut from F to E, round from F to C, and from C, through Y, and B, to A, curve A Z F.

The crown or head-piece, Fig. 12, is thus formed; let your paper be six nails wide, by seven nails and a half long.

SCALE.

	Nails.
From H to G	2¼
From the corner to G	¾
From the corner to K	2¼
J is from the corner..........................	1
From the corner to I	2

Slope G to K, shape according to the Plate from K to J, cut from J to I, curve from I to H.

The top or circle is cut exactly to fit this crown.

This bonnet is made of glazed calico; the poke is of pasteboard. If many of them are required, it is the best economy to cut out all the pokes at once, and then all the crowns, as they will fit into each other. Make it up as follows:—

After joining the two ends of the head-piece, wire and sew the circle into it, then tack the calico on the crown or circle; then tack a piece of calico outside the head-piece, piping it up the joinings; run on the lining of the poke, after which the outside cover is put on and tacked strongly at the edge; the trimming will conceal the stitches; sew the trimming, which is merely a cross-way hem one nail deep and piped to the inside of the edge of the poke with small stitches, then turn it over on the outside and sew it neatly down to the upper calico, taking care not to go through the pasteboard. Fasten the poke to the crown, and then put in the lining, making it to draw, and sewing it on the inside. The trimming, piping and bow, are all cut the cross-way; the strings are half a yard long, cut straight. One bonnet takes one sheet of 3d. pasteboard, and about one yard and a half of 4d. glazed calico, including the trimming; with the wire it comes to 9d. prime cost.

For winter wear, it is desirable to line both poke and crown with wadding or flannel.

A neat simple trimming for children's bonnets, is made as follows:—

Cut strips of glazed calico, one nail wide, fold them so that the raw edges shall lie at the back; making each strip somewhat less than half a nail broad, and then with a long needleful of coloured thread, run on the right side of it, up and down in vandykes; when done, draw it up, and it forms a pretty sort of edging.

OILED SILK HOODS.
PLATE 20. FIG. 17, 18.

These hoods are convenient for persons who travel much, or go excursions in open carriages, as a protection against rain; they are made of oiled silk, either black, or light coloured, the former looks best.

The shape is very simple, the hood consisting of four parts: the front is a straight piece, one yard long, and six nails and a half broad. The horse-shoe, Fig. 18, which is rather a different shape to the usual one, is six nails and a half long, four nails wide at the top, and five nails at the bottom; the curtain or tippet is half a yard deep, and one yard and three quarters long; the band is one nail broad, ten nails long.

In making up, the head-piece is run to the horse-shoe quite plainly, and the front, or part round the face is hemmed or bound; it is then set into the band, the horse-shoe being plainly put in, and the rest plaited in small folds; the curtain is sewed on in small plaits all round, the band lined with silk or ribbon, and a large hook and eye or chain is put on. The curtain is either hemmed or bound all round.

CALECHE.
PLATE 20. FIG. 19, 20.

These are worn by ladies who walk short distances to evening parties, and are better than a bonnet as they do not crush or disturb the cap or head-dress.

A calèche is best made of dark silk or satin, and lined with the same colour; it is in three parts. The front, or head-piece, is seven nails and a half wide, and one yard long; the horse-shoe, Fig. 19, is five nails and a half long by four nails and a half broad, at the widest part, sloped down to four nails at the bottom; the curtain is one yard and a quarter long, and one nail and a half deep. A lining is cut out exactly similar to the outside; and it is made up as follows:—

Run the edges of the head-piece and lining together on the wrong side, and turn them, put in a piece of whalebone the whole length of the front, viz:—one yard, about half a quarter of a nail broad, and run on the other side of it, to secure it, leave a space of one nail and a half broad, and make a runner the proper width to receive a second whalebone, and then, leaving the same distances, make runners for two more; the spaces between are quilted, as in the Plate, to give a little firmness to the whole.

Between the fourth whalebone and the outer edge is an interval of two nails and a half, and this is not quilted like the rest. The horse-shoe is then made, the outside and lining being run together, a whalebone is put in, (see Fig. 19), at the edge, and again another, one nail within. The head-piece is then gathered (the rough edges of both the satin and lining being turned within, so as to make it perfectly neat at the inside), and sewed to the horse-shoe, the fulness being chiefly towards the top. It is then gathered at the neck, and bound with ribbon, or a piece of the same material, which form a string-case; and the curtain is set on, lined or not, according to pleasure. A ribbon, about one yard long, is sewn on the front of the caléche, three nails from the bottom on each side, forming a kind of loop, by which to hold it forward when it is worn.

CLOAKS.
PLATE 20.

Cloaks may be made of satin, silk, cloth, merino, shawling, both the real and the imitation, Scotch-plaid,

Orleans or common stuff. The choice of materials is of course influenced by the purpose for which the cloak is intended to be used; for instance, carriage or travelling cloaks are plain of a thicker substance, and have less work in them than those used for walking in.

Satin cloaks have frequently a velvet cape or collar, sometimes they are trimmed with broad velvet hems, laid on all round, or with fur, and occasionally lined with fur also. Silk and merino cloaks may likewise be trimmed with velvet, cut or uncut, plush or fur, and lined with the same, or they may be made perfectly plain. As a silk cloak is at all times a costly article of dress, and, with care, will last a long time, it is worth while to have the silk a very good one; it should be soft and rich, not liable to crease: levantine, satinette, or satin silk, are the best; and the colour should be one that will not easily fly, change, or spot; dark shades generally look the best, as black, violet, myrtle-green, or deep marone.

Satin, silk, and fine merino cloaks should be lined with sarsenet, either the same colour, or some well chosen contrast: but as these sarsenet linings cost a good deal for a full sized cloak, two old silk gowns, nicely picked to pieces, and either washed or dyed, would be a good substitute, where economy is an object: when this is done, it is a good plan to turn a deep hem of the outside silk over the edge, on each side in front, or it is better still to let the two front breadths of the lining be of new silk.

Cloaks may either be simply lined with a piece of flannel between the silk and the lining, which makes them light and suitable for walking in the autumn and the spring, or they may be lined and wadded; this is done by laying breadths either of thin flannel or lining muslin, cut the same size as the breadths of silk on a table, and placing upon them sheets of wadding, so as to cover them entirely; then with a long needleful of thread, the wadding should be tacked or basted in wide stitches backwards and forwards in sort of vandykes upon the muslin or flannel, in order that it may always keep in its place, which otherwise it would not do. The flannel with the wadding thus sewed to it, is then put between the two silks and the seams run up.

LADY'S SILK CLOAK.
PLATE 20. FIG. 21.

It consists of six breadths of silk, the proper length to fit the person for whom it is made, i. e. from the collar-bone to the top of the shoe. Cut a shoulder-piece the shape of Fig. 1, or 4, Plate 13, making it to fit, with flannel and silk lining to suit; next cut a collar, Fig. 7, Plate 13, with a stiff muslin and silk lining; then cut the cape, Fig. 15 and 16, Plate 13, with only a silk lining.

In making up, having laid the lining and wadding together as described above, run up the seams; cut the arm-holes one nail and a half from the seam between the first and second breadths, and two nails and a quarter below the shoulder-piece; each arm-hole is three nails and a quarter long.

The shoulder-piece is next made, by running the silk and lining together, with the wadding and flannel between them on the wrong side, and then turning it to the other; the three back breadths of the skirt are then hollowed out to fit the shoulder-piece, next full the whole into the shoulder-piece, letting the two front breadths, reach to the shoulder only, while the rest is sewed to the back. A hem one nail and three quarters deep of cross-way velvet, cut or uncut, or an edging of fur may be put on, up the fronts according to pleasure. The back is then plaited in behind, at a proper distance below the shoulder-piece, to suit the waist, say four nails, and a band long enough to go round the waist is laid upon these folds, and drawn through two large button-holes, one at each end of the plaiting; this band hooks or buttons in front, inside the cloak. Another way of confining it at the waist, is, by laying a ribbon along the inside of the back breadth, at the proper distance from the top, thus forming a kind of string-case, through which two ribbons are passed, fastened at one end, and drawn out at the other, of the runner; these ribbons tie round the waist at the inside. The collar having previously been lined, is then set on, and small pieces, three nails and a quarter long and half a nail broad, are lined, piped all round, and sewed on one side of each arm-hole, so as to lay over and cover it when the arms are not in. The cloak is fastened at the throat either by long silk cords the same colour, with tassels at the ends, or by a gilt or bronze chain.

The capes of these cloaks are frequently made loose from them, in which case they may be worn separately as mantles or short cloaks; when they are fastened on, they are sewed to the shoulder-piece.

LADY'S MANTELET OR SHORT CLOAK.
PLATE 20. FIG. 22.

These are made of velvet, satin, silk, cloth, merino or shawling; they are lined with silk, muslin, or glazed calico, and trimmed with lace, fringe, velvet, satin or fur; they are very convenient and light for walking, or going out in an evening. A mantelet reaches to a little above the knee, and fastens in the front with hooks and eyes; it is made exactly like the cape of a large cloak, with five breadths in it, a little hollowed round the neck, and set into a band, or a collar turned over.

LARGE CARRIAGE CLOAK OR ROQUELAURE.
PLATE 20. FIG. 23.

Used by ladies in an open carriage, to put on in case of rain. It is made of plaid or some woollen material, and consists of five breadths of eleven nails wide, and one yard and a half long; two arm-holes are made five nails from the top of the cloak, and five nails long, to these arm-holes are sewed loose sleeves, eight nails long, and four nails wide, when sewed up; they are merely attached to the cloak by being sewed to the top of the arm-hole, so that they may be put on, or left to hang down at pleasure. The cloak is lined with flannel and glazed calico, or calimanco, it is set into a band at the neck, of about ten nails long, and a collar and one or more deep capes put on. It fastens at the throat with a gilt or bronze chain.

LADY'S NEAT GARDEN OR SERVANT'S CLOAK.
PLATE 20. FIG. 24.

This may be made either of merino or Scotch plaid; if the former, it has three breadths in it, of seventeen nails wide; if the latter, it requires five breadths, eleven nails wide.

The shoulder-piece is like Fig. 3 or 4, Plate 13; it is lined and wadded, as are also two capes the same shape as the shoulder-piece cut larger; the collar is like Fig. 7, Plate 13. The whole cloak is lined with black or coloured glazed calico; arm-holes are left between the first and second breadths; they are four nails long, and three nails and a half from the bottom of the shoulder-piece; a small piece of the material, four nails long and three quarters of a nail wide, lined and piped all round, is set on along each slit or arm-hole.

These cloaks can be purchased ready made at the mercer's shop, and are from 9s. to 18s. each.

OLD WOMAN'S CLOAK AND HOOD.
PLATE 20. FIG. 26, 27.

These are generally made of scarlet cloth, or grey duffel, and have only one breadth in them. The cloth is about three yards wide, and it is cut as follows:—

The width of the cloak is made in that of the material, therefore, when the proper length for the cloak is cut off the piece (say one yard and eight nails), it is doubled exactly in half the width, and then the selvages being laid together, they are sloped off at the top, perhaps from four to five nails gradually to about four nails above the bottom; the two corners in front are also rounded off at the bottom, so that a great part of it, as well as the two fronts are slightly on the cross, which renders binding or hemming not absolutely necessary, though the cloak looks much better when finished with a neat binding of scarlet or black ribbon; the top is set into a band the proper length to go round the neck, and a few plaits are made.

When two cloaks are cut out together, which is the most economical plan, the hoods will come out of the sloping at the neck, but this cannot be, if there is only one.

The hood is very simple, and is thus formed. Cut a paper pattern of half the hood, exactly like Fig. 27, and lay it on the cloth, taking care that D is upon the doubled part of it. In making it up, it is gathered or plaited from the top, or doubled part to A; the rest to B, is simply sewed up; B to C, is the part attached to the cloak, and the front, or what goes round the face, is neatly bound with ribbon. These hoods may be lined or not, at pleasure.

SCHOOL GIRL'S CAPE OR CLOAK.
PLATE 20. FIG. 26.

These are made of plaid or other stuff, lined with flannel and calico, and are good things for school girls to wear at church and elsewhere.

SCALE.

	1st. Size	2nd. Size	3rd. Size	4th. Size
	Nails.	Nails.	Nails.	Nails.
Usual width of plaid	11	12		
Number of breadths	2¼	3	3½	4
Depth to be cut down the selvage	8	10	12	13
Collar like Fig. 7, Plate 13, cut according to size				

The skirt of the cloak having been lined with coarse flannel and glazed calico, and the shoulder-piece being piped all round with a pretty thick piping, the skirt is plaited evenly to the shoulder-piece in handsome plaits, and the flannel being laid against it, the calico linings are neatly felled down over the plaits, so as to hide the rough edges; the collar, lined also with flannel and calico, is sewed on, and a piece of tape or strong calico laid upon the part where it joins the shoulder-piece at the top. A button is put on at the throat, on the right hand side, and another, four nails below, and small squares of plaid doubled, with each a button-hole made in them, put to correspond on the other side.

By lengthening the skirt, this would make a very suitable cloak for a woman.

A more economical cloak, of this pattern, may be made of green baize; without a collar, it costs very little, but of course it does not wear nearly so well as the plaid ones.

BOY'S CLOAK.

A cloak or deep cape for a boy, may be made very simply as follows:—

Cut a large circle of cloth or plaid, the size you wish the cloak to be, and in the centre of it, make a smaller circle for the neck; cut from this small circle to the edge in a straight line, which will form the opening in front. Gather or plait the neck into a broad band, and it is completed. A cloak thus made will hang in full handsome folds, and be very warm.

THE WORKWOMAN'S GUIDE.

SHAWLS.

Shawls may be made of various materials, velvet, plush, silk, cloth, duffel, plaid, or printed flannel, and they may either be square or in the form of a half-handkerchief; they are variously lined and trimmed, according to taste and circumstances.

CARRIAGE OR DRESS SHAWL.

This is either velvet, plush, or satin, and is half a square of one yard, twelve nails, or less, to suit the figure of the person, and the width of the material. It is lined with white or coloured sarsenet, and trimmed at the edge of the two straight sides, with a satin or silk hem, from one to one nail and a half deep, cut crosswise, lace, fringe, or fur.

LADY'S WALKING SHAWL.

Silk, cloth, or merino, are equally appropriate for this purpose. It may either be a square of one yard, twelve nails, or half of it, and is lined with silk. When the whole square is preferred, and when a hem of velvet, satin, or silk is laid on, care must be taken to arrange it so that when the shawl is doubled handkerchief-wise, the hems of both folds shall be seen at the same time, one lying nearly over the other, for which purpose, after laying the border on two successive sides of the square, turn your shawl over before sewing the border of the remaining two sides on. Thus half the trimming is on one, and half on the other side of the shawl.

These shawls, like the one mentioned above, may be trimmed in various ways.

SHAWL FOR A MEMBER OF THE SOCIETY OF FRIENDS.

This is a square of about one yard, twelve nails, and is made either of fine white, or very pale drab, grey, or other quiet coloured cloth, with a satin ribbon, the same shade and one nail broad, laid on all round it. It may be lined or not, according to pleasure.

QUILTED SHAWL.

This is half a square of silk of about one yard, twelve nails, and has a very neat appearance, besides being both light and warm. It is thus made:—

Lay wadding, demet, or flannel between the outside silk and the lining, which should be either white or some pretty suitable colour: it must then be run in three or four rows round the edge, and the middle quilted in diamonds, or any other pattern, according to taste.

CASHMERE SHAWL.

Purchase a piece of coloured Cashmere or Indiana, one yard, six nails square, to form the centre of the shawl, and make a very narrow hem all round it; then take shawl bordering, or four strips of Cashmere of some other colour, which will harmonize, or contrast well with the centre; these should be from two to three nails broad, and one yard, twelve nails long; they are likewise hemmed on both sides, and then sewed to the square; the corners are joined obliquely, or from point to point. A fringe should be set on all round. This coloured border must be put on, so that when the shawl is worn, the two corners shall fall properly over each other, as described in the "Lady's Walking Shawl." Coloured gimp is sometimes laid on over the joinings.

MOURNING SHAWLS.

These may be made in two ways, according to the depth of the mourning. The first and deepest kind is half a square of black silk, entirely covered with black crape, and lined with black sarsenet.

The other is also a half square of rich, but not very bright black silk, with a hem of crape from one to two nails deep, laid on the two straight sides.

PLAIN WALKING SHAWL.

This may be made of plaid, printed flannel, or duffel, and is suitable for ladies, children, and servants.

Cut half a square of the proper size, line it with silk, or calico, and run it at about one nail from the edge, on the two straight sides, so as to keep it flat, and make a sort of hem: this shawl is made to fit the neck, for this end, instead of hollowing it out, run on the cross-way part in the centre, a little string-case, in a semi-circular form, and by passing a ribbon through, it is drawn up to fit the neck, making a sort of frill or standing up collar. This shawl is plaited in at the bottom of the waist, and strings, or a band sewed on at the inside.

Arm-holes may also be made in it at pleasure.

TRAVELLING SHAWL.

A warm shawl or handkerchief for travelling, may be made of a square of wadding doubled in half, and covered with silk or muslin.

SPENCERS.

PLATE 20.

Spencers are made of silk, cloth, muslin, and print, and are worn with low frocks, by children, to walk out in.

PLAIN SPENCER.

PLATE 20. FIG. 28, 29.

From its simplicity, this is suited to very young children, as well as to school girls, or young servants.

SCALE.

—	1st. Size.	Child of 4 years.	Child of 6 years.	Girl of 12 yrs.
	Nails.	Nails.	Nails.	Yds. nls.
Length of the body, cut width-wise of the material	12	15	16	1..5
Depth of ditto, cut selvage-wise	3	3½	4	5
When doubled in four, cut for shoulder................	1	1½	2	2
Depth of arm-hole..	1¼	1½	1¾	2¼
Arm-hole cut into the stuff	½	½	¾	¾
Width of sleeve..	4	6	8	8
Length of ditto	4	6	8	10
Neck hollowed out	¼	¼	½	½
Length of band or collar	6	6	8	9
Depth of ditto	1	1	1½	2

In making, sew up the shoulders, make up the sleeves, and set them in, a little fulled at the top. Make a string-case at the wrist at about half or three quarters of a nail from the bottom of the sleeve, which, when drawn, forms a frill. Gather it equally into the band or collar; for stout children, small gussets may be put in the neck. It is either hemmed or set into a band at the bottom; sometimes a frill is sewed on round the waist, sometimes the spencer is cut one nail longer to admit of a runner being put one nail above the bottom, so as to form a frill.

DRESS SPENCER.
PLATE 20. FIG. 30, 31.

This is a very pretty shape for ladies' children, but as it must be cut out to fit the figure, only one size, for a child from two to four years old, will be given. It may be made of kerseymere, cloth, cambric, or jaconet muslin.

SCALE.

	Yds. nls.
Length of body, width-way of the material	1...0
Depth of body cut down the selvage	2
When doubled in four, slit for the arm-hole	2
Cut into the material for the arm-hole	¾
For collar, see Plate 13, Fig. 17	
For sleeves, see Plate 12, Fig. 1	
Length of band	10
Depth of ditto	1
Length of robing, from the back over the shoulder to the front	12
Smallest width of ditto	¼
Greatest width of ditto	2
For shoulder-piece, see Plate 13, Fig. 5	

In making up, supposing the spencer to be of cambric muslin, sew a piece of strong insertion-work to the backs and front of the shoulder-piece, simply hemming that part of it which goes over the shoulder; full the body evenly into the insertion-work, both before and behind, leaving it perfectly plain under the arm-holes; the sleeve is next gathered into the shoulder-piece, and sewed plainly into the arm-hole; the body is next fulled into the band. In the band, on each side behind, is a little runner of about two nails from the ends, through which a bobbin is run, which comes out through an oylet-hole, at about a quarter of a nail from the end; it fastens also with a button or with hooks and eyes: up the backs of both shoulder-pieces and body a broad hem is made, in which are buttons and button-holes to correspond. The robings are next put on, a little fulled at the back and front, and a good deal over the shoulders: the robing at the back is sewed immediately below the insertion-work; it is one nail and a half deep, which increases to its fullest breadth over the shoulders, and is gradually narrowed off again to the band in front. The collar, which is trimmed with neat work or a frill, is then set on. The sleeves are made and put in.

TIPPET AND SLEEVES.
PLATE 20. FIG. 32, 33, 34, 35.

These are very convenient for children to wear in the summer, as they are easily put off and on. They are made of jaconet or cambric muslin, gingham, or print, to suit the frock.

To cut the front, Fig. 33, let your paper be five nails and three-quarters long, and three nails and three-quarters wide, when folded in two. D is the doubled part.

SCALE.

	Nails.
From the corner to L	2
Above the corner to T	1
From the side to V	½
From the top to V	¾
From the corner to S	1½
From S to Z	1¼
From Z to N	¼

Curve from L to T, again from T to V; cut from V to S; slope from S to N. The part marked N, is for the neck; S V, for the shoulder; V T, the flap or shoulder-piece.

For the back, Fig. 35, let your paper be three nails wide and four nails long.

SCALE.

	Nails.
From the bottom to A	1¾
From B to C	¾
From C to F	2
Leaving to G	1
From H to K	1

Cut from H to A; slope from A to B; cut from B to F; curve from F to half a nail below G; N is the neck; S the shoulder.

For the little flap or shoulder-piece, Fig. 32, take a piece of paper, letting it be one nail and three quarters long, when doubled, and one nail and a half deep; at the opposite side to the doubled part, mark the point A one quarter of a nail from the side, and one third of a nail from the bottom; cut in a straight line from the top to A, and slope gradually from A to the bottom.

In making up, sew the shoulders of the two backs to those of the front, set in the two shoulder-flaps, fulling them in the middle, gather the front into the space of one nail, setting it into a band, which is about one-third of a nail, when doubled, and nine nails long, made to button behind; the backs are also gathered, and sewed to the band at each end, at a proper distance, say about three nails from the middle. The Plate represents the tippet as if the sides were not attached to the band, observe, however, that the bottom, A, is to be sewed to the part marked B, of the band. On the top of the tippet is set a collar, according to fancy; Fig. 19, Plate 13, is that generally preferred. Sleeves cut according to Fig. 1, Plate 12, are then made; they are set into a band at the top, and then sewed on to the fullest part or middle, under the flap, for the space of half a nail.

These tippets may be trimmed with braid, if made of cloth or kerseymere; when they are of muslin, with narrow work or edging.

NECK HANDKERCHIEFS.

Many persons wear net or muslin handkerchiefs within their dress, and under the collar or habit-shirt, and for those liable to be soon heated, or who are engaged in warm or dusty employments, it is a particularly good plan to do so, especially if the dress is not of a washing material, as it keeps the body clean and nice much longer than it otherwise could be. Elderly persons should always wear these handkerchiefs, as there is something delicate and cleanly in their having what will wash next the skin.

Muslin handkerchiefs may be purchased, woven for the purpose, with borders, at from about 6d. to 2s., but the cheap ones are not worth buying, they soon tear in the washing, and look thick and cottony; the fine ones are so costly that it is better economy to have squares of muslin cut from the piece; these, like the bordered ones, may either be worn double, or the square may be cut in two, which most people prefer. The muslin should be yard wide, not very coarse, nor yet extremely fine, if wanted for common wear, but a thin transparent muslin should be selected; that which is called India book, having a yellowish white cast, is preferable to the blue muslins, which are apt to look heavy and clothy when washed. Real India muslin is the best, but it is too costly for general wear.

The extreme points of the half square should be cut off, or turned up, which is a good plan for the back, as it makes it stronger; and after hemming the handkerchief all round, a tape is set on behind, to go round the waist and tie in front.

For net handkerchiefs, the best width of the net is from one yard and two nails to one yard and four nails; it should be of a medium fineness, not too close, or it will lose its clearness after washing. In making net handkerchiefs, it is a good plan to run a hem of book muslin, of about half or a quarter of a nail broad, on the two straight sides, which prevents the handkerchief running up in the washing; on the cross side, of course, a narrow hem is made, as the muslin would shew in the wearing, and would look untidy. The points should be cut off, and a tape sewed on behind.

Net handkerchiefs are, on the whole, more economical than muslin, as they wear longer.

POCKET HANDKERCHIEFS.

These are made of French cambric, fine lawn, Scotch cambric, cotton, or silk; the former are chiefly worn by ladies, and the latter by gentlemen; lawn and Scotch cambric are used by young persons and children; cotton handkerchiefs are confined to the working classes.

Ladies' pocket handkerchiefs are usually eleven or twelve nails square; they are purchased woven on purpose with borders. Sometimes very fine cambric may be procured eleven nails wide, which many persons prefer to the bordered handkerchiefs; these are often made with broad hems, half or three quarters of a nail deep, and a row of open veining worked at the bottom of the hem, or a narrow edging of lace is sewed all round.

Cambric handkerchiefs for gentlemen are larger than those for ladies, say fourteen or fifteen nails.

Gentlemen's silk handkerchiefs should be of India silk, and are about 5s. 6d. each; they are far preferable to British silk, as they are much softer, and keep the dye to the very last. British silk handkerchiefs should be dipped in gall the first time they are washed. Printed cotton handkerchiefs, for poor children, may be bought at a penny and even a halfpenny each.

BRIDAL FAVOURS.

The customs respecting favours and bridal paraphernalia differ so much in different places, that no general rules can be given respecting them.

Sometimes white ribbons, gloves, and handkerchiefs are given, and sometimes only the former. Favours for the higher orders are usually of lace, flowers, silver ribbon, or cord, and those for the middling classes, of satin ribbon; they are worn on the left side. The usual quantity given to servants, both men and women, coachmen, &c. is three yards, which is worn as a trimming for either the cap or bonnet by the women, and made up into very large bows for the men, to pin on their coats.

SHOES AND SLIPPERS.
PLATE 20.

No shoes will be here described but such as are soft, and therefore easily made at home, or those worn by children.

Slippers may be made of velvet, silk, cloth, kerseymere, carpet, wrap-rascal, or frieze, and worked canvass, any of these materials, together with ticking, having a pattern worked on it, may be used for children's shoes.

Cut a paper pattern of half the shoe, as follows, according to the size required. Fig. 42.

SCALE FOR ALL SIZES.

	Man.	Woman.	Girl of 9 or 10 yrs.	Child of 5 or 6 yrs.
	Nails.	Nails.	Nails.	Nails.
Length of paper	5¼	4¾	3¼	3
Width of ditto	2	1¾	1¼	1¼
Size from A to the bottom	1¼	1¼	⅞	⅞
Size from B to the bottom	¾	⅝	½	½
From the side to B	¼	¼	¼	¼
From the corner to C	2	2	1½	1¼
From C to E	3¼	2¾	2	1¼
From E to F	1¾	1	¾	¾
From F to H	3	2½	1¾	1¼
From H to G	⅜	¼	¼	¼
From G to I	a bare nl.	½	⅜	½
From F to the side	¼	¼	¼	¼

Cut from I to A, and again from A to B; curve from B to C, cut from F to H; H to G being only a slit; cut off from G to I; from I to A is the doubled part.

MEN'S SLIPPERS.
PLATE 20. FIG. 42.

These may be made of carpet, cloth and frieze, or wrap-rascal.

In cutting them out, the material should be doubled at D; these slippers should be lined with flannel, and either silk or cloth; the linings are tacked to the outside, and the three bound together all round with silk ferreting or binding; the sole is of strong leather or pasteboard, if the latter, it is put between two pieces of carpeting or cloth, as no needle is strong enough to go through it, and the edges of these pieces being bound round, the sole thus formed is attached to the slipper.

It is, however, better in general that men's slippers should be made by a shoe-maker, as it is hard work for women.

LADIES' SLIPPERS.

There are many neat and ornamental ways of making ladies' slippers, or toilette shoes; the following are the most generally approved:—

Canvass, worked in tent or cross-stitch, silk, jean, or print quilted, cloth, or soft leather, braided or embroidered.

Care should be taken that the braid is very fine and flat; gold or silver twist may be sewed at the edge of it, which improves the effect very much.

When made up, these slippers should be lined with flannel, or wadding, and silk, and bound round with silk binding or galloon. A pasteboard sole, put between two pieces of thick cloth, or carpet, is bound round, and sewed to the upper part of the shoe, and a warm lining of flannel, or fleecy hosiery, put upon it, on the inside. A trimming of fur is sewed round the edge.

QUILTED SLIPPERS.
PLATE 20. FIG. 43.

Some of these are made of strong silk, with a silk lining and soft flannel between; they are quilted all over in vandykes, octagons, or diamonds.

Some are made so as to wash, and look very well, if the material is of blue, or any lively coloured print or jean. They should be lined with flannel and good strong calico; the whole is then quilted together, with thread or coloured silk. The initials of the owner may be worked in button-hole or chain-stitch, on the top or side of the slipper; it is slit down in the front, for about three-quarters of a nail, and the two sides of the slit, as well as the whole shoe, bound with ribbon; purple galloon is the best, if it suits the prints, as it washes well.

A string is made to draw from about the middle of each side, which ties in the front.

LADIES' SLIPPERS.
PLATE 20. FIG. 44, 46, 50.

This slipper is in two parts, the back and the front, which is by some persons considered an advantage, and it certainly enables it to be cut out with more economy.

Fig. 44 represents the back-piece when doubled.

SCALE.

	Nails.
Greatest length of back-piece	6¼
Shortest length of ditto	6
Width of ditto	1⅛
Depth of front-piece, when doubled	1¾
Width of ditto	3
From A to B	2½
From B to C	¾
From C to the bottom	¾
From F to the side	½
From F to G	1
From H to A	½
From the bottom to E	¾

Cut from B to C, from C to E, from E to F, and from G to H.

This shoe is made like those described before, excepting that, being in two pieces, the ends of the back-piece, SS, Fig. 44, are bound as well as the top and bottom of it, and the corresponding parts, E F, of Fig. 46, being bound also, they are sewed together very securely with strong silk.

TRAVELLING OR OVER SHOES.

These are useful to wear on a journey, or to put over dress shoes, to keep the feet warm in going out to dinner, &c. They are very easily made.

ON LINEN. 173

Cut out the shape of the slipper (see Fig. 42), in frieze or wrap-rascal, and also a lining of soft flannel, and of silk; tack the linings to the outside, and then bind them round with silk-ferretting the colour of the wrap-rascal; make a sole of the material, bind it also round, and sew them altogether; then cut out a sole of strong millboard, which must be covered with thick flannel, and as this is too hard for the needle to pass through, it must be tied down within the sole of the slipper, by means of a halfpenny ribbon passed through holes made at the toe and heel, which must be so contrived as to secure it effectually.

LADY OR GENTLEMAN'S HALF SLIPPER.
PLATE 20. FIG. 45.

There is also a manner of making a slipper by merely sewing on a front to a sole, and leaving it without any back-piece at all, as shewn in the Plate.

CARRIAGE SLIPPERS.
PLATE 20. FIG. 49.

These are particularly desirable for invalids, especially on long journies. They consist of a mat, or small rug, either of sheep-skin, or worked in rug-stitch; upon this are sewed two large morocco shoes, without soles, which are lined with soft flannel, or fleecy hosiery, and trimmed round the top with fur, the rug itself acting as soles to the slippers, which should be large enough to admit of any person's foot.

BABY'S FIRST SHOES.
PLATE 20. FIG. 51, 52, 53, 54.

These look very well made of crimson cloth, with soles of black cloth, or they may be of silk or satin, quilted. The shoe is in two parts, each of which is lined with flannel, and bound with crimson ribbon, which is stitched on very neatly; between the cloth and the flannel of the sole, is laid one of pliable leather, to give it a little firmness. The front part, Fig. 51, is first sewed on to the sole (see Fig. 54), after which, the back, Fig. 52, is put on, and being so cut as to overlap the front, oylet-holes are made at A, Fig. 54, and at E, Fig. 52, through which a ribbon is passed, which serves at once to tie the shoe, and to keep the front and back of it together; the sides not being sewed up at all.

BABY'S SECOND SHOES.
PLATE 20. FIG. 47.

This is made of soft velveteen, strong jean, or thick cloth, lined with fine calico. It is cut all in one piece, as follows:—let your paper for the pattern be two nails and a half long, and one deep.

SCALE.

	Nails.
From the top to A	$\tfrac{1}{2}$
From the side to A	$\tfrac{1}{4}$
From the bottom to B	$\tfrac{1}{2}$
From the corner to C	$\tfrac{1}{4}$
From the bottom to E	$\tfrac{3}{4}$
From the side to E	$\tfrac{1}{2}$
From the top to F	$\tfrac{1}{2}$
From H to G	1

Lay B A, which is the folded part, on a double piece of the material. Cut from F to G, slope from G to E, curve from E to A, round from C to B, cut from B to A. This shoe should be bound with ribbon; it looks pretty made of drab or grey, and bound with blue or rose colour. A little bow is put on in front, and strings are sewed to the ends of the straps, or passed through oylet-holes made in them, to tie round the ancle, and thus keep the shoe in its place.

BABY'S TICKING SHOE.
PLATE 20. FIG. 50.

This is also in one piece, and makes a pretty variety, it is cut according to the scale given before, and care must be taken in the cutting out to place the ticking on the pattern, so that the stripes lie properly, i. e. straight from the middle or front of the shoe, to the toe. The ticking is then ornamented by being worked in the intervals between the dark stripes, either in herring-bone, or some other fancy stitch, in coloured netting silk, either in one colour, or in two well chosen contrasts, as blue and brown, crimson and dark green. It is then lined all through, bound with ribbon to suit the work, and sewed up behind. The sole is of thick but flexible leather, lined and bound. Oylet-holes are made on each side of the slit in the front, through which a ribbon is laced, to tie it up, and a bow put on at the top of the slit, completes it.

ON COVERING SHOES.

It is sometimes very good economy to cover white or light coloured silk or satin shoes, but it requires great exactness, both in the fitting and sewing the new cover on; black silk or satin is generally found to answer the best, as from its dark colour any inaccuracies are less likely to be observed. The quantity required for covering a full sized pair of lady's shoes is six nails, cut the straight way.

Lay a piece of soft paper upon your shoe, and cut an exact pattern, divided of course in two parts, the front and the back. Place the pattern upon your satin or silk, so that the material lies the straight way, and so as to economize the satin.

The shoes must be first well rubbed and cleaned with a cloth; the binding should, if possible, be picked off, and every little crack or thin place neatly darned.

When you put the satin on the shoe, begin with the front, and be careful that it lies perfectly straight and even, pin it with small pins very near together, all round the front, next to the sole, keeping your hand in the shoe, so as to fill it out, almost as when the foot is in it; whip or sew it over at the inside round the edge, with a tacking thread, and pretty close stitches; then with a stout needle and strong but not coarse black silk, sew the satin to the shoe, as close to the sole as possible, with small neat stitches, taking very great care not to draw or confine it in any part, for fear of hurting the foot, and trying it on from time to time, to make sure. The back is done in a similar manner, and then a ribbon is laid on up the sides, where the front and back join, and double stitched. The binding is next put on, this must also be neatly back-stitched, and is broad enough to conceal the tacking, or sewing-over threads; you must observe not to hold it in too much, or all your work is wasted; for if the binding is tight, the shoes can never be worn. Small bows and strings complete the whole.

Shoes that have been wetted by sea water, should be washed with soap and water, which prevents their spoiling.

For cleaning white satin shoes, see Receipt, No. 41.

Patent leather shoes should be well rubbed with oil outside, to clean them, and prevent their cracking.

The soles of shoes should be cut straight-wise, as when cut on the cross, they will crack.

GLOVES.

The chief kinds are kid, doe-skin, Berlin, Woodstock, and Limerick. The principal manufactures for the former kinds, are at Worcester, Dundee, and Jersey; the latter take their names from the places where they are made. French gloves are by some preferred to the English make, as they are considered to be more elastic. The Berlin gloves look like Woodstock, and wash and wear beautifully; a little pearl ash in the water makes them look as well as new. Others are made of cotton, silk, and worsted, and woven, net, or knit; for the latter, see "Knit Gloves."

Cotton gloves are worn by men servants when waiting at table, and are very good for the purpose, as they are easily washed.

It is impossible to give any shapes or scales for gloves; the best plan to get an exact pattern is to pick an old glove to pieces, and cut out by it. Gloves are sewed with a peculiar kind of silk, prepared on purpose, which is finer and less twisted than ordinary sewing silk; it is between floss and round silk. The needles are small, very sharp, and three-sided towards the point.

For cleaning gloves, see Receipt, No. 40, 45.

ON DOWN AND FUR.

As it may be a matter of economy to some persons, especially to those who live in the country, to understand something of the making up, cleaning, and keeping of down and fur, such hints as are essential to those not regularly employed in the business, are given in the following pages.

DOWN.

The down of the swan, from its high price, is rarely used; as it is not plucked from the skin, there is little to be said about it, excepting that, after being well cleaned, the skin is cut into strips or squares of the size required, and at once sewed upon the article to be trimmed or ornamented.

Christmas is the prime season for goose-down, and a great difference is made in the waste, if it is gathered out of season, when there will probably be a mass of pen feathers, or new quills, growing under the breast, which must all be picked out, before the down can be got at, which of course adds much to the trouble and expense. That down which lies under the wings has no quill, therefore it cannot be sewed at all, but is kept for stuffing cushions, coverlets, &c. Down should be kept in paper bags or boxes, in a very dry place; damp spoils it.

A little while before it is used, it should be laid in paper bags before the fire, to lighten or separate it.

For sewing on down, to be used as trimmings, &c., the following instructions should be attended to. Choose a small empty room, with as few drafts of air as possible in it; wear a black silk pinafore or apron, and have a silk cover, or old apron on the table, to prevent the down adhering to it, or to the dress.

Begin by sorting your down into a box, keeping the refuse, or that without quills, in another box or bag by itself; in sorting it, draw a handful out of the bag, holding it fast in the palm of the hand, pulling it out piece by piece, by which means there is little waste; the hands of the workwoman should be very clean and cool. When all those pieces which have quills to them have been carefully picked out, lay them in pairs upon the table.

Cut your strip of calico to the proper size, whether for a boa or muff, it must be the straight-way. Pin the calico, beyond the part where you are going to work, to your waist or dress, and have some strong thread in your needle; double your calico in regular rows or creases, rather less than one quarter of a nail apart; then begin to sew the down upon the first crease or fold, pass your needle through the ends of two of the small quilled pieces, which you must hold in your hand, push them down upon the calico, and sew three stitches strongly upon them, taking care not to pull the thread too tight, or it will not wash well; then take another stitch, a little further on the line, before beginning with the next piece of down. When the row is finished, go on to the next line marked on the calico, keeping that already done, next to you, so as to lie inside, or under your hand.

Observe, that for a boa, the rows of down go width-wise of the calico, while for a muff, the rows must be in a downward direction or round it; in short it should always be sewed in that way which will make it shew to the best advantage when made up, and so as to conceal the rows of sewing.

Upon an average, six ounces of down will make a boa, with nearly three ounces waste. The best goose down is about 2s. an ounce; it chiefly comes from Lincolnshire.

Turkey down is also at its prime at Christmas, and is sometimes used for cuffs, neck-ruffs, or operas, and other small articles.

IMITATION ERMINE.

Sew tails of false black sable into white Spanish rabbit skin, cut a little V and let the tail in, covering it over with the flap, and sewing the tail firmly in.

The following is a list of the furs in general use:—

    Sable, which is black and brown.
    Ermine, black and white.
    Chincilla, greyish blue.
    Bear, black, brown, and Isabella.
    Otter.
    Fox, black, brown, and white or Arctic.
    Wolf, yellow or sandy.
    Wolverine.
    Lynx, black.
    Squirrel, brown, or silver, which is also called Minever.
    Racoon.
    Fitch, brown.
    Weazel.
    Rat, Norwegian or Russian.
    Rabbit.
    Martin.
    Cat.

TO MAKE A MUFF.

A full sized muff is about nine nails wide, and fourteen nails long, before it is sewed up. To make a foundation for a muff, lay a piece of Jersey on the table, and upon it a layer of curled horse-hair, next a sheet of wadding, roll it round, and sew it up the proper size, put it inside the muff and tack round the edge at each end, then make the lining, slip it in neatly and fasten it. One yard and a quarter of silk will line a full sized muff.

TO MAKE A BOA.

After sewing the down on the calico, as before directed, or the skins of fur together, turn it to the wrong side, and sew the seam up neatly and strongly, turning it out to the right side as you go on, then fill it with Jersey to a proper thickness.

The usual length of a boa, is from two yards and three quarters to three yards.

TO MAKE A TIPPET.

A tippet is lined with flannel and wadding between the silk and the fur.

TO MAKE AN OPERA, OR RUFF.

This is lined with flannel and wadding, within the silk lining.

Fur is always cut at the back, with a knife and rule.

TO CLEAN FUR.

Unpick the seam, but not the skins. Place it on a large deal table, and tack it slightly down with small nails. Pound white French chalk, add some bran to it, and keep rubbing it on with the hand and a clean flannel very hard backwards and forwards, take it out with a brush, and when done, shake it well. When a grub or moth is in the fur, put it in a stove hot enough to bear the hand.

TO CLEAN DOWN.

Open the seam, and wash with white soap and warm water; shake it before a gentle fire till dry.

TO PRESERVE FUR.

With respect to keeping furs, it is well to bear in mind the old adage that

"A little neglect may breed a great mischief:"

great care should be taken to preserve them free from moths and damp; the following are the best methods of doing so:—

On laying furs by for the summer, they should be put into brown paper bags, with clean hops scattered over them, and once or twice during the season, they should be exposed to the air and well combed or shaken, or they may be put away in tin boxes, or sewed up in strong linen; pepper, Russia leather, or a piece of mould candle are very good preservatives against moths, when put in the box or bag with the fur.

When fur has been wetted, it should not be wiped, but only shaken, and laid in the sun or a warm room till dry.

The best method of cleaning or preserving fur, is by washing the skin with a solution of corrosive sublimate in as much spirits of wine as will dissolve it, and gently shaking it, dry near but not close to a fire. After this process has been gone through, the moth will not touch it, but it requires care, as corrosive sublimate is a strong poison.

CHAPTER VII.

HOUSE LINEN.

House linen appears to be a branch of domestic economy little understood and considered, in comparison with its importance.

Many persons are little aware how much the good washing and wearing of their house linen depends on the choice and adaption of it to the purposes for which it is intended, as well as of the different methods of cutting and making it up, so as to have a handsome appearance, with due attention to economy. The following suggestions, though not adopted in all families, may, it is hoped, prove useful to some.

House linen may be classed under four heads, namely, bed-room linen, table and pantry linen, housemaid's linen, and kitchen linen, to which may be added stable linen.

The following is a general table of all the linen necessary in a gentleman's house, together with the price, width, and quality. Each article will afterwards be entered upon at large.

BED-ROOM LINEN.

SCALE.

Number required.	——	Kind of Linen.	Length.	Width.	Price.
			Yds. nls.	Yds. nls.	
From three sheets to two pairs to each bed.	Best sheets, double bed	Fine linen	4...0	3¼ .0	8*s*. to 6*s*. 6*d*.
	Family sheets, double bed	Coarser linen	3...8	2¾ .0	4*s*. to 5*s*. 9*d*.
	Calico sheets, double bed	Fine strong calico ...	3...0	2½ .0	3*s*. or 22*d*.
	Servant's linen sheets, double bed	Stout unbleached linen	3...0	2½ .0	2*s*. 6*d*. to 4*s*.
	Best sheets, single bed	Fine linen...............	2¾ .0	2½ .0	3*s*. to 5*s*.
	Family sheets, single bed	Coarser linen	2...0	2½ .0	3*s*. to 4*s*.
	Calico sheets, single bed	Fine strong calico ...	2...0	2½ .0	20*d*.
	Servant's sheets, single bed.........	Stout unbleached ditto	2...0	2½ .0	10*d*. to 1s. 6*d*.
	Ditto, ditto	Ditto	2...0	1...0	4*d*. to 8*d*.
	Crib sheets	Fine calico or linen...	2...0	1½ .0	1*s*.
	Cradle sheets	Fine calico	1½ .0	1...0	1*s*.
Two to each pillow.	Best pillow cases	Finest linen	1...0	19 nls. before sew'd	3*s*.
	Family pillow cases....................	Fine linen...............	1...0	19	2*s*.
	Calico pillow cases	Fine calico	1...0	19	14*d*.
	Servant's pillow cases	Soft strong linen	1...0	19	11*d*.
From six to twelve towels each washing stand.	Best fine towels	Finest pinafore diaper	1...0	12	20*d*.
	Family fine towels	Fine check diaper ...	1...0	12	1*s*. 6*d*.
	Best coarse towels	Fine huckaback	1...0	12	1*s*. 4*d*.
	Family coarse towels	Coarser huckaback ...	1...0	11	1*s*. 2*d*.
	Servant's towels	Coarse huckaback ...	1...0	11	1*s*.
Two to each or three to two toilets.	Toilet table covers	Diaper or quilting ...			3*s*.
Two to each toilet.	Pincushion covers	Dimity or muslin......			

ON HOUSE LINEN.

TABLE LINEN.

SCALE.

Number required.		Kind of Linen.	Length.	Width.	Price.
			Yds. nls.	Yds. nls.	
	Breakfast cloth....................	Damask	1¼ .0	1¼ .0	3s. 6d. to 6s.
	Ditto	Ditto	1½ .0	1½ .0	4s. to 8s.
8 or 10	Ditto, large size, or small dinner cloth	Ditto	1¾ .0	1¾ .0	6s. to 12s.
	Ditto square	Ditto	2...0	2...0	8s. to 20s.
	Common table cloth...............	Ditto	2¼ .0	2...0	10s. to 25s.
	Table cloth	Ditto	3...0	2¼ .0	18s. to 40s.
8 to 10	Ditto	Ditto	3¼ .0	2¼ .0	21s. to 60s.
	Ditto	Ditto	4...0	2¼ .0	30s. to 40s.
	Ditto	Ditto	5...0	2¼ .0	80s. to 120s.
1 to 3	Largest size ditto	Fine damask	8...0	2½ .0	80s. to 160s.
	Table linen in the piece, per yard	Damask		1¼ .0	2s. 9d. to 4s.
	Ditto	Ditto		1¾ .0	3s. 6d. to 5s. 6d
	Ditto	Ditto		2...0	4s. 6d. to 10s.
	Ditto	Ditto		2¼ .0	6s. to 12s.
	Ditto	Diaper................		1¼ .0	1s. 6d. to 2s. 6d
	Ditto	Ditto		1¾ .0	2s. to 3s.
	Ditto	Ditto		2...0	2s. 6d. to 3s. 6d
	Ditto	Ditto		2¼ .0	3s. 6d.
3 to 6 doz.	Dinner napkins	Fine damask		14	18s. to 60s. per dozen.
3 to 6 doz.	Breakfast napkins	Damask		12	12s. to 24s. per dozen.
3 to 6 doz.	Doyleys	White or coloured do.	6	Square	6s. to 12s.
6 to 12 doz.	Large tray cloths	Damask or diaper ...	1...6	2..6	Prices too variable to notify.
6 to 12 doz.	Small ditto	Ditto	1...3	13	

PANTRY LINEN.

SCALE.

Number required.		Kind of Linen.	Length.	Width.	Price.
			Yds. nls.	Yds. nls.	
6 to 12	Knife-box cloths	Linen.......................	6	6	7d. per yd.
6 to 12	Pantry knife cloths	Coarse linen	8	8	7d. ditto
	Pantry dresser cloths ...	Coarse diaper		11	9d. ditto
3	Plate basket cloths	Linen.......................			11d. ditto
12 to 24	China cloths...............	Soft linen or diaper......	1...0	¾ .0	11d. ditto
12 to 24	Glass cloths	Soft fine linen	¾ .0	¾ .0	11d. ditto
	Lamp cloths	Linen and silk............	¾ .0	¾ .0	
4 to 6	Aprons	Leather and linen.........	See aprons		
6 pr. & upwards	Waiting gloves.............	Cotton wove			1s. per pr.

HOUSEMAID'S LINEN.

SCALE.

Number required.	—	Kind of Linen.	Length.	Width.	Price.
			Yds. nls.	Yds. nls.	
12 to 36	House dusters	Linen	1...0	12	1s. per yd
2	Scouring flannels	Coarse flannels	½.0	14	7d. ditto
6 to 12	Paint cloths	Soft old linen	½.0	12	
6	Chamber bottle cloths	Linen	¼.0	12	9d. ditto
6	Chamber bucket	Checked blue or lilac linen	1...0	12	9d. ditto
4 to 8	Clothes bags	Calico or linen			8d. ditto
2 to each maid	Pinafores	See pinafores			Pl. 16. Fig. 8.

KITCHEN LINEN.

SCALE.

No. required.	—	Kind of Linen.	Length.	Width.	Price.
			Yds. nls.	Yds. nls.	
6 to 12	Table cloths	Coarse diaper	2 or 3 yds	2...0	at 2s. 6d.
4 to 12	Dresser cloths	Diaper or huckaback		11	at 20d.
6 to 12	Cooking cloths	Huckaback	3...0	12	at 1s.
6 to 12	Roller towels	Ditto	4...0	11	at 1s.
12 to 24	Dusters	Blue linen check	1...0	12	at 11d.
24 to 36	Tea cloths	Soft linen	12	12	at 1s. 1d.
24 to 36	Knife cloths	Linen	8	8	at 1s.
6 to 12	Pudding cloths	Old linen	12	12	
2	Jelly bags	Flannel			at 1s. 4d.
	Ham and bacon bags	Brown earn			at 1s.
6 to 12	Cheese cloths	Canvass or cheese cloth	12	8	at 8d.

STABLE LINEN.

SCALE.

—	Kind of Linen.	Length.	Width.
		Nails.	Nails.
Carriage cloths	Soft linen	12	12
Paint ditto	Old silk		
Flannels	Soft but coarse		
Saddle-cases	See " Cases "		

Plate 21

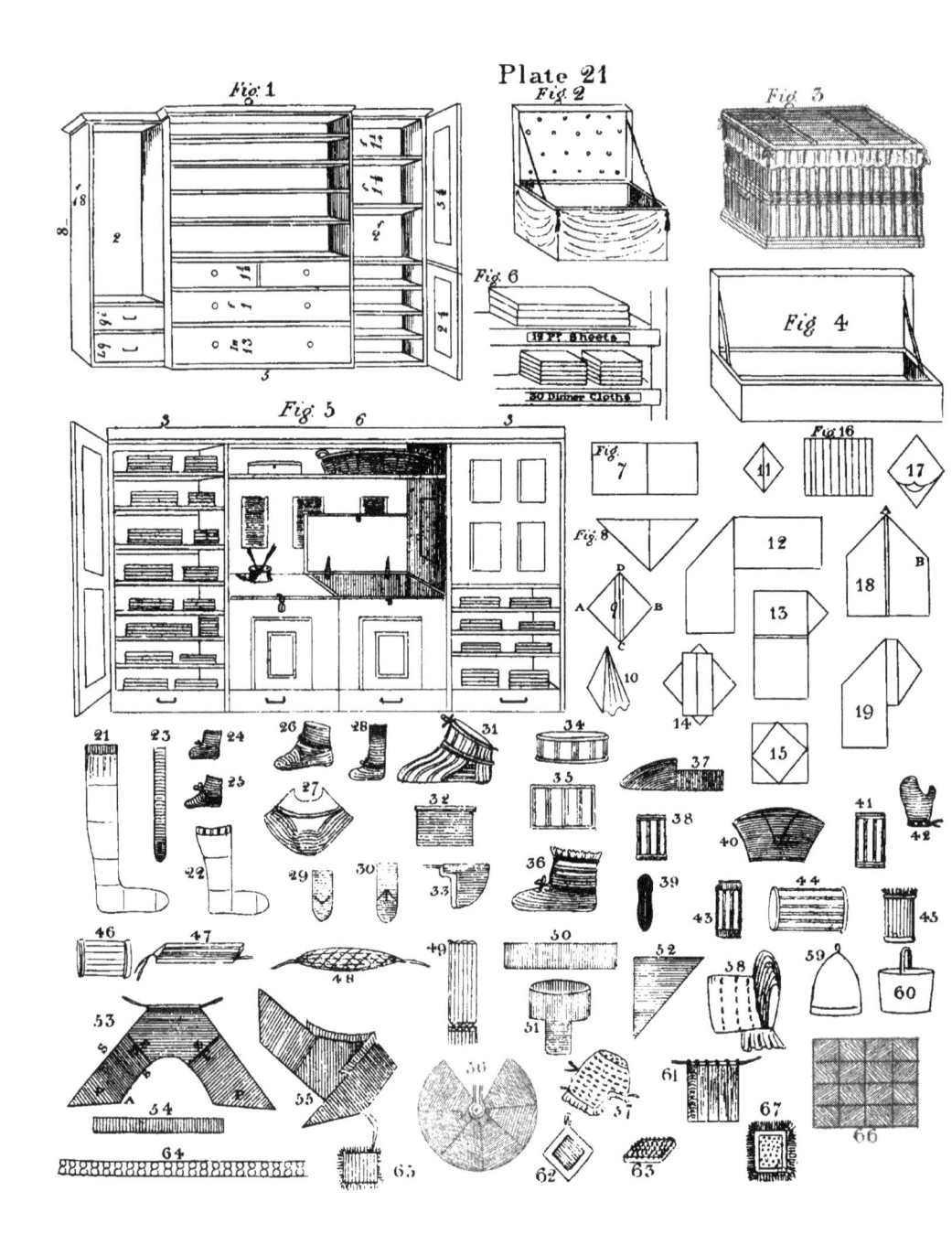

SHEETS.

These are of different sizes and qualities, which are regulated by the size of the bed, and other circumstances.

Gentleman's families generally have three and sometimes more qualities of sheeting. The finest and best for the spare beds; the second quality for the general use of the family; and the third, of a commoner kind for servants; where there are several children, it is good economy to have bed linen of an intermediate quality, for their use.

For those families who are in the habit of going periodically to the sea-side, it is a good plan to have calico sheets for the express purpose, for several reasons; in the first place, they take much less room than the linen in packing; secondly, if lost during the journey, they, not being of such value as linen, it will not be of so much importance; and thirdly, as very indifferent washerwomen are usually met with at watering or sea-bathing places, it would be a pity that linen sheets should run the risk of being badly washed or discoloured.

Invalids, infants, and young children should have sheets and pillow-cases of fine calico, as they are warmer and considered more wholesome, especially in hot weather, when persons are liable to perspire.

Sheets should, if possible, be of such a width as to avoid a seam in the middle, but they seldom can be procured of more than two yards and three quarters wide, which size, though wide enough for a good double family bed, is still rather within that usually adopted for spare beds.

In making up, if they are in two breadths, sew them together firmly, but with neat small stitches, the ends are turned down, as if for hemming, but they are sewed in the same manner as the tops of shifts.

Sheets should be marked at the corner with the initials of the master of the house alone, or with those of the master and mistress, with the set to which it belongs, the number and the date, for instance:—

H. M. S.
F.
4
..38

Signifies Henry and Mary Saville, family sheets, the 4th pair, 1838.

B may be put for the best sheets, F for family, S for servants.

The stock of sheets should depend on the number of beds, allowing, upon an average, either three sheets or two pair for each bed.

When worn in the middle, sheets should be turned, that is, unpicked down the seam, and the two outer selvages sewn together, so that the inner selvages thus become the outer, and the sheet is equally worn.

Best sheeting, four yards wide, costs per yard		6s. 6d. to 8s.
Ditto, three yards wide, costs per yard		5s. 3d.
Second best sheeting, four yards wide, costs per yard		4s. 6d. to 5s.
Ditto, three yards wide, costs per yard		2s. 9d. to 4s.
Servants' common, one yard wide, costs per yard		8d. to 1s. 6d.
Ditto, two yards wide, costs per yard		1s. 6d. to 2s.
Ditto, two yards and a quarter wide, costs per yard.	2s.	to 3s.
Ditto, two yards and a half wide, costs per yard		2s. 6d. to 4s.

Servants' common sheeting, two yards and three quarters wide, costs 3s.   to 5s.
Ditto,   three yards wide, costs per yard .... 4s.   to 7s. 6d.
Fine calico, two yards wide, costs per yard .... 1s. 8d. to 2s. 3d.
Ditto,   one yard and a half wide, costs per yard .... 1s. 2d. to 1s. 8d.
Unbleached calico, one yard wide, costs per yard .... 4d. to 8d.
Ditto,   wide width, costs per yard .... 10d. to 1s. 6d.

There is a common kind of calico sold in the piece, or whole sheet, for the poor, which is both warm and cheap.

PILLOW CASES OR SLIPS.

These are made of fine linen for the best, and of coarser linen and calico for the family and servants' use.

Procure your material of a width which corresponds with the length of the pillow; cut it one yard and three nails down the selvage. Fold the piece in half its length and sew it up; one end is also sewed up to form the bottom; at the other end, a broad hem is made, say half a nail wide, and strings or buttons sewed on to fasten in the pillow. It is a good plan, followed by some managing housekeepers, to cover the pillows with linen or calico, which is slightly sewed on, and the pillow cover is slipped over it. The advantage gained is, that it makes the pillow-case look particularly white, and as it is of no consequence whether it is of linen or calico, the first cover may be made of any old pieces of either that happen to be in the house.

The stock of pillow-cases must depend on the number of pillows to each bed; some beds have four belonging to them, while others have only two; each pillow in daily use, should have two slips belonging to it, and spare beds might have a cover to each pillow, and half the number besides, for the washing.

In addition to the full-sized pillows, some persons have small ones made of down, five or six nails square; they are a great comfort to those who are in delicate health, or who suffer from cold.

TOWELS.

These are always a yard long, and eleven or twelve nails wide; they may be bought singly, with fringe at the edges, or in the piece, in which case the ends are sewed, or very strongly hemmed. Nursery or school towels have sometimes loops sewed to the ends by which they may be hung to the wall.

Best towels are made of fine diaper, similar to that used for pinafores, and fine huckaback.

The second quality is of diaper, of a different pattern, and rather a coarser huckaback.

Servants' towels are of coarse huckaback.

The stock of towels should depend upon circumstances, such as the frequency or otherwise of washing; but upon an average, from six to twelve should be allowed to each washing stand.

DRESSING-TABLE COVERS.

These are of various kinds; sometimes merely a piece of diaper of the proper size is used, at others, a kind of Marseilles quilting made on purpose, and muslin or dimity, trimmed with fringe or frills. Much depends on the shape of the toilet table; some have merely the cover laid on the top, others are bordered along the sides and front with frills or work. Some persons have merely a piece of oil-cloth, the proper size, and bound with ribbon round the edge, upon their dressing-tables and washing-stands they look neat and are very durable.

ON HOUSE LINEN.

PINCUSHIONS.

For these and their cover, see "Pincushions." One cushion and two covers should belong to each toilet table.

TABLE CLOTHS.

These vary in quality, according to circumstances. The finest are the most expensive, and are only used for company. The price varies not only with the size, but also with the pattern.

The material of which they are made is called damask, and may be purchased up to a certain size in single table-cloths, after which it must be bought in the piece.

Care should be taken in choosing a table-cloth, to see that the edges are even, and the threads regular.

DINNER NAPKINS.

These are also made of damask, and vary in quality and price, according to the pattern.

The best are from 50s. to 60s. per dozen.

The second quality from 18s. to 45s. per dozen.

Dinner napkins are folded in various ways, and are generally put upon the plate, enclosing the roll or bread. The following modes are those usually adopted.

THE HALF-PYRAMID SHAPE.
PLATE 21. FIG. 7, 8, 9, 10.

1st. Take the cloth as it comes from the wash, and open the square length-wise, drawing the folded napkin to its fullest extent.

2nd. Turn up the ends to meet in the centre. Fig. 7.

3rd. Turn the napkin thus folded, so that the turned up ends are below, or underneath.

4th. Turn up each corner, half-handkerchief-wise, towards the centre. Fig. 8.

5th. Turn the cloth again the other side uppermost, and again turn the corners up to the centre. Fig. 9.

6th. Take hold of the corners, A B, and by drawing them under, make the napkin stand on its end, so that C stands up, and the cloth is supported by A B D. The bread is within the hollow, or between the folds thus formed.

THE DIAMOND SHAPE.
PLATE 21. FIG. 7, 8, 9, 11, 17.

1st. Open the square length-wise, drawing out the napkin to its full length.

2nd. Fold the ends to meet in the centre. Fig. 7.

3rd. Turn up each corner, half-handkerchief-wise, towards the centre. Fig. 8.

4th. Turn down the corners towards the centre. Fig. 11.

5th. Turn the cloth entirely over, and it is ready. Fig. 9. The bread is put in the mouth of the napkin, which should be turned on the plate towards the person. Fig. 17.

ANOTHER MODE.
PLATE 21. FIG. 12, 13, 14, 15, 18, 19.

1st. Open the napkin length-wise.

2nd. Fold it down from the centre, half-handkerchief-wise, at the centre, leaving two long ends. Fig. 12, 18.

3rd. Take the right-hand piece, and draw it over towards the left hand, making the point, B, lie upon the point, A, thus forming a second half-handkerchief, Fig. 13; turn the end back towards the right from the centre, fold it back again in several neat straight folds towards the centre, Fig. 19; do the same with the left hand piece, Fig. 14, turn the napkin, and it resembles a diamond on a square, Fig. 15.

Napkins are often used to lay under fish, pastry, or sweet things, in which case, they may be folded in the shape of a diamond, or else the whole napkin, being first laid open, is plaited in regular and very small folds till reduced to the proper width; it is then doubled down a little at each end to secure the folds, and to make it fit the dish, Fig. 16.

DOYLEYS.

These may be either white or coloured, and are sometimes open, of six nails square; they are generally fringed.

    The best linen doyleys are about 11s. 6d. per dozen.
    The second linen quality, 8s. per dozen.
    The common sort or cotton, 4s. to 5s. 3d. per dozen.

KNIFE-BOX CLOTHS.

These are used to lay in the knife boxes, to prevent their being creased, and should be of thick but soft linen.

PANTRY KNIFE CLOTHS.

These are for wiping knives and forks with, when cleaning them; they should be of common but strong material.

PANTRY DRESSER CLOTHS.

These are useful and neat in appearance; they save the paint of the dresser from being scratched. The length and width must of course depend on that of the dresser. They are made of coarse damask, or tolerably fine huckaback.

PLATE-BASKET CLOTHS.

This is a sort of bag to place within the plate-basket, in order to prevent the sides being greased by the plates, which would cause it to smell disagreeably. These bags are made of linen and fit the basket; a circle is cut the size of the bottom, and the sides are equally well fitted, and sewed to it; these sides are made to hang over outside the basket, a sufficient depth to allow it either to have a tape run through the hem, to draw it round under the rim, or it should have slits to fit over the handles, by which it is secured tolerably firmly to the basket.

PANTRY CHINA CLOTHS.

These are used for washing and wiping china, they should be of a soft and rather thin material, as linen or diaper.

PANTRY GLASS CLOTHS.

These are used for glass, and should be as thin, or thinner than the china cloths. Old silk handkerchiefs are sometimes allowed in addition, to give the finishing polish to glass.

ON HOUSE LINEN.

PANTRY LAMP CLOTHS.

These are for cleaning lamps and candlesticks, and are of flannel, linen, and silk.

PANTRY APRONS

Are worn by men-servants, whilst at their work; for a description of them, see "Aprons."

WAITING GLOVES.

These should belong to the pantry linen, as they give a clean appearance, and are particularly desirable for coachmen, and out-of-door servants, who are occasionally required to wait at table. These gloves are of woven cotton, and should be marked with their number, &c.

HOUSEMAID'S LINEN.

DUSTERS.

These are used for dusting furniture, &c.; they should be of strong and good quality; linen is generally used, though some persons have a kind of blue cotton check, but it wears badly, and therefore, though cheap, is bad economy in the end.

SCOURING FLANNELS.

These should be made of strong coarse flannel, not of a very open texture, or they wear out soon. As they do not last long, it is of no use to mark them further than by over-casting them with different coloured worsteds, to prevent the edges becoming ragged, and to distinguish the kitchen ones from those used up stairs.

PAINT CLOTHS.

These should be of old soft linen, as, if they are new and hard, they are apt to scratch the paint.

CHAMBER BOTTLE CLOTHS

Are used for wiping the jugs, glasses, and basins; they should be soft and not too thick.

CHAMBER BUCKET CLOTHS.

These are for the slop-bucket, and should be of a different colour and pattern to any other, for fear of getting them mixed, and employed for other uses. Blue or lilac checks or stripes are good for the purpose.

CLOTHES BAGS.

The size of these must depend entirely upon the use for which they are destined. They are generally made of linen, especially when large. The largest size is two yards long, of two breadths before sewed up; the small ones, two yards long, of one breadth before sewed up.

PINAFORES.

These are worn by servants while making beds, as, after emptying slops, cleaning grates, dusting rooms, &c., the clothes are apt to soil the bed-linen, which is very unpleasant and untidy.

KITCHEN LINEN.

TABLE CLOTHS.

These should be made of coarse and often unbleached diaper; the size must depend on the number of servants, or rather on the length of the table.

DRESSER CLOTHS.

These are laid on the dressers and cooking tables, and are of huckaback or coarse diaper; they should be merely the width of the dresser, and long enough to fall over a little at each end.

ROLLER CLOTHS.

These are very useful, and are fastened upon rollers fixed against the kitchen doors or walls. They are one breadth, and four yards long, the ends being sewed together; they are put upon the roller, and are used by servants after washing their hands in the kitchen.

KITCHEN DUSTERS

Are made of strong cloth; often of blue linen check.

KITCHEN TEA CLOTHS

Are of thin linen, and used for wiping tea things, &c.

KITCHEN KNIFE CLOTHS

Are made of any common old linen, used for wiping the knives and forks.

PUDDING CLOTHS.

As these are liable to be stained, they should be made of old towels or other coarse linen.

JELLY BAGS.
PLATE 24. FIG. 2.

These are made of flannel, and are in the shape of a half handkerchief cut from the square of a yard, the sides being sewed together, it resembles a reversed sugar loaf. The top is hemmed and has three loops sewed to it, which loop on to the corners of a frame which is made on purpose.

HAM BAGS.

These are made of earn, strong canvass or sacking, and are made of the same shape as a ham, or else are square, as a common bag; if the former is preferred, the wide end or mouth is hemmed, and has strings drawn through it, so that when the ham is put in, the bag is drawn up and hung up by them to the hooks in the ceiling. Bacon is also put into bags, which must be open at the long side, with an ample space to admit of the bacon being put in.

CHEESE CLOTHS.

These are made of a material usually called in the shops "cheese cloth"; it is a kind of thin canvass.

STABLE LINEN.

No remarks are necessary under this head, excepting as respects saddle-cases, which should be furnished always for ladies' saddles, as they are liable to be moth-eaten, being stuffed. They should be of linen or brown Holland, like a bag, cut out a little to the shape of the saddle they are to contain.

Harness should always be hung against matting or drugget, instead of against the naked wall; those parts of the harness not in general use, may also be put in bags.

GENERAL OBSERVATIONS ON LINEN.

House linen should be purchased of various patterns, according to the use for which it is intended, and a great difference should be made between kitchen, housemaid's and pantry linen, so that they may not easily be mixed, for servants frequently forget to look at the marks, and the tea-cloths should be easily distinguishable from the glass or china cloths.

House linen should be marked very clearly and fully for this purpose; ink is better than silk: it is well to mark all pantry things P, kitchen K, house H, and stable S, but the use should be more fully marked, thus "P china cloth," or "K duster," is not at all more than is useful.

Plate 21, Fig. 5, is a drawing of a very convenient linen press, being a kind of bin or chest, to contain dirty linen, placed between two cupboards, three feet wide and twenty inches deep, and from six to seven feet high. The doors of these cupboards may be in two parts, if preferred to one, so that the pantry linen may be divided from the kitchen on the one side, and the housemaid's from the bed-room on the other; the stable-linen and any that is old may be put in the two drawers under the cupboards; the apparent drawers under the bin are false.

The bin is four feet and a half long, twenty inches deep, and three feet high; it should have two lids on hinges, and a division inside down the centre, so that wearing apparel may be kept separate from the house linen; over the bin is a shelf, on which may be kept clothes-baskets, &c., and beneath the shelf, lists of the linen may be hung; an inkstand and washing books might also stand there.

The cupboards should have moveable shelves, with slides all down the sides. It is an excellent plan to paste on the edges of these shelves, tickets of card-board, on which are written the name and number of the article upon the shelf. Thus, a ticket with "best sheets, 6 pair," is placed on the edge of the shelf on which they lie; perhaps, "best pillow-cases, 12 pair," will be side by side with the sheets, the ticket belonging to them will therefore be on the edge of the same shelf. This arrangement is useful both to mistress and servant, particularly when a change takes place in the household. Fig. 6.

House linen should be counted over once a year at least.

A card containing a list of articles, together with the number and the mark, should be fastened within the cupboard, together with another list containing the quantity of linen allowed per week for the laundress, and the price to be paid the washerwoman for each article.

A linen-press should be kept in the most perfect order.

REMARKS.

In purchasing house-linen, it is a good plan to buy it in the piece, whether wanted at the time or not; by this means, you have always plenty of new linen by you, which being cut up, may be made by the servants when there is any spare time, they should also be marked, so that when a towel or any thing wants replacing, it can be done immediately, and it does not appear nearly so great a tax on the purse when several things are wanted at once; much time is thus saved, and when things are bought in the piece they are charged less.

Shirt fronts, collars, and wristbands, children's shifts, shirts and pinafores, with several other articles might also be cut out in the same manner, so that there is a constant supply of new linen ready-made when wanted. This plan, of course, only answers with large families where children of all sizes are to be fitted.

Very convenient washing books may be printed for families who pay for their washing by the piece, with the prices affixed, of which the following is a specimen.

It is the best economy to wash by the year, or by the quarter, in places where it can be done, and by the score or dozen in preference to the piece. A calculation may easily be made so as to be quite fair both to the washerwoman and her employer.

COUNTRY PRICES.

NURSERY WASHING BOOK.

Betty Powell,   *For Mrs. Wilson.*

Date. March 1st. Number	Date. March 1st. Number.		Price. d.	£.	s.	d.
8	8	Aprons	½			4
2	2	Bands	½			1
5	5	Caps	1			5
7	7	—— Night	½			3½
		—— Flannel	½			
		Cloaks	3			
		Frills	1			
		Frocks	2			
		Gowns, Night	2			
		—— Flannel	2			
		—— Dressing	3			
		Handkerchiefs	½			
		—————— Neck	½			
		Long Infant's Robes	3			
		—————— Petticoats	2			
		—————— Day Flannels	2			
		—————— Night Flannels	2			
		—————— Day Gowns	2			
		—————— Night Gowns	2			
		Napkins	½			
		Petticoats	1			
		—————— Flannel	2			
		Pinafores	½			
		Saccarines	2			
		Stockings, pairs of	1			
		Socks, pairs of	½			
		Shifts	1			
		Shirts	½			
		Shawls	1			
		—— Flannel	1			
		Spencers	1			
		Tippet and Sleeves	1			
		Trowsers	2			

ON HOUSE LINEN.

Number.	Number.		Price. d.	£.	s.	d.
		Leglets	¼			
		Waistcoats	1			
		Cradle Covers	2			
		—— Sheets	1			
		—— Blankets	2			
		—— Coverlets	3			
		—— Pillow Cases	½			
		Towels	¼			
		Pincushion Covers	¼			
		Pieces of lace	1			
		Mending				
March 4. £1. 11 2½ Settled, E. P.				£ 1	11	2½

LADY'S WASHING BOOK.

Number.	Number.		Price.	£.	s.	d.
		Aprons	½			
		Caps, Bonnet	1			
		—— Night	1			
		Collars	1			
		Dresses	4d. or 6d.			
		Dressing Gowns	3			
		Flannel ditto	3			
		Drawers	1			
		Flannel Petticoats	1			
		Flannel Drawers	2			
		Flannel Waistcoats	1			
		Frills	1			
		Habit Shirts	½			
		Jackets	2			
		Night Gowns	2			
		Neck Handkerchiefs	½			
		Pocket ditto	½			
		Napkins	¼			
		Pockets	½			
		Petticoats	2			
		Socks, pairs of	1			
		Stockings, pairs of	1			
		Shifts	2			
		Stays	6			
		Skirts	2			
		Shawls	2			
		Tippets	1			

GENTLEMEN'S WASHING BOOK.

Number.	Number.		Price.	£.	s.	d.
		Breeches, pairs of	3			
		Dressing Gowns	3			
		—— Flannel	3			
		Drawers	2			
		—— Flannel	2			
		Flannel Waistcoats	1			
		Jackets	1			

Number.	Number.		Price.	£.	s.	d.
		Nightcaps	½			
		Nightshirts	2			
		Neck-handkerchiefs	1			
		Pocket ditto	½			
		Socks, pairs of	1			
		Stockings, pairs of	1			
		Shirts	3			
		Shirt Collars	1			
		Waistcoats	1½			
		Under Waistcoats	1			

HOUSE LINEN WASHING BOOK.

Number.	Number.		Price.	£.	s.	d.
		Bed Furniture	2s. 6d.			
		Blankets, per pair	8d. or 1s.			
		Counterpanes	1s.			
		Chair-covers	½d.			
		Dusters and Cloths	¼d.			
		Doyleys	¼d.			
		Jack or Roller Towels	1d.			
		Kitchen Cloths	¼d.			
		Napkins	¼d.			
		Pillow Cases	½d.			
		Sheets, pairs of	2d. or 4d.			
		Sofa Covers	3d.			
		Table Cloths	2d. or 4d.			
		Towels	½			
		Window Curtains	2			

CHAPTER VIII.

ON UPHOLSTERY.

As some knowledge of upholstery is of importance to the head of every establishment, a few general observations relating to the fitting up of beds, windows, and other articles of furniture requiring much drapery; also, blinds, carpets, &c., may be advantageously inserted in this work; as, in families of limited income, it is a great saving to make up the above mentioned articles at home.

The Author has only introduced those patterns which, from their simplicity, may always be used, without being decidedly in or out of fashion. It is strongly recommended to those who can afford the expense, to employ an experienced upholsterer, as the patterns will not only be more in fashion, but more tastefully and regularly put up, than they could possibly be by any one unaccustomed to the business.

Great accuracy is necessary for the graceful arrangement of drapery.

BEDSTEADS.
PLATE 22.

There are various shaped bedsteads, and consequently numerous modes of fitting them up, the most simple of which will be explained in their proper order.

PLATE. 22

ON UPHOLSTERY.

In providing bedsteads, it is always better to purchase them quite new, even when required for the commonest purposes, as those which are second-hand are liable to harbour bugs, which it takes both time and patience to get rid of.

It is desirable that all bedsteads should have castors to roll upon, that they may be the more readily moved about. Observe likewise that there are valance sticks, curtain rods, and a good head board.

The best bedsteads are made of mahogany and oak: the commoner sorts, of beech, stained red or painted. Those for hospitals or prisons, of iron; supposed to be a preventative against bugs.

Brass bedsteads are used abroad, especially by travellers, and are ornamental and durable, but very expensive.

The following is a list of the different kinds of bedsteads in general use:—

The four-post bed, from	£2. 10s. upwards,	Plate 22,	Fig. 2.
The tent bed,	— £2. 0s. ——	— 22,	— 15.
The camp,	— £2. 0s. ——	— 22,	— 16.
The half-tester,	— 18s. ——	— 22,	— 19.
The French pole,	— £1. 18s. ——	— 22,	— 21.
The French arrow bed—	£1. 10s. ——	— 22,	— 22.
The canopy bed,	— £2. 0s. ——	— 22,	— 25.
The French block bed—	£2. 0s. ——	— 22,	— 24.
The turn-up bed,	— £2. 0s. ——	— 22,	— 26.
The stump bed,	— 9s. ——	— 22,	— 31.
The trestle or ×	— 9s. ——	— 22,	— 27.

Besides which may be added, hanging beds or cots, hammocks, cribs, sofa or chair beds, &c.

HINTS ON PUTTING UP BEDS.

So few ladies or servants understand how to put up or take down bedsteads, that the following instructions are entered upon at full length. An instrument called a bed key should be procured for the purpose (see Plate 22, Fig. 1), after which proceed as follows:—Divide the high upright posts for the head of the bed, from those intended for the foot; the former are easily distinguished from the latter, being usually square and perfectly plain, whereas those for the foot are generally circular and ornamented.

Place the two head posts near that part of the wall where the bed is to stand. Lay the foot posts below them on the floor, first observing whether there are any marks or numbers upon them, by which you can be directed to place the proper foot post opposite to its corresponding head post; next lay the side and end pieces in their proper places; the longer ones for the sides, and the shorter for the ends; these should also be marked to point out their relative situations. Lay the head board at the top, and the foot board at the bottom, and afterwards put one long and one short screw at each corner of the bedstead. Assistance must now be procured to rear up the four posts and set in the sides. Three persons are necessary to effect this, but four are better for a full sized bed.

Raise up the posts and set between them the side pieces, taking care to slip into the groove, both the head and the foot boards, as they cannot be put in after the posts are screwed together, unless they button against them. The four long screws are intended to screw into the sides, and the four short ones into the ends. The screw holes are placed behind the little brass plates usually put on the legs of the posts. Proceed with the bed key to turn each screw till firmly fixed in the hole.

The sacking is next tightly laced up with strong cord, and ought to be pulled together and knotted by a man, as a woman is scarcely strong enough to do it effectually. The top-rails are next put on by slipping the holes at the ends over the spikes at the tops of the bed posts.

The curtains are generally put on before the outer cornice, this last is generally fastened on by a spring, or by hooks, or some other simple contrivance.

Camp or tent beds have ribs or bars across the roof of the bed to keep the curved top firm, but in other respects, differ little from the four-post bed.

Observe, on taking down a bed, to mark carefully upon the pieces, before removing them, different numbers, so as easily to place them in their proper situations when next put up.

The head of a half-tester bedstead, should be very strongly attached to the back, as its weight will endanger its falling, if not firmly secured.

The other shapes will be entered upon when the mode of furnishing them is explained.

ON FURNISHING BEDS.

Beds are furnished with the following articles, which with the addition of sheets and pillow-cases, explained in the article of house-linen, make them complete.

> The drapery, including curtains.
> The straw mattress.
> The wool or hair mattress.
> The feather bed.
> The bolster.
> The two or three pillows.
> The quilt or counterpane.
> The blankets.
> The watch-pockets.

Beds for common use are hung with linen or cotton check, or stripe, print or stuff, but for better purposes, with dimity, fine stuff, moreen, damask, chintz, Turkey twill, and lined with glazed calico or muslin of various colours, and for state-rooms, fine silk, satin, or velvet is employed.

The modes of fitting up beds are various, according to the shape of the bedstead, as well as to the taste. The most usual and simple methods alone will be treated of here, all best beds and drapery for sitting-rooms should be put up by regular upholsterers, as it requires much correctness of eye, added to taste and knowledge of the prevailing fashion.

The following observations on taste, on the choice of materials, and arrangement of drapery, generally speaking, will be found worth attending to.

Beds that are placed in small and low rooms should be hung with as little drapery, as is consistent with comfort. Large valances, deep fringes, high mattresses look bustling, and are not so airy and therefore not so healthful as plenty of open space.

Beds placed in lofty rooms should be high, and have deep fringe and valances, otherwise they will have a mean appearance, still if the room be narrow, the less bulk of drapery the better.

Beds situated in dark gloomy rooms should be furnished with a cheerful airy material, at the same time avoiding too violent a contrast with the character of the room, furniture, or carpet. Every thing must be taken into consideration and is worth attending to, for with a little judgment, a room may be more elegantly furnished than another where six times the money has been laid out, if not under the direction of taste.

Blue is pretty, but rather cold; yellow gives great cheerfulness, as also pink, but the latter is apt to fade soon and is perhaps a little too shewy. Crimson, claret, stone-colour, buff, and light green all look well; a darker green is very refreshing to the eye, and therefore suitable for very light sunny rooms.

ON UPHOLSTERY.

Beds that are furnished with thick drapery, as stuff, moreen, damask or linens, seldom, if ever, require linings, while chintzes and sometimes dimities are lined with glazed calico, in which case, care should be taken that the colour of the lining harmonizes not only with the bed-furniture, but with the papering of the room. The fringe, tassels, ribbons, cord, and other decorations, should match in colour with the lining. The pattern of the material should also be a consideration. Stripes or small patterns are suitable for small rooms, while large flowers or patterns best accord with large ones.

ON THE VARIOUS MODES OF DECORATING BED FURNITURE.

Beds are generally decorated with tassels or fringe, if the latter, lace is usually laid on, at about a nail above the edge upon the hem which is turned up. Sometimes the lining is cut larger than the outer part, and brought over the edge to form a hem of a nail deep all round the material outside. This looks pretty and simple. If the cornice be a common one, the valance may be made with a kind of frill or heading above, or a band or rouleau of the material laid above the valance round which may be wrapped strips of the coloured lining of half an inch, or even a nail in width. Cords in festoons, cut velvet, binding and ornamental gimp or open work, are often employed. White dimity furniture is sometimes lined with coloured calico with turned up hems, sometimes merely coloured hems, at others finished with white fringe, or frills with white cords and tassels.

ON FURNISHING A FULL SIZED FOUR-POST BED.

Bed furniture is composed of a top, a back, two head curtains, two foot curtains, one top outer and one top inner valance, one bottom valance, and sometimes extra drapery laid on the back of the bed.

When beds are lined, the lining is put inside the curtains, and within the top and back of the bed. If there is any drapery laid upon the back, it is generally composed of the outer chintz, as is also the inside top valance.

Large sheets of coarse brown paper pasted together in lengths should be laid over the beds to catch the dust. Some persons lay hurden or coarse linen between the head of the bed and these sheets of paper.

The furniture for beds must be cut differently, according to the pattern of the material. If it is in stripes down the selvage the valances are cut in breadths, if otherwise, upholsterers generally cut them along the selvage, as they are less liable to shrink when cleaned or washed.

PLAIN DRAPERY FOR A LARGE SIZED FOUR-POST BED.
PLATE 22. FIG. 3.

	If in Breadths.	If cut down the Selvage.
Width of head curtains, each	2 breadths	2 breadths.
Width of each foot curtain	4 or 5	4 or 5.
Width of foot valance all round	9 or 11	11 yards.
Width of the top outside valance	15 breadths	16 yards.
Width of the top inside valance	11 breadths	11 yards.

The back and head must be exactly measured, letting the selvage-way run from head to foot of the bed. The curtains should just touch the ground, as also should the foot valance. The inner top valance should be half a nail narrower than the outer. In making up, the curtains are bound round, or if lined, sometimes the lining is brought outside to form a hem all round. Lace is often laid on at about one nail from the edge. The valances accord with the rest, having often fringe added to give a greater finish.

FESTOON HANGINGS.
PLATE 22. FIG. 4.

In making festoon valances or hangings, measure as follows:—

Divide the side of the bed in half, driving in a small tack as a mark. Hang a piece of tape from the middle of the side to the end, Fig. 7, making it fall in the droop or curve desired (see A B C, Fig. 7). Do the same with another piece of tape, making it fall in the direction of the upper part of the droop (see D E). Lay the material, Fig. 5, on the table, and after taking down the pieces of tape, measure the material from A to B, the length of the lower droop. Put a pin (see D) immediately above B, upon the other selvage as a mark, and then measure from the end, R, upon the selvage, the length of the upper droop or shortest tape, which will fall at E, at some distance within the mark D. Divide the space between D and E, exactly in half at G, and cut from B to G; cut three other pieces to correspond, which, as they exactly fit one with another (see Fig. 5), prevents waste. These four pieces or breadths are for part of each of the four festoons, which require a breadth and a half in each. For the half-breadths fold the material in exactly half its width, laying selvage along selvage, and measure for the rest of the festoons (see Fig. 6). Upon the selvage side, H, measure the length of the shortest part of the first breadths already cut, and on the doubled side, measure the *exact* length of the smallest tape for the upper droop, L, and cut from H, to within a nail of L, thus, when the doubled part is slit down, forming two half breadths to correspond with the two whole breadths, making in all two complete festoons. Cut two others, and the four festoons are complete, and when the half breadths are sewed to the whole breadths, they appear each similar to Fig. 10. Lay them one upon another, and slope off from the straight end at the bottom A, about two nails from the sloped side, B, and the festoons are ready to be made up. The bottom of the bed must be measured with tape, and cut out in a similar manner.

The corners of the festoons are cut as follows:—

Measure off from the end, A, Fig. 8, down the selvage, the length desired, putting a pin, B, in one of the selvages as a mark. Measure the half of the length, A B, on the opposite selvage at D, and slope off from D to B. This forms one head, post corner, or half a foot post corner, so that it requires six of these sloped lengths to complete the four corners of the bedstead, and if cut properly to fit into each other, no waste occurs. The Plate, Fig. 9, represents a head corner, and Fig. 8, a foot corner or two breadths sewed together.

Sometimes a double corner is also made to hang between the two festoons, in which case, it is cut similarly to the above, excepting that it is much shorter and rounder. When the festoon is carried over a pole, it is all in one piece (see Fig. 11), the pieces being shaped at the ends, as in the separate festoons above.

ANOTHER UPPER DRAPERY.
PLATE 22. FIG. 12.

This is simply a deep fringe, and looks exceedingly plain and handsome. A back-piece or very narrow valance should be put outside, the inner valance to accord exactly with the outer, to which the fringe is sewed. The rod or pole should be handsome, and should be put outside this valance, so as just to conceal the part where the fringe is attached. The curtains are suspended to the rod by handsome rings, and draw outside the valance and fringe. Cord and tassels may be added, if preferred.

ANOTHER UPPER DRAPERY.
PLATE 22. FIG. 13.

This is simple and pretty, and takes less material than the full valance; it is cut selvage way of the material of such a depth as will accord with both room and bedstead, and exactly to fit round the cornice. This valance is cut in various shapes, either pointed, rounded, vandyked, gothic or otherwise, and usually with tassels fixed to each point or angle to give a finish. Cords may be hung in festoons at pleasure.

ANOTHER UPPER BED DRAPERY.
PLATE 22. FIG. 14.

This is equally simple; it is cut in breadths and takes about nine on each side, and seven at the bottom, to go round the bedstead; it is sloped or cut nearly to a point in the middle of each of the three sides, where a bow or ornament of some kind may be put.

ANOTHER UPPER BED DRAPERY.
PLATE 22. FIG. 15.

This is suitable for tent beds, and is hung with a succession of festoons, made as explained before.

ANOTHER UPPER BED DRAPERY.
PLATE 22. FIG. 16.

This is intended for a camp bed, and is hung in festoons, having however a back valance of plaited or plain material, which, together with the curtains may, if preferred, be of a different colour to the valances.

ON THE HEADS AND TOPS OF BEDS.

These vary very much, being sometimes plain and at others ornamented. The material must always lie selvage way from head to foot, and never cross-wise of the beadstead.

When plain, the material is stretched across so as to shew neither crease nor wrinkle. Gimp is often laid down the seams and along the sides.

When the head is plain, it is usual to put two festoons to give it a more finished appearance. These festoons should be of the same material as the outer drapery.

When full, Plate 22, Fig. 20, it takes four or more breadths, and is set evenly into a band of webbing, which is tacked on to the bed, or with loops hung firmly to hooks, so as not to tear the furniture.

When starred, Plate 22, Fig. 17, it generally takes eight breadths, four at the corners, and the other four top and bottom, and the sides, these must be shaped to form the square. It is all drawn to a centre and fastened with a brass star. Sometimes they are half starred, as in Fig. 18, where the plaits radiate from just above the pillow.

ON FOOT BOARDS.

These are generally entirely solid wood, but sometimes the foot board is merely a handsome frame of mahogany containing the same material as the lining of the bed furniture.

Fig. 11 represents a foot board of wood only.

Fig. 15 represents a foot board starred within the frame with chintz or calico.

THE HALF-TESTER.
PLATE 22. FIG. 19, 20.

These may be trimmed in a variety of ways, either festoons, as in Fig. 19, valances, or plain, and cut out in vandykes and scollops, as in Fig. 20. This last looks pretty and simple, and as it gives the appearance of great lightness to the head, it is preferable to the others. The backs should be hung to accord with the outside.

Fig. 19 may be plain, with festoons of the outer material.

Fig. 20, with a simple inside valance, or the back fulled or gathered into a half star, or set in flutes.

FRENCH POLE BED.
PLATE 22. FIG. 21.

This is a compact, pretty shaped bed, and as it can be easily moved about, or taken to pieces, it is convenient in an invalid's room as an extra bed. Two poles which rise from the head and foot board, support the curtain rod which should be handsomely finished, and might be fastened on by pushing the ends through the rings or circular holes formed at the top of the supporters, and large ends screwed on to fix it firmly. The four curtains have three breadths in each, and are bound together firmly at the top. Rings must be fastened on, through which the rod is drawn, and fastened to the supporters. Tassels may be hung, and cords if preferred. Valances being put round, the drapery is complete. Sometimes the two curtains, falling one on each side, are sewed together behind.

THE FRENCH ARROW BED.
PLATE 22. FIG. 22.

This beadstead is much the same shape as the pole bed, excepting that it has no supporters or curtain rod, and therefore, when hung with drapery, requires being placed near the wall, into which a pin or arrow is driven, over which the drapery is hung. This shaped bedstead, when not hung with drapery, is particularly desirable for servants, or for schools, as the danger of fire is lessened, and if nicely finished and painted looks neat and respectable, besides being economical and clean. When hung, sew nine or eleven breadths together according to the size of the bedstead. Measure the length with a piece of tape, allowing it to droop as it lies from the top of the pole over the foot board to the floor. Sew the breadths up all the seams, and then, after dividing the whole width in half, marking it with a pin, hem the whole, and draw it up folded in two, sewing it firmly to a case which should be made to slip on the pole, something like an umbrella case. Another, and perhaps a better mode, is that of sewing rings to the doubled part thus drawn up, which will slip on to the pole, the head or knob of which when screwed on, would prevent the rings from falling off.

FRENCH BED.
PLATE 22. FIG. 23.

The drapery to this bed is exactly similar to the arrow French bed, excepting that it is passed over a hook secured to the ceiling, in preference to a pole from the wall.

FRENCH BLOCK BED.
PLATE 22. FIG. 24.

The drapery for this is also similar to that of the arrow French bed, excepting that it is fastened with tacks round four sides of a handsome mahogany block fixed to the ceiling. To this should be added a handsome valance or deep fringe to hide the fastenings of the drapery.

THE FRENCH CANOPY BED.
PLATE 22. FIG. 25.

The bedstead and drapery are as the preceding, but fastened to a head or crown secured to the wall having round it festoons as a finish.

Sometimes the head is supported by rods from the bedstead. A valance is added to complete it.

THE TURN-UP BED.
PLATE 22. FIG. 26.

This is also useful as an extra bed for invalids, or for small rooms, as it takes up but little space, can be easily moved, and when turned up, looks neat and tidy. In the one here represented, the sides are made to draw out, the legs to unhook, and the top to take to pieces, so that the whole can be packed in a small compass when not wanted. In making up the drapery, the back may be full, plain or starred; the sides plain or plaited, and two curtains sewed on, so made as to overlap each other a little in front. These curtains loop up at the sides with cords.

THE PRESS BED.
PLATE 22. FIG. 28.

This shuts up still more completely than the turn-up bed, and forms a chest or toilet table, when not in use; it looks very neat with a simple toilet cover over the top. These beds are useful on some occasions, in towns and in small houses, although they are not generally considered wholesome, being low and rather confined. They are sometimes lined with glazed calico, and a cover put outside of dimity, frilled round the top, to which is sewed a piece of the same material, very much fulled all round, to open in the middle of the front, down each side of which is put a frill or fringe.

THE STUMP BED.
PLATE 22. FIG. 31.

These are principally used by cottagers, and men-servants, and require no drapery, they are called stump bedsteads because the head posts are short, not being higher than is sufficient to admit of a head board.

Sometimes cottagers attach a kind of curtain to a hook in the wall, which adds much to their warmth and comfort, and would appear like a half French bed. This drapery might be two breadths behind, and two on each side, making six in all, which should be doubled and gathered to a strong webbing. Baize, calimanco, or cotton check would be very suitable.

THE TRESTLE BED.
PLATE 22. FIG. 27.

This is the most simple and most common kind of bedstead made, and from its construction, is not calculated to support a very heavy person, all the strength depending upon the power of the two pins or screws which fasten the legs. No drapery is used unless fastened to the wall as in the above stump bedstead. A head board, with two pins, slips into the holes at the top.

THE HANGING BED OR COT.

PLATE 22. FIG. 29, 30.

These are excellent things for children, especially where there is a large family of sons; for officers' families who are often obliged to change their residence, they are particularly desirable, on account of their cheapness, durability, and the little space they occupy. They are only proper for single beds, but are sufficiently strong for a grown up person. They would answer exceedingly well for cottagers, as in the day time, they might be drawn up to the ceiling, thus affording more room in the apartment for washing, or performing other household duties. They are made for the higher classes as follows:—

Procure a strong frame of wood, of about six feet long, and two feet and a half wide, also two round poles of wood, two feet long and about two inches in diameter. Get some strong ticking, or if it be covered and lined, a kind of thick sacking would do, which might have a cover of chintz, and lining of glazed calico. This sacking must be cut according to the Plate 22, Fig. 29, allowing in addition to the size of the frame, three feet at each end, and eighteen inches at the sides. The ends have a strong hem or case sewed to them, into which the poles are slipped. The four sides have lace holes large enough to admit of strong coloured cord to lace them together. The frame is let into the square thus formed, having previously fastened to the sides two pieces of ticking, one sewed on each long side at the bottom.

Put the frame into the square, having, however, first firmly fastened at the bottom of the square, another piece of ticking, which shall lace over the frame, down the length of the cot, so as to make a kind of straight waistcoat, which keeps the frame firmly in place. Observe that the cot, which is two feet six inches wide at the frame, is sloped off to two feet at the ends where the poles are admitted, in order to contract the sides a little, this keeps the clothes in place, and if for a child, adds much to its safety. Crimson or other coloured ropes should be employed to hang the cot from under the frame through hems up the high ends, and out through holes made in the poles, afterwards to meet at the hook in the ceiling on each side. A strong cord is also run in at the hem along the long sides of the cot. Fringe may be added at the bottom, if preferred. They should be hung at the same height from the ground as common beds, the ropes should be very strong, and be constantly looked at. They are better when fitted up with two thin mattresses than with a mattress and bed. When not wanted, they will, if unlaced, lie flat against a wall in a closet and take but little room. They are hung from a ring on a hook in the ceiling.

Very little cots might be made with advantage to hang in a carriage, or within a very large four-post bed, where the mother might attend her infant without rising in the night to the danger of taking cold.

The expense of a handsomely fitted up cot would be about £2., but a common one might be made for eight or ten shillings.

There are no further observations to be made on beds, excepting that the more readily the drapery can be taken off and put on to the bedstead, the less will be the wear and tear, so that if small loops or rings could be sewed on the valances, so as to loop over the cornice, it would be desirable. Once or twice a year bed furniture should be taken down and well dusted, rubbed with crusts of bread, and sometimes calendered to keep it in order. On leaving home, the curtains should be rolled up to the top of the bed and put into linen bags, and the cornices and valances taken down and covered up.

MATTRESSES.

The first mattress usually laid on the bedstead is made of straw, it is very thick, and as hard as a board; as these are never made at home, nothing more will be said about them, excepting that they are made in a frame, and should be covered with a very strong good tick or Holland.

The second mattress is made of horse hair or wool for large beds; and for children, of chaff, sea-weed, beech leaves, cocoa nut fibre, paper, and many other things of the sort; chaff and horse hair appear the most desirable, from being cool, and neither too soft nor too hard for comfort. These mattresses are made of various sorts of ticking, of which linen or cotton stripe, and a kind called cranky tick are most in use. For the poor, mattresses are often filled with mill-puff, or flock, and for children, bran might be a good substitute. Mattresses are made exactly to fit the bedstead, being cut out at the corners to surround the post, if they intrude into the square of the bedstead. They have sides sewed all round of one nail and a half or two nails deep.

In cutting out a mattress, the rule is to allow an extra inch to every foot, to give room for the stuffing both in length and in width.

These sides are usually cut the selvage-way of the ticking, and are attached to the top and bottom by means of ferreting or webbing, which is stitched with strongly waxed whitey brown thread, after which, the mattress is filled with the stuffing, and then is tufted, as it is usually called, which is done by passing a packing needle threaded with strong thread entirely through the thickness of the mattress and again passing it back at a little distance, and tying the two ends firmly together. This is repeated at intervals of four nails or more apart, in a straight row along it. A second line of tufting is now done, still at four nails apart, letting the stitches fall opposite the middle of the spaces in the last row, and so on. This secures the stuffing of the mattress, and keeps it in place, little tufts of worsted are sewed to these parts thus stitched, to hide the stitches and ornament the mattress, sometimes mere circles of red leather are sewed on instead.

The price of a straw mattress is from................ 10s. to 30s.
The price of a wool mattress is from................ 35s. to 60s.
The price of horse hair, per lb., is from .... 1s. to 2s.
The price of mill-puff, per lb. .... 2d.
The price of linen tick, per yard, is from .... 9d. to 2s. 9d.
The price of cotton tick, per yard, is from .... 4½d. to 1s. 6d.
The price of wool, per lb., is from.................... 6d. to 1s. 2d.

BEDS, BOLSTERS, AND PILLOWS.

These are filled with chicken, turkey, goose feathers, and down, for the higher classes, and mill-puff, which is a kind of cotton, for the lower classes. The following prices are an average of the expense of the various articles for making up beds.

Mill-puff, 2½d. per lb., of which fifty pounds make a large bed.
Flock, at 3d. per lb.
Chicken feathers, at 10d. or 1s.
Grey goose, or turkeys', at 2s. or 2s. 6d.
Best goose, white feathers, at 2s. 2d. to 3s. 6d.
Down from geese, for pillows, 6s. per lb.
Cotton ticking, for beds, at 6d. or 8d.
Linen ticking, for beds, at 1s. or 1s. 3d.

Beds are made sometimes with sides, and sometimes without; in the latter case, nine yards of ticking are sufficient, otherwise eleven yards. Divide one yard and two nails into four, to make the long sides, and another yard, divided into four, to make ends; the bed is two yards and a quarter in length, two breadths above, and two below. The ticking is waxed with white wax, or rubbed with brown soap, and when the feathers are in, the sides are bound with the usual binding, or what is still better, piped thoughout.

In making up mill-puff beds, care should be taken to separate dust, and disentangle it well, before putting it into the ticking.

For a bolster, two yards are required, and for each pillow, one yard. These should be filled with the softest feathers, and the ticking well stitched.

Pillows are sometimes covered with calico covers, which tack or button on underneath the usual pillow cases, mentioned in the article "House Linen," and make them look beautifully white and clean.

Every double bed should have three or four pillows, and single ones, either one or two. Bolsters sometimes have also covers to preserve the ticking. Pillows are often stuffed with down, or torn pieces of paper of a quarter of an inch square; this last is said to be particularly soft and cool.

BLANKETS.

Every bed should have one under blanket, and two or three upper ones. These last are usually the Witney, whilst the under blanket is of an inferior sort; they should be thick and light, with a soft nap or wool upon them. Blankets are generally sold in pairs, or two woven together. These, for beds must be cut, in which case, the edges are sewed over in a very wide kind of button-hole stitch, with red, or other coloured wool, also a kind of circle or star is often worked in the corner with various coloured wool.

For cribs, it is better not to divide the blankets but lay them on the crib double, as they come in more usefully as under blankets for beds afterwards, when uncut. The Witney blanket is considered the best.

The Rose and the Bath are the other varieties.

When not in use, blankets should be folded, and laid under those beds in use, to keep them aired. Some persons lend blankets to the poor, in which case, on their being returned, they should be scoured well and baked in an oven, before they are put by in brown paper bags with pepper sprinkled over them.

COVERLETS OR COUNTERPANES.

There are various kinds of quilts or counterpanes. Those most known are,

The Marseilles, which sell from............	6s. to 25s.
The Imperial, which sell from............	9s. to 30s.
The Summer, which sell from............	25s. to 58s.
The Toilet cover, or cradle quilt............	15s. to 42s.

Those used for servants, are of a dark brown, violet, or grey colour.

Those used by cottagers, are often of patchwork made by them at school, or in their leisure moments. These quilts are sometimes made of a succession of hexagons or six-sided pieces of print, at others, birds, figures, and other devices are cut out and sewed up with various shaped bits of calico, prints, &c. These quilts are durable when lined, and may be good work for school-children, though they certainly take up a good deal of time in making.

All counterpanes not in constant use, should be either put by in drawers, or laid on the bed with the wrong side uppermost.

Having now entered upon each article belonging to the beadstead, it only remains for us to make the following observation.

ON UPHOLSTERY.

It is advisable to cut several small squares of linen, and having wet them with the marking liquid, to mark upon them the list of every article belonging to the bed to which the square of calico is to be attached. These squares should be washed and ironed, and sewed upon the mattress, bed, bolster, pillows, blankets, and coverlet of each bedstead, thus:—

> **BLUE ROOM.**
> One straw mattress.
> One hair ditto.
> One feather bed.
> Four pillows, one bolster.
> One under and three upper blankets.
> One counterpane.
> Two watchpockets.

By this method, the bed furniture, if mixed, can easily be sorted and counted by the mistress or housemaid.

WATCH POCKETS.

These are often made of the same material as the bed curtains, or of white muslin, or dimity, or tick ornamented. A few shapes are mentioned hereafter, in the chapter on cases, bags, &c.

CARPETS.

Those generally known, are as follows:—

Superb Axminster.	Kidderminster.
Saxony.	Venetian.
Royal velvet pile.	Danish venetian.
Tournay.	Scotch.
Brussels.	Druggets.
Turkey.	Rugs, &c.
Imperial.	

All these carpets are expensive and durable, the Brussels is that most in use for best apartments, and best stair-cases in the present day, being very durable, and less expensive than most of the others mentioned in the same list. Their price varies from 4s. 6d. to 10s. 6d. per yard. Turkey carpets were formerly in great request for dining-rooms, and were sometimes used as table cloths in libraries, which gave a remarkably rich and handsome, though heavy appearance. The great objection to them is their great weight, which renders it difficult to shake them. These Turkey carpets look well for years, and are made in the piece, measuring sometimes ten or more yards long, and five or more wide. The expense varies according to their size, from £10. to £80. or more.

Those carpets generally employed for common sitting-rooms, stair-cases, servants' apartments, &c. are the following:—

Kidderminster.	Scotch.
Venetian.	Druggets.
Damask Venetian.	Baizes, &c.

The Kidderminster and damask Venetian are the most desirable of these inferior carpets; the Scotch and common Venetian being used for school-rooms and servants' apartments.

These vary much in price, from 2s. to 6s. per yard.

Druggets are very wide, being sometimes two yards, and sometimes four yards. They are chiefly employed to lay over another carpet, to preserve it when the room is in daily use, and only removed for company. Sometimes druggets alone are laid, and when of a handsome brown or marone colour, look exceedingly well. They should be very tightly stretched on the floor, so as not to present a wrinkle to view.

Carpets are often made in worsted-work upon canvass, and are considered durable, though the time occupied in making them is great.

A worked border upon canvass, with the arms or crest, with drugget sewed between, has a very pretty effect for a stair carpet, and might be quickly done. Borders can be purchased in shops for the same purpose.

There are various modes of making up rugs, but as this belongs more properly to fancy work, it will not here be mentioned.

Rugs may be knit in various ways also, as will be seen in the chapter upon knitting.

In making up carpets, observe the following directions, as they are necessary for their appearance and durability.

Brussels, when made up, should be turned with the wrong side outwards, with the selvages just touching each other, but not laid one upon the other. The carpet needle is then passed backwards and forwards, always taking up both seams at a time, first pointing the needle from, and next towards the chest. Observe, the alternate stitches are always taken behind, or at the back of the last stitch, so as to work along the seam from right to left in a kind of back-stitch fashion. The seam will be close together and tread down flat. Observe, carefully to cut out the carpet, and sew it up to match the pattern properly and exactly, as the slightest mistake or pucker will ruin the appearance of the whole carpet. There is a kind of thread, called carpet thread, sold for the purpose, of every colour.

Kidderminster and other carpets are sewed in the usual mode of sewing seams together, taking care to secure the selvages very firmly together, taking up every thread.

Druggets. These are turned down once, and herring-boned at the edges, and sewed up at the seams, as above.

All carpets should be bound with the regular carpet binding at the edges, or the carpet simply turned down with the binding laid on. This last plan is the flattest, and answers for that end of the room where the doors are situated, for them to open and shut more easily upon.

Expensive carpets should be cut as little as possible, therefore, when a piece is obliged to be cut for the hearth stone, it is better to slit the piece only at the sides, and having caught the edges over to prevent their ravelling, the piece or lip should then be turned in underneath the carpet. By this means, if the carpet is wanted for another room, the lip might be sewed up neatly and form the square again.

Carpet rods are very useful things, not only for stair-cases, but for bed-rooms, or sitting-rooms, to fasten and stretch the carpets on the floor with. In this case, the rod should be a little longer than the breadth of the carpet, and a Holland or linen case sewed very firmly underneath the carpet so as just to come to the edge of it, or even strong tape loops would answer as well. Run the rod along them, and let it pass at each end into two or more brass rings or hooks fastened to the floor.

Matting is used for halls, passages, and sometimes laid beneath the carpets to preserve them. It should always be neatly bound with red, green, or other coloured leather.

Carpets should always be mended with a loose kind of untwisted worsted, called thrums.

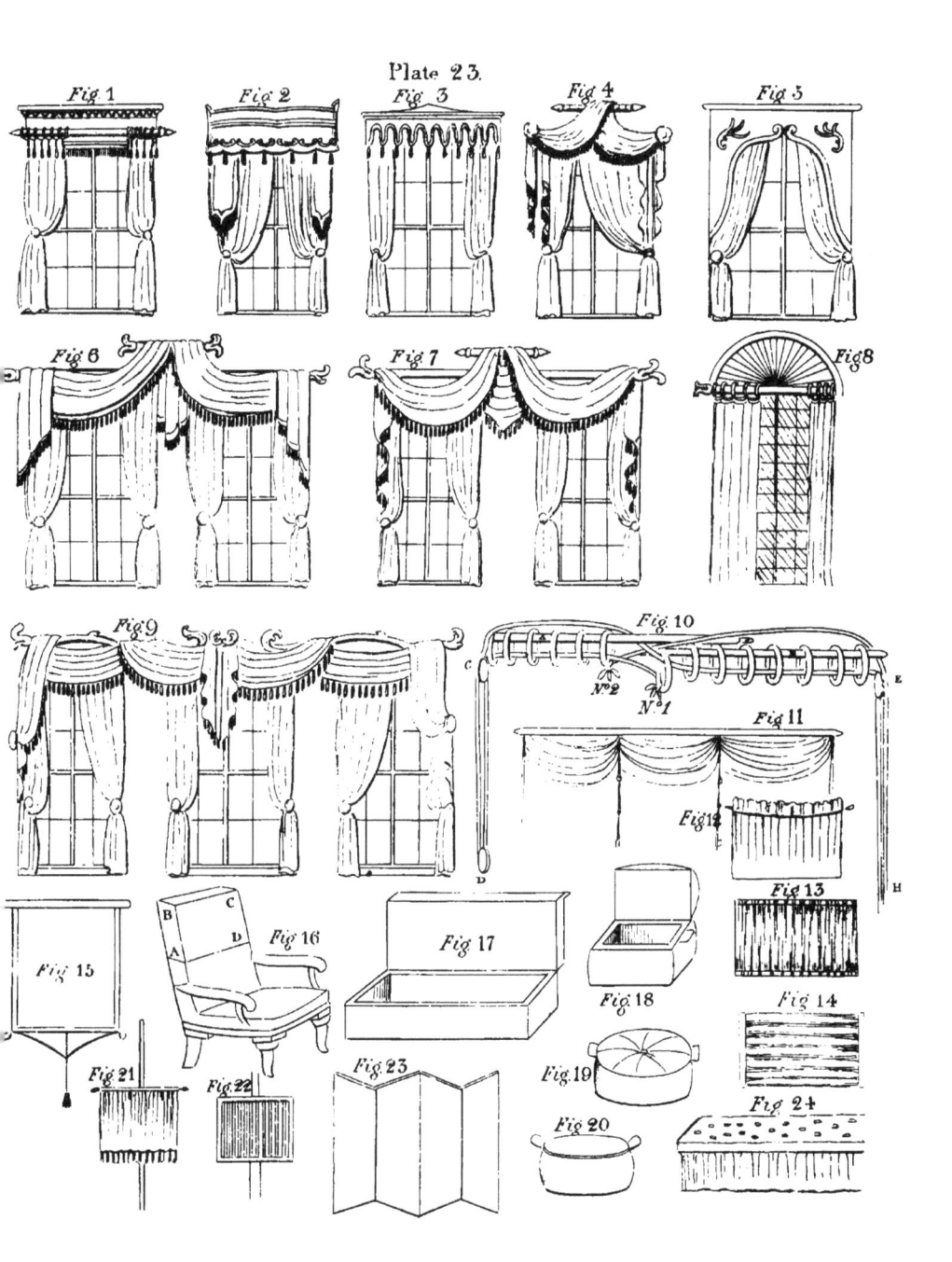

Plate 23.

ON UPHOLSTERY.

WINDOW CURTAINS.
PLATE 23.

The drapery for window curtains, if for sitting-rooms, is generally attached to one cornice, whether for two, three, or even four windows; but for bed-rooms, the drapery is always separately hung. Observe for bed-rooms, that the window curtains should always accord with the hanging on the bed, both in colour and material, as also in shape. Those hangings already drawn for bed furniture will be a sufficient pattern by which to form the corresponding window curtains, therefore but a few additional patterns for bed-rooms will be explained.

It is desirable to have as little window drapery as possible to family or secondary rooms, particularly nurseries and servants' rooms, on account of their liability to catch fire, especially as toilet tables are so often situated within the window. In an upper story, curtains might be dispensed with, using only the valance and corners.

Windows have generally two brass pins or hooks on each side, over which the curtains are hung or looped.

Curtains should always be cut six or eight nails longer than the length of the window, to allow for their touching the ground when looped upon the pin. For a window of three panes, two breadths are sufficient in each curtain, but for four or five panes, two and a half, or three breadths, will be necessary for each. They should be often dusted, and in hot summers, bed-room and even sitting-room curtains might be taken down and put by till wanted for winter, as the sun fades and makes them look shabby.

PLATE 23. FIG. 1.

This is very handsome for a sitting-room, or even for a drawing-room, a kind of straight valance is put behind a rod, to which a deep fringe is sewed. The curtains with tassels sewed to them at the top, draw along the rod with large rings. A lace may be laid down the curtains, at one nail from the edge: this curtain in green and gold looks very handsome.

PLATE 23. FIG. 2.

This style is more suited to a sitting-room or bed-room, being rather too heavy for a drawing-room.

The cornice is of mahogany or painted wood, to which a plain valance, cut selvage-way, is fastened. This valance is either scolloped, vandyked, or cut in any other form at the bottom, and a pattern in cut velvet or lace is sewed on at the edge, and also at about a nail above it. Two plain corners are cut, and with the curtains, are also ornamented at one nail from the edge, with the same decoration as the valance.

PLATE 23. FIG. 3.

This is very neat for a bed-room, or for a common sitting-room, but unless of very handsome materials, might be considered too plain for a best room. To a mahogany cornice is fastened a straight valance, cut down the selvage, and shaped according to the Plate, or otherwise, according to taste. It must be bound with another coloured binding, and handsome tassels sewed on at each point.

PLATE 23. FIG. 4.

This is a very handsome drapery for any room, and is simply a festoon thrown over a pole, as before explained, with double corners. Fringe and lace add to the finish.

PLATE 23. FIG. 5.

This is suitable for gothic windows, or for a study or library, it is very simple, and may be formed to any shape, according to the style of the room.

The corners are in a piece with the valance, and are cut down the selvage; a pattern of cut velvet may be laid on at the corners, to give it relief.

PLATE 23 FIG. 6

This is a handsome drapery for a drawing or dining-room, and might be adapted to any number of windows, by continuing the lower cornice, and providing one or more upper rods, in addition to the one represented in the Plate. The corners should reach more than half way down the window, but the middle double piece should be much shorter. Lace and tassels are required to finish the whole.

The cornice may be black, with brass ends, or entirely brass.

PLATE 23. FIG. 7.

Another very pretty festoon, and suitable for a drawing-room or elsewhere. The middle part is a festoon, with a point attached to it, and, on this account, would require two breadths instead of one and a half, to form the depth required.

PLATE 23. FIG. 9.

This is a beautiful drawing-room window festoon, and requires a more ornamental brass cornice than usual.

The festoons are all very simple, being cut out as before explained, excepting that the corners are longer than ordinary, being looped upon a high curtain pin, so that the ends must be sloped off from one third, instead of one half of the material.

Sometimes with three windows, the two inner curtains of the outer windows are simply muslin, and the middle window has two of muslin, as well as of the material.

PLATE 23. FIG. 8.

Passage or church windows are generally circular, unless pointed; in the former case, they should be hung at the top with a piece of straight material of the depth of half the diameter of the circle, and sufficiently long to be a little fulled to the outer part of the circle. The inner part is gathered to a point in the middle; the curtains simply hang to the rod, ornamented by a little frill, valance, fringe, or tassels, as taste may direct.

There are many ways of drawing curtains together, but the one now most adopted is that of bringing them forwards or backwards by means of one string which at once draws both curtains; the following is an explanation.

PLATE 23. FIG. 10.

Let A B represent the two rods under the cornice, and behind, or concealed by the valance. After putting the rings of each curtain upon its own rod, tie the cord to the ring, No. 1, and pass across through the rings marked No. 2, over the side pulley of the window, down the side, C, round the pulley, D, up the side again, and under the top pulley, and then take it across above the rings, till it comes to the first ring, No. 1, when it is also passed through it and all the others towards E, it is next taken round the pulley, H, and outside the rings, and fastened to the ring, No. 2, in a hard knot.

PLATE 23. FIG. 11.

This is an old fashioned simple curtain still in use in churches, small houses, and for housekeepers' rooms. The curtain is in as many breadths as is required for the width of the window, and of the proper length. The top is nailed to the cornice, and small loops or rings are put down the seams of the breadths, at equal distances (say about four nails from each other). Through these rings are passed cords which unite in one long cord, and on pulling this cord, the whole curtain draws up, forming as many festoons as there are breadths, or rather lengths of rings down it. This cord must be wound round and round two pins or hooks placed at the side of the window, at about six nails apart.

Other curtains are passed backwards and forwards like bed-curtains, or have a cord on each side, to draw them separately; in which case, it is passed through all the rings, being fastened to the last or innermost ring.

MUSLIN CURTAINS.

These are put within the outer curtains in drawing-rooms, dining-rooms, and sometimes even for bed-rooms. They serve as a great shade to the best curtains, both from dust and sun, and have besides a neat, clean, and rather dress appearance. Many persons take down their chintz curtains when they put up muslin ones.

Muslin curtains are generally made of book-muslin, though sometimes mull or jaconet have been employed. They are made with deep hems and rings at the top, and so arranged as to fall towards the inside of the window. Curtains are sometimes knit or net of cotton, they look very neat and pretty, and are besides very durable.

LITTLE HALF CURTAINS.
PLATE 23.

These are much in use for the lower windows of town houses, to prevent persons from looking into the rooms, and are generally made to reach half way up to the second pane, or merely to the first. They are made of muslin, or a kind of canvass, and sometimes, though very rarely of chintz.

FULL CURTAIN.
PLATE 23. FIG. 12.

This is simply cut in as many breadths as wanted to full it to the window, a frill is made near the top by turning down a nail or more, and making a runner, into which the tape is run, to draw it up to the size required, this tape is looped at each end and fastened on to two hooks at the sides.

ROD CURTAIN.
PLATE 23. FIG. 13.

This is a favourite and very neat pattern, and is made by sewing six or more breadths together according to the size of the window, of eight or ten nails deep. They are hemmed at the top and bottom, and two gilt or wooden rods are passed through the hems, fulling the curtain well upon them, after which, the rods exactly fit into the window frames.

PLATE 23. FIG. 14.

By way of variety these rods are sometimes put in at the sides, instead of top and bottom.

PLATE 23.

Sometimes these curtains are fixed in a frame, exactly to fit the width of the window, in which case they are often starred like a bed foot board, and look exceedingly neat and pretty.

WINDOW BLINDS.
PLATE 23. FIG. 15.

These are generally made of linen or long lawn, and sometimes of Holland, calico, painted print, green canvass or gauze, or calimanco. If possible, procure the material of the exact breadth of the window, allowing for a good turning in, to herring-bone down, as blinds wear and set far better without seams, and with the side herring-boned.

They should have tape loops or a case for the rod to slip in, and not be nailed on, as the blind is so apt to wear and tear when taken off for washing. Sometimes a small ring is fastened to the blind at the bottom on each side, through which a cord runs, and is nailed tightly top and bottom of the window, this contrivance always makes the blind draw up straightly. A hem is made at the bottom, to admit of the stick, and a cord and tassel generally fastened to the middle, by which it may be drawn down. A cord moving round a pulley at the top, and a window crank at the bottom, enable it to be drawn up and down at pleasure.

CHAIR, SOFA, AND OTHER COVERS.

When chairs and sofas are fitted up with damask, merino, stuff, horse hair, or other material that does not wash, they are generally covered with Holland, chintz, or glazed calico, which protects them from dust and dirt, and are easily removed, when required for company. Holland covers are the most durable, but look cold ; chintz, unless very strong, should be lined with thin glazed calico. The cover should be made exactly to fit the chair or sofa, with or without piping at the edge, and with loops sewed on three of the sides underneath, and a pair of strings on the fourth side ; the cover is firmly fastened down by passing one of the strings through the three loops, and making it tie. Ottomans generally have the covers to fit along beneath the edging of wood, in which case, they must be pinned to the stuffing with very strong pins, which from their length are called sofa pins.

ARM CHAIRS.
PLATE 23. FIG. 16.

It is a good plan to make a kind of case of Holland to fit half way down the cushion, A B C D, which protects the cover from being soiled by the head, on leaning back. Each arm chair should have two or three of these cases for wash and wear.

SOFAS.

These, besides being covered, should have a length of Holland of one breadth, and about one yard, or more long, for the feet of any person lying down to be placed upon.

Where there is an invalid in the house, constantly resting upon the sofa, it is very desirable to make a little flat pillow, put into a muslin cover, frilled all round, to lay the head upon, thus keeping the cushions perfectly clean and neat.

DIVAN.
PLATE 23. FIG. 17.

This is a kind of long sofa, without either back or sides, and may be made to open, which forms a

ON UPHOLSTERY.

very convenient box for large engravings, drawings, &c., &c. The cover should be all in one piece behind, but in front, and at the sides, the top should be unconnected with the lower part, to admit of its opening, so that in fact, the cover must look as much like a box that opens as possible; loops sewed to the edge might fix it into some hooks inside. These divans are very useful for bed-rooms, and would hold bonnets or furs, or mourning, or any thing else, and at the same time, act as a sofa also.

FOOTSTOOLS AND HASSOCKS.
PLATE 23. FIG. 18.

These are made in various ways, and may be got up very cheaply at home. The most simple and one of the prettiest for a bed-room or even a sitting-room is a cloth or velvet hassock braided over, or otherwise ornamented. It is cut circular both top and bottom, a straight side is sewed in between, and ears or handles fastened on, by which they may be carried. These are very soft for young children to sit upon.

ANOTHER KIND.

This is made of two or four bricks tied firmly together, wrapped round with strong sacking, and then neatly covered with cloth, and if not in good shape a little extra stuffing may be added. These footstools are very useful for nurseries, school-rooms, or for servants at work.

CHURCH BASSES.
PLATE 23. FIG. 20.

Flat circular ones are often in use. Sometimes straw ones are covered with green or crimson cloth, and look very neat. Basses may be filled with mill-puff, straw, chaff, bran, or bits of cloth, &c. Some persons prefer a simple cushion or flat pillow to kneel upon, in which case, they may be filled with feathers.

CHURCH SEATS.
PLATE 23. FIG. 24.

Church pews are generally lined with cloth, and fastened by brass nails and binding laid on. The cushions, Plate 23, Fig. 24, are oblong, and made like a very soft mattress.

They have pieces of cloth, bound round and sewed to them in front, to give an air of comfort and neatness to the seat.

The ground or floor is generally covered with a drugget of the same colour as the lining of the seat.

TABLE COVERS.

These may be made variously at home, or else cloth or linen covers may be procured at the mercers' shops. Those made at home are generally of cloth or silk, and sometimes, though very rarely, of satin or velvet. Cloth ones are generally bound with binding, and a lace laid on at a nail from the edging. Velvet, cut in leaves or patterns, is sometimes laid on; different kinds of coloured cloth, cut in the shape of oak leaves, or according to taste, sewed on round the edge look very pretty. Patchwork of silks on a black ground also looks handsome.

SCREENS.
PLATE 23. FIG. 21.

These may be made by merely hemming a piece of rich silk at the top, through which a rod is passed, which is secured to the pole of the screen. The bottom of this silk is hemmed neatly and has a deep fringe set on. The silk should be a good deal fulled, when on the rod, to look handsome.

Others are made by plaiting or fluting rich silk in straight lines, Fig. 22, or to radiate from the centre, which is confined within a frame of rose-wood or mahogany.

Large folding screens are made for putting near to doors, to prevent draughts of air, and are useful to place near a warm bath, especially for infants or delicate persons, so as to enable them to dress free from cold air: small screens of two folds are very convenient to place by every washing stand, when two persons occupy the same room. The frames, after being made by a carpenter, should be finished up at home. They are usually covered with canvass, Holland, calimanco, chintz, twill, or other material. Black Holland looks very neat. These screens make very good scrap books for children, by being pasted over with riddles, prints, caricatures, &c., &c.

CHAPTER IX.

ON COVERS, CASES, &c., &c.

NIGHT-GOWN BAG.
PLATE 24. FIG. 1.

This is made of Holland, calico, or thick cambric, or glazed muslin, and sometimes trimmed all round with a frill, or piped with coloured calico. It is intended to contain the night-gown, cap, also the dressing-gown, and perhaps a change of linen, and the tidy or dressing-case, and may be made to any size, according to the number of things it is intended to contain.

Its chief use is in travelling, especially in a large family, when the separate case, containing each individual's night things are easily found together, and as easily put up in a large carpet bag. Each bag should bear either the name or the initials of the person to whom it belongs.

A TRAVELLING DRESSING-CASE OR TIDY.
PLATE 24. FIG. 3.

These are most useful things, and no one who has once used them will travel without them, unless they can conveniently carry a dressing-case with them.

They are made of Russia duck, ticking, or stamped cloth, or any other firm material.

In making up, the greatest exactness is required to make the parts fit truly. The back, which is all in one piece, is lined with strong calico, and the various pockets are then laid on, the bottom of one being sewed a little below where the top of the next will come, so that the whole has a neat appearance: the sizes of the pockets, given in the Plate, allow for this wrapping over. The top of each pocket is bound with purple or other coloured galloon, and the divisions for the smaller ones are formed by stitching a piece of narrow galloon neatly down upon them. The whole is then bound round with galloon, and strings of the same colour fastened to the pointed end, so as to tie round the dressing-case when it is full. As purple galloon will wash well, it is best for this purpose, as most other colours fade. On each pocket is written with marking ink, the name of the article to be contained in it; these of course differ according to the fancy of the owner, but the most usual are curl papers in the triangular pocket at the top, H for hair-pins, W for thread, tapes, buttons, &c., S for soap, P for tooth-powder,

Plate 24

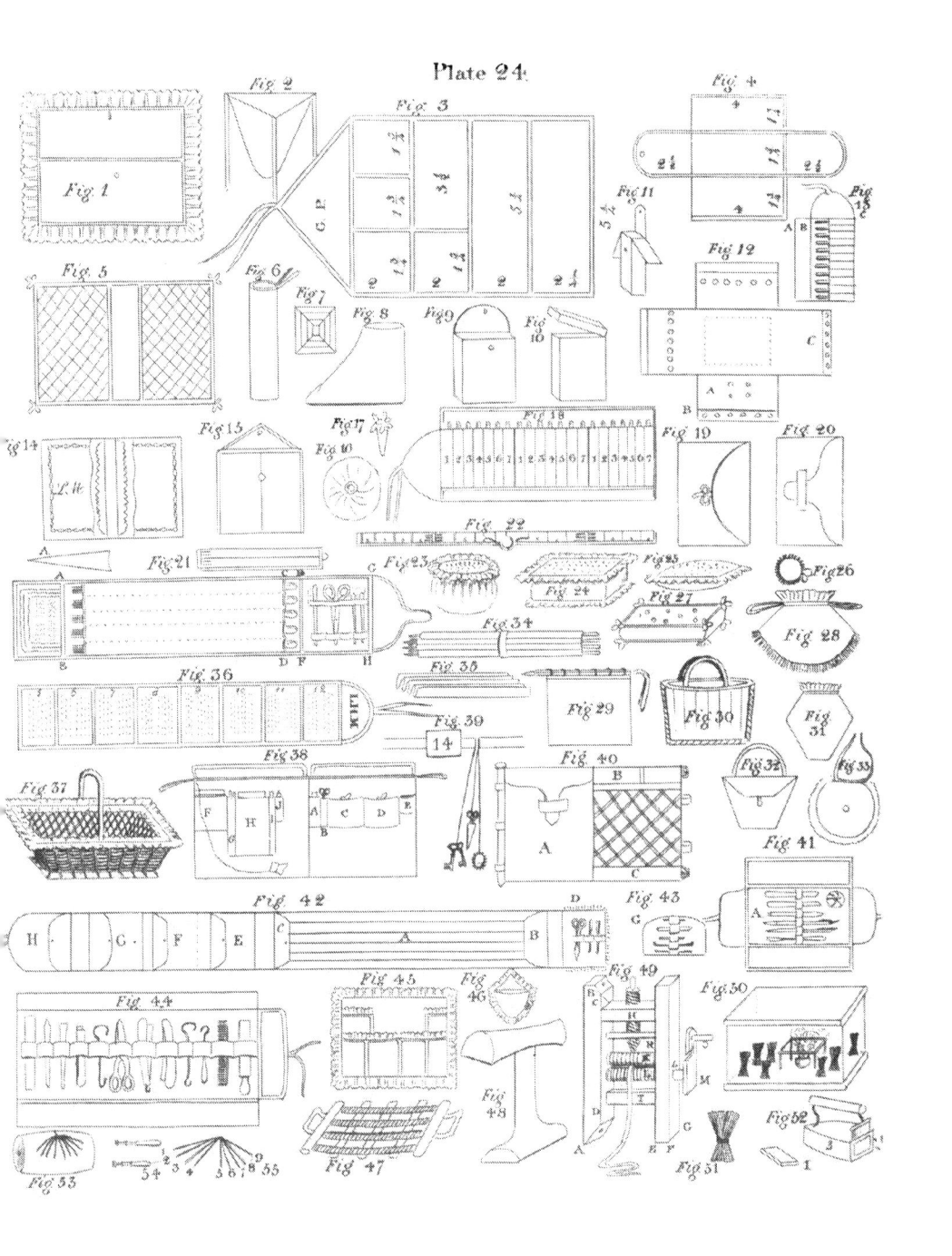

T for tooth-brush, which ought also to be enclosed in an oil silk bag; C for comb, and B for hair brush.

GLOVE CASE.
PLATE 24. FIG. 4.

Gloves easily become soiled, if not covered carefully, and as white gloves, coloured, and black should be kept in separate cases, it is better to make bags for the express purpose of keeping them nicely. It is also advantageous to buy several pairs at once, as they are cheaper when sold by the dozen or half dozen.

For ladies' gloves, take a strip of the material, about four nails wide, and five nails and a quarter long, and pipe or bind it all round with coloured glazed calico, or ribbon; cut another strip, one nail and three quarters wide, and nine nails long, this is also piped and bound; the ends may be finished according to fancy, either left square, rounded off, or turned down to form a triangle. Crease both strips in half their length, and lay the middle of the first strip cross-wise upon the middle of the other, so that the longest piece lies underneath, after pinning them very evenly together, stitch them firmly with small stitches in the piping, so as not to be seen. Strings, or a button and button-hole are fixed to the ends of the longest strip.

White gloves may be put between the two strips and the coloured ones above, when they are laid in, fold the side of the smallest piece over first, then the long one, and button it together.

On the outside mark the name, and the colour of the gloves.

Gentlemen's glove cases vary only in being larger.

POCKET HANDKERCHIEF CASE, COMMONLY CALLED PORTE MOUCHOIR.
PLATE 24. FIG. 5.

This is usually made of silk, and is lined with muslin or sarsenet, having perfume between the silk and the lining, and when put in ladies drawers, with the handkerchiefs laid in, gives them an agreeable scent. It consists either of one or two pockets, generally the latter, so that in folding up, the case is merely doubled over.

The case is about four nails wide, and if intended for double pockets, nine nails and a half long, each pocket being full four nails, and allowing half a nail for turnings in, and a nail space between them, cut out the lining, and two pieces of fine muslin the same size, and lay them as follows:—

First the silk, next one piece of muslin, then sprinkle the scent freely all over it, after which place the other piece of muslin, and then the lining, pin them evenly, and run them round at the edges. Quilt it or not, according to pleasure.

The quilting keeps the scent in place; the ends are turned up the two nails on each side, and the whole is bound with ribbon. Sometimes the initials of the owner are marked on the outside. For a suitable perfume, see Receipt, No. 14.

SHOE OR BRUSH AND COMB BAG.
PLATE 24. FIG. 6.

These are very convenient in travelling, as they save much paper, and take up little room, they are made of different materials, according to the shoe to be put in. If for walking shoes, a coarse brown canvass called earn, is the most suitable. For house shoes, calico or Holland, and for satin slippers, old silk. The bags are made to draw up at one end in the usual way, and should be just wide enough to contain the shoes, but as they are useful to put in one's muff, or to carry in the hand when going out to dine or spend the day, it is as well to leave sufficient space at the top for a pair of stockings above the shoe. The name of the owner, and the quality of the shoe, should be put outside.

ANOTHER SHOE BAG.
PLATE 24. FIG. 15.

This is a better shape for large shoes or ladies' boots, as they lie flatter when packed in separate pockets. The bag is therefore back-stitched up the middle, and a button put on for the upper flap to button upon.

A MAT.
PLATE 24. FIG. 7.

These are very useful to put on handsome tables, or to use as kettle holders. They are made with wool, which forms a fringe similar to that on a rug. Procure a piece of coarse flannel, the size wanted for the mat, which must be hemmed or herring-boned down to make it firm at the edges. Choose a mesh of the width required for the depth of the fringe, and then after fastening the wool at one of the outer corners, commence working by carrying the wool round the mesh and fastening the loop thus made by a cross-stitch to the flannel. Observe always to work along the thread, to keep it straight, and make the fringe lie very much thicker at the corners. Continue working, never fastening off, letting the second square be about four or five threads from the outer one, and connected at the corners to the outer square by fringe added diagonally. This makes the corners full and handsome. When the fringe is all sewed on, fasten off, and then proceed to cut the fringe neatly all round, and with the scissors spread it out, or comb it, to make it look rich and full. Afterwards procure some stiff muslin or buckram and tack it behind, and then sew on neatly the silk or glazed calico lining, and the mat is complete.

BOOT BAGS.
PLATE 24. FIG. 8.

These are very useful for gentlemen whose boots take much room when wrapped in paper, which they often burst, and soil the clean linen ; a boot when packed is generally rolled up from the top about half the leg, the bag should be made to fit it when thus rolled, and is on an average, about the following size :—

- The width at the top of the case, about three nails.
- The width at the bottom, about five nails.
- The length of the case when doubled, about four nails in front, sloped down at the top to three nails and a quarter.

NURSERY BAG.

This is used by nurses while travelling, and is very convenient for the purpose of carrying infants' soiled linen. The bag should be of dark coloured silk, or washing material, made in two divisions, and lined throughout with oiled silk, or Indian rubber cloth, so as to be waterproof. They should be six nails wide, and five or six nails deep. The oil silk bag should be made to draw out of the silk or outer bag. The one pocket or division holds the soiled linen, and the other pocket contains a damp sponge.

BOOK COVER.
PLATE 24. FIG. 5.

Bibles or other valuable books are often covered with cloth, leather, wash leather, Holland, &c., and for books in every day use it is far better than wrapping them in paper. Purple or claret coloured cloth looks very handsome, and when bound with ribbon, ribbon strings, and the initials marked outside, it looks finished and particularly neat. The case is merely a long piece of cloth of the width of the book, and of such a length as to lie outside, and turn in a piece to cover the inside of each flap with the book shut about two-thirds of the way. The book, when shut, takes more than when open, therefore it should be measured when shut.

ANOTHER BOOK CASE.
PLATE 24. FIG. 9.

This is a simple cover made usually of leather or Holland. One piece is sufficient to go before and behind the book, allowing an extra piece for a flap to turn over. Two strips for side-pieces complete the case. If of leather, the pieces are back-stitched neatly together; but if of Holland, &c., the sides are bound up with ribbon.

ANOTHER BOOK CASE.
PLATE 24. FIG. 10, 11.

This is made with a regular lid, as in the drawing, and buttons over.

Fig. 11 has fly pieces or bits, to lay over the book, but beneath the outer flap or lid.

A TRUNK CASE.
PLATE 24. FIG. 12.

This is made of coarse sacking or earn, and is most useful for covering large trunks, and is composed simply of two lengths of the stuff, laid one across the other, and stitched firmly together, exactly where they fall upon each other, forming an oblong or square of back-stitching, as in the Plate, of the size of the bottom of the trunk. Four holes should be made in one of the sides, on which the direction card may be more easily fastened (see A).

The ends are turned down with a broad hem, and button-holes made on the hems of the two ends, B and C, and at two or more nails from the hem at the opposite sides. In packing up the trunk, it is simply laid upon the back-stitched square of the sacking, and the sides being turned up, two at a time, they are laced up with cord, without the trouble of getting a packing needle and sewing it up every time.

A KNIFE OR FORK CASE.
PLATE 24. FIG. 13.

This is usually made of green baize, and is used for wrapping up knives and forks (both steel and dessert or silver), when not in daily use. The knives are put in one case and the forks in another. These cases are made out of half or a whole breadth of the baize, according to the width. After cutting sufficient length to hold six or twelve knives, allowing at one end enough to tie over, cut it at the top straight from A to B, which is to turn over as a side flap, and shape the rest from B to C, in a semi-circular form. Cut another long strip of baize, half the width of from B to C, lay it along and stitch it down at proper equal distances, and when done, bind it along the outer edge, and all round the case.

The knives are then put in, with the blades between the pieces of baize. The flap turns over the handles, the whole rolls up, and is finally tied round with strings, sewed at the circular end.

A SACHET OR CARD CASE.
PLATE 24. FIG. 14.

This is very similar in shape to the porte mouchoir, excepting that four little gores or hinges are put in at the sides of the pockets, to enable it to open wider and contain more cards (see A). This hinge should be creased in two, after being sewed in, and when once creased *well*, will always set properly. They are made of morocco paper, silk, rich satin, or velvet. A piece of flannel or demet may be put between the outside and the lining. They are sometimes embroidered or braided round the edge, with the initials or crest put in the middle. A cord or twist is sometimes put round the edge, to give a finish.

A CANDLESTICK CASE.
PLATE 24. FIG. 16.

Covers for bed-room candlesticks, teapots, cream jugs, sugar basins, dish covers, salvers, and indeed all plated or silver articles may either be made to the shape or circular. The advantage of the latter plan is, that by hemming it round and putting in a string, it will draw up and suit any shaped article, whereas cases made to fit one particular article will do for no other.

A NOSEGAY CASE.
PLATE 24. FIG. 17.

Flowers, especially geraniums, are apt sadly to injure the dress and waistband when worn; it is therefore very useful to put flower stalks in a kind of case, similar to a scissors sheath, which protects the dress completely. It should be cut out of card-board, in the shape of a wide scissors sheath, and covered all over with silk.

A WOOL CASE.
PLATE 24. FIG. 18.

This is made of thin muslin or of Holland, and is most useful for holding and preserving wools. It is made something like a housewife, having runners for the wool, side by side. The wools should be put in in shades and numbered; each colour might have six or seven shades allowed, so that it would require a long piece to admit three or four colours, with their various shades. The flaps at both ends turn over, the whole rolls up when not in use, and ties round.

ANOTHER WOOL CASE.
PLATE 24. FIG. 34, 35.

This is made to resemble thread papers, and is usually formed of muslin. It is plaited along, or doubled, like Fig. 35, and all the doubles sewed along together, thus forming a bunch of runners, for the wool to be drawn through.

A HOUSEWIFE.
PLATE 24. FIG. 19, 20, 21.

This is made of leather, stamped paper, silk, ribbon, satin, velvet, white dimity, Holland, or any other material, even common print.

Two pieces, the size of A B C D, are first of all cut out and back-stitched along, to form the thread runners, after which, another piece, E F G H, is cut out, and the places for the scissors, bodkin, &c.

ON COVERS AND CASES. 213

made, and then a long strip is cut, not only sufficient for the whole length, but to turn over at the end to form a pocket. The other pieces are neatly bound to it, and the flannel or kerseymere for needles is added. The initials may be put at the sloped end. The case may wrap up like Fig. 19 or 20.

A YARD MEASURE.
PLATE 94. FIG. 21, 22.

This is very convenient, from the small compass in which it goes, when folded up. It is similar to a carpenter's rule in shape, and is marked with nails on one side and inches on the other.

PINCUSHIONS.
PLATE 24. FIG. 23, 24, 25, 26, 27.

Pincushions may be made of every variety of shape and material, and stuffed with bran, wool, hair, flannel, chaff, &c., &c.

Fig. 23 makes a very nice toilet pincushion, and is circular at the top, with a deep length sewed all round, which is hemmed at the bottom; it draws neatly beneath the cushion, and ties firmly on it.

Fig. 24 is very neat for a toilet pincushion, and is made to button and unbutton from beneath.

Fig. 25. Another very neat toilet pincushion, made with a fringe or frill round it.

Sometimes the cushion is of glazed calico or coloured silk, and the cover of muslin, with a handsome worked edging all round. These are very handsome for spare rooms, but too good for daily use. The colour of the cushion ought to correspond with the paper or drapery of the room.

Fig. 26 is a flat pocket pincushion, and may be circular, square, diamond, oblong, or any other shape. Cut out the form in two cards, both of which are covered with silk. Flannel is put between, and the two sides neatly sewed together.

Fig. 27 is a drawing-room pincushion, usually made of silk or satin, and is tufted like a mattress with bows or tufts of silk. Bows are attached to all the corners.

BAGS.
PLATE 94. FIG. 28, 29, 30, 31, 32, 33.

Bags are made of silk, satin, velvet, and many other materials, and are almost always lined; in which case, they are done in a similar manner to sleeves.

There is a great variety of shapes, and they are trimmed with fringe, lace, ribbon, silk cord, &c., &c. The Figures represent the shapes most in use at present, and need little description.

Fig. 32 is a double bag, being two pockets or bags, which, being sewed together up the sides and along the bottom, form a third pocket between them, which may either be left open, or have a regular silk bag sewed above.

In one pocket may be kept pencil, knife, Indian rubber, and other writing materials; in the other, money, bills, memoranda, &c.; and in the middle part, scissors, thimble, cotton, and other materials for work.

NEEDLE CASE.
PLATE 24. FIG. 36.

This is made of a strip of kerseymere, one nail and a quarter wide, which is marked out in the required number of divisions, to separate the different sized needles from each other. Each space between the divisions should be half or three quarters of a nail, so that the length of the strip must depend upon the number and size of these divisions. After fixing upon the length and width, cutting off the strip, and marking in pencil the lines for the divisions, work over the lines in chain-stitch in silk, or lay on braid, marking at the top of each space, the number of the needles to be put in; then bind the kerseymere down with some broad ribbon, which serves likewise for the back of the case. This ribbon should be stiff and rich, and when turned over the edges of the kerseymere, should be back-stitched down very neatly. The end of the strip is usually rounded, as in the Plate, and the initials worked on. Ribbons, or a button and loop are attached to the end, to fasten it up by.

WORK BASKET.
PLATE 24. FIG. 37.

These are very pretty, light, and useful. Purchase a suitable size, of the shape of the pattern, about twelve inches long, eight wide, and three and a half deep, or smaller, are the usual sizes. As they look neater and keep better when painted, it is advisable to send them to the coach-maker's to be coloured the shade desired (the darker, the more handsome); when quite dry, procure a good silk of a suitable colour, and also satin ribbon to match, of two thirds of a nail wide, and line the basket, putting first muslin, and then a layer of fine flannel, and afterwards silk. It should be made exactly to fit, and be quilted in some pretty pattern all over, after which, the satin ribbon, neatly quilled, is sewed round at the top. Sometimes ladies put little pockets or bags all round, to contain a knife, scissors, money, pincushion, &c.

TRAVELLING BAG.
PLATE 24. FIG. 38.

A travelling bag is very useful for ladies, when taking long journeys, especially when they are fond of working or sketching while in the carriage.

The Fig. represents both sides of the bag complete, excepting that it requires the sides to be sewed up. It is thus laid open, or unsewed, in order to explain the plan more clearly.

The bag should be made of rich strong silk, and on one side pockets are made to contain as follows:—

  A. Needle book or housewife.
  B. Scissors.
  C. Work and cotton.
  D. Pocket for money.
  E. Ditto for watch, or gold, &c.

On the other side, the pockets are as follows:—

  F. For a note book, or journal.
  G. For two pencils.
  H. Sketch book.
  I. Rules.
  J. Knife.

A piece of Indian rubber is fastened to a bit of galloon and confined to one end of the bag. The pockets should be put in rather lower from the top than is represented in the Plate, else the bag will not close neatly, when the strings are drawn.

SCHOOL GIRL'S BADGE.
PLATE 24. FIG. 39.

This band is made of webbing, black tape, calimanco, or any other firm material.

To the middle of the band is attached a square piece of pasteboard, or tin covered with flannel and calimanco, on which the girl's number is marked.

On this band are put several strings of galloon or tape, to which are tied scissors, keys, pincushion, &c. A simple band of Holland, or tape would be very useful for servants, especially housekeepers, lady's maids, and housemaids, to attach the keys belonging to their department, also scissors, cushion, pencil, &c. These bands might have button-holes, or large oylet-holes worked in them, to receive the ribbons to which the things are attached, and they should be made to button neatly behind.

Shoulder-straps might be added of the same material.

CARRIAGE CASE, OR PORTE FOLIO.
PLATE 24. FIG. 40.

This is very useful for those ladies who drive about constantly in a town, and who have much shopping, or many calls, &c. to make.

The left hand side of the case marked A, is a porte folio to carry paper, bills, &c. with a long pencil at the side, which, when the book or case is shut, secures the two sides together, by being passed through the loops.

The other side is made with two pockets above, at B, for visiting cards, one pocket below C, for a rule, and crossed narrow ribbons between, to hold bills, &c. in. This case may be made of leather, cloth, or stamped paper, and should be laid on millboard, or pieces of tin to form the sides.

TRAVELLING PORTE FOLIO.
PLATE 24. FIG. 41.

This is convenient for travelling, when there is not sufficient room for a desk; it is made of card or book board, and covered with black silk or paper. Under the part marked A, is a porte folio for paper, the two parts being connected together by means of a wide ribbon all round. The four flaps lay over and tie across with ribbon. On the part, A, are places for sealing wax, pencil, pens, knife and paper knife, all in one, and at the corner a piece of ribbon sewed on in a circle, and made to draw up like a bag, to contain wafers.

SEAMAN'S OR TRAVELLER'S CASE.
PLATE 24. FIG. 42. 43.

This sort of case is very useful for men in all classes when travelling, and for school boys, and is usually made of Russia duck, or of leather; it is one yard long, and about one nail and a half or two nails wide. The pockets and thread-case must all be prepared before sewing them to the back. A is divided, according to the Plate, for the thread case as in a housewife, it is about four nails long, and has two flaps, C and B, at the ends, to keep the thread neat. The flap, C, is finished inside, as seen in Fig. 43, with boot-hooks, &c., &c. The thread should be strong white, strong black, whity brown, carpet thread, pack thread, and other kinds, also white and black silk.

D is a square pincushion with divisions for scissors, tweezers, stiletto, &c. Inside this pocket should slip a needle book and sticking plaister case, both in one; the flaps of E F G H, all hook and eye down to their respective pockets, which contain fish-hooks, buttons, hooks and eyes, &c., &c.

GENTLEMAN'S TRAVELLING DRESSING CASE.
PLATE 24. FIG. 44.

This is made of leather of any length, according to the number of things put in. It should be the width of the longest of the articles to be put in (say the razors). A row of divisions of the proper sizes are made by a strap of leather carried all along the case in which the razor strop, boot hooks, razors, scissors, knife, tweezers, pencil, tooth brush case, shaving brush, and soap case are put. The flaps fold over, and the whole wraps up and ties round. The articles should be bought before the case is made, as the divisions can then be formed exactly to fit.

WATCH POCKET.
PLATE 24. FIG. 45.

These may be made of silk or cambric muslin. The one here represented is composed of one large and two small pockets, the latter are to hold the watch and smelling bottle, and the large pocket is for the handkerchief. The large pocket is supported by three runners of whalebone or ribbon wire. These should be put in so as easily to draw out, if the watch pocket is of a washing material. Whalebone is also put at the top of each of the three pockets.

The whole should be frilled round or ornamented with narrow lace or fringe. The size must greatly depend upon the size of the bed, but five nails long by four deep is a good average size for a large bedstead.

ANOTHER WATCH POCKET.
PLATE 24. FIG. 46.

This is the usual shape, and intended merely to contain the watch. They may be made of silk, dimity, ribbon, or any other material. Some are composed of bed-ticking, which is worked in the light stripe with coloured silk in chain-stitch, herring-boning, or any other fancy stitch. They are ornamented round with fringe, lace, or frilling.

AN INVALID'S CHAIR.
PLATE 24. FIG. 47.

This is very convenient for carrying invalids about when they have lost the use of their legs, especially for conveying them down steps, to the carriage, &c.

The two outer pieces of wood should be of beech or some other strong kind, to which handles may be attached. These pieces of wood are connected together by four or more pieces of very strong double webbing, between which three slips of strong wood are firmly secured. When used, a simple cushion is put upon this webbing, and two servants, one on each side, can carry it with ease and safety. When not in use, it can be rolled up in a very little compass.

It is particularly useful for invalids while travelling.

CHAPTER X.

RECEIPTS.

The following receipts have all been tried either by the Authoress herself, or by her immediate friends, and are thoroughly to be depended upon.

A few have been introduced not immediately connected with the work-book, but from their value, no apology is necessary for their insertion.

No. 1.
PERMANENT INK FOR MARKING LINEN.

1 ounce, 5 drachms, 1 scruple of lunar caustic nitrate of silver,
2 ounces of gum arabic, powdered,
1 pint of distilled water,
½ an ounce of sap green,

For the liquid pounce with which the linen is wetted, previously to the application of the ink, mix
4 ounces of carbonate of soda,
2 ounces of powdered gum arabic,
1 pint of distilled water,

and a little cochineal, to colour it.

In marking linen, after applying the liquid pounce with a common small bristle brush, to the part which is to receive the mark, and wetting it very well, let it dry by the fire, and then after rubbing it with a glass calender or glazing stone, to make it smooth, mark it with a fine hard steel pen. It should then be exposed to the air, which makes the letters turn quite black. The place should be washed soon after it is dry, as the liquid pounce injures the linen, if left on it long.

No. 2.
PERMANENT RED MARKING INK.

Take half an ounce of vermillion, and a drachm of salt of steel, let them be finely levigated with linseed oil to the thickness required. The mixture must be well shaken before used.

Inks of various colours may be made, by using sap green, Prussian blue, gamboge, &c. instead of vermillion.

No. 3.
TO REMOVE MARKING INK FROM LINEN.

When linen is erroneously marked or spotted with marking ink, an application of chloride of lime with either cold or hot water, will efface it. It should be applied over and over again till the marks are obliterated; but as the chloride of lime spoils linen, it is advisable to wash the part well, immediately after each application, so as to prevent its eating away the linen.

Chloride of lime being poisonous, the mixture should be carefully thrown away after being used.

No. 4.
TO REMOVE COMMON INK FROM CLOTHES, &c.

Rub the place immediately with lemon juice, and hot soap and water, and if this does not succeed, have recourse to salts of lemon, which seldom fails.

No. 5.
SALTS OF LEMON.

They are used to remove ink and iron moulds from linen, calico, all articles of dress and furniture, and even from wood, books, &c.

It is made as follows:—

    A quarter of a pound of salts of sorrel,
    A quarter of a pound of cream of tartar,

Well mixed and rubbed together in a mortar, and it is then ready for use.

It should be kept locked up, the salts of sorrel being a strong poison.

In using salts of lemon to an inked carpet or table, merely rub it on with the top of the finger, having previously dipped it in hot water.

If it is a piece of linen, or an article of dress that has been inked, it is best to stretch it over a pewter or other vessel full of hot water, and when wetted through with the steam, apply a small quantity of the salts on the ink or iron-mould, rubbing it well at the same time with the finger, and a spot will, on repeating the application, disappear.

No. 6.
TO TAKE OUT INK, WHEN SALTS OF LEMON ARE NOT AT HAND.

Dip the spotted part into some melted tallow from a mould candle. Send it to the wash thus greased, and it will return clean and white.

Of course this is only applicable to articles that will wash.

No. 7.
TO REMOVE INK FROM CLOTH OR CARPETS.

Take up the ink instantly with a spoon, and pour on water in abundance, while still applying the spoon constantly, till it is removed; rub afterwards a bit of lemon upon the place, which will brighten any colour that may be deadened.

No. 8.
BLEACHING LIQUID

Is used to remove iron-moulds, or restore discoloured linen, and calico to its former whiteness.

Pour it into a basin, one part of the liquid to six parts of water; the cloth is dipped into it, allowed to lie in it, and well rubbed, till the mark is effaced, when the part is washed in clear water.

The bleaching liquid is made as follows:—

A solution of chloride of carbonate of soda; this cannot be procured in powder, but a preparation of lime in powder can be had, which will do equally well. Unless much diluted, this is apt to injure the texture of the linen.

Another receipt for making it is the following:—

Chloride of lime, the powder to be put into water, a part of it will dissolve, and a part will not;

decant the clear fluid, and keep it in a dark place. The powder is apt to attract moisture from the air, and to lose its chlorine by exposure, it must be kept in a bottle with a glass stopper, as it corrodes corks.

No. 9.
TO REMOVE STAINS MADE BY ACIDS.

Wet the part, and lay on it some salt of wormwood; rub it, without diluting it with more water.

No. 10.
ANOTHER RECEIPT.

Let the cloth imbibe a little water without putting it in, and hold the part over a lighted match at a proper distance, to avoid its catching fire. The spots will be removed by the sulphureous gas.

No. 11.
ANOTHER RECEIPT.

Tie up in the stained part, some pearl ash, then scrape some soap into cold soft water, to make a lather, and boil the linen till the stains disappear.

No. 12.
TO REMOVE STAINS OF WINE, FRUIT, &c. WHEN THEY HAVE BEEN LONG IN LINEN.

Rub the part on each side with yellow soap, then lay on a mixture of starch with cold water, very thick, like paste; rub it in well, and expose the linen to the sun and air till the stain comes out; if not removed in three or four days, take the starch off, and renew the process. When dry, sprinkle it again with water, and send it to the wash.

Many other stains may be taken out by dipping the linen in sour buttermilk, and drying it in a hot sun, then wash and dry it two or three times in the day.

No. 13.
TO REMOVE STAINS OF PORT WINE.

Directly the wine is spilt, spread common salt all over the stain, and wash it with water.

No. 14.
TO TAKE STAINS OUT OF SCARLET CLOTH.

Take soap wort, bruise it, strain out the juice, and add to it a small quantity of black soap, wash the stains a few times with this liquor, suffering the cloth to dry between, and in a day or two they will disappear.

No. 15.
TO TAKE STAINS OUT OF BLACK CLOTH, SILK, CRAPE, &c.

Boil a handful of fig-leaves in two quarts of water, until reduced to a pint; squeeze the leaves, take them out, and put the liquid into a bottle for use. The articles need only be rubbed with a sponge dipped in it, and the stains will soon disappear.

When black is stained by fruit or other acids, the spotted part turns yellow or red, touch it with a little spirits of hartshorn, which immediately restores the colour.

No. 16.
SCOURING DROPS

Are used to remove stains and grease from all silks; they are rubbed on with a bit of flannel, and generally answer perfectly well. They are prepared as follows:—
Mix equal quantities of spirits of turpentine, and essence of lemons.

No. 17.
TO REMOVE GREASE FROM SILK.

Rub it for some time with a split card, or a piece of cap paper, or if much greased, lay under it a piece of soft paper, or blotting paper, and the same over it, and place a warm iron upon it, which causes the paper to imbibe the grease from the silk; after repeating this, taking care each time the iron is applied to furnish clean bits of paper, then rub it with split card, or soft paper. Cloth may be cleaned in the same way.

Or, dip a clean piece of flannel into spirits of turpentine, and rub the spots until they disappear; the silk should not be made very wet with turpentine, or it will lose its lustre.

No. 18.
ANOTHER RECEIPT.

Rub the part with French chalk, or with part of the back of the cuttle fish scraped, which may be bought at the druggists for one penny each.

No. 19.
LIQUID FOR REMOVING SPOTS OF GREASE, PITCH, OR OIL FROM LINEN AND CLOTHES.

In a pint of spring water, dissolve an ounce of pure pearl ash, add to the solution a lemon cut in small slices. This being properly mixed and kept in a warm state for two days, the whole must be strained, and the clear liquid kept in a bottle for use.

A little of this mixture being poured on the stained part, removes all spots of grease, pitch, or oil, and the moment they disappear, the cloth is washed in clear water.

No. 20.
TO REMOVE GREASE FROM SILK OR WOOLLEN.

Mix together three ounces of spirits of wine, three ounces of French chalk powdered, and five ounces of pipe clay.

Rub the mixture on the stain, either wet or dry, and afterwards take it off with a brush.

Sometimes an equal quantity of spirits of turpentine and pipe clay mixed, and used as above, will have the desired effect.

This will remove stains from silk, woollen or cotton.

No. 21.
PORTABLE BALLS FOR REMOVING GREASE SPOTS.

Dry fuller's earth so as to crumble easily into powder, and moisten it well with lemon juice, add a small quantity of pure pulverized pearl ash, and work the whole up into a thick paste; roll it up into small balls, let them dry in the heat of the sun, and they will be ready for use.

The manner of using them is by moistening with water the spots on the cloth, rubbing the ball upon them, and leaving them to dry in the sun; on washing the places with water, and very often, with brushing alone, the spots will disappear.

No. 22.
TO TAKE OUT MILDEW.

Mix soft soap with powdered starch, half as much salt, and the juice of a lemon. Lay it on the mildewed part, on both sides, with a brush. Let it lie on the grass day and night till the stain comes out.

No. 23.
TO TAKE OUT IRON MOULDS.

Rub them with sulphuret of potash; then bathe them well with citric acid (lemon acid), afterwards wash the places well in water, and the linens will be completely restored.

No. 24.
TO REMOVE PAINT SPOTS FROM SILK, &c.

Apply spirits of turpentine repeatedly, when the article is silk.
If it is muslin or linen, cover it with butter, and then wash it.

No. 25.
TO CLEAN SILKS AND COTTONS WITHOUT INJURY TO THEIR COLOUR OR TEXTURE.

Grate two or three raw potatoes into a pint of clean water, and pass the liquid through a sieve, when it has stood to settle, pour off the clear part, and it will be fit for use.

Dip a clean sponge in the liquid, and apply it to the silk till the dirt is well separated, then wash it in pure water.

The coarse pulp of the potatoes which does not pass the sieve, is of great use in cleaning worsted curtains, carpets, and other coarse goods.

No. 26.
TO WASH BLACK SILK AND CRAPE.

Warm some small beer, and mix some milk with it, then sponge the silk with this liquid, and it will freshen the colour very much.

A strong decoction of fig-leaves, a little gin, or spirits of wine, will have an equally good effect.

No 27.
TO RESTORE RUSTY SILK.

Boil some green tea in an iron pot, nearly a cup full of tea to three quarts of water. Sponge the silk with it, and iron it while damp.

No. 28.
TO CLEAN BOMBAZINE.

Use the liquid mentioned, No. 25, and sponge the bombazine with it, and then with water, remembering to rub width-wise, not selvage-wise, or the bombazine will be frayed.

No. 29.
COMPOSITION FOR RESTORING SCORCHED LINEN.

Boil to a consistency two ounces of fuller's earth, half an ounce of cake soap, and the juice of two onions, in half a pint of vinegar. Spread it over the damaged part, and suffer it to dry on, then give it one or two washings, and if the scorching is not so great as to injure the threads, the part will appear white and perfect.

No. 30.
TO CLEAN CALICO FURNITURE.

Shake off the loose dust, and slightly brush it with a small long haired brush; after which, wipe it with clean flannels, and rub it with dry old bread. If well done, the furniture will look nearly as well as at first.

Bran is also an excellent cleanser.

While furniture remains up, it should be preserved as much as possible from sun and air, which injure delicate colours; the dust may be blown off with bellows.

No. 31.
TO CLEAN CHINTZ.

Chintz may be cleaned as follows:—

Boil two pounds of rice in two gallons of water till it is soft, when the whole is poured into a tub fit for use.

Wash the chintz till it is quite clean in soap and water, and then rinse it in the rice water, which will act like starch. In drying, it must be hung very smoothly, and rubbed with a glazed stone, but not ironed.

An upper crust of bread or bran, are very good for cleaning also.

No. 32.
TO SCOUR CARPETS.

Shake the carpet well.

Dissolve one ounce and a half of alum in a quart of warm water, also one ounce and a half of fuller's earth in another quart of warm water, put a little of each into a bucket full of soft water, adding a very little gall, and rubbing in some common brown soap. Then wash a small piece of the carpet with a flannel dipped in this mixture, so as to make it rather wet, and to shew the colour, brush it over with soap, which must be well washed off, and the carpet rubbed over with a coarse cloth. Then wash it over without soap, and with water in which alum, gall, and fuller's earth are mixed, and rub it as dry as possible with a cloth. When the whole carpet is washed over in this manner, piece by piece, it will appear as fresh and bright as a new one. The quantities here given are sufficient for a large sized carpet.

If a carpet is not very much soiled, it may be cleaned by being first well shook and beaten, and then scoured with gall, and soap and water, after which, it must be laid on the grass, or hung up to dry.

No. 33.
TO WASH SILK HANDKERCHIEFS.

These must be first washed in cold water, and the second lather must be only lukewarm, then rinse them in cold water, dry them gradually, and send them to the mangle.

No. 34.
TO WASH COLOURED MUSLINS, PRINTS, &c.

Coloured muslin, washing silk handkerchiefs and aprons, should have a little spirits of wine in the water, about a dessert spoonful to a gallon.

For prints, a little gall will fix the colours; if the principal colour is lilac, pearl ash put in the water will refresh it. If green prevails, put in a few half pence.

No. 35.
TO MAKE LINEN WHITE THAT HAS TURNED YELLOW.

Heat a gallon of milk over the fire, and scrape into it one pound of cake soap, when it is quite dissolved, put the linen in, and let it boil some time, then take it out, put it into a lather of hot water, and wash it properly out.

No. 36.
TO MAKE LINEN WASHED IN THE TOWN AS PURE AND WHITE AS THAT WASHED IN THE COUNTRY.

In great towns where linen cannot be exposed to the air and sun upon the grass, let it be steeped for some time before it is washed, in a solution of oxmuriate of lime; let it then be boiled in an alkaline lye. Linen or cotton thus treated, will not become yellow from age, as is too often the case with town washed linen.

No. 37.
TO WASH CHINA-CRAPE SCARFS, &c.

Make a strong lather of soap and boiling water, suffer it to cool, and when nearly cold, wash the scarf quickly and thoroughly; dip it immediately afterwards into cold hard water, in which a little common salt has been thrown, to preserve the colours; rince, wring and hang it out to dry in the open air; pin it at the extreme ends to the line, so that it may not be folded together in any part. The more rapidly it dries the clearer the colour will be.

No. 38.
TO WASH BLONDE.

If the blonde be very narrow, it should be slightly run to the edge of either net, or old tulle, in order to make it easier to iron, tack it together in the same way that lace is done, in a length of three or four nails, and wash it clean, in a light lather of white soap and water; then put it into a bason in which there is powder blue mixed with cold water, of a sufficiently deep colour to remove the yellow tinge of the soiled blonde.

The iron should be getting ready whilst the blonde lies in the blue water, which must be a few minutes, and it must only be taken out piece by piece, to be pulled out and ironed whilst it is still damp. The iron must be moderately warm.

The tulle, which is spoiled by the washing, is then taken off, and the blonde will be found to have a brightness similar to new.

The following is another method, which has been found to answer equally well:—

Tack the blonde together as before; prepare a lather of fine white soap and hot soft water, in which a little powder blue is mixed. Dip the blonde into this hot water, and squeeze it in the hand, so that it shall be wetted through and through, it should not be allowed to remain in the water, lest the blue should settle upon it unequally. When the colour is restored, take it out, and clap it between the hands, while still folded, until it is nearly dry, when it must be opened out, and ironed with a moderately hot iron.

No. 39.
TO WASH LACE.

The best methods of washing fine, and valuable lace, are as follows:—

Take a pint bottle (which is better than a larger one, being more easily held), wrap a piece of clean muslin or linen round it, and fasten it with a few stitches, then wind the lace round the bottle, avoiding the neck, and wash it in a light lather of white soap and water.

When it appears clean, rinse it in fresh water, and put the bottle in the sun, or in a warm room, to dry the lace.

On taking it off, pull it out with the first and second finger and thumb, taking care not to tear it, at the same time to pull it open to its full width; then lay it between the leaves of a blank book, or pieces of thin card board, not allowing one piece to fold over another, and put it under a weight, till it is properly pressed.

The soap should be cut in thin slices, and boiled in the water, to make the lather; this is particularly adapted to Mechlin lace.

The following plan is chiefly useful for Valenciennes or Lisle lace, or for the borders of infants' caps.

Fold the piece of lace evenly backwards and forwards (not round and round), the length of about three or four nails, and when done, tack it together down the middle with long loose stitches; then wash it thoroughly in a lather of white soap and water, rinsing it repeatedly, and squeezing it in clear water, then, while still wet, dip it in a mixture ready prepared of beer and water in equal quantities, let it remain about a minute, and then wring it out.

It must now be unstitched, and pulled out two or three times, until nearly dry, this must be done width-wise of the lace, and very thoroughly. Lay it on a table covered with a linen cloth, and glaze it with a glass calender, or, if one is not at hand, with a glass phial bottle.

The beer gives the creamy colour of new lace, and a little stiffness besides; some persons dip it in water, in which they put a little snuff tied up in a muslin bag, to colour it, instead of the beer.

Starch should never be put into lace, as it tears and spoils it.

No. 40.
TO WASH KID GLOVES.

Kid gloves, if they are good ones, and have never been touched by Indian rubber, may be washed so as to look like new, in the following manner; and some will bear the operation more than once; it answers equally well both for white and coloured gloves.

Lay the gloves on a clean towel, and with a piece of flannel dipped in warm water with a good deal of white soap, rub them thoroughly till all the dirt is removed; take care to use as little water as possible. Hang them up to dry gradually, at a distance from the fire, and the next morning, they will appear shrivelled and yellow, pull them out the cross way of the leather, and they will soon resume their colour and shape.

No. 41.
TO CLEAN WHITE SATIN SHOES.

Rub them with stale bread. Or rub them with a piece of new flannel dipped in spirts of wine.

No. 42.
TO KEEP BLONDE, WHITE SATIN, SILK, &c.

The above, and all articles which are apt to be discoloured by lying by, should be wrapped up and covered with the coarsest brown paper, as the turpentine contained in it, is an effectual preservation.

No. 43.
TO DYE GLOVES LIKE YORK-TAN OR LIMERICK.

Put some saffron into a pint of soft water boiling hot, and let it infuse all night; next morning, wet the leather all over with a brush.

The tops should be previously sewed up, to prevent the colour getting in.

No. 44.
TO DYE WHITE GLOVES TO PURPLE.

Boil four ounces of logwood, and two ounces of rock alum, in three pints of soft water, till it is half wasted; strain, and let it stand till cold. Then wet the gloves all over with a brush dipped in this mixture, and repeat it when dry.

Twice is sufficient, unless the colour is to be very dark. When dry, rub off the loose dye with a coarse cloth, beat up the white of an egg, and rub it over the gloves with a sponge.

The hands will be stained in the process of dyeing, but wetting them with vinegar before they are washed, will take it off.

No. 45.
WASH FOR LEATHER GLOVES.

If you wish to have your gloves quite yellow, take yellow ochre; if quite white, pipe-clay; if between the two, mix a little of each; if dark, take rotten stone and fuller's earth.

By a proper mixture of these, you may produce any shade you desire; mix the colour you fix on with beer or vinegar, *not water*, and apply it to the gloves, having previously washed them, let them dry gradually, rub and pull them out cross-wise.

After applying the mixture equally all over, let them dry very gradually, not in the sun or near a fire, lest they should shrink. Rub and pull them out before they are quite dry.

No. 46.
TO DYE COTTON A NANKEEN COLOUR.

Keep old nails and rusty iron for fifteen days in good vinegar; apply this dye to the cotton with a brush, it will give an excellent colour, which improves by washing.

No. 47.
TO DYE THE LININGS OF FURNITURE BUFF OR SALMON COLOUR, ACCORDING TO THE DEPTH OF THE HUE.

Rub down on a pewter plate two pennyworth of Spanish annatto, and then boil it in a pail of water a quarter of an hour. Put into it two ounces of pot-ash, stir it round, and instantly put in the lining; stir it about all the while it is boiling, which must be five or six minutes; then put it into cold pump water, and hang the articles up singly without wringing; when almost dry, fold and mangle it.

PINK.

The calico must be washed extremely clean, and dried. Then boiled in two gallons of soft water, and four ounces of alum; take it out, and dry it in the air. In the mean time boil in the alum water two handfuls of wheat bran, till quite slippery, and then strain it.

Take two scruples of cochineal, and two ounces of argall, finely pounded and sifted; mix it with the liquor, a little at a time; then put the calico into the liquor and boil it till it is almost wasted, moving it about.

Take out the calico, and wash it in chamber lye first, and cold water after; then rinse it in water, starch, strain, and dry it quickly without hanging in folds. Mangle it very highly, unless you have it calendered, which is the best.

BLUE.

Let the calico be washed clean and dried, then mix some of Scott's liquid blue in as much water as will be sufficient to cover the things to be dyed, and put in some starch to give it a light stiffness. Dry a bit to see if the colour is deep enough; then put the linen, &c. into it, and wash it; dry the articles singly, and mangle or calender them.

No. 48.
TO CLEAN GOLD AND SILVER LACE.

Sew the lace in linen cloth, and boil it in a pint of water, and two ounces of soap, then wash it in water.

When it is tarnished, apply a little warm spirits of wine to the tarnished part.

No. 49.
TO PRESERVE LINEN FROM MOTHS.

When well washed and dried, fold it up, and scatter in the folds powdered cedar wood, having previously perfumed your chest or drawers with storax; this will effectually prevent damp or moths from injuring the linen.

No. 50.
TO PRESERVE WOOLLENS AND BLANKETS.

They should first be properly washed in a lather of soap and water, and well dried, then pepper must be sprinkled over them before they are folded up and put away.

It is a good plan to keep them in brown paper bags.

No. 51.
TO PRESERVE FURS AND WOOLLENS FROM MOTHS.

Let the former be occasionally combed, while in use, and the latter brushed and shaken. When put away, dry them very well, then mix among them bitter apples from the apothecary's, sewed up in small muslin bags, or pieces of Russia leather.

No. 52.
TO VARNISH OLD STRAW OR CHIP HATS.

Take half an ounce of the best black sealing wax, bruise it, and put to it two ounces of spirits of turpentine, melt the sealing wax very gently, by placing the bottle that holds it in boiling water, near the fire, taking care the spirit does not catch fire; when all the wax is melted, lay it on the hat warm, with a fine hair brush, near the fire, or in the sun. It will not only give a beautiful gloss and stiffness to the hat, but will make it resist wet.

No. 53.
TO RAISE THE SURFACE OF VELVET.

Warm a smoothing iron moderately, cover it with a wet cloth, hold it under the velvet, and the vapour arising from the heated cloth will raise the pile of the velvet, especially with the assistance of a rush wisk. Velvet should be cleaned either with a bit of old velvet or crape.

No. 54.
TO MAKE STARCH.

Peel and grate a quantity of potatoes, put the pulp into a coarse cloth, between two boards, and press it into a dry cake; the juice thus pressed out of the potatoe, must be mixed with an equal quantity of water, and in an hour's time it will deposit a fine sediment, which may be used as starch.

No. 55.
TO MAKE COURT PLAISTER.

Lay some thin black silk on the table, and put on it with a brush some dissolved isinglass, or gum water, and let it dry, then dip it several times in the white of an egg.

No. 56.
TO MAKE LAVENDER WATER.

To one pint of spirits of wine, add eight pennyworth of essence of ambergris, and one shilling worth of oil of lavender.

No. 57.
TO MAKE EAU DE COLOGNE.

Spirits of wine (rectified at 36 degrees), one pound and a half,
Essence of bergamot, two drachms,
Essence of rosemary, half a drachm,
Essence of cedras, half a drachm,
Essence of lemon, half a drachm,
Essence of orange flowers, twenty drops,
Essence of mereby, twenty drops,
Spirits of melisse, one ounce and a half,
Of soft water, boiled and dropt slowly through clean blotting paper, one quart.

No. 58.
POWDER FOR INFANTS' DUST BAGS.

The skin of infants is so apt to chafe, if not thoroughly dried after washing, that powder is put upon all the folds of their skin, and rubbed by the hand upon them.

This is either put on with a powder puff, or dusted out of little muslin bags.

Lapis calaminaris, a fine yellow powder, is that generally used.

Fuller's earth is particularly adapted, from its cooling nature, to check inflammation. It is dusted on when the skin is not sore, but when the chafing has taken place it is put on mixed with cold water.

Violet powder is often used, but this is frequently mixed with some hurtful ingredient, which irritates and inflames the skin, and is therefore objected to by medical men. It can be procured perfectly harmless, but the druggist of whom it is purchased should be told for what purpose it is intended.

No. 59.

POT-POURRI, OR SWEET SCENT JAR.

Put the following ingredients into a large china jar, in layers, with bay salt between each layer; two pecks of damask roses, part in buds, and part blown; of violets, jessamine, and orange flowers, a handful each; two ounces of orris root sliced, storax, and gum benjamin; a quarter of a pound of angelica root sliced; a quart of the red part of clove gilly flowers, two handsful of lavender flowers, half a handful of rosemary flowers, bay and laurel leaves; three Seville oranges, stuck as full of cloves as possible, dried in a cool oven, and pounded; half a handful of knotted majoram, two handsful of balm of gilead dried.

Cover all quite close for some weeks, and the perfume is very fine.

No. 60.

A QUICKER SORT OF POT-POURRI.

Take three handsful of orange flowers, three of clove gilly flowers, three of damask roses, one of knotted marjoram, one of lemon thyme, six bay leaves, two handsful of rosemary, a handful of myrtle, half a one of mint, one of lavender, the rind of a lemon, and a quarter of an ounce of cloves.

Chop them all, and put them in layers with pounded bay salt between them, up to the top of the jar.

If all the ingredients cannot be procured at once, put them in as you obtain them, always throwing in bay salt, after each fresh layer.

No. 61.

SCENT BAGS TO LAY IN DRAWERS.

Half a pound of coriander seeds, half a pound of damask rose leaves, half a pound of sweet orris root, half a pound of calamus aromaticus, one ounce of mace, one ounce of cinnamon, half an ounce of cloves, three ounces of verbena powder, four drachms of musk powder, two drachms of loaf sugar, three ounces of lavender flowers, and some rhodium wood; beat them well together, and sew them up in muslin or silk bags.

No. 62.

TO MAKE SHOES WATERPROOF.

One pound of mutton suet, four ounces of bees-wax, two ounces of Venice turpentine, mixed altogether; the bees-wax being melted and strained.

Put on the composition with a hare's foot or brush, drying it before the fire, and repeating it at intervals of time, till all the seams and little cracks are filled up.

RECEIPTS.

No 63.
REMEDY AGAINST FLEAS.

Sew the leaves of fresh penny-royal, in little muslin bags, and put them between the blankets, or mattresses. Wormwood, or dried moss, will have the same effect.

No. 64.
TO PREVENT BEING BITTEN BY BUGS.

Put a sprig or two of tansy at the head of the bed, or as near the pillow as is not disagreeable. Pieces of camphor sewed to the bed, or mattress, will also drive them away.

No. 65.
TO DESTROY BUGS.

Mix some quicksilver in a mortar with the white of an egg, till the quicksilver is all mixed, and there are no bubbles; then beat up the white of another egg, and put it to the mixture in the mortar, till it becomes a fine ointment.

Anoint the bedstead all over in every crack, with a brush, and put it also about the cord lacing, head-board, &c. When repeated for the two or three following days, the cure will be effectual, and the bedstead uninjured.

No. 66.
TO DESTROY FLIES.

Ground black pepper and moist sugar mixed in equal quantities, and diluted with milk, put into saucers, adding fresh milk, and stirring the mixture when required.

No. 67.
TO DESTROY BUGS FROM FURNITURE.

Wash the bedstead or floor with water thoroughly saturated with glauber salts, once or twice a year, and the bugs will shortly be effectually destroyed.

The following receipts have been taken from that useful and interesting work, called the Magazine of Domestic Economy, which is strongly recommended to the notice of all those who are engaged in the management of a household, as containing a great variety of directions and useful knowledge in every branch of domestic economy.

No. 68.
TO PREPARE RABBIT SKINS.

To be good, the skin should be in season.

Take the skin as fresh as possible, and having mixed a quantity of salt and water, till it will bear an egg, saturate it with alum; put your skin into this mixture, blood warm, and let it lie and soak twenty four hours; then take it out, and having tacked it upon a board, the fur inwards, scrape the skin, and a thin membrane will come off; then having warmed up the liquor again, put your skin again into it, and let it remain five hours more, after which, take it out and nail it upon a board to dry, the fur inwards as before; and rub it well with pumice stone and whiting.

No. 69.
FRENCH POLISH FOR BOOTS, SHOES, AND HARNESS.

A quarter of a pound of glue, half a pound of logwood chips, a quarter of an ounce of indigo, powdered very fine, a quarter of an ounce of soft soap, a quarter of an ounce of isinglass.

Boil these ingredients in two pints of vinegar and one pint of water, during ten minutes after the ebullition begins.

Then strain the liquid; when cold it is fit for use, and may be put into either pint or half pint bottles.

The dirt must be sponged off the boots and shoes, and the polish afterwards put on with a clean sponge; should the polish ever become too thick, it must be held near to the fire to warm a little, when the heat will give it the proper liquescence.

No. 70.
TO PRESERVE GILT FRAMES AND LAMPS.

It is usual to clothe all frames and lamps with gauze, Holland, muslin or chintz bags, to protect them from damp, but this practice has been stated to be very injurious to them, as these bags are known to retain any moisture for so long a time as to be of great injury to the gilt; whereas, when left uncovered, though more exposed to the air, it becomes sooner dry.

The following is a good method of

REVIVING GILT FRAMES.

Beat up three ounces of eggs, with one ounce of chloride of potash, or soda, lay it over the frame with a soft brush dipped in the mixture.

No. 71.
TO MAKE CLOTH WATERPROOF.

Take half an ounce of isinglass (Russian is best), put it into one pound of rain water, and boil until dissolved; take one ounce of alum, put it into two pounds of water, and boil till it is dissolved; take a quarter of an ounce of white soap, with one pound of rain water, and boil till it is dissolved. After each of these ingredients has been separately dissolved, strain them separately through a piece of linen; afterwards mix them well together in a pot, put it on the fire again till it simmers, then take it off, and while thus near boiling, dip a brush into it, and apply it to the wrong side of the cloth intended to be waterproof.

The cloth must be spread out on a table during the operation, and remain there until it is dry; after it is dry it must be brushed on the wrong side against the grain; and then dipping the brush in clear water, pass it lightly over, and leave it again to dry.

After that, the gloss caused by the application of the ingredients can be taken off.

Three days after the operation has been done, the cloth will be imperious to water but not to air.

No. 72.
TO EXTRACT GREASE SPOTS FROM LINEN.

The following method is not generally known, and is the best we ever met with.

Take magnesia in the lump, wet it, and rub the grease spots well with it. In a little time brush it off, and no appearance of grease will be left.

No. 73.
TO CLEAN MERINO CURTAINS.

Remove the dust as much as possible with a brush, and lay the curtain over a large table, and having procured three or four pieces of flannel, and a quantity of bran, sprinkle a handful of the latter on a portion of the furniture, and proceed to rub it round and round with a bit of the flannel. When the bran becomes soiled, take more bran and a fresh piece of flannel, and thus continue till the merino becomes bright and clean.

No. 74.
METHOD OF CLEANSING SILK, WOOLLEN, AND COTTON.

Take raw potatoes in their natural state, and when well washed, let them be rubbed on a grater over a vessel of clean water, to a fine pulp; pass the liquid matter through a coarse sieve into another tub of clean water; let this mixture stand till the fine white particles of potatoe are precipitated, then pour off the liquor, which preserve for use.

The article to be cleaned should be laid on a table, and well rubbed with a sponge dipped in the liquor until clean, when it is washed several times in clean water, and then dried and ironed.

Two middle sized potatoes will suffice for a pint of water. The coarse pulp of the potatoe, which will not pass the sieve, is of use in cleaning worsted curtains, tapestry, carpets, and other coarse goods, while the liquor prepared as above, will clean silk, cotton, and woollen goods.

No. 75.
TO BLEACH WOOL.

To one pound of wool yarn, take two pounds of powdered white chalk, mixed with river water, to the consistency of paste; knead the yarn thoroughly in it, that it may be completely saturated, and let it dry for twenty four hours, then rub it well, and wash it in cold water, to remove all the chalk, and the yarn will be quite clean, and very white.

Warm water spoils the colour of the wool.

No. 76.
BALLS FOR REMOVING SPOTS FROM CLOTH.

Mix well four ounces of fuller's earth, dried so as to crumble into powder, with a piece of lemon; when well incorporated, add two drachms of common pearl ash powdered. Work up the whole into a stiff paste, and form it into balls.

Set them to dry on a gently heated stove, and when dry, they are fit for use.

When using this preparation, first moisten with cold water, the spots you wish to remove, and rub a ball all over them. Let the place dry in the sun, or near the fire, and when quite dry, wash the spots with a sponge and water, and they will disapear.

No. 77.
MODE OF WASHING A SILK DRESS.

If the dress is made up, the seams need not be separated, but the body should be removed from the skirt, and the lining taken away from the bottom. Trimming and ornaments should be taken off.

If dirty, let the dress be simply washed first in soft, cold clear water, and if black, a pint of gin should be added to every gallon of water, then proceed as follows:—

Lay the dress on a clean smooth table, a flannel should be well soaped, being made just wet enough with lukewarm water, and the silk rubbed one way, being careful that this rubbing is quite even. When the dirt has disappeared, the soap must be washed off with a sponge, and plenty of cold water. As soon as one side is finished, the other must be washed precisely in the same manner.

Observe that not more of either side must be done at a time, than can be spread perfectly flat upon the table, and the hand conveniently reach; likewise, the soap must be sponged off one portion of the dress, before the soaped flannel is applied to another.

The dresses should be hung up on a linen horse, in the shade, and when dry, if of a black, or dark blue colour, another sponging of gin, or whiskey, is highly advantageous.

Washed silks are spoiled if ironed with a hot iron, therefore use one of moderate heat, with a sheet of paper between.

No. 78.

INDIAN RUBBER VARNISH.

Put in a bottle two ounces of Indian rubber, cut very small; add one pound of spirits of turpentine, and stop the bottle close, that the spirit may not evaporate; leave it two days without moving, then stir the liquor with a wooden spatula, and if the India rubber is swollen, and has absorbed the spirit, add a sufficient quantity for it just to swim in the liquid. Stir it every forty eight hours, till the India rubber is quite dissolved, which is ascertained by squeezing a little of it between the fingers; when in this state put it into a glass bottle and keep it well corked till wanted for use; the longer it is kept the better it becomes.

No. 79.

TO CLEAN PAINT THAT IS NOT VARNISHED.

Put upon a plate some of the best whiting, have ready some clean warm water, and a piece of flannel, which dip into the water and squeeze nearly dry; then take as much whiting as will adhere to it, apply it to the paint, when a little rubbing will instantly remove any dirt or grease; wash it well off with water, and rub it dry with a soft cloth.

Paint thus cleaned looks equal to new; and without doing the least injury to the most delicate colour, it will preserve the paint much longer than if cleaned with soap; and it does not require more than half the time usually occupied in cleaning.

No. 80.

HINTS ON PURCHASING FURNITURE.

A misfortune of not very rare occurrence, is the splitting of valuable tables that are veneered. We have known the infliction, and we guard others from a similar annoyance.

One of the causes may be traced to the cabinet makers; it is not unusual for them to make use of wood for the foundation, that has not been sufficiently seasoned, and is besides of an open porous texture, so different from the close hard grained wood, which is to form the veneer, that a very long time is requisite before they can manufacture their goods without risk of shrinking.

In order to ensure this certainty of seasoning, a larger stock of wood is required than is always convenient to be on hand by a cabinet maker, either from want of capital or accommodation; hence, the purchase of new furniture requires circumspection.

In this, as well as every other requisite, we would enforce the oft repeated advice, that a preference is always given to the trader of known probity.

Chance bargains, cheap to the eye, almost always become dear and unsatisfactory in the end.

Veneered furniture which is purchased from a damp warehouse, and brought suddenly into a well aired warm room will almost infallibly fly.

Chests of drawers, particularly if they be made of coarse Honduras mahogany, scarcely fail to crack, and throw up from their edges slips of veneer, which snap off, and are swept away, leaving unsightly white gaps; these have to be replaced, and look shabby and patched.

Spanish mahogany, though much more expensive in the first purchase, is far more certain, hard, rich-coloured, and durable.

It is essential that new furniture should be inured by degrees to a change of temperature, in order to prevent this hazardous warping, and unequal contracting of the wood. Tables in particular, if intended to occupy a station opposite a fire, should be kept with the grain of the wood lying longways; not the ends of the grain and the joint pointing to the fire; for want of this simple precaution, we have known a beautiful rosewood table entirely spoiled.

Spanish mahogany was the beautiful wood which was first known in England, and which was said to be of so hard and close a grain as to turn the edges of our workmen's tools; but since our possessions and commerce have been extended to the North of America, we have been stocked with vast quantities of that open grained inferior kind, that is made into almost all our household goods, and which, from its facility of working, is so cheap, that purchasers are continually deceived by unprincipled tradesmen, by the substitution of one for the other.

No person can well be deceived, however, to whom the two sorts of wood have been explained; the one (Spanish) being rich coloured, of an even texture, like satin, when polished, with no grain visible; the other pale, rough, and uneven when highly polished, shewing the coarse grain like threads; the latter too is so soft, that it is dented with the slightest touch, a pencil-case falling upon it, six inches from its surface, will leave a dent that never can be removed, unless the whole is plained over.

No. 81.

TO CLEAN SPONGE.

Wash them in very dilute tartaric acid, rinsing them afterwards in water; it will make them very soft and white. Be careful to dilute the acid well, as it is very corrosive.

No. 82.

A USEFUL GLUE.

This is excellent for joining wood, in furniture, &c., as it forms so tenacious a union of the parts, that the point of junction is stronger, and is more difficult to break, than any other part of the wood. Also if sawdust is mixed up into a ball with the glue, it becomes solid and elastic, so as to be fit for turning.

Beat an ounce of isinglass to shreds, and put it into a small skillet, and pour over it a pint of brandy. Set the skillet over a very slow fire, so that a very gentle heat may be applied to the mixture. When all the isinglass is dissolved, strain the solution, and put it in a wide mouthed bottle with a glass stopper, which must remain constantly closed.

At the time it is required for use, it must be liquified by a moderate heat, which renders it thin and transparent.

This solution in brandy never corrupts, and is therefore the best form of dissolved isinglass for fining wines, and other liquids.

This solution likewise serves admirably for taking impressions of coins and models, over the surface of which, a very thin coating must be poured of the melted glue.

This coating being left on the coin, medal, or seal, during several days, until it is hard, is then a tough, horny, transparent substance, bearing the impression in relief on one side, and in intaglio on the other.

Nothing can injure this glue excepting water, which dissolves it, therefore it will not serve as a cement for china, or any thing holding or coming in contact with water

No. 83.

TO PRESERVE BRASS ORNAMENTS.

Brass ornaments, when not gilt or lackered, may be cleaned, and a fine colour may be given to them by either of the two following simple processes.

The first is, to beat sal-ammoniac into a fine powder, then to moisten it with soft water, rubbing it on the ornaments, which must be heated over charcoal, and rubbed dry with bran and whiting.

The second is, to wash the brass work with roche alum boiled in strong lye, in the proportion of an ounce to a pint; when dry, it must be rubbed with fine tripoli.

No. 84.

CHEAP SCOURING DROPS.

Take a wine-glassful of the rectified oil of turpentine, half a tea-spoonful or more of essential oil of lemons, mix them well, and preserve in a well stopped phial. If you have not oil of lemons, oil of cloves, or of cinnamon, or of peppermint, will do.

The scouring drops thus prepared, are of a pleasant odour, and will take out of silk, woollen, linen, or cotton stuffs, all sorts of grease spots, oil, paint, pitch, tar, fruit stains, &c. by rubbing a little on the satin, with a piece of flannel or woollen cloth.

A bit of silk velvet is the best rubber for silks; the drops do not affect the colour of stuffs.

No. 85.

IMITATION OF MAPLE WOOD.

For frames or furniture. The stain is merely aquafortis, washed on with a brush; as soon as it has been hastily brushed over, hold the article to the fire, it will become yellow in a few minutes. It is then to be brushed over with copal varnish, and left to dry in the sun or open air; two or three coats completely fill the pores of the wood; then rub it gently with a bit of flat pumice-stone, and give it another coat, perhaps two, letting it be completely dry between each; then polish again very gently, and finish off with flour and a soft rag. It is as good as French polish, and may be washed at any time.

No. 86.

RECEIPT FOR FRENCH POLISH.

One quart of rectified spirits of wine,
Two ounces of seed lac,
One ounce of shell lac,
One ounce of gum sandrach,
One ounce of gum copal,
One ounce of camphor,

Pound the gums together and put them with the whole of the other articles into a stone

stone bottle; cork it securely, and place the bottle in hot water, shaking it often, till all be dissolved.

A very small quantity is said to be used at a time, and only a small surface of the piece of furniture is covered with the liquid, and that is rubbed off immediately; a little more is then applied, which is also rubbed off, and this is repeated till the desired polish is attained. Another part of the table &c. is then treated in the same manner, till the whole surface is polished.

No. 87.
TO CLEAN HAIR BRUSHES.

The best mode is to use soda, dissolved in cold water, instead of soap and hot water; the latter very soon softens the hairs of the brush, and the rubbing completes their destruction. Soda having an affinity for grease, cleans the brush with very little friction. Hair brushes are generally chosen by the whiteness and delicacy of the hair, it is therefore prepared (which is injurious to them) to suit the taste of purchasers. Dark white, coarse thick Foreign bristles make the most durable brushes.

No. 88.
TO CLEAN KID GLOVES, WHITE OR COLOURED.

Have ready a little new milk in one saucer and a piece of brown soap in another, and a clean cloth or towel folded three or four times. On the cloth spread out the glove smooth and neat; take a piece of flannel, dip it in the milk, then rub off a good quantity of soap on to the wetted flannel, and commence to rub the glove downwards, towards the fingers, holding it firmly with the left hand. Continue this process till the glove, if white, looks of a dingy yellow, though clean; if coloured, till it looks dark and spoiled; lay it to dry, and the old gloves shall look nearly new. They will become soft, elastic, smooth and glossy.

WASHING AND IRONING.

As the appearance of many articles of dress depends greatly upon the skill of the washerwoman, it is thought that a few hints on the subject may not be misapplied; these have been collected from experienced laundresses, and from that excellent little work "Cottage Comforts." The first things to be attended to are, the articles required for both wash-house and laundry, which are as follows:—

1st. LARGE AND SMALL WASHING TUBS.—These should be of smooth wood, with no nails, or iron hoops outside, lest the linen should be torn or rusted.

2nd. A COPPER FURNACE in which to boil the Linen.—If required for large washings, it should be capable of holding eighteen or twenty gallons of water.

3rd. A MAID OR DOLLEY.—These are sometimes circular like a barrel churn, and sometimes upright, they are used for shaking and rinsing dirty and coarse linen.

4th. LINES.—These should be of worsted, if not too expensive, otherwise soft flaxen lines answer well. When they are done with, and dry, they should be taken down, wound on a skein, and put carefully aside until wanted.

5th. LINE PEGS.—These should be of white soft wood; they must be kept very clean for use, and counted before being put away.

6th. As RAIN WATER is essential for many articles, if none is at hand, a cask should be kept, to catch what falls from the house.

FOR THE LAUNDRY.

The following articles are in use.

1st. Ironing cloths or blankets; these are generally made of proper kind of flannel called fearnought; they should be carefully dried when put away, lest moths should destroy them.

2nd. A mangle for heavy linen.

3rd. The common irons for lighter articles.

4th. The Italian iron for frills, &c.

5th. The sleeve iron.

6th. The box iron.

7th. The gaufiering iron.

ON WASHING LINEN, &c.

A good washer-woman will examine carefully the linen she has to wash, and rub soap on to such parts as require it the most, as the collars and wristbands of shirts, taking care that the water is not too hot, otherwise it will set in the dirt.

She afterwards twice thoroughly washes out all her white things in plenty of white warm lather, shaking each article out, and examining if every spot or stain is removed. She then boils them, taking care not to put too many into the copper at once.

A small quantity of soft soap thrown in to the boil, helps to give a good colour to the linen, and if well washed out of the boil, as all linen ought to be, and afterwards well rinsed in plenty of spring water, no unpleasant smell will be retained.

The rinsing water should be made moderately blue, by means of stone blue tied up in a flannel bag, and squeezed in.

Such things as are to be starched, will be much clearer if they are first dried; then dipped in the starch before it is quite cold; then dipped in cold water and dried again; then once more dipped in cold water, spread upon a coarse dry cloth, and rolled up; by this mode also, their sticking to the ironing cloth, will be prevented.

The best way to make starch, is, very gradually to moisten with cold water, a table spoonful of starch; when quite smooth, stir it into a pint of boiling water, with a morsel of white wax, and let it boil gently for several minutes, stirring it all the time; when poured out, cover it over with a plate, to prevent a skin forming at top, which is both troublesome and wasteful.

To prevent flannels or woollen stockings from shrinking, pour over them, when new, boiling water; suffer it to remain till cold, then hang them up without wringing; and when dry, shake them well.

Greasy spots may be taken out of all kinds of woollen cloths, blankets, scarlet cloaks, or table baizes, without injury to the colour, by washing them with gall, instead of soap; the gall may be had at the butcher's, at 3d. a pint.

A pint mixed up in a good sized tub of soft water, will be sufficient for several articles; it will lather exactly like soap.

This is the process used by the scourer. The articles so washed, will require to be several times rinsed in water, to remove the smell of the gall; when dry, they should be removed, and suffered to remain in the mangle all night, after which, they will appear as good as new.

In washing prints the colours should be rubbed as little as possible, for which reason it is a good thing to boil a lather of soap till it is like a jelly, mix this jelly with cold water, and wash them in it.

It is a good plan also to wash coloured things the first time, in the suds in which flannels have been washed, if it is not too dirty. They should be taken immediately from one water into another, and not suffered to lie together damp, or they will dry streaky.

When washed, rinse them twice in spring water, and hang them out immediately, without wringing.

Blankets are washed with soft soap.

Gall is used for bombazines and stuffs.

Any thing that has been singed in the ironing should be wetted with cold water, and laid in the air.

Soda may be put in the water in which very greasy cloths are washed, but it is liable to spoil other things.

Grease may be taken out with cold water and suds.

Men and boy's stockings should be steeped, and stewed in cold water and soap, in a slow oven, or boiled.

HANGING TO DRY.

Stockings should be hung by the toe, to prevent the feet becoming thick.

Gowns should be pinned up by the shoulders, rather than by the bottom of the skirt, or the body lining becoming discoloured.

MANGLING AND IRONING.

Damp over the things, and iron or mangle them; the latter is used for heavy linen, such as sheets, towels, table cloths, &c.

Those articles which have buttons or thick plaits should not be mangled; the mangle is injured by them; besides the buttons are broken to pieces, and the plaited articles cannot be made smooth.

In ironing, be careful first to rub over something of little value, lest fine things be either scorched or smeared.

The Italian iron is used entirely for puffs, frills, &c.

The sleeve iron, which resembles a mushroom, having a half circle at the top, to which is attached a handle or stalk, is put up through the opening of the sleeve towards the wrist, and the sleeve is drawn or passed over the iron backwards and forwards until it is all properly ironed. This only suits some kinds of sleeves, but is remarkably good for them.

Let every thing be thoroughly dried, and aired by the fire, otherwise they will have a tumbled, half finished appearance, besides exposing the wearer to the risk of taking cold.

CLEAR STARCHING.

Wash out the articles to be clear starched, and then in a very clean vessel, put about two table spoonsful of water to two ounces of starch, wet it and mix it well up into a paste, pour about half a pint of boiling water upon it, keep stirring it all the while, till of the proper consistency, then boil it up well for a quarter of an hour, and by adding a little white wax, it prevents the starch sticking to the iron.

Dip the articles in, and wring the starch out again very dry, spread the things on a clean cloth, and then roll the cloth and articles together very tightly. It should remain thus about two hours, and then be ironed nicely.

The iron should be very clean; to effect this, rub it each time on taking it from the fire, upon a little sand paper and a cloth.

GAUFIERING.

This may be done either with gaufiering irons, or by means of straws, which are brought in bundles prepared for the purpose.

The following is the manner in which the straws are used:—

Procure a board about a yard long, and six nails broad, cover it with flannel, and fasten two tapes lengthwise, leaving about a quarter of a yard between them; then pin the net to the flannel at one end, and place a straw over the tapes (between which the net is lying) and under the net, the next straw is laid under the tapes and over the net, and so on alternately, taking care that the upper strawers are put close to each other, upon the under ones, forming two layers of straws. When all the net is folded, dip a coarse cloth in water, and wring it as dry as you can, lay this upon the net, and iron it dry, pressing on the board as much as you can without splitting the straws; remove the cloth, and place the board before the fire for half an hour, when you may draw out the upper straws, and run in some cotton to secure it, after which, the remaining straws may be taken away, and the work is complete.

Some persons hold the board in the steam of a kettle for some time and then dry it before the fire, in preference to ironing it.

Some others sprinkle it with very weak starch water, gum water, or rice water, before ironing.

CHAPTER XI.

KNITTING.

GENERAL OBSERVATIONS.

Knitting is the art of uniting worsted, or any other material together, without the aid of a loom. This work is applied to stockings, socks, boots, coverlids, and various other articles of wear or ornament, and is generally done with worsted, cotton or silk, but as the latter material properly belongs to fancy work, it will not be often mentioned.

KNITTING PINS OR NEEDLES,

As they are variously called, are made of iron or brass, for common use, and steel for best. They can be procured of every size and thickness, and are sold in sets, each set containing four pins. These sets cost from ½d. to 2d. each, according to the metal and size.

Ivory, bone, whalebone, steel, rosewood, ebony, and cane pins, of a larger size and thickness, are employed for knitting coverlids, boots, carpets, and other thickly knit articles. These are sometimes twenty inches, or two feet long, and have a knob at one end to prevent the stitches from slipping off. Of these pins two or three form the set. For schools, common pins may be procured from a carpenter or turner, for 2d. a set, whereas the former are charged at from 1s. 6d. to 8s. or 9s. the set.

MATERIALS FOR KNITTING.

Worsted, lambs' wool, or fleecy wool, is used for stockings, and other wearing articles.

ON KNITTING.

Cotton is employed for curtains, window blinds, bags, fringe, &c.

These materials are always sold by the weight; one pound contains sixteen ounces.

The expense of wools and worsteds varies so materially, that an average price can hardly be stated. It has been sold as low as at 2s. per pound, and as high as 6s. 6d. Crimsons are the most expensive colours, greens and oranges the next, blue is more moderate, and black, grey, purple, and pepper and salt are the least expensive, always excepting white, which is the lowest of any.

Grey and white common worsted contain a good deal of turpentine, and are often preferred by the poor on that account.

Black should be well soaked in strong vinegar, to set the colour, and prevent its coming off on the hands while being knitted.

Worsteds are more suitable for men's and women's stockings.

Wools for children's stockings, or for muffetees, ruffs, and other lighter articles of wear, which should be soft and warm.

All worsteds and wools should be carefully wrapped up in the coarsest brown paper, which also contains turpentine, and keeps out the air. They should be often looked to, as the moths are apt to get at them and spoil them.

Worsteds in use should be neatly wound in small balls, about the size of an orange.

ON KNITTING STITCHES.

In knitting, keep the ball in the pocket, or in a bag hung to the arm, or a basket, and do not allow it to roll on the table or floor, to get dusted.

There are a great variety of knit stitches, all of which, are founded on the following kinds, beginning with casting or setting on stitches, all of which will be explained in due order.

CASTING ON STITCHES.

This must be first learned, and signifies putting the stitches on the pins, in order to begin working. There are two or three modes of doing this.

Hold the worsted at about a quarter of a yard from the end, together with one of the pins in the right hand, between the finger and thumb.

Next, hold the worsted at some distance from the end, and lay it across the palm of the left hand, holding it down with the fingers while you make a loop, by bringing the worsted before the thumb, and carrying it outside and back again, between the thumb and first finger into the palm, taking care to cross it over the other worsted; with the right hand put the pin under the loop, and take it off from the thumb upon it, drawing the end of the worsted tight at the same time. Continue making loops with the left thumb, and taking them off on the right hand pin, until the proper number of stitches be set on.

Another and a better mode, is that of knitting on the stitches. For this purpose, after making the first loop with the left hand thumb, as above, and slipping it off the thumb upon the right hand pin, continue as follows:—

Take another pin in the right hand, and put it under the loop on the pin, making this right hand pin lie across under the left. Next, put the worsted between the two pins, and press the end of the right hand pin upon the worsted, till it is brought through the first stitch, and forms a loop upon the pin. Take this loop off upon the left hand pin, by putting the end of it under the loop, which gives it a kind of twist; continue thus increasing the stitches on the left-hand pin until the proper number is formed.

THE COMMON KNITTING STITCH.

After setting on the number of stitches in the manner before mentioned, begin to knit them off from one pin to the other, as follows:—

Hold the pin with the stitches on, in the left hand; with the right hand, put the other pin under the first loop, making the pin lie across behind the left-hand pin, while with the first finger, the worsted is drawn in front between the pins. Then with the end of the right pin, press this worsted till it is brought through the stitch in the form of a loop upon the right hand pin. Keep it on the right pin, taking the loop quite off from the left pin. Continue knitting the stitches off the left upon the right hand pin, till the row is completed, when change pins, putting the one with stitches in the left-hand, and the disengaged pin in the other.

DUTCH COMMON KNITTING.

This is another mode of knitting the common stitch, and is more simple, and more quickly done than the usual way.

Hold the pin-ful of stitches in the left hand, as also the worsted, which should be wound once or twice round the little finger, to keep it firm, and allowed to pass over the first finger to the pins. The right hand pin is then simply passed through the stitch, and catching the worsted outside, draws it through, and forms the loop on the right pin, and so on.

THE TURN OR SEAM STITCH.

This is also called back-stitching, or pearling, but when alluded to hereafter, it will invariably be called turn-stitch. It is simply bringing the worsted between the needles, and taking up the loop, by putting the needle into the stitch from behind, and knitting it off by putting the worsted round the pin, and pressing the loop through the stitch.

WIDENING.

This is increasing the number of loops, and is generally done in the middle of a pin-ful of stitches.

There are various modes of widening. One is, that of simply passing the worsted in front, before knitting the loop, and is termed making a stitch. Another, is effected by taking up the cross loop, below the next stitch belonging to the row before, and afterwards continuing the plain knitting.

In some cases where the widening occurs at the end, in order to form a gradual slope, knit the last stitch without taking the loop off the pin. Again put the right hand pin into the loop, but in order to give a twist to the worsted, put it in under the side furthest from you, and knit it off.

NARROWING.

This is decreasing the number of stitches, by simply knitting two together.

SLIPPING A STITCH.

This is merely taking the stitch or loop off one pin upon the other without knitting it.

FINISHING OFF.

In finishing off a piece of knitting, knit two stitches from off the left hand pin, upon the right, and then with the left pin, take up the first stitch and put it over the second, slipping it off the pin at the same time, so as only to leave the second stitch upon it. Knit a third stitch, and slip the second loop over it also off the pin, and so on till the last stitch or loop remains on the left hand pin, and none on the right; when, after breaking off the worsted, pass the end through the loop and draw it up, and the whole is completed.

Observe, in finishing off, not to pull the worsted too tight, as the end will curl up, and look puckered.

WELTING.

This is usually knit at the tops of stockings, socks, muffatees, &c. and tends to confine the article to the leg or arm of the wearer, from its tendency to contract.

Knit three or more plain stitches, and the same number of turn stitches alternately for several rows, observing always to knit one row or bout exactly to correspond with the other, so that the welts or ribs are regular.

BINDING.

In binding, or joining two stitches together, as for instance, in the heel of the stocking, lay the two pins together in one hand, and with a third pin knit a stitch, first off one pin and then off another, after which, put the first knit stitch over the second, slipping it off the pin as in fastening off, already described. Continue knitting a fresh stitch to it, first from one pin and slipping the loop over it, and then from the other. Pass the worsted through the last loop and the whole is completed.

There are many terms used in knitting which ought to be familiar to all knitters, as they are constantly introduced into knitting receipts.

The following will be described, but there are probably many more peculiar to different counties.

A Row is one line or length of knitting.

A Rib is two rows, or a row forwards and backwards, and is sometimes called a turn.

A Bout is one round of knitting, as in stockings.

A Welt is that part ribbed at the top of the leg of the stocking.

A Seam is that open line in a stocking, formed by a continuation of turn-stitches.

FANCY STITCHES.

The following are the various fancy stitches commonly employed by knitters for useful articles:—

No. 1. Double knitting.
2. Another ditto.
3. Another ditto.
4. Open hem.
5. Honey-comb stitch.
6. French stitch.
7. Fan-tail stitch.
8. Imitation net-work stitch.
9. Open cross stitch.
10. Insertion work, or Berlin wire.
11. Plain open stitch.
12. The crow's-foot stitch.
13. The chain stitch.
14. The embossed hexicon stitch.

No. 15. The common plat.
16. The elastic rib.
17. The rough-cast, or huckaback stitch.
18. The embossed diamond stitch.
19. The ornamental ladder.
20. Imitation double knitting.
21. The knit herring-bone stitch.
22. The purse stitch.
23. The lace-wave stitch.
24. The herring-bone bag stitch.
25. An improved open stitch.
26. The shawl stitch.
27. The cross-stitch pattern.
28. The curb stitch.

No. 29. The two coloured rib stitch.
30. A beautiful diamond stitch.
31. The raised French stitch.
32. The two coloured chain stitch.

No. 33. The rug stitch.
34. The nondescript.
35. A new stitch.
36. The new muffatee stitch.

KNIT FRINGES.

No. 1. Fringe.
2. Fringe.
3. Shawl fringe.

No. 4. A beautiful fringe, and border.
5. A very pretty fringe.
6. Fringe for curtains.

No. 1.
DOUBLE KNITTING.

This is very suitable for blankets, coverlets, comforters, socks, sleeves, ruffs, shawls, &c. There are three kinds of double knitting; the first is as follows:—

Put on an even number of stitches,
Knit a few plain rows,
Then begin a fresh row as follows:—
Knit a stitch,
Pass the worsted between the needles in front;
Take off a stitch, putting the needle inside the loop;
Pass the worsted back again,
Knit another stitch, as before, and so on.

No. 2.
DOUBLE KNITTING.

Another mode is as follows:—
Put on an even number of stitches,
Knit the first stitch plain, putting the worsted twice over the pin,
Pass the worsted between the needles before,
Slip a stitch,
Pass the worsted behind again.
Again knit a stitch, putting the wool twice over the pin, and so on.
In the next row, knit those stitches that were slipped, and slip those which were before knit.
It is advisable to knit the first three or four stitches plain in every row, as it confines it down neatly at the sides.

No. 3.
DOUBLE KNITTING.

This is worked on the wrong side, and is particularly simple, and far quicker work than the former method, but, as when completed, it requires turning inside out, it must be knit with plain knitting at the ends or sides, which to some, is an objection.

Set on an even number of stitches,
Proceed at once, without knitting a plain row,

ON KNITTING.

Put the worsted in front of the pins before beginning to knit, observing always to keep it so.
Turn the first stitch,
Take off the second stitch, and so on throughout.

No. 4.
OPEN HEM.

Use very fine pins and sewing cotton,
Set on any number of stitches, divisable by four,
Slip the first stitch at the beginning of each row,
Knit the second stitch,
Put the cotton over the pin, to make a stitch;
Knit two loops together,
Continue by knitting the next stitch,
Making a stitch, &c. &c., as before.

No. 5.
HONEY-COMB STITCH.

This is very applicable for shawls, purses, muffatees, and other fancy articles.
Knit the first stitch,
Put the cotton over the pin, to make a loop,
Knit two stitches together,
Continue making a loop, and knitting two stitches together, till the row is completed.
Knit the second row plain, and so on, every other row honey-comb stitch.

No. 6.
FRENCH STITCH.

Set on the stitches in fours, leaving two over.
Turn the first stitch,
Turn the thread back,
Knit two stitches together,
Bring the thread in front,
Knit a stitch, thus forming a new loop,
Bring the thread again in front,
Turn a stitch, one rib or pattern is then complete.
Begin the next in a similar manner, by turning the thread back, and knitting two together at the end of the row, turn the thread, and knit the last stitch.

No. 7.
FAN-TAIL STITCH.

This is very suitable for gloves, mits, purses, &c.
Set on fourteen loops,
Make a loop, by putting the cotton over the pin,
Knit a loop,
Make a loop, and so on,

Knit each of the two last plain,
Then narrow at the second and third stitches, both at the beginning and ending of each row, until it is reduced to the original number of fourteen stitches.

No. 8.

IMITATION NET-WORK STITCH.

Set on any even number of stitches you please.
Knit a row plain,
Commence the next row by putting the free pin on the wool, and twisting the wool round it, by bringing it from behind over the pin, and putting it behind again, then knit two loops together, putting the pin into the one nearest to you first, then twist the wool round the pin in the manner described above; knit two together, and so on to the end. Every succeeding row is knit in the same manner.

No. 9.

OPEN CROSS STITCH.

This is generally knit with two colours (suppose blue and brown); each colour is worked along two rows alternately. In changing colours, observe that the fresh colour crosses from *under* the last one, which prevents its leaving a hole.
The first row of each colour is turn-stitched the whole way, and the second row of each colour is worked as follows:—
Knit a stitch,
Make a stitch,
Slip a stitch,
Knit two stitches together,
Draw the slipped loop over the two knit loops   Continue to the end of the row, and then commence two rows with the fresh colour.
This is a very suitable stitch for a shawl-handkerchief, round which, another pattern of knitting should be made.

No. 10.

INSERTION-WORK, OR BERLIN WIRE STITCH.

If knit with fine thread, and finest needles, it forms beautiful insertion-work for collars, capes, frocks, &c.
If knit with large pins, and lamb's wool, it is useful for comforters and shawls, and looks very pretty.
Set on an even number of stitches,
(If for insertion-work, eight, every four stitches forms one pattern.)
Knit three plain rows or more,
Take off the first stitch,
Knit a stitch,
Knit off two together,
Make a stitch,
Again knit a stitch,
Knit off two together,

Make a stitch, and knit the last stitch, and so on to the end of the row,
Every alternate row should be knit plain.

No. 11.
PLAIN OPEN STITCH

Set on an even number of stitches.
    Knit two plain rows; then,
    Knit the first stitch,
    Pass the worsted in front,
    Knit two together, thus forming a new stitch,
    Again bring the worsted in front,
    Knit two together, thus forming a new one,
    And so on, till the last stitch, which is knit;
    Knit two more rows, and so on.
This is very suitable for shawls and caps.

No. 12.
THE CROW'S-FOOT STITCH.

This is very suitable for shawls, in which case, it should be begun at one of the corners, and added to at every row.

Otherwise set on any number of stitches divisable by three, allowing one over, to begin with.

After knitting one plain row, begin the pattern as follows:—
    Knit the first stitch,
    Make a stitch,
    Slip a stitch,
    Knit two plain stitches,
    Put the slipped stitch over the two plain ones,
    Again make a stitch,
    Slip a stitch, and so continue to the end.
For the next row, turn every stitch.

No. 13.
CHAIN STITCH.

    Set on thirteen loops,
    Knit two plain rows,
    Knit three stitches plain,
    Bring the worsted in front,
    Turn seven stitches,
    Turn the worsted back, and knit the remaining three stitches,
    Knit the next row plain,
    Continue as above, till you have knit in all sixteen rows;
    Next knit three stitches plain,
    Take off the four next stitches upon a third pin,
    Knit the next three stitches from behind the third pin, so as entirely to miss it, drawing the worsted very tight, so as to connect the pins close together;

Then, knit the four stitches off the third pin, and the twist is completed. Knit the remaining three and begin to form a fresh link, by knitting three stitches,
Turning seven,
Knitting three, and so on; making sixteen more rows before you twist again.

No. 14.
THE EMBOSSED HEXAGON STITCH.

Set on any number of stitches, divisable by six,
Knit a row plain,
Turn a row,
Knit a row plain,
Knit four stitches, and slip two to the end of the row,
Turn a row, slipping the stitches that were slipped in the preceding row,
Knit a row, still slipping the two stitches,
Turn a row, slipping the same two stitches,
Knit a row, slipping the two stitches,
Turn a row, slipping the same stitches,
Turn a row, taking up every stitch,
Knit a row plain,
Turn a row.

Commence the next pattern by turning a row, slipping the fifth and sixth stitches, taking care that the slipped loops come in the centre of the previous pattern, continue alternately knitting and turning a row, remembering to slip the two stitches, till you have done six rows, when knit a row, taking up every stitch and so on.

No. 15.
THE COMMON PLAT.

This is very pretty for coverlets, muffatees, &c.
Set on any number of stitches in threes.
After knitting a plain row, begin as follows:—
1st Row. Knit three plain, and turn three all along.
2nd Row. The same as above, observing to continue from where you left off in the last row, so that if the row ended in turning, you should begin with plain stitches and so on.
3rd Row. Observe as above.
These three rows form a succession of squares, of alternate inside and outside knitting.
4th Row. As the work of the squares should now cross or sit alternately with those above, like the squares of a chess-board, the first three stitches should be the same as those with which the last row is completed.
Continue turning and knitting plain every alternate three stitches, and varying the squares every three rows, till the whole is completed.

No. 16.
THE ELASTIC RIB.

This is very suitable for cuffs and garters, as it clings or contracts to the form.

Set on any number of stitches,
Knit a row,
Turn a row,
Knit two rows,
Turn a row,
Continue knitting two, and turning one row to the end of the work.

No. 17.
THE ROUGH CAST, OR, HUCKABACK STITCH.

Set on any uneven number of stitches.
Knit plain and turn stitch alternately, observing to begin every row with the plain stitch.
This is very pretty, and firm, and suitable for borders.

No. 18.
THE EMBOSSED DIAMOND.

Set on any number of stitches, devisable by seven,
Knit a row plain.
Turn a stitch, then knit five, and turn two alternately to the end,
Knit two, then turn three, and knit four, alternately to the end,
Turn three, then knit one, and turn six alternately,
Knit a row plain.
Turn two, and then knit two, and turn five alternately,
Knit two, then turn four, and knit three alternately,
Knit six, and turn one alternately,
Knit one, and turn six alternately,
Knit five, then turn three, and knit four alternately,
Knit three, then turn two, and knit five alternately,
Knit a row plain.

No. 19.
THE ORNAMENTAL LADDER STITCH.

Set on your stitches in elevens,
Knit two plain stitches,
Knit two together, again knit two together, draw the first loop over the second, knit one plain, and then knit two together, knit two more together, draw the first loop over second, knit one plain, and so on to the end.
In the second row, turn two, pass the thread twice over the pin, turn two, and so on,
In the third row, knit two, pass the thread twice round the pin, knit two, and so on,
Continue alternately knitting one row and turning one, till it is the length required, observing always to slip the loops, formed by passing the thread twice round the pin off, without knitting them.

No. 20.
IMITATION DOUBLE KNITTING.

Set on any even number of stitches.
Turn a stitch, and knit a stitch alternately.

As the stitch that was knit before is now to be turned, commence every row with a turn stitch; this makes both sides alike, and though single, gives it the appearance of double knitting.

No. 21.
THE KNIT HERRING-BONE STITCH.

Set on any number of stitches, allowing three stitches for each pattern, and one besides at each end.
Knit a plain row,
Take off the first loop,
Knit two stitches together in turn stitch,
Make a stitch by passing the wool before, and knitting one,
Turn two stitches together,
Again make and knit a stitch, and so on,
Every row is begun and continued the same.

No. 22.
THE PURSE STITCH.

Set on ninety or an hundred stitches,
Knit the first stitch,
Make a stitch by putting the silk over the pin,
Slip a stitch,
Knit a stitch,
Turn the slipped stitch over the knit one,
Repeat this till the row is finished,
Knit the next row in turn stitch,
Repeat as above, alternately knitting a row in turn stitch, till the whole is completed.

No. 23.
THE LACE WAVE STITCH.

Set on an even number of stitches,
Slip the first stitch,
Knit a stitch,
Make a stitch (by putting the cotton over the pin,)
Knit two stitches together to narrow,
Again knit a stitch,
Make a stitch, and narrow till the row is complete,
Knit the next row plain,
Next row, knit two plain stitches, make a stitch, narrow two stitches in one, knit a stitch, make a stitch, and narrow to the end of the row,
Next row, knit plain,
Next row, knit three plain stitches, and continue as above, by making a stitch, narrowing two stitches in one, and knitting a stitch,
Next row, knit plain,
Next row, knit four stitches, and continue as above, by making one, narrowing two, and knitting one stitch.

Next row, knit plain,
Next row, knit five stitches plain, and do as above,
Knit two rows plain.

This forms one wave or pattern. Continue as above to any length required; this, knit with fine thread, forms beautiful lace for nightcap borders.

No. 24.
THE HERRING-BONE BAG STITCH.

Set on your stitches by fours,
Knit two plain stitches,
Turn the silk twice over the pin to make a long stitch,
Knit two stitches together,
Repeat this till the whole is finished.

No. 25.
AN IMPROVED OPEN STITCH.

Knit the first row plain,
Knit the second row like the usual open stitch, by knitting the first stitch, putting the worsted in front, to make a stitch, and knitting two stitches together, and so on;
Next knit one row plain,
Turn-stitch three rows, and
Knit one row plain,
This is particularly suitable for muffatees, bags, and reticules.

No. 26.
THE SHAWL STITCH.

This is very suitable for shawls, caps, and handkerchiefs, knit with soft wool, and large pins, and for mittens, with fine black thread or silk, and is done as follows:—

Set on an even number of stitches,
Knit the second row in the Hole-stitch, the next row in Turn-stitch, and so on.

No. 27.
THE CROSS-STITCH PATTERN.

This is very suitable for bags, purses, gentlemen's caps, &c.
Set on an even number of stitches,
Put the wool over the pin, and make a stitch,
Put the needle into two stitches, and knit them backwards, and so on.
Observe to throw the wool properly over the pin, as, if wrongly twisted, it is apt to make two stitches.

No. 28.
THE CURB STITCH.

Set on an even number of stitches,
Knit a plain row,

Next row, knit the first stitch, after which continue as follows :—

Bring the wool in front, turn a stitch, put the wool back, knit a stitch, putting the wool twice over the pin.

Observe, in the next row, the long stitch is the turned stitch.

No. 29.
THE TWO-COLOURED RIBBED STITCH.

This is a very pretty stitch for cuffs, mits, or muffatees, and should be done in two colours, or one colour with white.

Set on an even number of stitches, and continue knitting, letting every other stitch be of one colour, and the alternate loops of the other.

Observe, in crossing the worsteds, always to keep the white wool uppermost.

No. 30.
A BEAUTIFUL DIAMOND STITCH.

Set on the stitches in threes, and one over,

Slip off the first stitch. Then knit all along as follows, always keeping the wool in front,

Slip one stitch, holding the loop, as if going to turn-stitch,

Put the wool over the pin, to make a loop,

Knit two turn-stitches in one.

Next row, it is to be turn-stitched all the way, excepting that the formed stitch of the last row is always to be slipped, taking hold of it as in turning.

After the beginning of this alternate row, there will be always two single turn-stitches, and one slipped stitch all along.

No. 31.
THE RAISED FRENCH STITCH.

Set on an even number of stitches,

Turn the wool over the pin to make a stitch,

Knit two together, and so on to the end of the row:

Next row, turn-stitch the whole way,

Next row, knit plain,

Next row, turn-stitch, making in all three plain rows;

Repeat the whole as above.

If this is for a shawl, increase one stitch at two loops from the end of the needle, always at the same place, once in every rib.

No. 32.
THE TWO-COLOURED CHAIN STITCH.

This is a very pretty stitch, and is suitable for muffatees, bags, and mats. It is knit with two wools, coloured and white, and is done as follows :—

Set on the required number of stitches, and knit in the coloured wool alternately with the white. To form the chain-like appearance, observe to cross the wool, with which the loop is being knit, over the wool of the last loop. Observe to knit off the white loops with the coloured wool, and the coloured loops with the white wool.

No. 33.
THE RUG STITCH.

This is knit with fine pins and worsted of a common kind, and the rug or woolly part is composed of soft thick wool.

Set on any number of stitches, and knit one plain row, after which, begin with the wool, knitting first one plain stitch, and then pass the wool between the pins, round the second or third finger, according to the depth required, and in front between the pins. Knit another plain stitch, and again carry the wool between the pins, round the fingers in front, and make another stitch, and so on to the end of the row, when cut off the wool, and knit the row back with the worsted, which secures the fringe.

Lay the wool between the pins again, after knitting the first plain stitch, and continue as before, making a loop of fringe between each plain stitch, and so on. After knitting the number of rows required, cut the fringe and open the wool as much as possible, taking care not to pull it out.

No. 34.
THE NONDESCRIPT.

Set on any number of stitches, knit as follows, always slipping the first stitch;
Make a stitch, by putting the wool over the pin,
Knit a stitch;
Next row, knit two stitches together all along the pin;
Continue as above.

No. 35.
A NEW STITCH.

Set on any number of stitches,
Put the wool over the pin to make a stitch,
Turn a stitch, and so on:
Next row, turn-stitch, taking two loops at once the whole way.

No. 36.
THE NEW MUFFATEE STITCH.

Set on any even number of stitches,
Slip the first stitch, then knit as follows :—
Put the wool in front of the pin, then take up a loop of the former row on the pin, then turn a stitch, take up a loop as before, turn a stitch as before, and so on;
Next row, turn-stitch all along, taking two loops at once.

No. 1.
FRINGE.

Set on eight stitches,
Knit a plain round,
Slip the first loop,
Double the wool, and put the knot over the pin; knit two loops, put the wool behind, knit one, bring

it in front, knit two, turn it behind, and knit one; turn it again in front, and knit the last loop, then knit a plain row. In the third row, slip the first loop, put the little finger of the left hand through the fringe, and pass the wool for the next loop, round the finger also, then turn it over the pin, and knit the row as before.

No. 2.

ANOTHER FRINGE.

This is very suitable for doyleys and pincushion covers; in which case, it must be knit with cotton.
Set on twelve stitches,
Knit a stitch,
Make a stitch, by putting the cotton over the pin,
Knit two stitches in one,
Continue this till the row is finished.

Proceed onwards until a strip of sufficient length is made to go round the doyley or article for which it is intended. Then fasten off six of the stitches, letting the other six drop off your pins, and unrove it down the whole length of the strip, to form the fringe. Sew it on with coarse white cotton.

No. 3.

A SHAWL FRINGE.

Cast on five stitches,
Slip off the first stitch,
Knit the second stitch,
Make a stitch,
Knit two stitches together,

At the last stitch, twist the cotton three times over the pin and the second finger, or over the pin and a mesh of the proper depth of the fringe, and knit it firmly on. Let every alternate row be plain.

No. 4.

A BEAUTIFUL FRINGE AND BORDER.

Set on an even number of stitches of any depth sufficient to allow for the fringe, and for the head of the fringe, and knit thus:—

Make a stitch, by laying the wool over the needle. Put the needle in two loops, and knit them in one, just contrary to the usual way.

Continue thus, row after row, until a strip of sufficient length is done. Fasten off, letting four, six, eight, or ten stitches drop off the pin to unrove for the fringe.

No. 5.

A VERY PRETTY FRINGE,

For mats, handkerchiefs, mits, &c.

Use fine pins and common worsted for knitting the fringe, which should be of thick handsome wool.

Set on as many stitches as are required for the length of the peice of fringe,
Knit one plain row,
Next row, knit one stitch,

Lay the wool (either singly, or doubly, or even trebly, if required very full) between the pins, from the front towards the back, round the second or third finger, according to the depth required, and back again through the pins in front. Knit the next stitch, and again carry the wool behind round the fingers, to make another loop of fringe, and when brought forward between the pins, make another stitch and so on, to the end of the row, after which, knit a plain row back, to secure it more firmly, knitting alternately with the wool and worsted, fastening off as you go along.

No 6.
FRINGE FOR CURTAINS.

This is a useful and very pretty fringe for toilet tables, curtains, pincushions, &c., and is made of cotton, wool, worsted, silk, or any other material; the first, however, is more useful, because it washes well.

Set on ten stitches, and knit every row as follows:—

Slip the first stitch,
Knit the next stitch,
Put the cotton over the pin twice,
Turn two stitches together,
Turn the cotton back,

Put the cotton or wool, for the fringe, over the pin, leaving the ends behind. Knit one stitch, turn the wool in front, knit two stitches, turn the wool behind, knit two stitches, again bring the wool in front, and knit the remaining stitch. Knit a row plain, taking the wool with the stitch when you come to it, to make it quite firm.

The fringe should be cut in pieces of the proper length, and three or four taken together, to be knit in at once.

STOCKINGS.

Knit stockings are considered so much better than woven ones for wear, that it is advisable for all servants, cottagers and labourers invariably to adopt them, as the former will last out three or more of the woven, which are more suitable for the higher classes.

The children of the poor should always be taught to knit, and each member of a family ought to have a stocking in hand to take up at idle moments, by which means many pairs might be completed in the year. It is difficult to make very correct scales for different sized knit stockings, as so much depends on the quality of the worsted and of the pins, as also on the knitter, as some persons work much slacker than others, so that two stockings knit with the same pins and worsted, may be of very different sizes when knit by different persons.

The following proportion for a general rule is good, and may prove useful, though to tolerably experienced knitters, it is recommended to procure a pair of stockings that fit very well, and to knit others like them, which can easily be done by means of constantly measuring and comparing them with the pattern.

GENERAL PROPORTIONS FOR STOCKINGS.
PLATE 21. FIG. 21.

Ascertain the proper breadth of the stocking.
From the top to the bend of the knee is one square, or the length of the breadth.
From the bend of the knee to the beginning of the calf is one square or breadth.
From the beginning to the end of the calf, is one square or breadth. (See note.*)

* In this square, we narrow as many stitches as are contained on one of our three pins, narrowing always twice on the same row, placing one of them on each side of the seam stitch. We calculate the number of rows intervening between each narrowing, by dividing *half* the number of stitches contained on one pin, with the number of stitches contained on the three, and abide by the result.

THE WORKWOMAN'S GUIDE.

For the small of the leg, one square or breadth; for the heel, half a square; for the narrowing on each side of the instep, one quarter of a square; from the heel to the narrowing of the toe, one and a half square; for the narrowing, a quarter of a square.

Observe, that the squares always relate to the breadth of the stocking, at the time the next square is begun.

In making up stockings, see that the pins and worsted are suitable to each other; observe also to knit regularly, and let but one person knit each pair, otherwise they will not match or look well.

Stockings are knit with four pins, three of which hold the stitches, and the fourth serves to knit with.

After setting on the number of stitches required, dividing them equally on the three pins (always observing, however, that one pin has an uneven number), commence knitting round and round, according to the scale, taking care always to make the middle or odd stitch in the one pin a turn-stitch, which forms a kind of seam down the stocking, and serves as a guide, by which the place of narrowing is more easily ascertained.

After welting several rounds or bouts, continue knitting and widening, or narrowing, according to the scale, observing to widen or narrow invariably on each side, within one loop of the seam-stitch.

For a description of welting, widening, narrowing, binding, &c., refer to knitting stitches and terms.

After knitting the heel and foot, the stitches are put upon two pins instead of three, and the narrowing begun and continued; after which it is fastened off, and the stocking completed.

SCALE FOR STOCKINGS.

Observe these are the proper proportions for stockings, when knit with coarse worsted and pins.

	Child of 4	Child of 6	Child of 9	Child of 12	Child of 14	Child of 16	Child of 18	Man's Small or Woman's	Man's Large.
Stitches on each pin, allowing one extra for the seam-stitch in the middle of one pin..................	16	18	20	25	30	33	35	42	45
Stitches altogether, including the seam stitch...............	49	55	61	76	91	100	106	127	136
Knit rows for welting.....................	8	8	8	10	10	12	16	20	24
Plain rows, or two squares...............	49	55	61	76	91	100	106	127	136
Number of double narrowings, one on each side of the seam-stitch, at three rows between................	8	9	10	12	15	16	17	21	22
Stitches altogether...........................	33	37	41	51	61	67	71	85	91
Plain rows to the heel..................	16	18	20	25	30	33	35	42	45
Stitches upon one pin for the heel.....	17	19	21	27	31	35	37	43	47
Knit rows for the heel.....................	9	10	11	13	16	18	19	22	24
Narrowings on each side the seam stitch, at one row between..........	2	.2	2	3	3	3	4	4	4
Bind down the heel.........................									
Pick up loops on each side of the seam-stitch................	9	10	11	13	16	18	19	22	24
Widen one row every third stitch on each side of the heel..................	4	5	5	6	8	9	9	11	12
Narrow at the two corners of the heel, at one row between.............	24	27	30	37	45	49	52	63	67
Knit of plain rows.........................									
Put half the stitches on one pin and half on the other, and narrow till there are stitches left on each pin	6	8	8	10	10	11	11	12	12
Bind down and fasten off...............									

ON KNITTING.

SOCKS.
PLATE 21. FIG. 22.

Socks are often worn by men and boys of all classes, and are made similarly to the stockings, excepting that the knitter begins immediately after the two squares knit for stockings; welting, of course, several bouts.

GARTERS.
PLATE 21. FIG. 23.

These are chiefly worn by females, and are merely narrow strips of knitting, of three quarters of a yard long, and a nail, more or less, wide.

They are made of worsted, cotton, or soft wool; the latter is most elastic and pleasant.

For garters, set on from twelve to twenty, or even thirty stitches, according to the fineness of the material.

Knit backwards and forwards till of the proper length, when fasten off. Some persons prefer a loop at the end; for which purpose, when near the end, divide the stitches equally upon two pins, and knit each pin about ten ribs, after which connect them together by binding them in fastening off.

Garters are sometimes knit by putting the material, which is fine, twice round the pin at every stitch, letting the pin be very thick.

Garters are sometimes ribbed, at others knit, in a succession of squares of different patterns.

BABYS' SOCKS.
PLATE 21. FIG. 24.

Set on thirty loops.	Knit three ribs.
Narrow each end.	Knit three ribs.
Narrow each end.	Knit three ribs.
Narrow each end.	Knit one row plain.

There are now eleven ribs and twenty-four loops on your pin. Put twelve on another pin, and add fourteen. Knit three ribs, and narrow at the toe. Knit three ribs, narrow at the toe. Knit three ribs, narrow at the toe. Narrow at the heel every other row three times. There ought to be thirteen ribs. Add fourteen loops to the twelve left on the other pin, and do the same. Join the two together and sew up the sock.

BABYS' SOCKS, ANOTHER KIND.

Set on twenty-four stitches. Widen at the beginning of each row, till there are twenty-eight stitches. Knit ten ribs, narrow at the heel, twice at one end. Take twelve on one pin and add twelve, make another side the same, and fasten off. Add fourteen stitches to the twelve that were left, widen each end every rib till there are thirty. Knit ten ribs and fasten off.

BABYS' SOCKS OR BOOTS.
PLATE 21. FIG. 25.

Set on twenty-two stitches.
Knit three ribs, widening at the beginning and end of each rib.
Knit five ribs, widening at the toe end of each rib.
Stitches altogether, thirty-three.

Knit three plain ribs,
Take off eleven stitches from the toe end upon one pin, and fasten off the rest.
Knit six ribs, widening every rib at the toe,
Knit six ribs, narrowing every rib at the toe,
Add twenty-two stitches to the eleven already on the pin, making thirty-three.
Knit three plain ribs,
Knit five ribs, narrowing at the end of each rib,
Knit three ribs, narrowing at the beginning and end of each rib, and fasten off.
This forms the shoe part of the sock, and is knit of some pretty colour, as green or blue.
For the sock or upper part, pick up twelve stitches from the front or top of the shoe, and knit with white wool.
Knit nine ribs, connecting it with the sides, by picking up the stitches at each edge, as you knit along
Pick up the remaining coloured stitches on each side,
Knit three plain ribs, and then one row widened at the beginning and end alternately, for four times;
Then knit two ribs, after which, one rib more of coloured work, and fasten off,
Sew up the seams, and the sock is completed.

BABYS' SOCKS, OR SLIPPERS.
PLATE 21. FIG. 26, 27.

This is a very pretty kind of sock, and from being worn in two colours with a kind of sandal, resembles slippers worn over stockings.

Set on twenty stitches of coloured wool,
Widen one at the beginning and end of each rib, four times,
Widen at the beginning, or toe end of each rib, for two ribs,
Knit two plain ribs,
Knit nine stitches at the toe end, and fasten off the remaining ones,
Knit the nine stitches, two ribs plain,
Widen at the beginning, or toe end of the three next ribs,
Knit three plain ribs,
Narrow at the beginning, or toe end of the next three ribs,
Knit two plain ribs,
Knit the next row, which should consist of nine stitches, and add twenty-one stitches,
Knit two plain ribs,
Narrow at the toe end of each rib, for two more ribs,
Narrow at the beginning and end of each rib, for four times, and fasten off,
Pick up thirteen stitches, in the front of the boot,
Knit eight plain stitches in white wool,
Widen at the beginning, and end of the next rib,
Knit one plain rib,
Pick up the stitches on both sides at the top of the boot on the same pin,
Knit two plain ribs in coloured wool, and continue afterwards in white wool,
Narrow at the beginning and end of the next rib,
Knit two plain ribs,

Widen at the beginning, and end of the next rib,
Knit three plain ribs,
Widen at the beginning, and end of the next rib,
Knit three plain ribs,
Knit another rib in coloured wool, fasten off, and put a little ribbon bow in front of the boot.
Sew or lace up the square in front of the boot all round.

CHILD'S LONG SOCK.
PLATE 21. FIG. 28.

This may be knit either of two colours, or entirely of white.
Set on thirty-four stitches,
Knit sixteen rows, turning every other stitch to form a welt,
Knit one rib of coloured wool and two of white, alternately four times,
Knit two ribs white,
Take fifteen stitches on one pin, and add fifteen stitches,
Knit twelve plain ribs in coloured wool,
Knit three ribs, narrowing at the beginning and end of each row, and fasten off;
Take up the fifteen stitches which project beyond the leg, and which form the top or front of the boot,
Knit twelve plain ribs,
Knit three plain ribs, narrowing at the beginning and end of each row, and fasten off.

The loose slit in front must be connected to the shoe part, by knitting two stitches in the centre, forming a hole on each side, through which the ribbon is drawn. Sew up the sock and it is completed. Sometimes the boot has a little white intermixed with the colour; in which case, the coloured wool is simply laid inside, and brought forward when wanted.

CHILD'S FIRST STOCKING OR SOCK.
PLATE 21. FIG. 29, 30.

This is commonly made with fine cotton, letting two rows be knit in stocking, and one in garter or turn-stitch, alternately the whole way.
Set on twenty-two stitches to each of three pins,
Knit round and round for fifty-four rows,
Put thirty-three stitches on one pin for the heel,
Knit thirty-three rows, and bind the heel,
Pick up the remaining stitches, so as to have twenty-two again on each pin,
Narrow once at each end of the heel for five rows,
Knit seventy-three rows,
Bind down the toe and fasten off.

THE RIBBED BOOT.
PLATE 21. FIG. 31.

Set on twenty stitches on each of the three pins,
Knit a square,
Put thirty stitches on one pin, and the remaining thirty on another pin,
Continue knitting the thirty stitches on the pin for the instep, towards the toe, which is generally about two squares,

Then narrow at each end till but five stitches remain on the pin, then fasten off;
Next, take the other thirty stitches, and knit a square for the heel and fasten off;
Knit two gores to put in between the front and heel on each side, for which purpose,
Set on twenty stitches, and narrow at the beginning of every other row till it ends in a point,
Set in the gores,
Next, make a sole by setting on fourteen stitches, or any number, according to the width of the foot. Knit it straight along, till of a sufficient length,
Sew the sole upon the boot, and the whole is complete.
This boot is generally ribbed by knitting two stitches and turning two.

THE OVER SHOE.
PLATE 21. FIG. 32.

This is very convenient to slip over a satin shoe, or as a house shoe.
Set on thirty-four stitches. Knit a plain square, double it, and sew it up one side to form the heel; sew up about three inches to form the instep, and pucker in the end for the toe.

THE SNOW HEEL.
PLATE 21. FIG. 33.

This is very useful in slippery weather for persons to put over their shoe or boot heels, to prevent their falling. It is particularly good for old people and children.
Set on sixty-six stitches on one pin,
Knit five ribs,
Finish off four stitches on each side, and continue knitting the middle part,
Knit fourteen ribs,
Knit twenty-five stitches, then narrow; knit six, again narrow, and then knit the remainder.
Continue narrowing every alternate row twice in the row, reducing the six centre stitches every time, so that at the sixth narrowing there are none of them left. Fasten off.

LITTLE NIGHT BOOTS.
PLATE 21. FIG. 34.

These are made by knitting a piece of six nails long, and a nail and a half or more deep. This, when fastened at the ends, is sewed to a sole, which is made by knitting an oval piece.
For this sole, set on about six stitches and knit on, widening at both ends, till about fifteen stitches are upon the pin; continue knitting till nearly of the proper length, and then begin narrowing down to the six stitches again. Fasten off.
The sides of the boot are generally ornamented by knitting four rows of garter stitch of one colour, and then four rows of stocking stitch of another, and so on throughout. About thirty stitches may be set on the pin.

A VERY PRETTY OVER SHOE.
PLATE 21. FIG. 35.

Set on thirty-six stitches on each of three pins;
Knit one plain round, after which knit fifty rows (more or less, according to pleasure) in the welt of three, by which means it is ribbed up and elastic, and will fit almost any person's foot.

ON KNITTING.

If for a child of five or six years old, set on eighteen stitches to each pin.

SOCKS FOR INVALIDS, OR THOSE WHO HAVE COLD FEET.

These are very useful for those who have cold feet, either to wear in bed, or slip over the stockings when dressing; and as they set quite close to the foot and ankle, they give a great deal of warmth.

They are best made of floss wool of five or six threads, and about two and a half ounces of wool is sufficient for each pair. Whalebone or wooden pins are used; they should not be very thick, considerably less than a drawing pencil.

For women's full sized socks cast on thirty-six stitches on three needles, and knit ten plain rows, then turn the first stitch of the next row; after this, for the thirty following rows, narrow thus—the two last loops of the last needle must be knit as one; turn the first loop of the next row, and take the two next loops off at once, taking hold of the loops at the back instead of in the usual way. After this you begin to welt, and the depth of the welting is regulated by fancy.

VERY PRETTY KNIT BOOTS,
PLATE 21. FIG. 36,

Commonly called Derby jail boots, at which place the female prisoners are employed in making them.

SCALE FOR KNIT BOOTS.

	Child of 8	Child of 10	Child of 12	Child of 14	Child of 16	Child of 18	Woman's
Loops set on one pin...............................	14	16	18	22	24	26	28
Widen every rib on one end till the number of loops are	17	19	21	26	28	31	33
Knit plain ribs..	2	3	3	3	4	4	4
Narrow every rib on one end, till the number of loops are........................	14	16	18	22	24	26	28
Number of loops to be added, half of which are to be set on the pin with the stitches already on, and the other half on a fresh pin immediately joining it.....	20	22	24	28	30	32	34
Pick up the stitches on the second pin, which were first set on for the toe............................							
Ribs knit for the side of the foot....................	7	8	9	11	12	13	14
Pick up loops to the toe................................							
Ribs for the bottom of the foot...................	1	2	2	2	3	3	4
Pick up the loops round the ankle, and narrow every rib on the right side three or four stitches from the front of the rows..	10	11	12	14	16	18	20
Fasten off..							

These boots may be knit in two wools, white and coloured. They should have leather soles sewed on, to make them more durable. They should have fringe, and worsted platted strings.

NIGHT SOCKS.

Coarse lamb's-wool and thick pins.

Set on thirty-six stitches, knit ten ribs, put eighteen on one pin, and knit twelve ribs; narrow each rib at the heel twice, making in all fourteen ribs. The other side the same. Pick up loops on both the side pieces; for the toe, knit ten ribs; narrow every rib on each side, so that the narrowings shall be on the sides of the foot, and not at the bottom; seven narrowings, and finish in a point.

VERY NEAT NIGHT SOCKS.
PLATE 21. FIG. 37.

Set forty-six stitches on one pin,
Knit twenty-seven plain ribs,
Add twenty stitches, setting them equally on three pins,
Knit twenty-six plain bouts or rounds,
Divide the stitches, letting half of them lie on one pin, and the other half equally divided between two pins. This arrangement makes it easier to knit than on two pins, and, at the same time, distinctly marks the half for the two narrowings;
Narrow on each side of the pin with half the stitches.

SQUARE NIGHT BOOTS.
PLATE 21. FIG. 38.

Set on forty loops, knit the two first stitches plain, the rest double knitting till it is a square bag; fasten it off, making it to open at the top; large pins and coarse; lamb's wool.

KNIT SOLE.
PLATE 21. FIG. 39.

This is a sole to put within a shoe or boot, and is made in double knitting and sewed to a piece of stiff muslin of the proper shape, and bound all round with ribbon.

For a good average size, set on fourteen stitches, knit in double knitting for twenty-three rows, and fasten off. The knitting must be brought into shape by taking it in with the galloon, when wanted to be narrowed.

KNEE CAP.
PLATE 21. FIG. 40.

Set on one pin forty-seven stitches,
Knit plain seventeen ribs,
Next row, knit twenty-three plain stitches, widen, knit a stitch, widen again, and knit the remaining twenty-three stitches.
Every alternate row, widen at each of the above widenings exactly in a straight line, so that the increase of stitches falls in the centre, forming a gore or half diamond.
Knit sixteen plain ribs,
Next row, knit twenty-three plain stitches, narrow, knit thirty-six stitches, narrow again, knit the remaining twenty-three stitches.
Every alternate row, narrow in a straight line, over each of these two narrowings, so as to reduce the stitches between by degrees to a point again, at the end of thirteen ribs.
Knit thirty-one plain ribs;
Next row, fasten off four stitches, and knit the rest of the row; knit a plain row;
Next row, fasten off four more stitches, and knit the rest of the row; knit a plain row;
Next row, same as above, and then fasten off, and sew up the seams.

KNIT GLOVES, LARGE SIZE.

Put eighteen stitches on a pin, leave about thirteen rows open (by knitting backwards and forwards instead of round) for the thumb; knit round till you come to the figures. Put half the stitches on one pin, and half on the other. Take nine stitches off each pin for the first finger, and add eight between the first and second finger to make a gore, then there will be twenty-six stitches on your pins altogether; knit two rows plain, narrow every other row at each end of the eight loops you added, for three times on each side; there should now be twenty stitches left. Knit plain till the finger is long enough. Then narrow twice at each end of the finger, leaving one stitch between the two narrowings on each side. Do this every other row three times, when there will be eight loops left, divide them on two pins and bind them down. For the second finger, take six stitches off each pin, and pick up eleven stitches for a gore, between the second and third fingers. Knit two rows plain; there should then be thirty-four stitches; narrow every other row on each side of *both* the gores three times. There should then be twenty-two stitches. Finish the finger like the other. For the third finger, take six stitches off each pin, pick up ten at the bottom of the last gore, and add ten for the new gore; there are then thirty-two stitches. Narrow as before, and there should then be twenty left. For the little finger, pick up ten stitches for the gore, and the six off the two pins make twenty-two, after the narrowings there should be sixteen stitches left. For the thumb, pick up three stitches at the bottom of the hole, and knit backwards and forwards, picking up an extra stitch each time, till there are sixteen stitches on a pin, then pick up three at the top, and knit backwards and forwards till there are eight. Join all together, and knit round; finish the thumb as the fingers.

DRIVING MITS.
PLATE 21. FIG. 41.

These are very useful for gentlemen or coachmen, in severe weather, being double on the out, and single in the inside.

Set on forty stitches on ivory pins, of thick soft floss wool. Knit several rows in double knitting until half the muffatee is completed, when knit the remainder in imitation double knitting, which is not so clumsy for the palm of the hand, when grasping reins, &c. When completed, sew it up, leaving a hole of a full nail for the thumb, at half a nail's distance from the end.

BABY'S MITTENS.
PLATE 21. FIG. 42.

Set on twenty stitches on each of three pins, and knit plain one square.

Knit backwards and forwards along two of the pins, letting every other row be turn-stitch, for another square, and fasten off.

Knit the other pin in a similar manner for thirty rows, and fasten off.

Sew up the hand and thumb, and add a fringe or a ribbon to tie, or, if preferred, it may be begun with a welt at the wrist.

MITTENS.

Set on twenty-two loops on each of the three pins, welt twenty rows, knit one row plain, next row alternate *turn and plain*, third row plain, fourth row alternate *plain and turn*, so that the plain stitch is over the one that was turned before, and so on till you come to the beginning of the thumb. Then knit backwards and forwards, leaving a hole for the thumb. Then knit round again, and finish with a welt. To make a thumb, pick up three loops at the top of the hole left, and knit backwards and forwards, picking up an additional loop at the end of each row, for about ten rows. Then pick up three loops at the bottom of the hole, and do the same till you meet the stitches at the top. Join all together and knit round and round till it is long enough; welt five or six rows and finish.

THE KNIT ARMLET.
PLATE 21. FIG. 43.

This is very suitable for school girls to wear over their arms, or for old persons, or people when travelling. They may be made as high as the elbow, or up to the shoulder. Little children, in severe weather, wear them over their little naked arms to prevent them from chapping. Fine black lamb's wool is most usually worn, in which case, it should be well steeped in vinegar, and then dried, to prevent the dye coming off.

For a grown up person, one hundred stitches will reach to the elbow. Knit plain, as you would a garter, backwards and forwards, using large ivory or steel pins. About twenty rows (more or less, according to the size of the arm) are sufficient. Sew down the whole length, leaving an opening of about a nail long to admit the thumb, sewing beyond it to the end, about half a nail or less. When worn, they cling to the hand and arm, keep them warm, and look particularly neat.

Some persons prefer them welted at the top and bottom, or ribbed the whole way.

KNIT MUFFATEE.
PLATE 21. FIG. 44.

This is made simply by setting on forty stitches, and knitting three rows plain and three rows turn-stitch, till wide enough, when it is sewed up, leaving a hole for the thumb. It looks very neat in black or light grey. Use finest wool and pins.

MUFFATEE.
PLATE 21. FIG. 45.

This is in plain knitting.
    Set on twenty stitches,
    Knit twenty eight ribs.

Fringe is sewed on with a carpet needle in a kind of cross-stitch, being wound over a mesh of the proper width.

MUFFATEE.
PLATE 21. FIG. 26.

This is extremely pretty, made of the two coloured ribbed stitch, or the two coloured chain stitch.

Set on thirty loops, and knit the first and last three loops of every pin plain knitting, of one colour, to make a kind of border. Continue this for about twenty two ribs, when sew up, and either add fringe, or not, according to pleasure.

MUFFATEES.

Use fine pins and merino wool. Set on seventy four loops, knit six rows, backwards and forwards, then six rows double knitting, and so on alternately three times of double, and four of plain; then knit twelve double, six plain, and finish off. Sew it up.

MUFFATEES.

Set on an even number of stitches (twenty for a child, thirty for a lady, or fifty for a man) on an ivory pin.

Knit four, six, or eight stitches plain, according to the above sizes, and continue the row in imitation double knitting stitch, making as many plain stitches at the end of the row, as at the beginning.

Continue knitting backwards and forwards until sufficient is done for the thickness of the wrist.

Sew or lace it up, and it is completed.

FRILL OR RUFF.
PLATE 21. FIG. 47.

These are very soft for children, and are generally knit of two coloured wools and with ivory pins of a middling thickness.

Set on thirty-five stitches for a child, and fifty for a grown up person.

Knit three plain rows with the coloured wool,

Knit ten rows, putting the wool twice round the pin, with white wool.

Again, knit four plain rows with the coloured wool, and ten rows putting the wool twice round the pin, with the white wool.

Knit three plain rows with the coloured wool, and fasten off.

Make up the frill as follows:—

Plat or double each white row, making the three sets of white rows lie side by side, so as to stand up, and have a square appearance. When done, lay the frill the wrong side uppermost, and sew the middle row of each set of stitches together, side by side, all along.

Sew a ribbon at each end, to tie.

A RUFF.
PLATE 21. FIG. 48.

This is particularly useful for children to tie round the neck, and is knit with fine wool and coarse pins. It may be knit in the raised French stitch, or the open hem, or any other elastic soft stitch.

Set a sufficient number of stitches on the pin to be about two nails wide, and knit six or eight nails long, and when done, sew up along the side, and after drawing a piece of rolled wadding through, draw it, or sew it up at each end, and attach ribbons, or worsted cord to tie it. It resembles a boa in shape.

A SCARF.
PLATE 21. FIG. 49.

Set on sixty stitches (more or less, according to taste), always choosing an even number, and knit along in the "Imitation Net-work Stitch, No. 8," to the length required, from one yard and a half to two yards. Next make a fringe by setting on eighteen stitches, and, after knitting a sufficient quantity in the same stitch to sew along the two ends, fasten off, leaving, however, fourteen stitches to unrove, to form the fringe.

These scarfs look beautiful in shaded colours, and may be knit of floss silk, netting silk, cotton, thread, or wool. The above number of stitches is calculated for wool.

ANOTHER SCARF.

This is made of the "French Raised Stitch, No. 31," and looks exceedingly beautiful, when made with fine wool and small pins.

The number of stitches depends, of course, on the quality of the wool; it is therefore impossible to set down any fixed number; suffice it to say it should be made of the usual width. At the ends fix some long fringe, of which there are various kinds given in this work.

COMFORTER.
PLATE 21. FIG. 50.

For one comforter, buy a quarter of a pound of lamb's wool. The six thread, untwisted, is the best.

Set forty stitches on a pin, and, if the pins are not very thick, put the wool twice round them while knitting every stitch, which should be knit in double knitting, and may have a border and fringe at the ends to give a finish, in which case, a little more wool will be required.

COMFORTER.
PLATE 21. FIG. 51.

Set thirty stitches on one pin,
Knit sixty-four plain ribs, backwards and forwards,
Pick up twenty-two stitches from the middle of the side of the piece, leaving twenty-one stitches on each side from the end.
Knit on backwards and forwards for twenty-two ribs, to make a chest piece, and fasten off.
Sew up the two ends of the long piece, and it is completed.
When worn, the comforter is drawn over the head, letting the chest piece hang down in front.
This is knit with soft wool and upon ivory pins.

ANOTHER COMFORTER, THE SAME SHAPE, BUT DONE IN DOUBLE KNITTING.
PLATE 21. FIG. 51.

Set on fifty-four stitches, and knit in double knitting, about sixty-six or seventy rows, and fasten off, by knitting or binding the two ends together.

From the middle of the length in front, pick up stitches for the chest-piece, and knit forty rows or more, according to pleasure.

A HANDKERCHIEF.
PLATE 21. FIG. 52.

This is a small and very warm handkerchief, to wear under a shawl or fur tippet, in the winter; it is knit with pretty thick floss wool, either white or coloured, in blue or crimson it looks well; the needles used are either of wood, whalebone, or cane.

Cast on 160 common stitches, and knit one plain row, then nine rows of double knitting with a plain stitch at the beginning and end of each row, continue this double knitting, narrowing at one end, until the handkerchief is brought to five or six stitches, then take it off like a garter. This bottom corner is bound with ribbon, and two strings put on to tie round the waist, the other two ends are also bound, and a ribbon loop put on each, the ribbon passes through these loops, and it fits neatly to the figure.

LITTLE KNIT HABIT-SHIRT.
PLATE 21. FIG. 53, 54, 55.

These are remarkably nice things to wear under the shawl, as they set close to the chest, and give a great deal of warmth. They are best knit with small wooden or thick steel pins, and with floss wool, about three or four threads, and in double knitting.

The habit-shirt is in four pieces, namely, one back, two fronts and one collar.

The back should be cut out to fit the person tolerably, and the fronts joined to it on the shoulder, and brought across over the chest.

Observe, in the Plate that in Fig. 53, S S represent the straight parts, and P P the sloped.

Begin to knit the front, by setting on as many stitches as will form the length required from S to A, or top, and observe, as you continue knitting, that one end of the knitting must be much more sloped than the other, for which purpose, at that end most sloped, increase at the beginning and end of the row, but at the side which is less sloped, widen only at the end of the pin. Having made the two fronts to match each other so as to be a pair, begin making the back. Begin it at the bottom or narrow straight part at the waist; increase it at the beginning and end of each row, till sufficiently wide to go from shoulder to shoulder; after which, diminish in the same way at each end of every row to the neck. Take off or finish the few centre stitches that may remain, and knit up first on one side, and then on the other, lessening each row till it is properly hollowed.

The collar is merely a straight piece.

In making up, sew the sides marked P, to each side of the back marked Z Z, and sew on the collar all round. Put a ribbon behind, to tie round the waist, and another at the throat.

A PRETTY KNIT HALF HANDKERCHIEF.

Begin the handkerchief from one stitch, knit as many rows, increasing one stitch every row at the same end, until there are seven loops upon the pin.

Begin the pattern thus:—
Make a stitch,
Slip off a stitch,
Knit two together,
Put the slipped-stitch over the two just knitted in one.
Again make a stitch,
Slip off a stitch,
Knit two stitches,
Put the slipped stitch over as before,
Continue thus until four stitches from the end of the row, then make a stitch, and knit the four remaining stitches plain.
Knit every alternate row in turn-stitch;
This alternate row must have the three last stitches knit plain, increasing it by making a stitch.
The handkerchief must be one yard and a quarter long on the straight side. When done, fasten off.

HONEYCOMB-KNIT SHAWL.

This is made of fine lamb's wool or yarn; it looks very well when the centre is white, with a shaded border of some bright colour.

For a small shawl, or a large handkerchief, the following quantity is required:—
Three ounces of fine white lamb's wool.
Two skeins of the darkest shade of colour.
Two skeins of the next.

Two skeins of the next.
One skein of the lightest.

The needles are of wood, rather fine, not so thick as a drawing pencil.

The centre is first knit, beginning with only two loops on your needle, to make the point fine; knit several plain rows, raising one loop in each row; the raising is merely knitting first the outside and then the inside of the last loop, and is continued in every row, whether plain or open, through the whole shawl.

When you have ten loops on your needle begin your pattern, which is done as follows:—

    Knit four plain stitches, bring the wool in front of the needle, and then, taking hold of two loops instead of one, knit them plainly together; continue this till within four loops of the end, which must be knit plain. Always begin and end every open row with four plain stitches.

    Knit three plain rows between each figured one. When you have from 200 to 250 loops, (which will make a good sized shawl), begin the border, which looks best dark at the edges, and shaded up to light in the middle. Before beginning the border at the top, it is best to knit three or four plain rows of the white wool; and observe, that as there is a right and a wrong side to the shawl, the first row of the border must be continued so as to suit it, by knitting one, more or less, of the plain white rows.

    Begin with your darkest shade of border, and knit three or more rows of it, according to taste; then the second, the third, the lightest, the third again, second, and darkest, increasing one loop in every row, both open and plain, as before; the last three or four rows should be plain, to make the edge firm. Then fasten off.

    Begin the side border by taking up all the inside loops, as those in the heel of a stocking are done, and begin with the dark shade as at the top, and in the *first row only*, raise a loop every fifth stitch, which may be easily done by taking up the little bars or loops that lie between the stitches; go on as before, raising one loop at the end of every row.

    Be careful to begin all the borders on the same side, as, in consequence of the manner of taking up the loops, there is a difference.

The raising the loops at the side border is done to make it set loosely to the shawl, as, if it were not thus enlarged, it would be tight and confined. The corners and point of the border are neatly joined with a needle and thread.

A TIPPET.
PLATE 21. FIG. 56.

Cut out a tippet or cape of the proper shape and size in paper, and then divide it into five equal portions; each portion may be considered a gore, and by measuring by the stitches put on the pin with the pattern the right number may easily be ascertained. These gores may be made to increase equally on both sides, as in the Plate, or only on one side. Sometimes long ends are continued with the two front gores, to make a sort of mantilla or pelerine.

Neat tippets might be made with advantage for school girls at times when worsteds are cheap.

FOR A PURSE.

Set on one pin ninety or a hundred stitches, knit the first stitch, put the silk over the pin, then slip a stitch and knit a stitch; turn the slipped stitch over the last knit one, and so on all through the pin; then seam the next row, and so on till completed, when fasten off.

FOR A PURSE

Use four pins. If the silk twist be fine it requires two skeins—if coarse, three skeins; or, if to be made of two colours, half that quantity. Cast on your three pins eighteen loops, if fine, or sixteen loops, if coarse, and begin (after one plain row) to knit in raised French stitch (see No. 31); and when sufficient rounds have been completed to form fourteen holes lengthwise, knit backwards or forwards on two pins in the same stitch, to form the opening; after complete fourteen more holes or batterns, join the purse again by knitting in three pins, as before, until fourteen more holes are done, when bind down and fasten off.

FOR A PURSE,

Two skeins of silk are sufficient (generally of two colours); use four pins, set on four stitches on each pin; begin to knit plain round and round, widen one stitch each round, until you have eighteen stitches on each pin (measure here how much silk you have used that you may know how much to reserve for narrowing with), then knit one stitch plain and one turned for every round, until time to make the opening, when put all your stitches on one needle, knitting backwards and forwards, taking care to preserve the stitch by knitting the back rows properly, by turning the stitches that were before knit plain, continue this till the one skein is used up, when you are at the middle of your purse; take the other skins as many rows again, backwards and forwards, then join the opening by putting the stitches on three needles, as before, and knit round and round until you have but enough silk left for the narrowing, when begin to knit plain, narrowing every round until reduced to four stitches, as before, on each pin, when fasten off.

FOR A PURSE.

Cast seventy-five stitches on one pin; two skeins of silk are sufficient, and very fine pins are best; after knitting one plain row, continue as follows: knit one stitch plain, and then knit the silk twice round the pin, knit two stitches together in turn stitch; again put the silk twice round the pin, and knit two stitches together in turn stitch, and so on to every row, remembering that the first stitch in every row is knit plain

PRETTY NEW PURSE PATTERN.

Use four pins and set on each of three pins eighteen or twenty loops,
Knit one plain round, and then continue for another round as follows:—
Bring the silk in front of the pin, slip a stitch, knit a stitch, then turn the slipped stitch over the knit one;
Again bring the silk in front of the pin, slip a stitch, knit a stitch, and turn the slipped stitch over the knit one, and sow on to the end of the round,
Knit the two next rounds plain,
And continue alternately knitting one round of the pattern, and two rounds plain, until the purse is finished.

RECEIPT FOR A ZEPHYRINE.

This is a very convenient thing to lie over the head instead of a bonnet, especially in travelling, and is generally knit of two colours. It should be knit with Berlin wool, on two rather fine pins, with knobs at the end.

Set on your pin 100 stitches,
Knit a row plain,
Turn, or purl a row,
Repeat this twice more each,
Then change the colour, and continue knitting and purling alternately, three rows each,
Again change to the first colour, and continue knitting and purling, three rows more each,
Continue thus changing colour until there are five stripes of one colour, and six stripes of the other, when it is finished,
Then gather the ends to a point, bind them with ribbon, and sew on strings to match the darkest colour.

A ZEPHYR.

This is a soft shawl to lay a baby on, or carry it out in, and is desirable on account of its warmth and lightness. Some are made square, others of a half handkerchief shape.

In either case, set on about 130 or more stitches, and knit in honeycomb or French raised stitch, the embossed, hexagon, or any other simple pretty pattern preferred. A border and fringe may be added, according to taste, and certainly gives a rich finish to it.

A BABY'S CAP.

Put on eighty stitches on the three pins, so as to have 240 stitches; knit twelve, turning every alternate stitch; in the next row turn the stitch which was plain before; take in eighty stitches, one at every fourth stitch, so as to leave a full border; then knit one row plain, one open row, three rows plain, and twenty-four rows double knitting; then knit three rows plain, one open row, three rows plain, twenty-four rows double knitting, three rows plain, one open row, and three rows plain.

Cast on twenty-four stitches at each end of the first three plain, to form the back of the cap; then knit forty-eight rows double knitting the whole length; then take in gradually to the size of the crown in one row, knit three rows plain, one open row; again three plain; fasten off at the top, join up the back, and knit three rows plain, one open row, and three plain.

The crown is made by putting on sixteen stitches, and increasing one at each end for sixteen rows; then knit sixteen rows; then decrease sixteen rows, which forms the circle.

A BABY'S CAP.
PLATE 21. FIG. 57.

Set on one stitch on each of three pins, and knit a circular piece of knitting in hole-stitch, until there are 110 stitches altogether on the three pins.

Knit six ribs of stocking knitting, one of holes, and one of garter rib,
Knit six ribs of stocking knitting, one of holes, and one rib of garter-stitch,
Knit six ribs of stocking, one of holes, and one of garter,
Knit six ribs of stocking, one of holes, one of garter, two of stocking, and two of garter,
Finish off twenty-two stitches, and divide the remainder of the stitches on two pins,
Knit three ribs of stocking, making holes at six stitches distance, which serve for ribbons,
Knit three ribs of garter-stitch, two of stocking, six of garter, three of stocking, one row of holes, four ribs of stocking, six ribs of garter, three ribs of stocking, one row of holes, four ribs of stocking, six ribs of garter, and three of stocking; after which three more of stocking, with holes at six stitches distance, to admit of a second ribbon.

For the border, continue knitting twenty rows in huckaback stitch; for the border behind, take up the stitches at the ear on each side, and knit sufficient rows in huckaback stitch till each strip is long enough to reach the middle of the back. Put in a ribbon behind, and the whole is completed.

A BABY'S BONNET OR HOOD.
PLATE 21. FIG. 58.

For the border, set on eighty stitches and knit in huckaback stitch, narrow one stitch at each end of every other row, till you have knit ten rows. Next, commence the head-piece, and knit six rows in double knitting, the one row of holes, eight rows of double knitting, one of holes, and six rows of double knitting, then begin to knit in honeycomb-stitch, fasten off two stitches at the end of each pin, every row until there are but twenty-four on the pin, then fasten off.

For the crown, set on five stitches, widen each row till you have sixteen loops, then knit twelve rows. Narrow at each end for two rows, knit fourteen rows and fasten off. Sew the crown to the head-piece with wool of the same quality.

Begin the curtain by taking up all the stitches at the back, and knitting six rows in double knitting, widening four stitches on each pin; then one row of holes, widening two stitches; then six rows of double knitting still widening, one of holes, widening two stitches, and double knitting, increasing till there are 150 stitches on the pin, then fasten off, and put in ribbons through the holes where wanted.

A GENTLEMAN'S NIGHT CAP.
PLATE 21. FIG. 59.

This cap has a very pretty appearance, something resembling old fashioned insertion lace, as there is an ornamented border round the head. It is done with fine needles and cotton, and knit round like a stocking. The plan is as follows:—

Cast on any number of stitches, divisable by thirteen.

1st Row. Turn one, knit one, turn one, slip one, knit one. Draw the slipt loop over, knit six plain, bring the cotton over, as though going to turn, knit one, bring your cotton to the top and knit one.

2nd Row. Turn, knit, turn, slip, and draw over, knit nine.

3rd Row. Turn, knit, turn, slip, and draw over, knit five, bring the cotton to the top and knit two.

4th Row. Turn, knit, turn, slip, and draw over, knit nine.

5th Row. Turn, knit, turn, slip, and draw over, knit four, bring the cotton to the top, knit one, bring the cotton to the top, knit three.

6th Row. Turn, knit, turn, slip, and draw over, knit nine.

7th Row. Turn, knit, turn, slip, and draw over, knit three, bring the cotton to the top, knit one, bring the cotton to the top, knit four.

8th Row. Turn, knit, turn, slip, and draw over, knit nine.

9th Row. Turn, knit, turn, slip, and draw over, knit two, bring the cotton to the top, knit five.

10th Row. Turn, knit, turn, slip, and draw over, knit nine.

11th Row. Turn, knit, turn, slip, and draw over, knit one, bring the cotton to the top, knit six.

12th Row. Turn, knit, turn, slip, and draw over, knit nine, knit two plain rounds, turn five rounds, knit one round, throwing the cotton twice over the needle; turn one round, repeat this until you have eighteen turned rounds. Knit two plain rounds, turn five rounds, take four needles, and knit and turn three rounds alternately, narrowing at each needle end, having a turn, knit and seam between each narrowing; continue this until there are four loops on each needle, which will draw round the tassel.

KNIT BAGS.
PLATE 21. FIG. 60, 61.

Very pretty bags may be made of fantail-stitch in silk twist, for which purpose set on as many stitches, divisable by fourteen, as are required for the width of the bag. About four times fourteen or fifty-six stitches will be a useful size, adding, if preferred, four extra stitches on each end, and between each of the fourteen stitches, to separate the pattern more effectually, and make it look richer. These extra stitches will amount to five times four or twenty, making in all seventy-six stitches. Knit the four stitches of any pattern preferred; supposing the open hem, No. 4, is selected, then knit as follows :—

Set on seventy-six stitches, knit four plain ribs, and six turn-stitch rows.

Open hem the first four stitches,

Fantail the next fourteen stitches,

Open hem the next four stitches, and so on, till the last open hemmed four stitches complete the row.

Continue as above till a sufficient length is done for both sides of the bag, after which, seam it up, and put cord and tassels to complete the whole, lining it or not, according to pleasure.

KETTLE HOLDERS.
PLATE 21. FIG. 62.

This is knit in double knitting, with a border of plain ribs round.

Set thirty-two stitches on one pin,

Knit four ribs plain,

Knit double knitting, letting the first four stitches and the last four stitches of every row be plain knitting.

When the double knit part is quite square, add the four ribs of plain knitting, to complete the border, and fasten off.

A little loop of twisted wool is put at the top to hang it by.

KNIT MATS, OR KETTLE HOLDERS.
PLATE 21. FIG. 63.

This is knit to resemble fringe all over, and when well done looks very pretty.

Use fine needles and a common kind of worsted for knitting the wool fringe, which must be thick and soft.

Set on any number of stitches, and knit one plain row, after which, begin the next row by knitting one plain stitch, then put the wool between the pins round the fingers, and back again between the pins in front, and so on, similar to the rug-stitch, No. 33.

KNIT OPEN BRAID.
PLATE 21. FIG. 64.

This is very simple, and if done with cord or thick cotton or worsted, might be very useful for sewing on, to ornament children's dresses; or if of silk twist, for putting round pincushions, curtains, &c.

Set on one stitch, and knit as many stitches as the longest pin will possibly hold. Knit two rows plain, and then unrove one row by pulling out the pin, and draw the wool through the last loop, to keep it from roving still further. The braid is thus formed, and must be sewed on at each top and bottom loop.

KNIT MATS.
PLATE 21. FIG. 65.

Set on thirty stitches or more, according to the size required, and knit in the two coloured chain-stitch till a square is completed, when make a fringe, No. 1, and sew it round. When completed, cut it and comb it out, taking care not to pull out the bits by drawing too hard.

COVERLET.
PLATE 21. FIG. 66.

This is knit with cotton, and is composed of several squares sewed together. These squares are begun at one corner, commencing with two stitches, and increasing to fifty or more, by widening at each end of each row. It is then decreased by narrowing at each end of each row, and fastened off when two stitches are left on the pins. These squares are often ornamented, sometimes by knitting one row turn-stitch, seven rows plain, backwards and forwards, and so on, so as to form three ribs garter, and one rib stocking-stitch.

Some persons ornament each square differently, others merely sew them, so that the rows shall run or lie in different positions. A border with fringe may be put round, for which purpose, refer to the stitches for fringes, &c.

The huckaback pattern is very suitable for coverlets.

BLANKETS.

These are usually made for infants' cradles and invalids, on account of their warmth and lightness; they should be knit with very large pins and thick wool, and in double knitting all the way, having a border of imitation double knitting or huckaback all round, to keep them more in place.

Set on from 100 to 200 stitches, according to the size required, knitting about ten ribs of border, after which the remainder is plain double knitting. Observe that the first and last eight or ten loops on each end of the pin be knit in the border-stitch.

COTTON DOYLEYS.
PLATE 21. FIG. 67.

These are very pretty, and may be made in various stitches.
The following is a particularly pretty way:—
Set on thirty-eight stitches,
Knit two plain ribs,
Continue knitting two plain stitches and two turn stitches, remembering every two ribs to knit plain stitches over turn stitches, and turn stitches over plain, so as to form a kind of ornamental knitting, resembling huckaback or checks.
Observe, the two last, as well as the two first stitches of every row are plain, to continue the border; also knit two plain ribs to correspond, before fastening off. Sew in the fringe, No. 2.

ANOTHER DOYLEY.

This is similar to the one before, excepting that it is knit in honeycomb or hole-stitch.

A HANDSOME BORDER AND CORNERS FOR A SHAWL.

This is a very beautiful pattern when properly done, and would answer well for a shawl, a baby's zephyrine, a mat, carpet, counterpane, or any other article enclosed in a square.

The border (which is a kind of fantail stitch) is ended at each corner by squares, which gives great lightness to the whole.

In beginning one of these corners, set on but two stitches on the pin to form the point; and observe, as you go on, to increase one stitch at the end of every row, until the square or diamond is knit to a sufficient width (say thirteen rows) when decrease every row one stitch at the end, until the number of loops on your pin is reduced to two again, when fasten off, and the square is completed.

The stitch with which the square is knitted is formed as follows; and the number of ribs at the side should be divisable by six and one over, to be the proper width for the border; thirteen is a very good number of ribs.

Begin the square by knitting plain every row until you have thirteen stitches on your pin (remembering to increase one stitch at the end of each row) and then continue as below.

1st Row.   Knit six stitches plain,
           Pass the cotton in front to make a stitch,
           Knit two together,
           Knit the remaining stitches plain.
Next Row. Knit plain,
           Knit six stitches plain,
           Pass the cotton in front, to make a stitch,
           Knit two stitches together,
           Pass the cotton in front again, to make a stitch,
           Knit two stitches together,
           Knit the remaining stitches plain.
Next Row. Knit plain.
           Continue the above, observing that every alternate row is knit plain, and the rows between knit in the above stitch; always leaving six plain stitches at each end of the pin, to make a kind of little border to the square.
           When complete, begin the border by picking up the stitches on one side of the square, and then continue thus :—
1st Row.   Seam a stitch,
           Knit a stitch,
           Seam a stitch,
           Knit two stitches,
           Pass the cotton in front to make a stitch.
           Knit a stitch.
           Repeat the same for six more stitches; then,
           Knit one stitch.
Next Row. Knit a stitch;
           Seam a stitch,
           Knit a stitch,
           Knit two together,
           Seam eleven stitches,

ON KNITTING.

    Knit two together.
Next Row. Seam a stitch,
    Knit one,
    Seam one,
    Knit two together,
    Knit nine plain,
    Knit three together.
Next Row. Knit a stitch,
    Seam a stitch,
    Knit a stitch,
    Knit two together,
    Seam seven stitches,
    Knit two together.

Continue these four rows successively, until the border is long enough to insert another corner or square, as before.

GENTLEMAN'S TRAVELLING CAPS.

These are remarkably pretty and comfortable, and should be made of shaded wool or silk, and are knit with two pins only.

  Set on an even number of stitches,
  Knit the first row plain;
  Observe to slip off the first stitch of every row throughout, and continue as follows:—

1st Row. (After slipping the first stitch) put the wool in front to make a stitch,
    Slip off a stitch the contrary way,
    Knit a stitch, as before,
    Continue this until at the end of the row,
Next Row. (After, as usual, slipping off the 1st stitch) knit two stitches together the whole way, leaving one at the end to knit plain. Repeat this.

SOFA FOOT COVERS, OR WARMERS.

These are useful for the feet of an invalid, when lying on the sofa, and are knit as follows:—

  Set on one pin 174 stitches, and knit one plain row, after which knit eleven or twelve rows in any fancy stitch to form a border, and then commence double knitting, remembering to continue the border pattern at each side, by knitting the first and last twelve stitches on the pin, every row in the same fancy stitch.

  Continue this until your work is square, when open it like a bag, which must be done by gently taking out your pin and picking up the loops on two pins, each pin taking up the alternate loops. Knit a similar border as that made at the beginning, to each pin of stitches, and fasten off. The foot warmer, or bag, is then completed, and may have a fringe sewn on all round, to give a finish to the whole.

RETICULE BAG.

This is knit in two colours, say violet and green.

  Set on your pin any number of stitches divisible by six, (about seventy-eight is a good size),

2 M

and, after knitting one plain row, fasten on the other colour and knit six stitches with the violet and six with the green, alternately, to the end of the row.

Next row, knit entirely turn-stitch, still knitting six stitches, alternately, of the two colours, taking care that each colour shall be knit in continuation of itself, so as to form distinct stripes.

Continue knitting alternate rows of plain-stitch and seam-stitch, until the work is so long, as when doubled will form a well-proportioned reticule bag. Observe, in passing the wool behind of one colour across the other, not to pull it tight; when completed, fasten off; line with buckram and flannel and violet green or gold silk; put a cord of silk or wool all round, with cord handles and tassels.

This makes a durable handsome bag, and may be knit of even more colours or shades, if preferred.

Reticules knit with other stitches look very pretty, as the herring-bone back-stitch,

The two coloured rib-stitch,

The two coloured chain-stitch.

Or the above striped pattern may be varied by arranging the stripes in checks instead.

Papier machée tops are now made for bags, which look very handsome.

KNIT PETTICOAT.

For delicate children, a knit petticoat is far warmer and lighter than a flannel one, and is knit in double knitting, or in imitation double knitting:—for a child of four or six years of age, set on 400 stitches and knit the proper length, when finish with a few plain rows and fasten off. Sew up the seam to the proper distance behind.

CHILD'S KNIT STAYS.

As stays vary so very much in size, according to the make of the child, it would be difficult to form a receipt, as they should fit well, and the styles of knitters vary so much. It is better to cut, in paper, the exact shape of the stay, and then knit your stay to match it, by constantly measuring. Set on sufficient stitches on your pin to form the depth of the end of the stay, and knit several plain rows until the rize of the shoulder.

Add a stitch at the beginning of every rib until it is sufficiently raised or hollowed, to form the beginning of the shoulder strap, then begin to hollow for the arm hole, decreasing one stitch at the beginning of one row, and the end of the next, and so on, until the hole is deep enough, when commence increasing in the same proportion, to form the rise inside the arm hole.

The body in front should be slightly hollowed towards the middle, and the remainder half of the body finished in the same manner, therefore, it is advisable to set down every widening and narrowing as you do it, in order that the one half may exactly correspond with the other.

These bodies generally have tape shoulder straps, but knit ones can easily be attached, by picking up six stitches on the shoulder, knitting a narrow strip.

They are generally straight at the bottom, and are usually knit of cotton, and are very elastic.

SILK WATCH GUARD.

Set on your pin seven or nine stitches, or even more if the silk is very fine.

Knit in common knitting a yard and a half in length.

Some thread their silk with beads, either black or gold, and introduce them in the knitting to form the initials or name of the wearer, or to make fanciful devices; others knit it entirely with beads of one or more colours, introducing one bead at every stitch, but the plain knitting is the neatest and handsomest of the three kinds, the other two being too gay for daily wear.

CHECKED NAPKIN RINGS.

Choose two colours, say green and gold, set on your pin with the green wool twenty-four stitches and knit one plain row, and then knit as follows:—

1st Row. Knit plain four stitches, alternately of each colour, to the end of the row.

2nd Row. Turn-stitch (four stitches alternately of each colour) to the end of the row, observing to keep the gold colour over the gold, and green over the green.

3rd Row. Plain knit, as in the first row.

4th Row. Turn-stitch, as in the second row.

Repeat these four rows.

The next eight rows are knit exactly the same way, excepting that the colours are arranged so that the green is placed over the gold, and the gold over the green.

Continue alternately changing the situation of the colours every eight rows, until about one and a half nail in length is knit, when fasten off, line with buckram or wire, and silk, putting a bow at the seam where the ends are sewn together, and it is completed. Some knit these in the two coloured rib and two coloured chain-stitch.

SOFA SHAWL.

These are very expensive, but useful for invalids, on account of their warmth and lightness.

Set on five or six hundred stitches and knit a square of double knitting, or imitation double knitting, either with or without a border, if the latter is preferred, the one which is explained with corners is the handsomest, unless fringe is also required, when one of the fringe borders may be added at once.

A BOSOM FRIEND.

Set on your pin seventy stitches, and knit in imitation knitting for about 100 rows, when knit twenty-five stitches of the next row, after which take another pin and fasten off the next twenty stitches, then knit the last twenty-five stitches on another pin.

Continue knitting the twenty-five stitches on one pin in the same stitch, fastening off one stitch at every end and beginning of each row, next to the middle, which forms the hollowing round the neck. When the stitches are reduced to four, fasten off.

Do the same with the other pin containing twenty-five stitches, and fasten off.

Sew pieces of white ribbon to the corners, to hang it by round the neck.

Some persons do not hollow out bosom friends, but knit them square or oblong.

BRACES FOR GENTLEMEN.

These may be knit in wool, cotton, or even silk. The following receipt is for cotton braces (the wool would require fewer stitches, and the silk more than the cotton).

The shape of a brace is wide in the middle, with two narrow ends.

For the first narrow end, set on twenty-four stitches, and knit two nails in length, in imitation of double knitting, or in huckaback-stitch. Widen to forty-eight stitches, and knit a length of nine nails.

Narrow at each end, till reduced to thirty stitches, when put half the loops on one pin and half on another; continue knitting each end separately until three nails long, when fasten off and the one brace is completed. These two last ends should be knit with a button hole in each, which is easily done by again halving the stitches on two pins, and knitting them separately a few rows (say eight or twelve), and afterwards joining them together on one pin again.

THE SPIRAL BOA, OR RUFF.

Set on any quantity of stitches to form an even number of threes, say thirty-six or forty-eight, and knit a plain row in one coloured wool.

Fasten on the other colour, and knit three stitches alternately with each colour.

Next row, turn-stitch back again, knitting each colour over its own shade.

Continue knitting one row plain, and turn-stitch back again, observing each plain row to alter the arrangement of the colours one stitch, which gives the shades a spiral direction.

For a clearer explanation, observe as follows:—

1st Row. Knit plain three grey and three scarlet stitches, alternately to the end of the row.

2nd Row. Turn-stitch back, keeping the colours over their own shades.

3rd Row. Knit two grey stitches, then three scarlet and three grey, alternately, to the end of the row, leaving one grey at the end.

4th Row. Knit the colours over their shade in the last row in turn-stitch.

5th Row. Knit one grey stitch, then three scarlet and three grey, alternately, ending with two grey at the end.

6th Row. Turn-stitch back again.

7th Row. Knit three scarlet and three grey, alternately to the end.

8th Row. Turn-stitch back again.

9th Row. Knit two scarlet, and three grey, and three scarlet alternately, leaving one scarlet at the end.

10th Row. Turn-stitch back again.

11th Row. Knit one scarlet, and three grey, and three scarlet alternately, leaving two scarlet at the end.

12th Row. Knit three grey and three scarlet, alternately and so on. Observe that you keep your wool (which is constantly passed across) always at the wrong side of the knitting, or that side which does not resemble the stitch of a knit stocking. Take care not to pull the wool tight when passing it across.

When a sufficient length is knit, fasten off and sew up, and fill with wadding or wool, which is pushed down with a stick or long knitting pin, and then sewn up.

Three or more colours may be used, but it is rather troublesome to prevent the wools from entangling, on account of their crossing each other so frequently.

SWISS CAP.

This is a kind of woollen tie or frill, to keep the head and ears warm when in an open carriage, and is put on over the border of the bonnet cap, and ties under the chin.

Its length is about six nails and a half, and the depth when double, one nail and a half.

The colours generally chosen are white, blue, and scarlet.

Choose two very thick wooden pins, also some very fine lamb's-wool, and some thick sewing silk of the same colour.

Set on about sixty stitches or more (according to the length desired) on one pin with silk, and knit a plain row, then knit another plain row with wool, putting it three times round the needle every stitch instead of once.

ON KNITTING.

Next row, knit exactly the same.
Next row, knit plain, passing the wool but once round the pin as usual.
Repeat the three rows twice more, and then finish off by knitting a plain row of silk.
Double the piece of knitting in half its depth, so as to form a kind of frill, and run in a ribbon along the third row of long stitches in and out through both the folds or frills, to keep them in place, which also serves as strings to keep the cap on the head by tying under the chin.

A LIGHT SCARF.

Set on 100 stitches, and knit either in one or two colours, seven nails of raised French stitch, or honeycomb-stitch, after which, knit a row plain, putting the wool six times round the pin at every stitch.
Next row, knit plain, taking care to keep the long stitches even.
Knit one row of honeycomb pattern.
Knit another plain row.
Repeat the row of long stitches, by again putting the wool six times round the pin.
Again the plain row, as also the row of honeycomb pattern, and the other plain row.
Continue this till the scarf is long enough to allow of your ending as you began, with seven nails of fancy stitch. A fringe should be added.
These scarfs are often made with the long stitches white, and all the rest coloured, and look very handsome.

AN IMPROVED SOCK.

Use coarse lamb's-wool and middle sized pins; cast on seventeen stitches of coloured wool, this makes the first row in reckoning.
At the end of the second row, make a stitch, which gives a better form to the heel than setting on eighteen at first.
At the end of the third row, add a stitch.
Add a stitch at the end of the fifth, seventh, ninth, eleventh, &c., until you have twenty-five loops on the pin.
Then with a third pin knit ten stitches only.
Continue knitting backwards and forwards the ten stitches only, until you have knit twenty rows.*
At the end of the twenty-first row, make fifteen stitches, so as to have twenty-five stitches again on the pin, and to make it correspond with the other side.
Finish this side of the shoe with as many rows as you knit on the opposite side, decreasing every other row by knitting the two first stitches together at the toe, until there are but seventeen left on the pin, and fasten off.
All this has been knit of red wool.
Then continue with the white wool for twenty-four rows, which will complete the sock, adding at the end of the two first sixth and seventh rows, one to enlarge the boot.
Sew up the shoe to the sock at the instep, and draw up the toe and sew it round the heel and up the leg. A bow may be added, if required, also leather soles.

* At the end of this twenty rows, take up ten stitches, and with white wool knit fourteen rows. Then take on to this middle pin, which has the white even upon it, nine stitches from each side (namely, from the top of the heel) of the red shoe, and knit two rows with coloured wool for the strap.

FLOWER STAND COVERS.

Take a tin can or jar, of the proper size for the flowers to be placed in, and make the knit cover as follows:—

Choose two middle sized steel pins, and rather fine wool of two colours, and begin as follows :—

Set on as many stitches as will measure to the depth of the flower stand, and knit six rows of one colour, letting the alternate rows be plain, and turn-stitch so as to make one side appear like knit stockings on the right side. The next six rows knit of the other colour, and altering the alternate rows of plain and turn-stitch, so as to throw the stocking-stitch inside. Continue thus ribbing the piece of work until you have knit sufficient to go round the base, when fasten off and sew up. Add a fringe at the top, and a circular piece of wire inside, both at top and bottom, is sometimes put to keep it in shape; though the jar generally is sufficient in itself when put inside. A leather or cloth bottom may be added.

KNIT PEN WIPER.

Set on your pin thirty stitches of black wool, and knit eight rows backwards and forwards for the border. The middle part is next begun in the embossed hexagon-stitch of red, or any other colour, still observing to continue the border, by knitting four plain stitches at the beginning and ending of each pin of the black wool.

End by knitting the eight plain rows of black wool as before, to complete the first enclosed square of the pen wiper, do not fasten off, but begin knitting another piece exactly to match the first, which when finished completes the pen wiper. Double it like a book and sew a bit of ribbon down the inside, under which may be passed bits of silk or rag to wipe the pens upon.

CHAPTER XII.

STRAW PLATTING.

GENERAL OBSERVATIONS.

THE precise period when the Dunstable bonnets, made of straw plat, were invented, is unknown, but is supposed to be probably a century and a half old.

The straw platting districts now, include Bedfordshire, Buckinghamshire, Hertfordshire, and Essex. In many other counties the platting is partially followed, and it may be well adopted in other districts for the supply of the neighbourhood.

There are markets for the sale of the large bundles of long straw, both rough and properly stripped; also the short straws, the straw plats, and the bonnets throughout the straw plat districts. The best bonnet market is at St. Alban's, but there are others at Luton, Dunstable, and Braintree. These markets are held only in the morning, from about eight to ten o'clock, when the plat buyers always attend.

ON STRAW PLATTING.

Experiments on the different straws of corn and grass, and on the precise times when they should be cut, whether before or at the time when the grass and corn are ripe, might lead to some discoveries which would add to the durability and beauty of the bonnets.

There are few manufactories in the kingdom in which so little capital is wanted, or the knowledge of the art so soon acquired as in that of straw platting; it is, therefore, particularly suitable for school children, from six years old and upwards, as also for the sons of cottagers to employ their spare moments.

The expense of a *perfect* apparatus for bleaching, rolling, pressing upon, &c., amounts to about three guineas, which will employ any number of persons from one to one hundred; but, by contriving with materials at hand, a guinea alone would almost provide those articles not to be procured at home.

The following are the articles required for platting, and making up the plats into articles for sale:—

	£.	s.	d.
Box for bleaching the straw and bonnets	0	18	0
Mill for rolling and glazing the plat	0	18	0
Bonnet stand for ironing and shaping the bonnet upon	0	11	0
Box-iron with two or three heaters	0	4	6
Tin kettle for dying	0	5	0
Tailor's measure	0	0	6
Earthenware jar for the brimstone	0	0	4
Cloths for ironing	0	0	6
Large iron bason tinned	0	1	6
Straw splitting machines, two at 4½d.	0	0	9
Stone brimstone, bone-dust, needles, &c., about	0	3	0
	£.3	3	0

THE BLEACHING, OR FUMIGATION BOX.

PLATE 24. FIG. 50.

If required to be large enough to hold several bonnets, two stories high and two rows in width, it should be made about three feet long, two feet wide, and two feet deep.

The earthen jar is put in the middle of it, in which the brimstone is put and set fire to when articles are to be bleached, as there is danger of some of the straw falling into the jar and catching fire; it is advisable to have four stout legs or wires about a foot high, fastened round the jar in the centre of the box, and, by carrying a wire round from peg to peg at the top, and the second a little lower, a kind of double railing would be formed round the jar as a protection to the straw (see Fig. 50). The box should be made to shut down very close, for which purpose the lid should have a ledge to fall over the sides of the box, something similar to the lid of a band-box.

MILL FOR ROLLING THE PLAT.

PLATE 24. FIG. 49.

This is difficult to procure well made, and is essential to give the gloss and finish to the straw plat. It should be made of the strongest oak or box-wood, and of the following size, or larger:—

	Inches
The upright sides, from A to B	15¼
Ditto sloped down to (as from C to D)	13¼
Width of these sides, from E to F	1½
Depth, or thickness, from F to G	3¼
The two bars of wood, H and T, in width and depth, to be	3¼
Distance between H and T	11
Circumference of each wheel, K L	7
Length of screw, not including handle	4½
Length of handle	3¼
Depth of bar across, R	½
Length of handle, L	3
Height of upright, M	5¼
Length of upper handle, O	5

The use of the screw is to press the upper wheel nearer upon the lower one, if wanted, as the thickness of the various plats vary materially, and what will press one kind, will not be close enough to do another properly.

The plat being put in at one end, is worked through between the wheel, till the whole is drawn through. The wheels should always be as near together as will just admit the straw without spoiling, as the greater the pressure the finer the gloss. It is a question whether glass rollers would not produce a still higher finish. The holes are made entirely through the wood at the end, A B, to admit of screws, by which the whole mill is fastened to the side of some chest, or press, or door. Care should be taken to place it at the proper height from the floor, for convenience. From three feet and a half to four feet and a half is about the best distance. It should also be placed in a situation where the handle may have free play when turned.

THE BONNET STAND.
PLATE 94. FIG. 48.

This is made of strong deal or oak, and is formed at one end smaller and differently to the other. The one end is circular, and so formed as to fit into the crown of a bonnet or hat; the other end is shaped like the poke, or front. This wood is mounted on a kind of stand, at a convenient height, and is used for ironing the bonnets upon, after being wet with the stiffening.

BOX-IRON.
PLATE 94. FIG. 52.

This is made much in the usual way, excepting that it should be particularly heavy, and have a large handle to enable the person, while ironing, to have a firm grasp.

THE TIN DYEING KETTLE.

This should be made as long as the longest bundle of straw, as also deep and narrow. To have a lid to fit tightly on, and a long handle to carry it about with greater ease. The following dimensions are very suitable:—

	Inches
Length	17
Width	5
Depth	6

ON STRAW PLATTING.

The eathernware jar should be like a little painter's pot.

The tailors' measure is used for measuring round a person's head, to work the crown of the bonnet by.

The ironing cloth is merely to lay between the iron and the bonnet; it might be of calico, or any other common material.

THE STRAW SPLITTER.

This is a useful little machine, for dividing or splitting the straws, and may be procured with almost any number of wires or divisions, from two up to seven or eight. The machine, which is nothing but crossed wires or divisions in iron, is set into a wooden handle, through which the straw is pressed, and thus divided into an equal number of splints or split straws. These machines cost from 2*d.* to 8*d.* each.

ON PREPARING STRAW.

In selecting the straw, great care should be taken as to the sort and the colour. Rye straw is considered the best for platting, but is more difficult to get than wheat, which is preferable to any other sort of common straw. As it should be picked carefully, it is advisable to go to the barn itself, or to send some experienced person thither, previous to the straw being thrashed. Soft good coloured straws should be chosen, as free from blight and spots as possible. The ears should be cut off with scissors (not pulled off), and then the straw is tied in bundles and removed. It is then prepared as follows:—

Cut off at the joint and pull off the outer or loose covering, which process is called shocking.

Each straw will generally cut into three lengths of different thicknesses and sizes. These lengths should be carefully sorted into bundles, taking care to put together not only those of the same thickness, but those also of the same length.

ON BLEACHING STRAW.

Take six quarts of water, and make a strong lather of soap; put in half an ounce of pearlash, and half an ounce of sugar of lead, and make it quite hot. Wash the straws well in it, (keeping it still tied up in little bundles) after which, place the bundles in the fumigating box, which should be air tight, and shut it down close, after having previously lighted the stone brimstone, which should be broken into small pieces in the jar.

Observe carefully, when setting the bundles round the box, that they stand firmly, so as not to fall upon the lighted brimstone and catch fire.

These bundles should not be tied very tightly, but sufficiently loose to stand out a little, as in Fig. 51, Plate 24, to allow of the steam gaining free access to them.

They should remain shut up for twelve or eighteen hours, after which, the bundles should be opened one at a time, cleaned with a cloth, and then tied up again, ready for platting.

ON DYEING STRAW BLACK.

One pound of logwood chips,
Four quarts of water,
A piece of copperas the size of a walnut,
One pennyworth of verdigris.

Let the logwood remain in the water three hours, then boil it half an hour over a slow fire, put in the articles, whether straw, silk, or any thing else, let it boil half an hour, then take out the chips, and the straw, add the copperas and the verdigris, previously dissolved over a slow fire, then put in the straw again, boil it half an hour, let it stand to cool three hours, wash the straw in cold water, and dry it in the air, without putting it in the sun.

To stiffen it, steep gum arabic in small beer, wet the straw with it, and dry it as before.

ANOTHER BLACK DYE.

Three quarts of water,
Three quarts of urine,
Three quarters of a pound of logwood,
Half a pound of alum,
Quarter of a pound of copperas,
Three or four nut galls.

Boil the water, urine, logwood, alum, and nut galls together a quarter of an hour, then add the copperas and boil the whole half an hour, afterwards put in the straw, and let it boil six hours. Let the straw remain in the dye till quite cold, then take it out, spread it on a tray or board to dry in the air, turn it every day for a fortnight, then rub each straw with an old linen duster, tie the straw in bundles, and keep it in a damp place. It should be used up quickly, or else it will decay, without being stiffened.

DIRECTIONS FOR PLATTING.

Each platter should have a separate bundle of straws, and great care taken that the straws in the bundle are exactly alike, unblemished, and equal in quality, as no good platter would work a tough straw with a pliant one. These bundles should have a piece of paper or calico round them to keep them clean, and they are generally kept by school children under the arm to prevent their being mixed with a fellow platter's straws.

Observe as follows:—

1st. Platters should use the second finger and thumb, instead of the forefinger, as this last is very useful in assisting to turn the splints, and thus facilitates the work.

2nd. The straws while being platted should be held with the long ends turned up above the hand, and not below towards the waist; this arrangement keeps the straws cleaner and they are less liable to be bent or broken.

3rd. The straws should be renewed before used too near the end, as the joining is more firm; also avoid if possible, renewing two straws at the same time as the plat will be weakened.

4th. Avoid wetting the straws unless absolutely necessary while platting, as water tends much to diminish the glossy appearance afterwards. In working double splints, there should be just sufficient moisture to make them stick together while being worked.

5th. Each platter should have a piece of board, about a quarter or half a yard long, and three or four inches wide, on which should be wound the plat worked, taking care to cut off the ends of the straw as the plat is worked along, previous to winding it on the roller, to keep it in nice order. These boards should be rounded at the sides, to keep the plat from cracking. Some use rollers, and this last is perhaps the better plan. The circumference of the rollers should be of some settled size, say half a yard, so as to enable the platter easily to ascertain by counting the turns of the plat wound round it, how many yards have been completed.

6th. When the number of yards required are finished, the plat is passed through a roller, as often as is necessary, till well flattened and glazed, when it is folded like a coil of ropes in an oblong shape, ready for making up. The coils should be kept perfectly dry and free from dust, until a sufficient number is made for use.

PLATS.

There are numerous kinds of plats of which the names vary so much in the different countries that it is needless to call them by their names, excepting those universally known by one term; they will therefore be simply distinguished by the number of straws employed in making them.

Plats are sometimes made with whole straws; sometimes with half straws; sometimes with a third or fourth or even seventh parts of straws, according to the quality required.

Another plat is made with double straws; that is laying two splints or part of a straw together with the polished parts outside.

Plats of whole coarse straws are applicable to mats, basket, matting, &c.

Plats with finer whole straws; are used for school children, servant's, or ladies' country bonnets, and are commonly called Dunstable.

The split single, or split double, are made of every quality and number, and vary in price, according to the labour.

Some bonnets are made of paper, of grass, of Tuscan plat, and even of rushes; also of whalebone, of chip, &c.

Plats made of coloured straw may be platted in various patterns, by varying the number or position of the one colour with the other.

The following names of plats, together with their prices per score, are those in general use.

	s.	d.
Whole Dunstable	0	6
Fine whole Dunstable	2	3
Patent Dunstable	2	6
Luton Dunstable	1	4
Devonshire plat of seven or eight	0	0
Bedford Leghorn	4	0
Mixture plats............ 1s. 2d. to	2	0
Tuscan ends	3	0
Rustic plats	0	6
Fine seven plats	0	0
Back-bone straw	0	0
Double seven	0	0
The eleven straw	0	0
The double eleven	0	0
The lustre, or shining, of seventeen straws	0	0
The wave of twenty-two (the straws appear as if worked one way)	0	0
The diamond of twenty-three straws	0	0

PLAT OF THREE.

Double one straw in two, letting the ends be unequal. Lay a second straw upright, between the two ends of the first ; thus forming three ends, which must be held with the points upright, between the finger and thumb of the left hand. Put the right hand straw over the middle straw, flatten it with the finger and thumb.

Put the left hand straw over the middle, also flatten it. Continue thus all the way along, remembering when joining on a new straw, to let the ends all lie on the outer side.

Observe, in platting, that the straw be always entirely folded over, as you would in platting paper, and the edges kept even.

This may be platted with whole straws, or split ones.

ANOTHER PLAT OF THREE.

This is done with very fine split straws, and is similarly platted with the one above, excepting that the straw is not flattened on folding in the patterns, but simply a little twisted, so as to keep the polished edge uppermost. This is called pearl plat, and is used by bonnet makers to form ornamental bonnets.

PLAT OF FOUR.

Double two straws, so that all the ends shall be of unequal lengths, and plat as follows:—
Put the right hand straw, over one, and under one ;
Put the left hand straw, under one ;
Again, the right hand straw over one, and under one, and so on.

ANGULAR PLAT OF FOUR.

This is sometimes called the corner plat,
Put the right hand straw, over one, and under one ;
Again, put the right hand straw, over two, and under the last straw, making it the left hand, or outside straw.
Put the left hand straw, over one, and under one.
Again, put the left hand straw, over two, and under the last straw, making it the right hand straw.

PLAT OF FIVE.

Double two straws, so that the ends shall be of unequal lengths, and add a fifth straw between the left hand, first and second.
Put the right hand straw, over one, and under one ;
Put the left hand straw, over one, and under one ;
Repeat this all along.

PLAT OF SIX.

Double three straws unequally, and begin.
Put the right hand straw, over one, and under two ;
Put the left hand straw, over one, and under one.

PLAT OF SIX.

Double three straws unequally, making six ends to plat with ;
Put the right hand first straw, over one, and under one ;

Put the left hand straw, over one, and under one;
Repeat this.

PLAT OF SEVEN.

Double your straws;
Put the right hand first straw, over one, under one, and over one;
Put the left hand straw, over one, under one, and over one.

ANOTHER PLAT OF SEVEN.

Put the right hand straw, over one, and under two;
Put the left hand straw, over one, and under two;
Repeat this all along.

ANOTHER PLAT OF SEVEN.

Put the right hand straw, over one, under one, and over one.
Put the left hand straw, over one, under one, and over one.
Repeat this.

PLAT OF EIGHT.

Put the right hand straw, over one, and under two;
Put the left hand straw, over two, and under two;
Repeat this.

ANOTHER PLAT OF EIGHT.

Put the right hand straw, over one, and under three;
Put the left hand straw, over one, and under two;
Repeat this.

ANOTHER PLAT OF EIGHT.

Put the right hand straw, over one, under one, and over two;
Put the left hand straw, under one, and over two;
Repeat this.

PLAT OF NINE.

Put the right hand straw, over one, under two, and over one;
Put the left hand straw, over one, under two, and over one;
Repeat this.

ANOTHER PLAT OF NINE.

Put the right hand straw, over one, under one, over one, and under one;
Put the left hand straw, over one, under one, over one, and under one;
Repeat this.

ANOTHER PLAT OF NINE.

Put the right hand straw, over one, under one, and over two;

Put the left hand straw, over one, under one, and over two;
Repeat this.

PLAT OF TEN.

Put the right hand straw, over one, under two, and over two;
Put the left hand straw, over one, under two, and over one;
Repeat this.

ANOTHER PLAT OF TEN.

Put the right hand straw, over one, under one, over one, and under two;
Put the left hand straw, over one, under one, over one, and under one;
Repeat this.

PLAT OF ELEVEN.

Put the right hand straw, over one, under one, over one, under one, and over one;
Put the left hand straw, over one, under one, over one, under one, and over one;
Repeat this.

ANOTHER PLAT OF ELEVEN.

Put the right hand straw, over three, under three;
Put the left hand straw, over three, and under one;
Continue thus all along.

ANOTHER PLAT OF ELEVEN.

Put the right hand straw, over two, under two, and over two;
Put the left hand straw, over two, and under one;
Repeat this.

ANOTHER PLAT OF ELEVEN.

Put the right hand straw, over one, under two, and over two;
Put the left hand straw, over one, under two, and over two;
Continue this.

PLAT OF TWELVE.

Put the right hand straw, over one, under two, and over two;
Put the left hand straw, over one, under two, over two, and under one;
Continue this.

PLAT OF THIRTEEN.

Put the right hand straw, over one, and under two, over two;
Put the left hand straw, over one, under two, over two, and under one.

ANOTHER PLAT OF THIRTEEN.

Put the right hand straw, over one, under one, over three, and under one;

Put the left hand straw, over one, under one, over three, and under one;
Repeat this.

ANOTHER PLAT OF THIRTEEN.

Put the right hand straw, over one, under one, over one, under one, and over one;
Put the left hand straw over one, under one, over one, under one, over one, under one, and over one.
Repeat the same.

PLAT OF FOURTEEN.

Put the right hand straw, over one, under two, over two, under two, and over one;
Put the left hand straw, over one, under two, and over two.

PLAT OF FIFTEEN.

Put the right hand straw, over one, under two, and over two;
Put the left hand straw, over one, under two, and over two.

ANOTHER PLAT OF FIFTEEN.

Put the right hand straw, over one, under one, over one, under one, over one, under one, and over one;
Put the left hand straw, over one, under one, over one, under one, over one, under one, and over one.

PLAT OF SIXTEEN.

Put the right hand straw, over one, under three, over three, and under one;
Put the left hand straw, over two, under three, and over three;
Continue this.

HOLLOW SPIRAL STRAW WORK.

This is used for ornamented bonnets, and when made with a great many straws forms a basket, into which may be put fruit, and other small light things.

Take any number of uneven straws, from five upwards, to fifteen or twenty-one.

If five are taken, tie them securely together in a knot, and spread out the straws, laying a pencil or other round thing upright upon the knot, and begin working, making each straw as it is folded over, lie across in a horizontal position.

Lay one straw, across over two straws,
Miss the next straw,
Lay the next again across over two straws,
Again miss the next straw,
Repeat this continually until sufficient is made, and fasten off.

THE TUSCAN HAT, COMMONLY CALLED LEGHORN BONNETS.

The manufacture of straw bonnets is a considerable employment in Tuscany. The platting is chiefly carried on in the neighbourhood of Florence, Pisa, and Sienna.

The straws used in working those flats, which is the term for large flat circular plats, is grown in barren and mountainous districts, and is produced from a kind of wheat, said to be like cape wheat, of which the grain is very small. This straw, though slender, has much consistency, and the upper part of the stalk being hollow is easily dried. It is pulled out of the earth before the grain begins to form. After being freed from the soil that adheres to the root, it is formed into small sheaves for winnowing. The part above the last joint of the stem is then plucked off, the ear remaining attached to it, this being done, it is bleached alternately by the dew and the sun-shine; rain is very injurious and destroys much of its proper colour. The lower parts of the straw are treated in the same manner, and employed in forming flats of an inferior quality. The upper parts, torn off just to the knot, are sorted according to their degrees of fineness. This stapling is made with much care, and usually affords straw of three different prices. A quantity of straw worth but 4½d. will, after undergoing this process, be sold for 4s. 7d.

The tress is formed sometimes of seven or nine straws, but generally of thirteen. For the latter number, tie them together at one end ; then divide them, placing six straws on the left side, and seven on the right. The seventh or outermost on the right, is to be turned down by the finger and thumb of the right hand, and brought up under two straws, over two, and under two, thus seven straws will be placed on the left hand ; then the finger and thumb of the left hand is to turn the seventh or outermost straw on the left side, and bring it up under two straws, over two, and under two, and seven straws will again be on the right hand, and so on alternately doubling and platting the outermost seventh straw from side to side until it becomes too short to cross over; then take another straw and put it under the short end at the point of the angle, and by another straw coming over and under the joined one from both sides of the angle, in the operation of platting, it will become fastened ; the short ends always being left out underneath the plat. Continue until a piece of about twenty yards or more, is completed. As fast as it is worked, it is rolled on a cylinder of wood : when it is finished, the projecting ends and ears are cut off, it is then passed with force between the hand and a piece of wood, cut with a sharp edge to press and polish it. The tresses, when prepared, are used so that a complete hat shall be made of one piece ; they are sewed together with raw silk ; the diameter the of various kinds of hat is in general the same ; the only difference being in the degree of fineness, and consequently the number of turns which the plat has to make, varies.

These hats have from twenty to eighty such turns, the number regulating the price from 9s. to £20.

The Tuscan plat, made from Italian straw, and Tuscan bonnets, have since become a considerable manufacture in this country.

ENGLISH IMITATION LEGHORN PLAT.

A kind of grass has been discovered in America, England, and in Ireland, which, upon repeated trials, has been found to answer as well, and is broke equally fine as the Tuscan straw. It is called the crested dog's tail, and grows on barren poor soils. Its flower stalks are so remarkably harsh and tough that cattle will not touch them, and they remain all the winter in the fields useless. They are called, in Irish, trawnyeens ; hence the Irish saying, " When a thing is useless," it is not worth a trawnyeen." This has been dried and platted, and made up by the Irish, and it said likely to become a productive manufacture.

ARTICLES MADE UP OF STRAW PLAT.

Bonnets of all descriptions and sizes.
Boy's straw hats.

Boy's straw caps.
Baskets and reticules.
Mats.
Basses.
Matting.

BONNETS.

In making these up, begin by preparing the plat for the crown by pulling out the edge, as the outer circle must be larger than the inner one Sew the plat, making long stitches on the wrong side, and laying one plat about half or more under the preceding one. No good directions for bonnet making can be given in writing, it is therefore recommended to the inexperienced to take a lesson from a bonnet maker, or to pick an old one to pieces, as a kind of guide. When made up to shape or pattern, the bonnet, if it requires it, is bleached in the sulphur-box, after which, when quite dry, it is sponged all over, inside and outside, with the stiffening prepared according to the receipt mentioned below; when dry, another wash of stiffening is put on, and then, when quite dry, spread a wet piece of jaconet muslin over the bonnet, and press it with the box-iron upon the bonnet block until it is quite in proper shape. This pressing is very hard work, and requires much strength and weight. The bonnet is then wired and papered.

RECEIPTS FOR STIFFENING.

The best stiffening is that made of buffalo's hide or vellum, which may be procured in London and Liverpool, cut in shreds, and sold at 8d. a pound. Others use bone-dust, ivory shavings, also isinglass for best, and white glue for common bonnets.

VELLUM STIFFENING.

Boil a quarter of a pound of vellum shavings in two quarts of soft water for six or seven hours, filling it up occasionally until quite glutinous, then let it stand a few minutes to settle, pour it out into a basin, and it will become a thick jelly. A second two quarts of water may be added to the sediment left in the pot, and after a second boiling, will form a second quantity of almost as strong a jelly.

When used, melt up a quart of the jelly, and add a sufficient quantity of oxalic acid to make it white in the degree desired, a table spoonful to a quart is a very good average measure for good bonnets, more is required for the very best, and less for servants and school girls, &c. This acid, if too strong, turns the straws a pink colour.

Observe, that oxalic acid is a most dangerous poison, and should be kept locked up in a safe place.

BONE DUST STIFFENING.

Put half a pint of bone dust to half a pint of water, and boil it eight hours; then strain it through a thick earn strainer into a basin, let it stand about five minutes, and pour it very carefully into another vessel, as there will be a sediment at the bottom. Put the stiffening on the straw articles with a clean brush, making them quite wet. Hold the bonnets before the fire a few minutes, pulling them into shape, and afterwards hang them to dry for six hours, then with a sponge damp them with warm water, and spread over them a fine cloth or handkerchief, and press them well with a box iron. Take off the cloth, gloss the bonnets, then wire and paper the crown.

N.B. The white bonnets should have a little sugar of lead put in the stiffening, and they should be steamed in the brimstone a second time, after being made up, previous to being stiffened.

ON CLEANING BONNETS.

Take out the wires, and wash the bonnet with common brown soap and water. Bleach them with stone brimstone, a bit the size of a walnut is sufficient for twelve bonnets; dry, and mend them if required, stiffen them according to the receipt and press them.

ON TURNING BONNETS.

The bonnet is picked to pieces, and the plat turned, so that which was inside is then outwards, the bonnet should be cleaned well before being unpicked.

HATS.

Men's and boy's hats are easily made of straw, and the brims may be narrow or broad at pleasure; baby's straw hats are generally looped up with a plat loop.

Boy's caps may be made of straw also, and are very serviceable.

MATS.

These are made of plats also, and may be made round or oblong for the table, as also for door mats. The latter requires a very wide plat.

Very pretty mats may be made of fine straws or rushes, about twenty taken in the hand at once, and connected together in a similar manner as the straw work of a bee-hive, either with very fine split osiers, which are passed through the straws easily when a hole is bored through with a kind of packing needle threaded with twine, braid answers very well indeed. The stitches should be very regular, and if for a circle or oval, observe to let the stitches radiate from the centre. Baskets look very pretty when made in this way, also church basses, which also are made of straw plats, and sewed over sackcloth after it is made to the shape of a cushion, and properly filled with bits of straw, bran, or flock, &c.

BOBBIN MAKING.
PLATE 24. FIG. 53, 54, 55.

This is done on a cushion, and with bobbin handles similar to those used by lace makers; Fig. 54, a cushion stuffed with wool is firmer than one of feathers, it is rather heavier, but that is not an objection. The cost of the bobbin handles is four-pence each, and there are nine required. It is preferable to have the handles made with two *necks*, any turner accustomed to make lace bobbins will know what is meant.

The best cotton for use is knitting cotton, and for very broad bobbin, a double thread of middling fineness is preferable to a single coarse one. It is done as follows:—

Let the nine threads be tied together, and fastened upon the top of the cushion with a stout pin; Fig. 53, then separate them so that five fall on one side, and four on the other. Fig. 55.

The object is to pass No. 9 *over* Nos. 7 and 8, and *under* Nos. 5 and 6; therefore, take up the two latter bobbins in the right hand, No. 5 between the thumb and first finger, and No. 6 between the first and second fingers; the thumb and first finger may, notwithstanding, grasp No. 9, and throw it over Nos. 7 and 8 to the left hand side of the cushion, next to No. 4. Lay Nos. 5 and 6 in the places from which they were raised, and perform the same process described with the left hand, taking up Nos. 9 and 4, and passing No. 1 across to the right hand. The bobbin, as it is made, may be wound several times round a card at the top of the cushion, and then passed under a large pin. Fasten on a single thread, by tying the two ends together, and looping it round a pin stuck just above where you are at work, it is thus perfectly strong, and a knot does not occur in the bobbin.

The outer thread to the left hand, over two, and under two; the same with the right hand.

INDEX.

	Page
ANGULAR STITCH, see *Stitches in Needlework* ...	
APRONS	76
——— Clear Muslin	77
——— Common for Ladies	78
——— Working	ib.
——— Cooking	79
——— Dress	76
——— Evening	78
——— Frilled	77
——— Gentleman's Working	79
——— Grocers'	ib.
——— Hollowed at the bottom	77
——— Muslin	ib.
——— Nursery	17
——— Pantry	79, 179
——— Silk	77
——— Pockets	78
——— with Bibs	ib.
——— with Shoulder-straps	79
ARTICLES USED IN THE LAUNDRY, see *Washing*	
ARTICLES USED IN THE WASH-HOUSE, see *Washing*	
BABY LINEN	16
——— General Observations on ...	17
——— Articles necessary for Wardrobe ...	16
——— ——— for lending the Poor ...	17
——— Band	28
——— Basket for Nursery	44
——— Bassinette Cover	41
——— Bib	38
——— Bodies, full, for Robes	33
——— ——— Plain	34
——— ——— Fancy	ib.
——— Bottle, Leather suck of	45
——— Caps, material for	17
——— ——— Day	20
——— ——— Flannel	19
——— ——— Foundling	18
——— ——— Full French	21
——— ——— French	ib.
——— ——— Horse-shoe	ib.
——— ——— with Runners	19
——— Cloak, Flannel	38

	Page
BABY Cloak, Silk or Merino	38
——— Cockades	22
——— Cot, Hanging	43
——— ——— Travelling	ib.
——— Cradle and Cover	42
——— Crib and Cover	ib.
——— Crib, or Cradle Furniture ...	44
——— Chair for Day	45
——— ——— for Travelling, Night ...	46
——— Frocks and Robes	32
——— Gowns, First Flannel	25
——— ——— Another	26
——— ——— for the Poor	ib.
——— ——— Second size Night Flannel	27
——— ——— First size Day Flannel ...	ib.
——— ——— Another	28
——— ——— First Calico Night Gown ...	29
——— ——— Another, ...	30
——— ——— Another	ib.
——— Hood, for Boy or Girl	40
——— Napkins	29
——— ——— Another sort	ib.
——— Pelisse	38
——— ——— Long, ...	39
——— ——— Summer	40
——— Petticoats	32
——— Pilcher	28
——— Pincushion	45
——— Pinafores	30
——— ——— with Lappets	31
——— ——— Waste Not	ib.
——— ——— Tidy, or Dress	ib.
——— Receiver	37
——— Robes	32
——— Rosettes	22
——— Savers	28
——— Shawl	37
——— Shirts, First Open	22
——— ——— Close, or Second ...	23
——— Sleeves, the Round	35
——— ——— the Common	ib.
——— ——— the Triangular	36

INDEX.

	Page
BABY Sleeves, Long	37
—— Skirts	33
BADGE, Clergyman's	149
—— School Girl's	214
BANDS, Clergyman's	150
—— Infant's	28
BAGS, Boot,	210
—— Brush and Comb	209
—— Clothes	
—— Family	1
—— Night Gown	208
—— Nursery	210
—— Rag	15
—— Travelling	214
—— Work	213
BASKETS, lending out for the Poor	17
—— Nursery	44
—— Work, how to line	214
—— —— for Servants	15
BATHING Gown	61
—— Cap	68
BEDS, see *Upholstery*	
BELTS, Men's	83
—— Hunter's	ib.
—— Coachmen's	ib.
BIASSING, see *Stitches in Needlework*	
BINDING, see *Stitches in Needlework*	
BLANKETS, see *Upholstery*	
BLEACHING LIQUID, see *Receipts*	
BLEACH Linen, Wool, &c., see *Receipts*	
BLINDS, see *Upholstery*	
BLUE CHECKS	12
BOA, fur	176
BOBBIN, making	290
BOLSTERS, making, see *Upholstery*	
BOOK Cases	211
—— Covers	211
BOMBAZINE, to clean, see *Receipts*	
BONNETS, Children's	150
—— —— soft, for young	ib.
—— —— drawn up	151
—— —— soft, for two years old	151
—— —— soft, for three years old	152
—— —— soft, for four or five years old	153
—— —— soft, for eight years old	151
—— —— soft, another sort	153
—— Women's	158
—— —— Another shape	159
—— —— Member of the Society of Friends	160
—— —— For a Servant	ib.
—— —— School Girls	161

	Page
Box Clothes, see *House Linen*	
—— Tin	15
—— Work	15
—— Carriage	16
BRAIDING, see *Stitches in Needlework*	
BRASS Ornaments, to preserve, see *Receipts*	
BREAKFAST CLOTHS, see *House Linen*	
BRIDAL FAVOURS	170
BROAD HEMS, rules for cutting out	14
BUGS, to destroy and prevent, see *Receipts*	
BUSTLES	83
BUTTON Holes, see *Stitches in Needlework*	
BUTTONS, to make	5
—————— How to keep	1
CALICO, on choosing, see *Purchasing Goods*	
CALICO FURNITURE, to clean, see *Receipts*	
CALECHE, or Woman's large Hood	162
CAMBRIC, on choosing, see *Purchasing Goods*	
CANDLESTICK Case	212
CAPS for Infants, see *Baby Linen*	
—— for Boys	153
—— —— Soft and Light	154
—— —— Porringer, Cloth	ib.
—— —— for a Young Child	ib.
—— —— Another	ib.
—— for an Infant Boy	ib.
—— for a Boy of six years old	155
—— Another	ib.
—— for a Boy of seven or eight	156
—— for an older Boy	ib.
—— Boy's neat	157
—— Gentleman's Travelling	156
—— Another	ib.
—— for a Lady or Gentleman	157
—— Lady's Riding	ib.
—— Workman's Paper	ib.
CAPS of Muslin, or Thick Material	61
—— Woman's, Day or Night	62
—— —— very neat Night	ib.
—— Young Servant's Day	63
—— Very neat shape	64
—— Another	ib.
—— School Girl's	65
—— Favourite Lady's Night	ib.
—— Neat Day or Night	66
—— Another	ib.
—— An Old Woman's	ib.
—— A Poor Woman's Night	67
—— A Neat Old Fashioned	ib.
—— Bathing	68
CAPS of a thin material, as Net, &c.	124

INDEX.

	Page
CAPS Day	124
—— for a Young Lady	125
—— Morning	ib.
—— Undress	ib.
—— Dress Morning	126
—— Plain, for an Elderly Lady	ib.
—— for a Member of the Society of Friends	ib.
—— for an Elderly Friend	127
—— Bonnet	ib.
—— another Shape	ib.
—— Helmet Morning	ib.
—— Bonnet Cap	128
—— another Shape	129
—— Handkerchief Bonnet	128
—— Bonnet Cap for a Child	129
—— Widows	ib.
—— Velvet	130
—— Silk	ib.
—— Half Cap, or Lappets	129
CAPES, see *Collars.*	
CAPETTE	129
CARE of a Lady's Wardrobe	119
—— of a Gentleman's Wardrobe	121
CARD-CASE, or Sachet	212
CARPETS, see *Upholstery*	
—— to Scour, see *Receipts*	
CARRIAGE Cloths, see *House Linen*	
Chain-Stitch, see *Stitches in Needlework*	
—— Fancy	ib.
—— on Gathers	9
CHAIR for Invalids	216
—— and other Covers, see *Upholstery*	
CHAMBER BOTTLE Cloths, see *House Linen*	
CHAMBER BUCKET Cloths, see *House Linen*	
CHEAT, Boy's	147
CHECKS, see *Purchasing Goods*	
CHEESE CLOTHS, see *House Linen*	
CHEMISETTE	97
CHINA CLOTHS, see *House Linen*	
CHINTZES, see *On Purchasing Goods*	
—— to Clean, see *Receipts*	
Church Seats and Basses, see *Upholstery*	
CLEAN, Curtains, see *Receipts*	
—— Gold and Silver Lace	ib.
—— Gloves	ib.
—— Shoes	ib.
—— Sponges	ib.
—— Hair Brushes	ib.
—— Paint	ib.
—— Cotton, Woollen, Silk	ib.
CLEAR STARCHING, see *Washing*	

	Page
CLERGYMAN'S Dress	147
—— Cassock	ib.
—— Gown	ib.
—— Surplice	149
—— Sash, or Badge	ib.
—— Scarf, or Hood	ib.
—— Bands	ib.
CLERK'S Gown	150
CLOAKS, Infants'	38
—— Womans'	163
—— —— Short, or Mantelet	164
—— —— Carriage	ib.
—— —— Garden	ib.
—— —— Servants	ib.
—— Old Woman's, and Hood	ib.
—— School Girls'	165
—— Boys'	ib.
CLOTH, see *On Purchasing Goods*	
CLOTHES BAG, see *House Linen*	
COCKADES	22
COLLARS, Gentlemens'	145
—— Boys'	146
—— General Rules for Cutting	14
—— Women's	93
—— —— Round	94
—— —— another	99
—— for Infants	94
—— Square	95
—— Mourning	99
—— for a Cloak	94
—— to wear over a Shawl	ib.
—— a very Pretty one	95
—— for Walking in	ib.
—— Morning	96
—— for a Habit Shirt	97
—— Pointed	ib.
COLLARETTE	98
COMB BAG	209
COMPLETING WORK, General Rules	10
COOKING CLOTHS, see *House Linen*	
CORONATION BRAID	8
CORSETS, see *Stays*	180
CORD, sewn on	8
CORAL PATTERN, see *Stitches in Needlework*	
COT for Infants	43
—— or Hammock	198
COTTONS, to Clean, see *Receipts*	
—— Sewing, how to keep	1
—— how worked	ib.
COVERS, CASES, &c.	208
COUNTERPANES, see *Upholstery*	

2 P

INDEX.

	Page
COURT-PLAISTER, to make, see *Receipts*	...
COVERLETS, see *Upholstery*	...
CRACK, on mending one	4
CRAPE, see *On Purchasing Goods*	...
CRADLE	42
CRAVAT	147
CRIB	42
CROSSWISE, how to Cut	14
CURTAINS, see *Upholstery*	...
———— Moreen to Clean, see *Receipts*	...
CUFFS, Tidy	75
———— Morning	ib.
———— Satin	ib.
———— Dress	ib.
———— Double	76
———— Mourning	ib.
———— Muslin	ib.
———— Mourning	ib.
———— another Shape	ib.
CUTTING OUT, General Rules	14
CUTTING OUT Dresses	107
DARNING, see *Stitches in Needlework*	...
DINNER NAPKINS	179
DIVAN, see *Upholstery*	...
DOWN, see *Fur*	175
DOUBLE HERRING-BONING	9
DRAWERS, see *Trowsers*	50
———— Women's	53
———— Women's	ib.
———— Men's	54
DRAPERY, see *Upholstery*	...
DRESSES, see *Gowns*	106
———— see *Frocks*	32
DRESSING-GOWNS, Men's	68
———————— Plain	ib.
———————— Cloak	70
———————— Ladies'	69
———————— Jacket	70
———————— Case, or Tidy for Travelling	208
DRESSER-CLOTHS, see *House Linen*	...
DUSTERS, see *House Linen*	...
DOYLEYS, ib.	...
DYE Cotton Nankeen, see *Receipts*	...
———— Furniture ib.	...
———— Gloves ib.	...
EAU DE COLOGNE, see *Receipts*	...
FANCY BOBBIN EDGING, see *Stitches on Needlework*	
———— Button-hole Stitch ib.	...
———— Chain-stitch ib.	...
———— Herring-bone Stitch ib.	...
FIANCEE, or Neck Tie	79

	Page
FLANNEL, see *On Purchasing Goods*	...
———— Scouring, see *Upholstery*	...
FLANNEL, Petticoats, Women's	72
———————— Small Size	ib.
———————— Girl's Large Size	ib.
———————— Smaller	ib.
———————— Ten years old	ib.
———————— Six years old	ib.
FLEAS, to Destroy, see *Receipts*	...
FLIES, to Destroy, see *Receipts*	...
FLOUNCES, Rules for Cutting	14
FOOTSTOOLS, see *Upholstery*	...
FRENCH POLISH, see *Receipts*	...
FRILLS,	74
———— General Rules for Cutting	14
———— Simple	ib.
———— Neat	ib.
———— Crimped	ib.
———— For Children	ib.
———— Dress	ib.
———— Otherwise called Ruche	ib.
FROCKS, Infant's, see *Baby Linen*	...
———— Child's simple	114
———— ———— full	ib.
———— ———— simple, three quarters	115
———— ———— plain	ib.
———— ———— full	116
———— ———— Morning	ib.
———— ———— for a Boy	ib.
———— ———— jean tunic	117
———— ———— surtout	ib.
FRONT for Shirts	147
FUNERAL, articles worn at	123
FUR AND DOWN	175
———— Muff	176
———— Boa	ib.
———— Tippet	177
———— Opera	ib.
———— How to clean	ib.
———— To clean Down	ib.
———— How to Preserve, see *Receipts*	177
FURNITURE, Hints on Buying, see *Receipts*	...
GAGING, see *Stitches in Needlework*	...
GATHERING, see *Stitches in Needlework*	...
GAUFERING, see *On Washing*	...
GENERAL OBSERVATIONS ON NEEDLEWORK	1
GENERAL OBSERVATIONS ON BABY LINEN	17
———————————— ON COMPLETING WORK	10
———————————— ON CUTTING OUT	14
———————————— ON GENTLEMAN'S WARDROBE	121

INDEX.

	Page
GENERAL OBSERVATIONS ON LADY'S WARDROBE	119
———— ON LINEN PRESS	187
———— ON NEEDLEWORK	1
———— ON PURCHASING WORK	11
———— ON PACKING	121
GENERAL RULES FOR COMPLETING WORK	10
GERMAN HEMMING, see *Stitches in Needlework*	
GINGHAMS, see *On Purchasing Goods*	
GLOVES	175
———— to Wash, see *Receipts*	
———— to Clean, ib.	
———— to Dye, ib.	
———— Cases	209
GLUE, How to make, see *Receipts*	
GOWNS	106
———— General Observations on	ib.
———— On Cutting out	197
———— Side pieces	108
———— Back Shoulder pieces	ib
———— Shoulder straps	ib.
———— Skirts	109
———— Plain high body	ib.
———— Full French body	ib.
———— Wrapping high body	110
———— High, to open in front	ib.
———— Another pattern	111
———— Plain low body	ib.
———— Another French low front	ib.
———— Trimming low bodies	ib.
———— French low full body	112
———— Grecian low body	ib.
———— A simple low body	113
———— Full low body	ib.
———— Select dresses	ib.
———— Nursing	ib.
———— Bathing	61
GOWN, Clergyman's	148
———— Clerk's	150
GRAVE CLOTHES	124
GREASE, to Remove, see *Receipts*	
GUSSETS, to Cut	14
HAM AND BACON BAGS, see *House Linen*	
HATS AND CAPS	153
HAT LININGS	14
HAT-BANDS	123
HABIT-SHIRTS	99
HEAVY PINCUSHIONS	15
HEMMING, see *Stitches in Needlework*	
HERRING-BONEING	ib.
HONEY-COMBING	ib.
HOOD, Oiled Silk	162

	Page
HORSE-SHOE STITCH, see *Stitches on Needlework*	
HOUSE LINEN	178
———— Bed Room Linen	ib.
———— ———— Sheets	181
———— ———— Pillow Cases	183
———— ———— Towels	ib.
———— ———— Toilet Covers	ib.
———— ———— Pincushions	ib.
———— Table Linen	179
———— ———— Table Cloths	183
———— ———— Dinner Napkins	ib.
———— ———— ———— how to fold	ib.
———— ———— Doyleys	184
———— ———— Large Tray Napkins	179
———— ———— Small ditto ditto	ib.
———— Pantry Linen	
———— ———— Knife-box Cloths	184
———— ———— Pantry Cloths	ib.
———— ———— Dresser Cloths	ib.
———— ———— Plate-basket Cloths	ib.
———— ———— China Cloths	ib.
———— ———— Glass Cloths	ib.
———— ———— Lamp Cloths	185
———— ———— Aprons	ib.
———— ———— Waiting Gloves	ib.
———— Housemaids' Linen	180
———— ———— House Dusters	185
———— ———— Scouring Flannel	ib.
———— ———— Paint Cloths	ib.
———— ———— Chamber Bottle do.	ib.
———— ———— ———— bucket do.	ib.
———— ———— Clothes Bags	ib.
———— ———— Pinafores	185
———— Kitchen Linen	180
———— ———— Table Cloths	186
———— ———— Dresser Cloths	ib.
———— ———— Cooking Cloths	180
———— ———— Roller Towels	180, 186
———— ———— Dusters	ib. ib.
———— ———— Tea Cloths	ib. ib.
———— ———— Knife Cloths	ib. ib.
———— ———— Pudding Cloths	ib. ib.
———— ———— Jelly Bags	ib. ib.
———— ———— Ham and Bacon Bags	ib. ib
———— ———— Cheese Cloths	ib. ib.
———— Stable Linen	180
———— ———— Carriage Cloths	ib.
———— ———— Paint Cloths	ib.
———— ———— Flannels	ib.
———— ———— Saddle Cases	ib.
———— General Observations	ib.

INDEX.

	Page		Page
House Linen, Remarks	180	Opera, or Ruff, see *Fur*	177
Housewife	212	Packing, Directions for	120
Infant's Wardrobe	16	Paint Cloths, see *House Linen*	
Imitation of Maple Wood, see *Receipts*		—— Spots, to remove, see *Receipts*	
India Rubber Varnish	ib.	Pelerines, see *Collars*	100
Ink, Marking, to Make	ib.	—— long	101
—— to Remove Spots of	ib.	—— Frill for	ib.
Iron-Moulds, to Remove	ib	—— Morning	100
Jacket, Woman's Night	55	—— Handsome	193
—— Dressing	70	Pelisse, Baby's, see *Baby Linen*	
Jelly Bags, see *House Linen*		—— Child's	118
Knife and Fork Case	211	Petticoats, Flannel	72
Knitting, see *separate Index*		—— Calico, &c.	104
Ladder, on taking up	4	—— Skirts for	ib.
Lamp Cloths, see *House Linen*		—— Bodies or waists	ib.
Lappetts	129	—— Nursing	105
Lavender Water, to Make, see *Receipts*		—— Pieces, fulled in bands, how to cut	15
Lawn, see *On Purchasing Goods*		Pillows, see *Upholstery*	
Lending Linen, for the Poor	17	Pillow Cases, see *House Linen*	
Leggets	52	Pinafores and Saccarines	130
Linen, see *On Purchasing Goods*		—— Child's Surtout	ib.
Linen, Baby	16	—— Close or Smock Frock	131
—— Men and Women's	46	—— Large sized	132
—— House	178	—— for Boys	ib.
—— Press	187	—— Saccarines	133
Linings	14	—— Housemaid's	134 & 180
Mantua-Maker's Hem, see *Stitches in Needlework*		—— School Girl's	135
Marking	ib.	—— Child's	135
Mantelet	164	—— Surgeon's	ib.
Mat	210	—— Waggoner's Smock	136
Mattresses, see *Upholstery*		Pincushions, Nursery, see *Baby Linen*	
Mending a Crack	4	—— heavy	15
Mildew, to remove, see *Receipts*		—— other sorts	213
Modesty	102	—— covers, see *House Linen*	
Mourning	122	Piping, see *Stitches in Needlework*	
Muff	176	—— how to cut	14
Napkins, Infants, see *Baby Linen*		Pitch and Oil spots to remove, see *Receipts*	
—— Dinner, see *House Linen*		Plaiting, see *Stitches in Needlework*	
Needles, How to keep	1	Plate Basket Bag, see *House Linen*	
Needle Case	15 & 213	Platting, see *Straw Work*	
Needle Work, Observations on	1	Pockets	73
Neck-tie	79	—— for Aprons	78
Neck Handkerchief	169	—— Watch	216
Night-jacket	55	—— Handkerchiefs	170
—— Gown	56	—— Case	209
—— Another pattern	57	Portfolio for a Carriage	215
—— Gored	ib.	—— for travelling	ib.
Night-gown Bag	208	Powder for Infant's Dust bags see *Receipts*	
—— Chair	45	Pot Pourri	ib.
Nosegay Case	212	Preserve Linen, Woollen, Furs, &c. ib.	
Nursery Bag	210	Prepare Rabit Skins	ib.

INDEX.

	Page		Page
PRINTS, see *On Purchasing Goods*	...	RECEIPTS ———— ———— blue	... ib.
PUDDING CLOTHS, see *House Linen*	...	———— Leather (wash for)	... 224
PUFFING, see *Stitches in Needle Work*	...	———— ——— Gloves like tan	... ib.
PURCHASING GOODS	... 11	———— ——— ——— purple	... ib.
———————— Blue Checks	... 12	———— Eau de Cologne	... 226
———————— Calico	... ib.	———— Fleas, to destroy	... 227
———————— Cambric	... ib.	———— Flies, to destroy	... ib.
———————— Cloth	... 13	———— French polish for Furniture	... 233
———————— Crape	... 13	———— ——————— Boots and Harness	... 228
———————— Flannels	... ib.	———— Fur, to preserve	... 225
———————— Lawn	... 12	———— Furniture, hints on buying	... 230
———————— Linen	... ib.	———— Grease to remove from Silk	... 220
———————— Muslin Checks	... ib.	———— Another Receipt	... ib.
———————— Prints, Chintzes, &c.	... 13	———— ——— from Silk or Woollen	... ib.
———————— Satins	... ib.	———— ——— from Linen	229 & ib.
———————— Silks	... ib.	———— Glue to make	... 232
———————— Stuffs	... ib.	———— Imitation of Maple wood	... 233
QUILTING, see *Stitches in Needle Work*	...	———— Indian Rubber Varnish	... 231
RAISE THE SURFACE OF VELVET, see *Receipts*	...	———— Ink, permanent marking	... 217
RECEIVER, see *Baby Linen*	...	———— ——— red marking	... ib.
RECEIPTS	... 217	———— ——— to remove spots of	... ib.
———— Balls to remove Grease	... 229	———— ——— to remove, common	... 218
———— Another Receipt	... ib.	———— ——— from Cloth, &c.	... ib.
———— Bleaching Liquid	... 218	———— Ironmoulds, to remove	... 222
———— Bleach Wool	... 229	———— Lavender water to make	... 226
———— Bleach Yellow Linen	... 223	———— Mildew to take out	... 221
———— Blonde to Wash	... 223	———— Paint spots, to remove	... ib.
———— ———— Town Washed	... 223	———— Pitch and Oil spots to remove	... 220
———— ———— Wool	... 229	———— Powder for Infant's dust bags	... 226
———— Brass Ornaments to keep	... 233	———— Pot-pourri	... ib.
———— Bugs to prevent	... 227	———— ——— quicker sort	... ib
———— Bugs to destroy	... ib.	———— Prepare Rabbit skins	... 227
———— Carpets to scour	... 222	———— Preserve Linen from Moths	... 225
———— Clean Bombazine	... 221	———— ——— Woollens and Blankets	... ib.
———— ——— Brass Ornaments	... 233	———— ——— Furs	... ib.
———— ——— Cotton Silk, Woollen	... 229	———— ——— Blonde, Satin, &c.	... 224
———— ———	... 221	———— ——— Gilt Frames	... 228
———— ——— Chintz	... 222	———— Raise the Surface of Velvet	... 226
———— ——— Curtains, Moreen	... 229	———— Restore rusty Silk	... 221
———— ——— Calico Furniture	... 222	———— ——— Scorched Linen	... 222
———— ——— Gold and Silver Lace	... 225	———— Revive Gilt Frames	... 228
———— ——— Hair Brushes	... 234	———— Another Method	... ib.
———— ——— Kid Gloves	234 224	———— Salts of Lemon, to make	... 218
———— ——— Paint	... 230	———— Scent Bags,	... 226
———— ——— Satin Shoes	... 224	———— Scouring Drops to make	... 220
———— ——— Sponges	... 232	———— Another kind	... 233
———— Cloth to make Waterproof	... 228	———— ——— Cheap	... ib.
———— Court Plaister, to make	... 226	———— Shoes to make Waterproof	... 226
———— Dye Cotton and Nankeen	... 224	———— Stains to remove, from acids	... 219
———— ——— Furniture buff	... ib	———— ——— Another Receipt	... ib.
———— ——— ——— pink	... 225	———— ——— Fruit or Wine	... ib.

INDEX.

	Page
RECEIPTS —— Port Wine	ib.
—— —— Out of Scarlet Cloth	ib.
—— —— Black Cloth, Silk, &c.	ib.
—— Starch, to Make	226
—— Varnish old Straw Hats	225
—— Wash black Silk or Crape	223
—— —— Silk Handkerchiefs	222
—— —— coloured Prints, Muslins	223
—— —— Blonde	ib.
—— —— Lace	224
—— —— Kid Gloves	224 & 234
—— —— Leather Gloves	224
—— —— Silk Dresses	230
—— Waterproof, to make Shoes	226 & 228
—— —— to make Cloth	228
RESTORE RUSTY SILK, see *Receipts*	
—— Scorched linen, ib.	
ROBES, Infant's, see *Baby Linen*	
ROLLER CLOTHS, see *House Linen*	
ROQUELAURE	164
ROSETTE, see *Baby Linen*	
ROULEAUS	8
RUCHE	74
RUNNING, see *Stitches in Needlework*	
SACCARINE, see *Pinafore*	
SATCHEL, or Card Case	212
SALTS OF LEMON, see *Receipts*	
SASH, or Badge	149
SATIN, see *On Purchasing Goods*	
SCARFS, Clergyman's	149
—— Dress, or Caprice	80
—— Cashmere	ib.
—— Simple	ib.
SCENT BAGS, see *Receipts*	
SCISSORS, Remarks upon	1 & 15
SCOURING FLANNEL	180
—— Drops, see *Receipts*	
SCREENS, see *Upholstery*	
SEAMAN'S CASE	215
SENTIMENT, or Neck Tie	79
SERPENTINE STITCH, see *Stitches in Needlework*	
SEWING SILKS, How kept	1
SEWING and Felling, see *Stitches in Needlework*	
SHOULDER Pieces, or Stays, how cut	15
SHIFTS Gored	46
—— Not hollowed	47
—— Crossed	48
—— Child's	ib.
—— To save a seam and two fells	49
SHIRTS, Infant's see *Baby Linen*	
—— For Labouring Men	137

	Page
SHIRTS Scales for	139
—— On making up	141
—— Gentlemen's	142
—— Fronts	143
—— Young Child's Front	ib.
—— A Boy's Front	ib.
—— An older Boy's Front	ib.
—— Another	ib.
—— A Gentleman's Front	ib.
—— Another	144
—— Shoulder Strap	ib.
—— Child's Shoulder Strap	ib.
—— Sleeves	ib.
—— Wristband's	145
—— Binders and Linings	ib.
—— Collars	ib.
—— Boy's Collars	146
—— Men's Collars	ib.
SHAWLS, Infant's, see *Baby Linen*	
—— Carriage	166
—— Walking	ib.
—— For a Member of the Society of Friends	ib.
—— Quilted	ib.
—— Cashmere	ib
—— Mourning	167
—— Plain walking	ib.
—— Travelling	ib.
SHEETS, see *House Linen*	
SHOES, SLIPPERS	171
—— —— Men's	ib.
—— —— Ladies'	ib.
—— —— Quilted	172
—— —— Ladies'	ib.
—— —— Half	173
—— —— Carriage	ib.
—— —— Infants' first	ib.
—— —— —— second	ib.
—— —— —— Ticking	174
—— To Cover	ib.
—— To Clean, see *Receipts*	
—— Bags	
SHOULDER PIECES	91
—— —— For Woman's Cloak	92
—— —— For a Child's Cloak	ib & 93
—— —— —— Woman's Cloak	ib.
—— —— —— Infant's Cloak	93
SHROUD	124
SILK, see *On Purchasing Goods*	
—— sewing, how to keep	1
SLEEVES, Infant's first, see *Baby Linen*	
—— General Rules	15

INDEX.

	Page
SLEEVES, Child's first	85
———— Older Child's	ib.
———— Long	86
———— Circular	ib
———— Plain long	87
———— Full	ib.
———— Another	ib.
———— Small	88
———— Old Woman's	ib.
———— Boy's	ib.
———— Woman's large	ib.
———————— short	89
———————— short	90
———————— circular	ib.
———————— tight	ib.
———— On lining	6
SLIPS, or Pillow Cases	182
SOFA, see *Upholstery*	
SPENCERS, Plain	167
———— Dress	168
STARCH, to make, see *Receipts*	
STAYS, or Corsets	80
———— materials for	81
———— making up	ib.
———— Woman's	ib.
———————— gores for	82
———————— shoulder straps	ib.
———————— lace holes	ib.
———————— modesty piece	ib.
———————— nursing	ib.
———— Men's	83
———— Coachmen's	ib.
———— Hunter's	ib.
———— Child's small	ib.
———————— large	ib.
———————— first, see *Baby Linen*	
STAINS, to remove, see *Receipts*	
———— from acids, ib.	
———— from fruit or wine, ib.	
———— from Port wine, ib.	
———— out of scarlet cloth, ib.	
———— out of black cloth, ib.	
STEEL, How to keep	1
STITCHES IN NEEDLEWORK,	1
———— Angular-stitch	9
———— Biassing	6
———— Binding	7
———— Braiding	6
———— Button-holes	3
———— Chain-stitch	8
———— Coral pattern	10

	Page
STITCHES IN NEEDLEWORK	
———— Darning	4
———— Double gathering	2
———— Fancy Chain-stitch	8
———— Fancy Bobbin-stitch	9
———— Fancy Herring-boning	ib.
———— Fancy Button-hole stitch	10
———— Gaging	7
———— Gathering	2
———— German hemming	3
———— Hemming	1
———— Herring-boning	4
———— Honey-combing	7
———— Horseshoe-stitch	10
———— Mantua-maker's hem	2
———— Marking	5
———— Quilting	7
———— Running	2
———— Serpentine-stitch	9
———— Sewing and felling	2
———— Stitching	ib.
———— Whipping	3
STOCKS,	147
STRAW PLATTING, see *Separate Index*	
STUFFS, see *On Purchasing Goods*	
SUCK, to Baby's bottle	45
SURPLICE	149
SURTOUT	117
TABLE CLOTHS, see *House Linen*	
TABLE COVERS, see *Upholstery*	
TAPES, How to keep	1
TEA CLOTHS, see *House Linen*	
THIMBLE, Remarks upon	1
THREAD, How to strengthen	1
———— How to keep	ib.
TIPPETS, see *Collars*	
———— School Girl's	99
———— Another	104
———— Another	168
TOILET Covers, see *House Linen*	
TOWELS, see *House Linen*	
TRAVELLING Dressing Case	215
———— Portfolio	ib.
———— Bag	214
TROWSERS, Child's	50
———— larger	51
———— Girl's	ib.
———— Boy or Girl's	52
———— Turkish	54
———— For a little Boy	ib.
TRUNK CASE	211

INDEX.

	Page
Tucks, Making	5
Tucker	97
Tunics, see *Frocks*	
Upholstery,	190
——— Arm chair Covers	206
——— Bedsteads	190
——— ——— Hints on putting up	191
——— ——— On Drapery	193
——— ——— On Heads and tops	195
——— ——— On Footboards	ib.
——— ——— On furnishing 4 posts	193
——— ——— On Prices	199
——— ——— On Coverlets	200
——— ——— On Blankets	ib.
——— Beds, the Tent	191 195
——— —— Camp	ib. ib.
——— —— Half-tester	ib. 196
——— —— French Pole	ib. ib.
——— —— French Arrow	ib. ib.
——— —— French	ib. ib.
——— —— French Block	ib. ib.
——— —— French Canopy	ib. 197
——— —— Turn-up	ib. ib.
——— —— Press	ib. ib.
——— —— Stump	ib. ib.
——— —— Trestle	ib. ib.
——— —— Hanging, or Cot	198
——— Mattrass	ib.
——— Beds	199
——— Bolsters	ib.
——— Pillows	ib.
——— Blinds, window	206
——— Chair, Sofa &c. covers	ib.
——— Carpets	201
——— Curtains, window	203
——— ——— Muslin	205
——— ——— Little Half	ib.
——— ——— Full	ib.
——— ——— Rod	ib.
——— Church Basses	207
——— Church Seats	ib.
——— Divan	206
——— Footstools and Hassocks	207
——— Screens	ib.
——— Sofa	206
——— Table Covers	207
——— Watch-pockets	201

Varnish, old Straw Hats, see *Receipts*	
Veils, common	
——— Crape,	
——— Demi-voile	
——— Mourning	
——— Riding	
——— Tulle	
Velvet, Dress	
——— Cap	
——— To raise the Surface of, see *Receipts*	
Vest, Boy's	
——— Night	
——— Day	
Waistcoat, Lady's Flannel	
——— Boy's	
——— Invalid	
——— Man's under	
——— Boy's upper	
——— Child's, see *Vest*	
Waiting Gloves, see *House Linen*	
Washing Books, for Nursery	
——— ——— Ladies'	
——— ——— Gentlemen's	
——— ——— House Linen	
Washing and Ironing	
——— Articles used in the Washhouse	
——— ——— Laundry	
——— Clear Starching	
——— Gaufiering	
——— Hanging to dry	
——— Ironing, Mangling	
Wash, Black Silk or Crape, see *Receipts*	
——— Silk Handkerchiefs	ib.
——— Coloured Prints, &c.	ib.
——— Lace,	ib.
——— Blonde	ib.
——— Kid Gloves	ib.
——— Silk Dresses	ib.
Watch Pocket, see *Upholstery*	
——— Another	
Waterproof, see *Receipts*	
——— Shoes and Boots, ib.	
Whipping, see *Stitches in Needlework*	
Work Box	
——— Basket	
Yard Measure	

INDEX.

ON KNITTING.

	Page
GENERAL OBSERVATIONS	... 237
KNITTING PINS, ...	... ib.
MATERIALS FOR KNITTING	... ib.
ON KNITTING STITCHES	... 238
——————— Binding	... 240
——————— Casting on stitches ...	... 238
——————— Common knitting stitch	... 239
——————— Dutch common stitch	... ib.
——————— Finishing off ...	... ib.
——————— Narrowing	... ib.
——————— Slipping a stitch ...	... ib.
——————— Turns for stitches ...	... 240
——————— Turn or seam stitch ...	... 239
——————— Welting	... 240
——————— Widening	... 239
FANCY STITCHES	... 240
——————— Berlin wire or insertion	... ib.
——————— Chain stitch ...	... ib.
——————— ———— two coloured	... ib.
——————— Cross stitch pattern ...	... ib.
——————— ———— Open ...	... ib.
——————— Crowsfoot stitch ...	... ib.
——————— Curb stitch ...	... ib.
——————— Diamond stitch ...	... ib.
——————— ———— Embossed	... ib.
——————— Double knitting ...	... ib.
——————— Another kind ...	... ib.
——————— Another kind ...	... ib.
——————— ———— Imitation ...	... ib.
——————— Fantail stitch ...	... ib.
——————— French stitch ...	... ib.
——————— ———— Raised ...	... ib.
——————— Hem open ...	... ib.
——————— Herringbone stitch ...	... ib.
——————— Another kind ...	... ib.
——————— Hexagon embossed ...	... ib.
——————— Honeycomb ...	... ib.
——————— Huckaback, or roughcast	... ib.
——————— Lace wave stitch ...	... ib.
——————— Ladder, ornamental	... ib.

	Page
FANCY STITCHES Muffatee stitch, new	... 240
——————— Network, imitation ...	... 244
——————— New stitch ...	... ib.
——————— Nondescript ...	... ib.
——————— Open stitch, plain ...	... ib.
——————— ———— Improved	... ib.
——————— Plat, common ...	... ib.
——————— Purse stitch ...	... ib.
——————— Rib stitch, elastic ...	... ib.
——————— Two colours ...	... ib.
——————— Rug stitch ...	... ib.
——————— Shawl stitch ...	... ib.
FRINGES KNIT	... ib.
——————— Plain	... ib.
——————— Beautiful on border ...	... ib.
——————— Very pretty ...	... ib
——————— For a Shawl ...	... ib.
——————— For Curtains ...	... ib.
ARMLET	... 262
BAGS, ...	... 270
BLANKETS, ...	... 271
BONNET, or hood	... 269
BOA or ruff, spiral knit ...	... 276
BOSOM FRIEND, ...	... 275
Boot, ribbed	... 257
—— For infants	... 258
—— Night	... ib.
—— Square night	... 260
—— Derby jail	... 259
BORDER AND CORNER, handsome for Shawl	... 272
BRAID, open	... 270
BRACES, for Gentlemen ...	... 275
CAP, Infant's	... 268
—— Another, ...	... ib.
—— Gentleman's night ...	... 269
—— Gentleman's silk travelling	... 273
—— Travelling knit silk ...	.....
—— Knee	... 260
—— Swiss	... 276
COMFORTER, ...	... 264

2 R

INDEX.

	Page		Page
Comforter Another	264	Shoe Another pretty kind	258
——— Another	ib.	Slippers, Infant's	256
Coverlet,	271	Snow Heels	258
Doyleys, Cotton	ib.	Socks, Night	259
——— Other sorts	ib.	——— For invalids	ib.
Flower-stand Covers,	278	——— For infants'	255
Frill,	263	——— For grown up persons	ib.
Garters,	255	——— Child's long	257
Gloves, Large size	261	——— Child's improved	277
Habit Shirt,	264	——— Neat night	260
Handkerchief,	ib.	——— Several kinds	256
——— Small half	265	——— Another sort	255
Heel, to wear in snow	258	Sofa, Foot warmer	273
Hood, or Bonnet for a baby	269	——— Shawl for Invalids	275
Kettle Holders,	270	Sole, For inside of Shoe	260
Light Scarf,	277	Stays For Children	274
Mats,	270	Stockings	253
——— Another kind	271	——— Proportions for	ib.
Mittens,	261	——— Scales for	254
——— For driving in	ib	——— Child's first	257
——— For Infants	ib.	Shawl, For a Baby	268
Muffatees	264	——— For a Sofa	275
——— Another kind	ib.	——— Honey Comb	265
——— Another kind	ib.	——— Fantail border and corners	272
——— Another kind	ib.	Spiral Boa or Ruff	276
Napkin Rings,	275	Swiss Cap	276
Petticoat, for a child	274	Tippet	266
Pen Wiper,	278	Purse	ib.
Reticule Bag,	273	——— Another	267
Rings, for dinner napkins	275	——— Another	ib.
Ruff,	263	——— Another	ib.
Scarf,	ib.	——— Another very pretty	ib.
——— Light	277	Whatch Gurad, Silk	274
——— Another,	263	Zephyr, or Baby's Shawl	268
Shoe, over	258	Zephyrine, or Soft Bonnet	267

INDEX.

ON STRAW PLATTING.

	Page
STRAW PLATTING	... 278
———————— General Observations	... ib.
BLEACHING BOX	... 279
BONNET STAND	... 280
BOX IRON	... 280
MILL FOR ROLLING THE PLAT ...	... 279
STRAW SPLITTER	... 281
STRAW, on Preparing	... ib.
———— on Bleaching	... ib.
———— on Dyeing Black ...	... ib.
———— Another Black Dye ...	... 282
TIN DYEING KETTLE	... 280
DIRECTIONS FOR PLATTING ...	... 282
PLATS IN GENERAL USE ...	... 283
———————————— of 3 ...	... ib.
———————————— another ...	... 284
———————————— of 4 ...	... ib.
———————————— Angular 4 ...	... ib.
———————————— of 5 ...	... ib.
———————————— of 6 ...	... ib.
———————————— another ...	... ib.
———————————— of 7 ...	... 285
———————————— another ...	... ib.
———————————— another ...	... ib.
———————————— of 8 ...	... ib.
———————————— another ...	... ib.
———————————— another ...	... ib.
———————————— of 9 ...	... ib.

	Page
PLATS IN GENERAL USE another ...	... 285
———————————— another ...	... ib.
———————————— of 10 ...	... 286
———————————— Another ...	... ib.
———————————— of 11 ...	... ib.
———————————— Another ...	... ib.
———————————— Another ...	... ib.
———————————— Another ...	... ib.
———————————— of 12 ...	... ib.
———————————— of 13 ...	... ib.
———————————— Another ...	... ib.
———————————— Another ...	... 287
———————————— of 14 ...	... ib.
———————————— of 15 ...	... ib.
———————————— Another ...	... ib.
———————————— of 16 ...	... ib.
HOLLOW SPIRAL PLAT ...	... ib.
ARTICLES MADE OF STRAW PLAT ...	... 288
BONNETS	... 289
———— On cleaning	... ib.
———— On turning	... 290
HATS	... ib.
———— Tuscan	... 287
LEGHORN, English imitation ...	... 288
MATS	... 290
STIFFENING	... 289
———— Made of Vellum ...	... ib.
———— of Bone-dust ...	... ib.

THOMAS EVANS, PRINTER, 30, COLMORE ROW, BIRMINGHAM.

Lightning Source UK Ltd.
Milton Keynes UK
UKHW021255310320
361126UK00005B/988